*Communication
and Culture in Ancient
India and China*

Communication
and Culture in Ancient
India and China

ROBERT T. OLIVER

Research Professor Emeritus of International Speech
Pennsylvania State University

SYRACUSE UNIVERSITY PRESS

MANUFACTURED IN THE
UNITED STATES OF AMERICA

for Margaret

Robert T. Oliver, Research Professor Emeritus of International Speech at Pennsylvania State University, is past president of the Speech Association of America and the Speech Association of the Eastern States. In 1942, he began twenty years of participation in the political problems of modern Korea, working on Korea's relations with Japan, India, China, the United States, and the United Nations. He became interested in the cultural foundations of Hinduism, Buddhism, Mohism, legalism, and Taoism. His professional involvement in the field of speech naturally led to inquiries into the roots of Eastern rhetorical and communication theory. In 1959, he received the Presidential Medal, the highest civilian award, from the Republic of Korea.

Professor Oliver discussed evolving concepts with such statesman-scholars as Pyun Yung-tai and Hollington K. Tong. Close friends—including Syngman Rhee, Pyo-Wook Han, K. N. S. Rao, and Pandharinath H. Prabhu —contributed to his understanding of Asia.

Among the books edited or written by Professor Oliver on speech and his experiences in the Far East are *Korea: Forgotten Nation, Why War Came to Korea, Verdict in Korea, Syngman Rhee: The Man Behind the Myth, The Psychology of Persuasive Speech, Conversation: The Development and Expression of Personality, Effective Speech, Leadership in Twentieth Century Asia, Making Your Meaning Effective,* and *The History of Public Speaking in America.*

Contents

Preface

EVERY PIONEERING INQUIRY has its own excitement and difficulties. This first attempt to identify the rhetorical theories and practices of ancient India and China is no exception. Rhetorical views—the principles which explained or governed the nature, functions, and effective methods of oral discourse of the ancient Indians and Chinese—are seldom explicit but are intrinsic in their religio-philosophical writings and in their political and social practices. Much undoubtedly remains hidden from so exterior a view as mine, and much that I have found will appear differently to inquirers having other backgrounds and interests. My best hope is that this initial effort to discern and describe the rhetorics implicit in these two Eastern cultures will lead to further and more definitive investigations.

If the subject matter of the following chapters appears to range broadly through religious and philosophical writings and social and political institutions, the reasons are twofold. First, with no more than one or two significant exceptions (Han Fei-Tzu and occasionally Gautama Buddha), the ancients of India and China viewed rhetoric not as a separate inquiry but as an inherent part of their over-all world view. And second, in their view, the manner of talk was less an aspect of life than a key revelation of the speaker and of the community's way of life. Rhetoric always is authentic only in its cultural matrix. Everywhere and always it is intrinsic as well as extrinsic. It is real only as it is an emergent from the philosophy and practice of its theorists and its practitioners. Rhetoric inevitably shares and stimulates the vitality of the society of which it is a dynamic part.

A rhetoric abstracted from its context appears as a decorative sheen applied exteriorly to communication, or as a set of devices and manipulative artifices employed by skilled and crafty experts to bedazzle, mislead, and dominate listeners. This has been well recognized by all true rhetoricians. Nevertheless, it is because rhetoric in the West has developed as a special and separate discipline that Western social critics have

ix

tended to derogate "mere rhetoric." It is only when rhetoric is viewed in the totality of its cultural coordinates that we can share such a critical insight as that of Wendell Johnson that "speech and personality are inseparable" or that of Hugh Dalziel Duncan that "man as a social being exists in and through communication."

The questions this book seeks to explore are answerable only as oral communication is considered in relation to philosophy and social customs. They are as follows: How did the ancient Indians and Chinese, prior to the third and fourth centuries B.C., conceive the problems of human communication? What significance did they attach to barriers that impede the communicative transaction? What in their view were the personal and social effects of success and of failure in efforts to exchange understandings? By what means and in what contexts did they consider such rhetorical problems? What sorts of communicative systems interested them? What motivational patterns did they discern? What communicative theories and practices did they foster? Who were the principal rhetorical theorists of their ancient civilizations, and what different views did they hold? By examining cultures so different from the rhetorical strongholds of the West, what new ways of looking at rhetoric may appear? Such questions as these are the guidelines for this effort to penetrate into the nature of the leading ancient Asian rhetorics.

My own efforts to find answers to these questions commenced in 1942, when I began a twenty-year participation in the political problems of modern Korea. Working on the Republic of Korea's relations with Japan, India, China, the United States, and the United Nations, it became apparent to me that some of our Western communicative perceptions and presumptions differ significantly from those of Asian statesmen. The drift of our frequent conversations to traditional Eastern value systems led to my interest in the cultural foundations of Hinduism, Buddhism, Confucianism, Mohism, legalism, and Taoism. My professional attachment to the field of speech naturally led to inquiries in the Oriental roots of rhetorical and communication theory.

As these inquiries gradually deepened and expanded, I was fortunately able to discuss evolving concepts with such scholar-statesmen as Pyun Yung-tai, Foreign Minister and Prime Minister of the Republic of Korea and translator of the Confucian *Analects;* and Hollington K. Tong, a leading publicist and diplomat of Nationalist China. Many close friends, including Syngman Rhee, Pyo-Wook Han, Insoo Lee, Young Soo Lee, K. N. S. Rao, and Ben C. Limb, contributed richly over a span of two decades to my understanding of Asian value systems. On some fifteen trips to the Far East, sharing experiences with many Asian acquaintances, and in broad and discursive reading on multiple aspects of Asian life, as well as in more concentrated research and the writing of five books on Korea and its relationships, my interest and hopefully my understanding of Oriental modes of thought continued and grew.

Meanwhile, at the Pennsylvania State University I was enabled to develop new courses in the rhetorical theory and practice of both the ancient and the modern Far East. A small number of graduate students undertook research under my direction leading to dissertations in the area. Students in my seminars helped to shape my investigations and budding conclusions through their questions, challenges, and insights. The Central Research Fund of the University contributed small funds annually to finance aspects of the work. More significantly, in 1965 the University granted me appointment as Research Professor of International Speech, with ample opportunity to devote virtually all my time to this project.

What should be stressed is the generous help I have encountered at every stage in the development of this work. No inquiry into the cultural and linguistic morass of ancient India and China could possibly proceed without considerable indebtedness to innumerable specialists and experts. Source citations only partly indicate the depth and breadth of my dependence upon translators and editors, historians and interpreters, both Eastern and Western. A debt of appreciation is happily acknowledged to colleagues and students who patiently listened and reacted to the early and fuzzy ideas that gradually grew into this study. Librarians and secretaries were endlessly and graciously helpful.

In its early stages this inquiry profited especially from the reactions of such departmental colleagues as Paul Holtzman, Carroll Arnold, Eugene White, and Thomas Olbricht; and from the questions and suggestions and encouragement of such scholars and activists from other areas as Hugh Kang, E Tu Zen Sun, Sun Fo, P. H. Prabhu, Tai Si Chung, Michael Prosser, and Otis Walter. Dean Stanley Paulson of Penn State's College of Liberal Arts and Professor H. B. Knoll of Purdue University thoughtfully and helpfully read the entire manuscript, with many suggestions for improvements of style and presentation.

I am grateful to my brother Egbert and his wife Helen for their aid in helping me to understand the spirit of India. And to the staff of the Syracuse University Press I am deeply indebted for an interest that went far beyond professional duty and for helpfulness beyond what any author might rightly expect.

Despite the extent of this help, the terrain of ancient Asian rhetoric proved to be wholly unexplored. Where to look, what to look for, and how to interpret what was found were all questions to be phrased and answered afresh. Leading Orientalists whose opinions I have sought have been surprised, and remained dubious, concerning my efforts to discern genuine rhetorical significance in such works as the *I Ching,* or in such Taoist concepts as *te, wu-wei,* and *wu-hsin.*

Quite aside from the primary difficulty of ascertaining the true rhetorical theories of ancient India and China was the additional problem of how to present these ideas in their proper social and historical contexts to readers who, for the most part, would not be familiar with the circumstances and personalities involved—or, if they were knowledgeable about the ancient East, would be unfamiliar and perhaps unsympathetic with rhetorical theory. To relate too little of the lives of the theorists, of the philosophical context, of the social and political matrix, and of the rhetorical problems requiring consideration would leave the framework of conclusions stark and meaningless. To report too much would impede the presentation and dissolve the focus. The problem is common to all historical analyses; but the failure of Orientalists to be even vaguely interested in rhetoric and of rhetoricians to acquaint themselves even cursorily with the Far East seemed to magnify the difficulties.

The difficulties are, perhaps, all too evident. As this volume is perused, it will be equally evident that not all these problems have been fully solved. Just as I shall be pleased with whatever credit may be granted for this pioneering endeavor to explore an important area hitherto unexamined, so shall I willingly accept full responsibility for errors of judgment. My highest claim is to have done my best. Hopefully, others will shortly be doing better. Perhaps the very shortcomings of this study will have the effect of encouraging others to follow through and do better what has here been commenced.

*Communication
and Culture in Ancient
India and China*

CHAPTER 1

Culture and Rhetoric

THE CULTURAL ORIENTATION OF COMMUNICATION

NEITHER INDIA NOR CHINA has ever had a public platform comparable with that of America or of those European nations inclined toward democracy.[1] Until very recently political debate in the whole area from Bombay to Peking was confined largely to court circles. There were no political parties, no election campaigns, no contending candidates arguing their issues before voters. Their courtrooms offered none of the inducements found in the West to affect judicial decisions through eloquent pleading. Although evangelism was prominent in some Eastern religions, their temples of worship contained no pulpits in which weekly sermons were delivered. Their education did not feature what the West would consider to be lectures, though it encouraged student discussions. Despite the prominence of lecturing in early India and the Chinese penchant for talk, Eastern communities developed nothing comparable to the lyceum, the chautauquas, or the commercial lecture bureaus of the Western world.[2]

Eastern legislative bodies debated public policies only in a strictly confined format, for carefully limited purposes. They called no conventions to draw up constitutions or to nominate candidates for public office through processes of discussion and debate. Their colleges had no debating societies; nor did their businessmen organize luncheon clubs in which to listen to speeches. Even on ceremonial occasions they made little use of such set orations of praise or blame, attack or defense, as made the eloquence of classical Athens a marvel of the Western world. There was none of the debating of civic issues that was among the highest literary achievements of Cicero's Rome.[3] There was none of the dialectical preaching that sharpened the wits of schoolmen and ecclesiastics in medieval and renaissance Europe. Nor even in modern times has skill in speech—in public forums, at conference tables, and in the persuasion of salesmen—had in the East anything like the currency attained in the West.

1

Despite this catalog of negative statements, it should not be presumed that the populations of India and China dwelt for centuries in stultified silence. For them no less than for the peoples of the West, their ability to symbolize and to communicate was the cardinal aspect of their humanity. It is a commonplace of sociological doctrine that "man as a social being exists in and through communication; communication is as basic to man's nature as food and sex."[4]

This is a sweeping judgment, and one that inevitably directs attention to the manner in which people communicate, if their culture is to be understood. What communication means to them—how important it is, how it is conducted, who the nominated speakers are, and to what groups they find it desirable to speak—these are questions not of incidental but of paramount importance for the study of any society.

Once this approach is undertaken, it must be accepted as a totally inclusive way of viewing the social scene. It is as though a photograph of the society were to be taken from a communicative stance. Everything will be considered from the perspective of communicative intentions and effects. As Margaret Mead, a dean among cultural anthropologists, has testified: "the whole mesh of human social life might logically, and perhaps, in other contexts, fruitfully, be treated as a system of human communication."[5]

The confident acceptance of communication—and most explicitly of spoken or oral communication, with its face-to-face directness—as the essential factor in the study of the "languagized mammal"[6] and of the kind of society which a particular set of people evolves is well nigh universal among philosophers, political scientists, humanists, and even the fabled man in the street. Perhaps nowhere has it been better stated than by Thomas Mann, in the magnificent sixth chapter of his *Magic Mountain,* where he wistfully attests that "Speech is civilization itself. The word, even the most contradictory word, preserves contact—it is silence which isolates."

It is inconceivable that oral discourse should be in the West "that web of signals and expectations and understandings that makes living together possible," and also "in its private manifestations, within the single mind, a controlling factor in personality,"[7] and that, at the same time, it should lack a comparable importance in the East. If "civilization itself might well be called that state of being in which communication is achieved,"[8] the highly civilized societies of India and China cannot have been mute. On the contrary, the key to understanding the Asian mind and Asian civilization is their *manner of talk: how they addressed one another and why, under what circumstances, on what topics, in what varied styles, with what intent, and with what effects.*

This is the key to the inquiry that comprises this book: an attempt to depict the manner of talk in ancient India and China. The method is through exploration of the communication theories implicit in the philosophical classics of their peoples and expressed in the life style of their societies. Since rhetoric inheres in the philosophy and way of life of its practitioners, it is necessary to examine the premises which underlie Oriental thought and feeling, as well as (a strange concept to Western minds) their non-thought and non-feelings. As guidelines for the inquiry, the following questions are always dominant: How have Asians conceived the problems of communication? What significance have they attached to barriers which impede it? By what means and in what contexts have they considered such questions? What sorts of communication systems—nonverbal as well as verbal—have they conceived? What theories and practices have they fostered? How have they institutionalized communication beyond the boundaries of talk?

In conducting this inquiry, primary attention is focused upon oral communication in all its forms: person-to-person conversation, as well as in the more formal situations of public address. There must also be serious consideration of the Asian recognition of the varied communicative functions of silence. Meanwhile, secondary and incidental consideration of written discourse is occasionally inevitable, for considerable segments of rhetoric apply without significant discrimination to speech and writing.

Should we attempt to conceptualize the nature of rhetoric and of public discourse in Asia in terms that have proved appropriate in the West, the results would be biased, inadequate, and misleading. The East is not the West. Cultures differ, and minds, feelings, and intentions in differing societies intermesh in differing ways. Discourse occurs, or is constrained, under different circumstances and has different styles for different reasons. The standards of rhetoric in the West which have had a unitary development since their identification by Aristotle are not universals. They are expressions of Western culture, applicable within the context of Western cultural values.

The premise that rhetoric is culturally based is the vantage point from which this exposition of ancient Indian and Chinese rhetorics is undertaken. Any attempt to discover in Asia prototypes of the Western rhetorical canons would be unavailing. It would resemble trying to measure the salinity of water with a ruler.

Orientals have long understood how cultural differences stamp themselves not only upon but also within human personality, dividing mankind into groups that in significant ways differ from one another. The point is emphasized in an old Chinese fable about a monkey and a fish that were caught in a devastating river flood. Luckily, the monkey was able to grasp an overhanging bough and pull himself to safety. Then, seeing the fish still tossed in the raging waters, the monkey generously reached down and pulled it up beside him in the tree. But the fish was not grateful. What is good for one kind is not necessarily good for another. "Like a fish out of water" is a saying that has relevance even to the varied provinces of rhetoric.[9]

How different a strange culture may be was well described by a Korean student reporting his feelings upon arriving in New York:

> To be a New Yorker among New Yorkers means a totally new experience from being Japanese or Chinese or Korean—a changed character. New Yorkers all seem to have some aim in every movement they make. (Some frantic aim.) They are like guns shooting off. How unlike Asiatics in an Oriental village, who drift up and down aimlessly and leisurely. But these people have no time, even for gossiping, even for staring. To be thrown among New Yorkers —yes, it means to have a new interpretation of life never conceived before. The business interpretation. Even the man who only goes to a show and is making arrangements about it, has a business air. His every action is decisive, orderly, purposeful. . . . he must know exactly what he wants to do in his mind. . . . His mind is like Grand Central Station. It is definite, it is timed, it has mathematical precision on clearcut stone foundations.[10]

A perceptive American diplomat, on his first mission to Tokyo at the opening of the twentieth century, found that "everywhere about lay a mystery that either lured or irritated, but one felt it and could not escape. The Japanese themselves, the islands in which they lived, their customs and their language seemed so utterly unlike anything ever imagined that they either absorbed the stranger in an attempt to understand, or he rejected it as impossible to understand."[11]

Decades earlier, a scholarly Chinese, seeing white men in his country for the first time, found them quite incredible. "These 'Ocean Men,' as they are called," he reported, "are tall beasts with deep sunken eyes and beaklike noses. The lower part of their faces, the backs of their hands, and, I understand, their entire bodies are covered with a mat of curly hair, much as are the monkeys of the southern forests. But the strangest part about them is that, although undoubtedly men, they seem to possess none of the mental faculties of men. The most bestial of peasants is far more human, although these Ocean Men go from place to place with the self-reliance of a man of scholarship and are in some respects exceedingly clever. It is quite possible that they are susceptible to training and could with patience be taught the modes of conduct proper to a human being."[12]

The significance of these attestations is clear: every society has its own culture—its own ways of thinking, behaving, and believing. And it is a truism of cultural anthropology that there is universal belief in the superiority of one's own culture. There is everywhere a lack of sympathetic comprehension of the unlike. What is *strange* is, to use the word the Greeks applied to it, *barbaric. Exotic* is psychologically if not semantically a synonym for *eccentric*. Ruth of the Old Testament is regarded as being of unique virtue because she could say to Naomi: "Your ways will be my ways, your people my people." Each person bears within himself the imprint of his own society—its values, its fears, its prejudices, its mannerisms. Every culture "is a body of ready-made solutions to the problems encountered by the group . . . that gives to the people who participate in it a certain style of life that is peculiarly their own."[13]

What happens when we try to understand a set of meanings in another culture is, to use a word coined by Gregory Bateson, *schizmogenetic,*[14] meaning, in effect, that one difference creates another. Strangeness begets strangeness. When foreigners confront one another across cultural barriers, the strange behavior that each notices causes him to alter his own behavior. He adjusts his manner of speaking and acting; concurrently he also adjusts his ways of interpreting what he sees and hears. Where ideally there ought to be a drawing together, there is instead a pulling apart. A socio-psychological chasm develops that is not readily bridged; indeed, clumsy efforts to bridge it result rather in its being pushed further apart.

The difficulties to be encountered in this attempt to discover, depict, and evaluate the rhetorics of ancient India and China are apparent. Every culture constitutes a unique value system. Any attempt to see inside a culture from the outside must be carefully guarded, with the difficulties understood. Indians and Chinese cannot be expected to think or to communicate as do Americans. They react to different stimuli in different ways. Their goals are not the same, nor are their ways of trying to achieve them.

To escape utter confusion, it is essential that the fact of the differences and the reasons for them be recognized. If the great thought systems of Asia—Hinduism, Buddhism, Confucianism, Taoism—are not quite religions (according to Judeo-Christian standards) or quite philosophy (according to Platonic or Kantian expectancies), the impulse to reject them should be replaced with a desire to discover what alternatives they do present. If their historic-sovereignty systems do not correspond with our Western concept of nationalism, we should be glad to explore with them the system of relations which they have used to make their societies cohesive. If instead of democracy we find them exalting propriety, and along with justice they acclaim decorum, we may at least pause to inquire the reasons for their choices of emphasis. If our technological forwardness keeps us aware of the "social lag" in adapting men to machines, perhaps we may be just as interested in the Asian "science lag," which for many centuries kept them more interested in mastery of social relations than in the mastery of nature.

The necessity of accepting differences not as barriers to understanding but as invitations to inquiry, and even to new modes or channels of investigation, is especially pertinent for a study of ancient Asian rhetoric. If their occasions for speech and their methods of speaking did not conform to ours, the reasons no doubt lay in the differing cultural patterns of their societies and of ours. If their rhetoric was not like ours, it is because they, like us, derived the principles of effective discourse from observation of what appears to have been required and what seems to have worked in situations being observed. The situations East and West were different; so were the rhetorics. This is why such an inquiry as we are undertaking is long overdue.

RHETORICS EAST AND WEST

A widely accepted encapsulated definition of rhetoric is "the function of adjusting ideas to people and people to ideas."[15] It should be added: and also of adjusting people to people. The function of rhetoric is not, like dialectic, to examine a given subject in order accurately to depict its nature. Nor is rhetoric, like logic, designed to discover and demonstrate inevitable conclusions about a subject. The province of rhetoric, as Aristotle pointed out, is the realm of probabilities. We do not argue about that which is certain or ascertainable; we try to persuade concerning propositions which have alternative acceptable conclusions.[16]

It follows that eloquence, the fruit of rhetoric, whether it be suasive or informative, is devoted to influencing the behavior of men concerning the matters of choice by which they are confronted. Rhetoric is the consideration of means by which eloquence is or may be rendered effective in influencing the reactions of listeners (or of readers). Whatever might be adduced to influence the unfettered actions of men is the proper inquiry of the rhetorician. The answers to be found depend on the personalities of the speakers and listeners and on the nature of their society. The *kinds of ideas* that interest or move people and the *reasons why they accept or reject them* are not universals; they are particular attributes of specific cultures.

Accordingly rhetoric may be universal in (and only in) the sense that "philosophy" or "religion" are universals. There is a genre of rhetoric, just as there is a genre of philosophy. But precisely as there are distinct philosophical systems and distinct religions, so, too, are there distinct rhetorics, each an integral part of its own culture, its own society.[17]

Although there was a long tradition of quasi-rhetorical thought in the Mediterranean basin prior to the Periclean Age, the foundation of Western rhetoric is properly found in the writings of Plato and Aristotle. Plato's most definitive statement about the nature of rhetoric is to be found in his *Phaedrus,* where he represents Socrates as saying:

> The conditions to be fulfilled are these. First, you must know the truth about the subject that you speak or write about; that is to say, you must be able to isolate it in definition, and having so defined it you must understand how to divide it into kinds, until you reach the limit of division; secondly, you must have a corresponding discernment of the nature of the soul, discover the type of speech appropriate to each nature, and order and arrange your discourse accordingly, addressing a variegated soul in a variegated style that ranges over the whole gamut of tones, and a simple soul in a simple style. All this must be done if you are to become competent, within human limits, as a scientific practitioner of speech, whether you propose to expound or persuade.[18]

This Platonic definition has been confidently asserted to encompass "all discourse which influences men."[19] Rather, it was specifically designed for the civilization that provided its context. Plato's injunction to "discover the type of speech appropriate to each nature" is indeed a rhetorical universal. But his insistence upon "knowing the truth about the subject," and thence proceeding to "isolate it in definition" and "to divide it into kinds" is based upon a particular view of the nature of truth and a particular concept of psychology.

Similarly, Aristotle posited a universal rhetorical principle when he declared: "So let Rhetoric be defined as the faculty of discovering in the particular case what are the available means of persuasion." He was, however, speaking for the free society of Athens when he further postulated that, "Of the means of persuasion supplied by the speech itself there are three kinds. The first kind reside in the character of the speaker; the second consist in producing a certain attitude in the hearer; the third pertain to the argument proper, insofar as it actually or seemingly demonstrates."[20] *Ethos, pathos,* and *logos* (or "the argument proper"), which Aristotle assumed to be the three *differentia* of persuasion, are indeed rhetorical universals. But Aristotle's particular inferences were drawn from his understanding of the nature of man and of the particular society with which he was familiar.

In the Platonic-Aristotelian tradition as it has developed in the West, rhetoric is all too commonly conceived as a pattern of manipulative devices or techniques by which a speaker (writer) may influence listeners (readers). In Aristotle's own view, rhetoric is a mode of thinking. It is a kind of thinking by which to try to determine the *relationships* that may be manifested among (a) the truth of the matter under consideration; (b) the personal goals or purposes of the speaker (writer, thinker); and (c) the needs or susceptibilities of those who are to be influenced in their attitude toward the subject and the speaker.

The logician is concerned with relationships that lie within a subject: if such-and-such is true about a proposition, what else must inevitably follow? Both logic and the scientific method undertake to *demonstrate inevitable conclusions.* So does dialectic, which searches into the nature of a subject, questioning its various aspects to enlarge and clarify understanding of its nature. All these are means of determining *what is true.*

Rhetoric is concerned with truth as it relates to human purposes. It does not demonstrate conclusions but seeks to *make motive appeals compulsive.*[21] The rhetorician's proper concerns are: in what sense is a particular proposition true for him, and by what means may it be made to appear as true and desirable to others? Thus, it is confined to matters concerning which there may be honest doubt. Its domain consists of probabilities rather than certainties. As Aristotle phrased it, "this art has to do with matters that may turn out in more than one way. Like ethics, rhetoric deals with variable relationships which may be adjusted, or interpreted, for good or ill, in terms of human desires. The end to be sought is the influencing of an audience."

According to Aristotle, the effectiveness of a speaker is limited by two factors which lie outside his control. The first is that truth and justice are realities; in the long run he cannot deny them, and in immediate circumstances it is his duty to uphold them. The second factor is human nature, both his own and as represented in the audience the speaker will address. In Aristotle's view, man is potentially or basically rational but tends to be governed by emotions. Hence, the speaker often finds it convenient to appeal to emotions, even though he or his listeners will ultimately insist upon determination of the issue by rational considerations. Meanwhile, the speaker finds that his listeners interpret the case he is presenting to them in terms of their conception of his character, personality, and reputation—or, to use the Greek term, his *ethos*.

Thus, in every circumstance the speaker is confronted by a threefold task. He must try to accomplish what he himself most desires, what the facts of the matter prescribe, and what the audience wishes or at least will accept. Such a tripartite rhetoric is basic in European and Anglo-American civilization. It has evolved for a society in which honest inquiry will lead to debate, by means of which propositions of fact and of policy may ultimately be decided by decision of the majority—or by those able to control the opinions of the majority. Truth and justice triumph when they are adequately championed. But "minds warped by emotion" (Aristotle's phrase) will accept whatever probability is made to appear most appealing to them. Obviously such a rhetoric evolved to serve a particular kind of man in a particular kind of society, rather than mankind in general. It was oriented to the culture of Athens and has served those peoples whose societies developed in the Hellenic tradition.

The conditions described here were not found in ancient times in either India or China. An Indian would not have reasoned from the same premises as a European, nor would his thinking have followed the same processes. Nor would a Chinese of the period have resembled either an Indian or a European. Each culture had different topical priorities; each used its own value system as its chosen standard of judgment. Not only in India were there "sacred cows" and "untouchables." In China as well, even as in Europe and America, there were compulsive prejudices and unreasonable dislikes. And as motivational patterns adhered in each culture in special ways, so too did rhetorical systems flourish to serve these differing needs.[22]

One striking difference that is highly relevant to our inquiry is in the kinds of attitudes toward rhetoric. In Euro-American literature rhetorics occupy a considerable space. From the outpouring of writings on rhetoric, it would appear that the West has been intoxicated with eloquence and the means of attaining it. In sharp and dramatic contrast, the bibliographies of Indian and Chinese writings are virtually bare of tractates on rhetoric. Everything published bearing directly on the subject in ancient India and China could be comprised in a slim anthology.

This does not mean that the inhabitants of ancient India and China did comparatively little speaking; nor does it mean that they neglected to theorize about the nature, means, and effects of discourse. On the contrary, as will become evident, in all the extensive populations subject to Indian and Chinese influences, speaking, discussing, arguing, and elucidating have been exceedingly important activities. They have dealt with these matters, however, in a way that was peculiarly their own, very different from the tradition that developed in the West.

In ancient India and China, in contrast to what happened in Athens and Rome, speculation about how truth and justice should be determined, interpreted, and rendered appealing to listeners was not considered to be separable from general religious, social, and political philosophy. It is a striking fact that Aristotle wrote separate treatises on *Ethics, Politics, Poetics, Logic,* and *Rhetoric.* However interrelated he may have thought them to be, he believed nevertheless that they could and should be treated separately. This was strictly in accordance with his and Plato's emphasis upon definition and classification as essential tools for dealing with the nature of truth.

To state the matter most simply, in the West rhetoric has been considered to be so important that it has had to be explored and delineated separately, as a special field of knowledge about human relations. In the East, rhetoric has been considered so important that it could not be separated from the remainder of human knowledge. Asian thinkers have consistently seen rhetoric as being inseparably interconnected with problems of ethics, psychology, politics, and social relations. Basic rhetorical considerations underlie much of the classical literature of the Eastern hemisphere. There are many reasons for this which will emerge in following chapters. Perhaps most basic of all is the cardinal devotion of the Asian mind to the related concepts of unity and harmony. In this view all things properly belong together and should coexist. Consequently, the ancient East has not been much interested in logic, which necessarily correlates unlike elements, nor has it favored either definition or classification as aids to clear thought. Indeed, clarity of thought itself has been far less favored in traditional literature of India and China than it has been in the West. Whereas the West has favored analysis and division of subject matter into identifiable and separate entities, the East has believed that to see truth steadily one must see it whole. If the outlines and the distinctions are dimmed, this possible loss is counterbalanced by the gain of viewing the object in its interrelated entirety. Hence, rhetoric, like philosophy and religion, penetrates all Eastern thinking and writing. The problem is not to find the rhetoric of the East but to find ways of identifying and depicting it in a fashion that will make it meaningful to Western minds without thereby denying its essentially holistic character.

Basic to both Hindu and Buddhist conceptions of reality is the mystery of the symbolic process. Moreover, even from its legendary beginnings Chinese civilization stressed communicative speaking as the principal means by which the actions of men might be harmonized.

It was Tzu-Ssu, the grandson of Confucius, who said that words are like colored glass: they obscure all that they do not clarify. The sentiment is often encountered in both Indian and Chinese cultures. The relationship between *what is* and *what appears* was as intriguing to thinkers of the ancient East as it has been in the West. In the East, as in the West, there has been much speculation about why some try to represent and some to misrepresent the nature of reality, and about the means by which both types of communicators do or may or should present their interpretations in order to make them effective. All the great Oriental philosophers—including Gautama and the anonymous authors of Hinduism, Confucius, Mencius, Hsüntze, Han Fei-Tzu, Mo-Tze, Lao-Tzu, and Chuang-Tzu—have also been rhetoricians. For in Asia rhetoric has been too important to be severed from its religio-philosophical context.

CHAPTER 2

India: The Rhetorical Milieu

CHARACTERISTICS OF INDIAN PHILOSOPHY

INDIA has popularly been considered a land of abstract spirituality, encouraging its impoverished masses to look beyond temporality to some ultimate nirvāna instead of demanding social reforms of its wealthy and powerful aristocracy. This view overlooks the practicality of the Indian mind that led to the invention of both algebra and the zero, thus making mathematical calculation flexible. It undervalues the rationality, or rationalization, that produced an intricate, if imprecise, system of logic. And it ignores the sophistication that invented and imposed on its population the most extraordinarily detailed and rigid social system known anywhere.

Whatever India has, it has had for a long time, for among nations it represents a high degree of conservative stabilization. One of its leading historians of ideas, Surendranath Dasgupta, wrote: "The laws which regulate the social, legal, domestic and religious customs and rites of the Hindus even to the present day are said to be but mere systematized memories of old Vedic teachings."[1] Amidst all the ambiguities, vagueness, and contradictions of Indian culture there is at least this much to comfort the outside inquirer: the basic ideas and customs tend to remain long enough to permit their examination in terms of widely varying social and political contexts. Rulers change; invaders come and go; inventions introduce different economies—but the basic faith and behavior remain remarkably stable.

The reasons are significant. The most preponderant idea animating Indian culture is a belief in the inevitability of both change and continuity. Far more than the French, the Indians have been devoted to what is depicted in the old French proverb: *le plus ça change, le plus c'est le même chose.* Or, as the idea is stated by Sir Charles Eliot, "everything passes away and changes but it is not true to say of anything that it arises from nothing or passes into nothing."[2] The consequences of this basic belief are evident everywhere in Indian society, religion, philosophy—and rhetoric.

Perhaps the most dramatic and significant exemplification of this fundamental Indian conviction is the belief in transmigration or reincarnation. To the Indian, birth and death are not the beginning and the end but are incidents in a continuous cycle of birth and rebirth. The notion of immortality of the individual soul would to an orthodox Indian be unimaginable. His skepticism would revolve around questions such as: Is there, then, a fresh beginning, or birth, for every person, but no ending in death? Does the soul represent the person as he existed in babyhood, or in youth, or in maturity, or in old age? If souls accumulate as rapidly as people are born, where and how could this vast undying population live? If individual souls are created out of nothing by God, why must He persist in making many of them evil and then in subjecting them to suffering on this earth and to eternal damnation? Most puzzling to the Indian mind is the thought that souls have a continuance that cannot be terminated but also have a beginning that is completely new. In the Indian view, perhaps the greatest hiatus in Western religion is the failure to explain birth.

In India such a problem is nonexistent since every individual goes through an immediately visible lifespan as only one stage in an unbroken succession of rebirths. A present life has been preceded by many others and will be followed by many more. The spirit of the newborn babe does not come from nowhere but is implanted in the physical fetus following its release from another body that has died. Thus there is maintained only a limited number of spirits which pursue a continuing hegira through eternity in one bodily form after another.

Of considerable rhetorical significance is the cardinal fact that each experience in life changes and affects the nature of the spirit, for better or for worse. Everything that is done or said, neglected or left unsaid, has consequences that stretch across generations. A good life well lived improves the quality of the spirit so that it becomes capable of transmigration to a better body, to live another lifespan in improved circumstances. A life badly lived, on the contrary, debases the spirit so that it becomes fitted only for a lesser life form and therefore retrogresses in its evolutionary pattern.

To the Indian mind this conception of cause and effect is both rational and moral. It is rational because it explains not only death but also birth, and also because it accounts for both continuity and change. It raises problems, of course, but it neatly provides answers for many more. And it is moral because it equates effect with cause: good results in good, evil results in evil. What is performed or neglected is inescapable. Causation is elevated to a preeminent role.

The continuity which Indians envision not only unites generation to generation but also individual to individual. All life, in their view, constitutes one indissoluble, unbreakable, and continuous unity. The useful cow and the loyal dog are not derogated below the value level of the scheming mendicant or the exploitative employer. Westerners might suspect that even the vegetable, since it, too, is a form of life, should belong to the same continuity which unites all. But the Indians observe a significant difference between sentient and nonsentient beings. To eat a carrot may be pardonable, as it also is necessary. But to eat an animal is neither necessary nor pardonable. It is a kind of cannibalism, and it marks a spirit debased below decency. Living creatures manifest many differences from one another; but all of them—spider, monkey, goose, and man—are fundamentally conjoined in one great family of life.

No less than the peoples of other cultures, however, Indians feel and have felt the limitations and suffering involved in life. In the great body of their classical literature, death is represented (as is true around the world) as in some sense a release—a positive good that ends suffering and provides relief when faculties have decayed and enjoyments palled. Beyond this, whereas the religions of the West picture an eternal life for the soul, the Indian nirvāna—precious to both Hindus and Buddhists—is a heaven of extinction, into which the soul may enter when it has become truly blessed through highly moral living, deserving finally to win surcease from the toil and trouble of continuing the round of existence.

The religious goal of orthodoxy in India is so to live that one need not live again. Eventually this is the reward which every living spirit yearns and hopes to achieve. So sectarian, modern, and in some ways Westernized an Indian as Jawaharlal Nehru could declare: "death is the birthright of every person born."[3]

An individual's entry into nirvāna may be delayed for a thousand or for many thousands of years. Even the saintly Gautama Buddha himself underwent a succession of twenty-four generations of purifying improvements after he had reached a state of grace that forecast his destiny, in his incarnation as a man named Dipankara.[4] Ordinary mortals may fully expect to slide backwards virtually as fast, or faster, than they progress forward, in view of the frailty of the human will and the seductive strength of temptation. Nevertheless, always tantalizingly beckoning the individual on is the ultimate fact that nirvāna lies at the elusive end of the trail. Earthly life is comparable to the current of water which bears onward its droplets (or individual spirits) by routes however circuitous and with whatever evaporation or diversion or interruptions by users, toward final absorption into the undifferentiated immensity of the sea.

But the Indians were not content to find an explanation for the ending of life; they were fully as interested in its beginning. Somewhere, somehow, it all had to commence. The Judeo-Christian tradition is that God created the world and man out of original chaos, which was something apart from Himself. In this view life, and indeed all matter, is essentially separate from God. Every individual soul has the problem of trying to win its way back toward eventual union with an entity that is immeasurably greater and entirely distinct from itself. The heart of the religion is its Christian view of separation of God from man, a chasm that could only be bridged by belief in a special Son of God, half man, half divine, whose sacrifice offered a means of redemptive reunion. The possibility of such a reunion exists because God originally created man in His own image, and because Jesus went to man, in human form, and brought him back to his original relationship with the Divine.

This religion of the West has made slow progress in the East. It leaves unanswered the question of how evil got into a world that was created by a God who is all-wise, all-good, and all-powerful. It leaves believers confronted with the puzzling paradox that God created all and governs all; yet it is individual man who must bear the responsibility for his sins and suffer punishment for them. These are questions theologians contemplate and lay believers seldom worry about.

Indians have sought to explain the beginning of created matter in a way that would avoid these particular awkwardnesses. With its great number of religious sects, Hindu India evolved a variety of explanations. An ancient concept that appeared in the early Vedic hymns and animated many of the Upanishad chronicles is that God created the world not out of chaos but out of Himself. The world and all its creatures are thus viewed as individual particles that possess essentially a primordial unity. Everything, no matter how special or particular or unique it may appear, is actually akin to everything else. Even contradictory elements or incidents or behaviors are really reflections of precisely the same inner reality.

Herein lies the key to Indian rhetoric. Opposites are coordinates. Contradictions are illusory. The world is a dramatic portrayal of God playing hide-and-seek with Himself, trying to reassemble all the divergent parts back into their original unity. There is no other principle in Indian philosophy that had so great a rhetorical significance.

In such a universe, the existence of evil is easily understood; evil consists of the apartness, the partiality, the imperfection of incompleteness. The wickedness that appears is a one-sided view, based on partial knowledge, accounting for but a portion of the total circumstances. If the doer of evil deeds could be all-knowing, he would do good instead of ill. If the victim of cruelty could understand all the circumstances, he would forgive, even as he suffered. Ultimate good can only be regained through a final amalgamation of all being back into its primary monism, the finally inescapable unity.

What is most self-evident about the Indian way of life is its complexity, the subtlety of its distinctions, and its interminable attempts to reconcile apparent contradictions.[5] Dharma, the central concept in Indian social philosophy, means the *way of life* which must be followed if the individual is to progress toward the ultimate goal of nirvāna. Yet for even the most thoughtful and knowledgeable Indians, dharma is "a subtle principle . . . unfathomably deep," and "we mortals are not likely to understand all its ramifications."[6]

In other words, Indians must seek to live in accordance with a pattern they cannot hope to understand. Moreover, each will be judged by his neighbors in terms of standards which are unclear to both the observed and the observer. The complexity and the contradictoriness of the social requirements are compounded by the fact that Indian philosophy places the highest value upon individuality. The individual must continue to exist through perhaps multiple thousands of incarnations until his own exertions and achievements may win for him release from the round of rebirths. But it is equally true that Indian philosophy also denies real individualism—for nowhere else on earth is so much emphasis placed upon the essential relation of the individual with all the remainder of creation.

One Indian social psychologist, Pandharinath H. Prabhu, confronts the contradiction squarely: ". . . the ultimate end of life . . . seems to be concerned mainly with the individual. . . . But, from the Hindu's point of view, we must also remember that the inner personality of the individual, at its best, is identified by him not only with the group, nor only with society, nor with the nation, nor the race, nor even with the entire human race, but with the whole creation, animate and inanimate, seen and unseen, which includes all these and is still much more than all these."[7]

It would probably be impossible to avoid contradictoriness in the life values and social systems of a people whose deepest conviction, as has been noted, is that everything remains, everything continues, and, concurrently, everything changes, everything passes away. In the midst of such a philosophy, the hallmark of the Indian mind is its subtlety.

Subtle, too, is Indian rhetoric. Nothing is as it first appears. What is said must be interpreted in terms of what has been left unsaid or what had been said before or might be said later or at least was thought—and if not thought, should have been. Behind what appears lies what really is. Words are counters for dealing with immediacy as it pushes into our affairs. But it is impossible for an Indian rightly to confront the simplest problems of work, play, or government until after he "first raises the fundamental question of the significance of man's existence on earth, gives consideration to basic questions of the relation between man and the possible ultimate purpose and fulfilment of his existence, and, upon such bases, seeks to define and formulate his relations with every other thing, person, event and circumstance in the world."[8]

Such a concentration of interest upon ultimates and intangibles indicates a cultural tendency toward theorizing, speculation, analysis, and explication. So it would appear was the character of ancient India. Sir Charles Eliot declared that "The love of Hindus for every form of argument and philosophizing is well known." Then, since the principal subject matter of their argumentation is utterly inaccessible to both logic and observation, he noted the result: "India's greatest contribution to religion is not intellectual . . . but the persistent and almost unchallenged belief in the reality and bliss of certain spiritual states which involve intuition."[9] So pragmatic a modern-day Indian politician as Prime Minister Nehru agreed that intuitive theorizing marked India's past and to some extent also its present, resulting in "an absorption in finding an answer to the riddle of the universe. This leads them away from the individual and social problems of the day, and when they are unable to solve that riddle, they despair and turn to inaction and triviality."[10]

This is the philosophical milieu within which Indian rhetoric is to be discovered, explicated, and evaluated. But there are many more influences affecting rhetoric than intellectual beliefs, however sincerely they are held or however comprehensively they may be expressed in action. Members of a society also develop ways of living together, of governing and being governed, of neighboring together, of dealing with the stranger at the gate. The nature of a people's society helps to explain their rhetoric just as truly as do their religion and their philosophy. Indian society, as we shall see, does not contradict the beliefs we have summarized. Instead it exemplifies, reinforces, and elaborates the consequences of the structure of ideas that has been presented.

ANCIENT INDIA'S SOCIAL SYSTEM

The role of persuasion in ancient Indian society was relatively minor. Social relations were not widely subject to the free play of competitive moral suasion. On the contrary the population was fitted into the world's most complex and rigid social stratification. Historically, ancient India did not seek to establish individual welfare through a system of free choice. Rather, it sought to maintain personal well-being through guaranteeing the stability of groups. The group became the unit of concern, far more than the individual.

The groups that mattered most in early Indian society were the village community, the caste, and the extended family. During the long hegira through multiple rebirths, every individual had to find his own way, but during each particular earthly incarnation, his mode of life was ruled by his family, his village, and his caste.

The governing principle of Indian social philosophy was that every individual is born into a form of life that accurately reflects the merits and demerits of his preceding incarnations. He is what he has become. He is what he deserves to be. He is what he must be until he shall regress or advance in a succeeding incarnation as a direct result of his actions, thoughts, and words. Meanwhile, although individuals come and go, society itself remains. Social systems have the invaluable function of regulating the relationships of individuals; they must, therefore, at all costs be preserved. Since the individual profits from their predominant influence in his life, he should not hesitate to make sacrifices, when necessary, to preserve their structure. The group thereby comes to have a life and importance of its own which clearly transcends the life and importance of its individual members.

The importance of the family as the primary disciplinary center in China has been well known in the West. In ancient India the family occupied a position even more important and dominant than it did north of the Himalayas. The Indian family was an entity in itself, much more significant than any of its individual members. The living members of a family were but the trustees of the home, acting in behalf of ancestors who had departed and in the interests of the unborn members who would later be entering it.

The extended family consisted not only of parents and children, together with uncles, aunts, and cousins, but also the entire membership of three or even of four generations. The family was patrilineal, with the sons bringing their wives to their father's (and grandfather's) abode. Property was owned not by individuals but by the family. No one felt that land or furnishings or personal effects belonged to himself. Debts were shared responsibilities—so also was punishment, including that meted out by the community when a crime was committed. Even murder was punishable by a fine which was levied against the family of the guilty person.

The philosophical view that all creation was monistic gave another function of vast importance to the family. It was impossible to live without guilt in a society which viewed the killing or injury of any creature, even an insect, as destruction of a fellow being. Every home, consequently, contained of necessity five slaughterhouses: the hearth, the grinding stone, the broom, the mortar and pestle, and the water vessel. Through their daily use many tiny, even microscopic, beings were destroyed. The guilt for this life-sacrifice had to be expiated, and this was accomplished through an elaborate combination of family rituals—including studying the sayings of ancient sages, offering water and food at ancestral shrines, and extending hospitality to guests and strangers. Only through cooperative family effort was it possible to live without serious sinfulness under the philosophical tenets which viewed all life as being indissolubly united.

The rhetorical significance of such a system is obvious. Personality itself came to be considered communal. Arguments or appeals that might be compulsive for one individual were diffused in their effect when they had to be considered by an entire family group. Individual motivation lost some of its potency. It would not often be considered of a person that he was bold, thrifty, irresponsible, or talented. Instead, entire families would be categorized as having certain traits. Under such circumstances individual ambitions and feelings of triumph, guilt, or shame were in one sense heightened, in another diminished. They were heightened since whatever one did or failed to do reflected credit or blame not only on himself but on his entire family, including their ancestors and their descendents. But they also were diminished since the glory of achievement or the guilt for offenses was ascribed to the entire family, not just to the individual.

It was difficult for an individual even to think of himself apart from the family. Prabhu declares that the individual could no more be separated from the family than a finger from the hand. A smashed finger hurts the entire person. A skilled hand helps the entire person. Each individual likewise is not a separate entity but an organic part of the whole.[11]

Families, in their turn, joined into communities; and in the early history of India villages were highly autonomous. The emergence around 600 B.C. of republics and kingdoms in northern India introduced somewhat larger units of government. But even then the public business was largely conducted in assemblies where heads of families or other representatives met to debate and decide on matters of common concern.

These meetings were distinctly forums for general discussion, not unlike the town meetings of colonial America. Typically, a *raja* presided—not as the people's ruler, but as chairman of the assembly. Each matter as it arose was debated until a consensus developed. Questions were not put to a vote unless it appeared impossible or unlikely that a general agreement would emerge. The spirit was highly democratic and equalitarian. Debating skill was highly valued, for communities were much influenced by persuasion in the depiction and interpretation of situations and events. A typical and historically important feature of ancient Indian villages, and of the capital towns of the small republics, was the Moot Hall in which the assemblies sat.[12]

Through membership in the autonomous community the personality of the individual was both enlarged and diminished, much as occurred through his family connection. A village consisted of a group of families that had intermeshing responsibilities. Failure by any family to perform its set tasks or prescribed duties would immediately and perhaps deeply injure the entire community. Similarly, the prosperity of a family would infallibly improve the lot of the community to which it belonged. A person would be proud or ashamed of his community, though the community would be unlikely to have feelings of admiration or of condemnation toward him, since such feelings were, as a matter of course, directed toward his family as a whole.

More impersonally, but also more importantly, every Indian belonged not only to a family and a community but also to a caste. Caste membership was absolutely crucial in determining the individual's manner of life; and it also deeply affected every individual's self-image. It represented what in the West is comprised by both status and role. Everyone was born into a particular caste and had no practical means of departing from it except by death.

The conviction of the whole society was that an individual was born precisely into the situation merited by his life in prior incarnations. As it was described in the *Brihadāranyaka Upanishad:* "As he has acted, as he has lived, so he becomes; he who has done good is born again as a good one; he who has done evil is born again as an evil one. He becomes good through good action, bad through bad action. Therefore, it is said: 'Man here is formed entirely of his desire, and according to his desire is his resolve, according to his resolve he performs the action, and according to the performance of his action is his destiny.' "[13]

Succinctly, the *Maitri Upanishad* summarizes the idea: "what a man thinks that he becomes." There could be no argument with what destiny had decreed for him, for he had created his own destiny. His caste position was an outward reflection of his inmost self—of his strengths and weaknesses, of his genuine characteristics, of his honest desserts. To question or to quarrel with one's caste position would have been equivalent to a renunciation of oneself. Of course there was no reason not to try to earn a higher caste role in the next incarnation, and every reason for trying to do so.

In the kind of society that existed in ancient India, there would not be outstanding individuals. A person was not valued for his idiosyncratic characteristics but for his compatibility with his group. *Ethos* in ancient India did not arise from special merits of the individual but from his quality of representation of his family, his community, and his caste. What was admired was typicality. What was most valued in human personality was what in the West has most commonly been deemed an ineffective personality; namely, the lack of any striking evidence of individuality. The rather cynical slogan attributed to run-of-the-mill American politicians, "To get along you have to go along," was in ancient India not a hope or a threat but a settled and acknowledged way of life. Strikingly and significantly, early Indian history is the history of societies rather than of persons. Even the great literary and philosophical masterpieces are all anonymous. Not who said it, but what was said— this was what mattered.

Naturally, Indian legend and literature are little concerned with biography. The rich collection of Vedic hymns and the philosophical Upanishads are not ascribed to individual authorship. Neither is the richly individualized *Bhagavad Gita*. Hinduism is a religion virtually unique in having no founder; nor does it have either doctrines or an organizational structure derived from the teaching of specific individuals. And even though the other great Indian religions—Buddhism, Jainism, Islam, and Sikhism—did have individual founders, there was notably little interest among their disciples for preserving factual or anecdotal records of the lives of Gautama, Mahavira, Akbar, and Nanak.

Among the leaders who gave significant redirection to Indian thought or to political and social developments, a few names of greatly influential leaders from later periods stand out, such as Asoka, Bimbisara, Chaitanya, Kanishka, Kautilya, Sankaracharya, Marathi, Nagarjuna,

Ramanjuna, and Sankara, for example. Of these and of others who might be noted along with them, it could be said of all as Sir Charles Eliot wrote of Sankara: "Had he been a European philosopher anxious that his ideas should bear his name . . . , he would doubtless have taken his place in history as one of the most original teachers of Asia. But . . . his whole object was to revive the traditions of the past and suppress his originality." Then Eliot stated what he believed to be Sankara's basic idea: "A man who has any pride in himself is *ipso facto* differentiated from Brahman [the monistic essence of all being] as much as possible."[13]

The lesson is clear. No man lives for himself. All creation is bound together. Most explicitly and immediately, every individual belongs to groups which transcend his own interests, but through such groups he finds wholeness and completion. Primarily, these are his family, his community, and his caste. Individualism in such a society is not the ideal. The ideal, rather, is communalism—being an inconspicuous and integral part of the group.

The Uses of Speech in Ancient India

The socialization of personality, especially when carried to such an extreme as in ancient India, necessarily depended upon effective communication. Coordinate group action could not just happen. Even when traditional patterns were strong and were followed faithfully, changing circumstances and new problems continuously required renewed consideration. In a society that fostered individualism, such reexamination could consist primarily of private and personal thought. But in a group-oriented society, the problems had to be talked to a solution.

Talk was needed particularly because the people of early India did not make much use of writing. Many experts on Indian history have noted that "it is a strange phenomenon that in India, from the oldest times up till the present day, the spoken word, and not writing, has been the basis of the literary and scientific activity."[14] Oral communication has served even more definitively the social, political, and commercial needs of the Indian people. The reason in part undoubtedly was the widespread illiteracy of the population. But, considering that India in earliest times had an efficient system of writing, one may assume that literacy would have been general if it had been held in high esteem. The choice to communicate largely through spoken rather than written discourse was a deliberate one.

Reasoning from the present to the past has obvious disadvantages, but the failure of written records from antiquity imposes on the historian a burden of presumption from available evidence. What is undoubtable is that in present-day rural India conversation is the principal means by which ideas and information are exchanged. Whatever of interest comes to the attention of villagers is sure to be quickly and widely discussed. Someone notices the peculiar dress of a stranger who passes through the town; not only is it thoroughly discussed, but the topic is enlarged to include dress in general, the uniforms worn by the police—then on to the laxity of police discipline, the presumed prevalence of bribery, and so on to broader questions of government.

In each village there were special locations—such as the blacksmith shop, the portico of a public building, a low wall along the public square, or benches in a park—that were recognized as "conversational sitting places." These were likely to be occupied from morning to night. But social discussion was not confined to any special places. "Anywhere and at any time that two or more people get together there is some topic of common interest to them. Man must talk and talk he does, at times too often and too much."[15] And so it was, two thousand years ago, very probably much as it is today.

Partly because of the choice of speech over writing as the common mode of communication, the spoken languages of India retained a high degree of localisms, while the written scripts developed greater uniformities. As a result, India came to have some fifteen major written languages and several hundred spoken variants. As late as the end of the sixteenth century, books in India were still inscribed on pressed leaves and sheets of grass, as they were in ancient times. These sheets were hung on lines or limbs of trees and were called "treasure houses of the Goddess of Speech."[16]

The earliest history and literature of India were preserved through oral rendition, memorized and repeated down through successive generations. In the dawn of the historic epoch, India was inhabited by a people called Harappa, whose culture flourished from about 3000 to about 1500 B.C. The Harappans were then conquered by an Aryan race that had dwelt for an undetermined period on the Iranian plateau. At first nomadic, these Aryans gradually settled down in agricultural villages. Their most notable production was the collection of hymns known as the *Rig-Veda,* which date from before 1000 B.C., and which comprise a rich source of information about the civilization of these early settlers in India. Two other major sources are the *Mahābhārata,* the longest poem in the world, which (like the *Iliad*) relates the chronicle of a war and of the psychological conflicts that accompanied it; and the *Rama-yana,* an account of the kidnapping of Princess Sita by the king of Ceylon and of her recapture by her husband, Prince Rama, who thereafter gave India a legendary utopian reign that is pictured as the country's Golden Age.

The political development of the early Aryan settlers may be traced in their literature and legends. Apparently the tribal villagers engaged in conflicts which required them to elect chieftains; eventually the chiefs assumed some monarchal functions and privileges. Their power, however, was limited by the operations of two types of legislative assemblies —the Sabha, which was composed of the tribal elders or heads of families, and the Samiti, which was a gathering of the entire tribal membership. By some of these councils kings were elected, with their authority kept subordinate to the councils. In large areas of India small republics were established, again with the councils being the main organs of government.[17] In this early period of Indian history (1500–1000 B.C.), there was no formal system of codified laws. Custom determined what could or must be done, with enforcement in the hands of the king or council chief, with the help of leading priests. The principal evidence upon which a verdict was based consisted of oral testimony, both by the accused and by witnesses. To impress the value of truthfulness, a person suspected of a crime might be required to prove his veracity by placing his tongue against a heated axe-head.[18]

Among the types of public speakers who were most notable for the amount and influence of their discourse in early India were the Brahmins and the priests of Jainism, Hinduism, and Buddhism, all of whom will be considered in following chapters. Also widely influential, though for shorter periods of time and in a more restricted area, were the Parivrajaki, or "Wanderers," and the members of local legislative assemblies.

The Wanderers were traveling Skeptics who roamed ancient India in large numbers, teaching a kind of sophistic logic that won for them such designations as "hair-splitters" and "eel wrigglers." Although the Skeptics challenged the whole belief system which was so deeply entrenched in India, their eloquence—adapted to villagers who delighted in listening to eloquent discourses—attracted huge audiences. Great halls were built to accommodate the debates they held with whomever would venture to oppose them, and princes offered large rewards to the winners of such debates. Little remained of their influence after the rise of Buddhism and the subsequent regeneration of Hinduism.

But from another source of public speaking, the debates in the assemblies, India was to reap a heritage of free discussion and of insistence on the right of government by consent of the governed which persisted through centuries of disruption and occupation.

Each village had its own elected council; a higher council represented a cluster of villages, with power to intervene in a local community's affairs when this seemed necessary. Council members had both legislative and judicial authority and were generally treated with high respect. They distributed land, collected taxes, and tried suspected criminals. Members were elected and also were subject to recall in case of misbehavior. To guard against nepotism, no near relative of a council member could be appointed to a public office. The assemblies zealously guarded their independence and power in their relations with the reigning kings. An old Indian proverb attests that "Public opinion is more powerful than a king, as a rope of many fibers is strong enough to drag a lion."

Debate in the assemblies was free and vigorous. Gautama Buddha was sufficiently impressed with their functioning that he adopted the principle of free debate in council as the means by which his monks should regulate their monasteries. On an occasion when the King of Magadha planned to attack and destroy the Vajjian tribesmen, Gautama warned him of the futility of such an enterprise, in the following colloquy:

"Have you heard, Ananda, that the Vajjians foregather often and frequent the public meetings of their clan?"

"Lord, so I have heard," replied he.

"So long, Ananda," rejoined the Blessed One, "as the Vajjians foregather thus often, and frequent the public meetings of their clan, so long may they be expected not to decline but to prosper."[19]

The normal relationship between a king and the council was depicted in the *Atharva-Veda,* a collection of poems contemporary with the better-known *Rig-Veda.* In the third of the poems, in section 4, an elder summons a newly elected king to crown him, with language designed to emphasize the honor of the choice being conferred on him: "To you has come the kingdom, with splendour rise forward; as lord of the people, sole king, rule." Then (in the seventh poem, section 12) the king made the expected response, accepting the limitations of his authority: "May the assembly and the council protect me; . . . may I speak pleasantly at the meeting, O fathers; of these seated here together may I take away splendour and discernment; of this whole gathering, O Indra, make me the possessor of fortune."[20]

The Sabha, or assembly of elders, is mentioned often in the *Rig-Veda* and seems to have been of considerable importance. The Samiti, or large gatherings of all the village men,[21] was presided over by the king. In both councils debate was extensive and free, the aim being to arrive at a consensus so that no vote need be taken. The concluding hymn of the *Rig-Veda* celebrates this aim of the councils:

> Assemble, speak together; let your minds be all of one accord. . . .
> The place is common, common the assembly, common the mind,
>   so be their minds united. . . .
> One and the same be your resolve, and be your minds of one
>   accord;
> United be the minds of all that may happily agree.

An example of the kind of speaking done in the Sabha is preserved in the *Rig-Veda,* Hymn X, section 117, where the eloquence is no doubt heightened by the poetic rhythm and meter, but the line of argument probably reflects the persuasive approach used by the speaker. The speaker was a Brahmin who was appealing to the wealthy men on the council for more generous grants to support the priesthood:

> Hunger (he said) was certainly not meant as a means of death by
>   the gods,
> For also him who has eaten his fill, death befalls in various forms;
> The wealth of the liberal is never exhausted,
> But the stingy person never finds a friend.
> He who, though possessing food, to the broken and destitute, ap-
>   proaching him, refuses a morsel,
> And hardens his heart against him even though he had served him
>   before, he, too, likewise, never finds a friend.
> He indeed is a patron who gives to the beggar, longing for food,
>   wandering and thin,
> Who then readily responds to the call to alms, and also thence-
>   forth becomes his friend.
> He is no friend who does not give to the friend—to the comrade
>   asking for food;
> Let him turn away from him, with him there is no shelter; rather,
>   seek shelter with a generous stranger.
> Let the wealthier person be generous to the applicant; let him
>   take a longer view;
> For life rolls on like the wheels of a chariot; wealth comes now to
>   the one, now to another.
> The food earned by the fool is in vain; truly say I that it is death
>   to him;

He feeds no comrade nor a friend; he eats alone and also bears
the burden of his sins alone.
Only when ploughing does the ploughshare produce food; only by
walking can a distance be covered;
A Brahmana who can speak [i.e., who will talk with the mendicant
at his door] is preferable to one who cannot;
A liberal friend should be better than an illiberal one.[22]

This speech makes it clear why consensus rather than a majority
vote was the goal of the ancient Indian councils. The appeal is not at
all directed to private motives or to special interests. The speaker is
making a serious effort to show that the point of view he espouses is
precisely the value system of the entire community. What he proposes
is not his own policy set forth in contrast to other policies that might
likewise be defended. Quite to the contrary, he is attempting to depict
inevitable conclusions that must arise from contemplation of the truest
principles of Hinduism. He is not arguing about probabilities but declaring truth.

With such an approach to debate, the question is not whether one
speaker may excel another in persuasive skills. The question, rather, is
whether the genuine sentiments of the assemblage are being rightly
stated. The tone is not argumentative, even though it clearly is exhortative; the mood is one of patient explanation. The appeal of the speaker
is not to his own authority or to his own powers of reasoning but to the
common beliefs which all reasonable men must share.

This approach takes the speech out of the category of controversy
or of advocacy, even though it is infused with strong moral urgency.
The speaker intends to leave his listeners no choice. In his view, he is
dealing not with a question of probability but with one of absolute certainty. The issue he discusses may appear to be in the realm of individual choice, leaving to his listeners the opportunity to make up their own
minds. But actually the appeal is to such basic common convictions that
the speaker clearly intends his conclusion to be inescapable. The appeal
could be countered neither by presentation of contrary arguments nor by
reinterpretation of the speaker's data. It could only be attacked by a flat
renunciation of his underlying assumptions.

Here is a major characteristic of Indian rhetoric. Matters worthy of
discussion should not be presented in such partial or personal terms
that the listeners find themselves becoming partisans who disagree with
one another, thereby leading toward a counting of votes on the specious

theory that solutions should represent "the greatest good to the greatest number," or at least the view having majority support. Far from it. Solutions should represent what the community truly understands to be essentially right. The discussion should concern itself with accepted or self-evident principles. Matters of fact which might appear to deny or contradict the principles ought to be ignored or brushed aside; for obviously if the principles are right, any factual item not in clear conformity with them must either be an accidental exception or improperly interpreted.

Such a rhetorical concept imbued Indian discourse with a quality of assured finality. It seemed to indicate: *agree with us or you must be morally and intellectually wrong.* Within the Hindu tradition, this approach seemed obviously and clearly the way to conduct a discussion. The assumption was that speakers should attempt to say only what was right and true, and that judgment of the speaking should be governed by this criterion. The concept was possible only in a culture that conceived of truth as being both ascertainable and ascertained. The ancient Indian society was rent and shaken by multiple contentious sects, each fiercely differing with all the others. Nevertheless, on the essentials which this chapter has sought to depict there was general agreement; and as has been indicated the fundamental tenets of Hinduism have proved tenaciously stable.

This is not to say that the ancient Indian philosophers believed truth was easily come by, or even that their acknowledged seers had license to speak with dogmatic assurance. Their strong devotion to the truth led them to renounce persuasion that was aimed merely to win adherents to some partial or personal preference. They were suspicious of verbal eloquence and of merely prolific verbosity. In the second of the *Katha Upanishads,* for example, a Brahmin is castigated when he speaks vaingloriously, to display his scholarship and the superiority of his knowledge. Scathingly, the advice is given: "Let a Brahmin renounce learning and become as a child. . . . Let him not seek after many words, for that is mere weariness of tongue."

In the *Brāhmanas,* which are instructions written by the Brahmins to regulate their own conduct, a dialogue is represented in which mind and speech debated whether it is better simply to know, or both to know and declare. In this particular dialogue mind is declared to be the winner, on the ground that it is more important to understand than it is to communicate understanding—though in the conclusion it is evident that in general the Brahmins also valued highly both skill in and effective use of communicative speech:

Now a dispute once took place between Mind and Speech as to which was the better of the two. Both Mind and Speech said, "I am excellent!"

Mind said, "Surely I am better than thou, for thou dost not speak anything that is not understood by me; and since thou art only an imitator of what is done by me and a follower in my wake, I am surely better than thou!"

Speech said, "Surely I am better than thou, for what thou knowest I make known, I communicate."

They went to appeal to Prajāpati [a supreme god among the Vedic deities, known as the creator and protector of life] for his decision. He, Prajāpati, decided in favor of Mind, saying (to Speech), "Mind is better than thou, for thou art only an imitator of its deeds, and a follower in its wake; and inferior, surely, is he who imitates his better's deeds and follows in his wake."

Then Speech, being gainsaid, was dismayed and miscarried. She, Speech, then said to Prajāpati, "May I never be thy oblation-bearer, I whom thou hast gainsaid!"

Hence, whatever at the sacrifice is performed for Prajāpati, that is performed in a low voice; for Speech will not act as an oblation-bearer for Prajāpati.

Thus, the principal factors of India's ancient rhetorical milieu are seen to have had a high degree of consistency and continuity, whether the consideration is conducted in terms of typical Indian philosophy, or of its social system, or of the uses which historically were then made of speech.

The early Indians were accustomed by their culture to believe that truth could be found by earnest searchers; that the essential truth is that all creation is unified and monistic; and that, therefore, speaking truth means the utterance of whatever tends to clarify relationships rather than differences, and whatever brings people into agreement rather than disagreement.

Such a point of view toward discussion is rendered practicable by the formation of a society in which individual responsibility for one's own status was strongly emphasized, while, concurrently, individualism —in the sense of asserting one's own preferences or seeking one's own special well-being—was not only deprecated but rendered extremely difficult by predominant influences of family, community, and caste.

Within this kind of rhetorical milieu one type of speech particularly flourished. This was the explication of meanings in a manner intended to lead to unanimous agreement, or at least to an acceptable consensus. Such discourse might often seem to be trite and platitudinous. Its tone appeared to be moralistic and dogmatically assured. Within the ancient Indian culture, however, this kind of speech appeared to be humble and non-assertive, for its aim was to serve truth rather than the self-seeking interests of the individual speaker. Both speaker and listener had but one shared criterion for judging the worth of the speech: was it true? Such a rhetorical milieu differed greatly from that of the West, which taught that truth is elusive, relative, and uncertain, and that speakers by right ought to advocate their own interpretations, seeking their own welfare through accomplishment of their own individual purposes. The differences in the context of the rhetoric of Athens and that of ancient India were considerable. So, too, as will appear, were the differences in the rhetorics that were formulated to meet the differing social and philosophical needs of the ancient societies of the Indian subcontinent.

CHAPTER 3

Caste as Rhetoric in Being

THE CASTE SYSTEM IN INDIA

RHETORIC is not necessarily confined to written treatises. The nature of a society and its operative structure determines significantly the range of choices an individual may exercise and helps to guide his decisions. Thus, there is a rhetoric that exists wholly apart from abstract formulations. This may be called "rhetoric in being." It consists of a set of rhetorically effective patterns—customs, folkways, habits, regulations—which shape communicative behavior, including thinking, speaking, listening, and responding.

The means by which ideas are adjusted to people, people to ideas, and people to people are not haphazard. They are regulated by societal needs and established traditions. Every culture has its own rhetoric in being. Each society determines the kinds of speaking which it permits and fosters. It prescribes who speaks to whom, under what circumstances, and in what modes or styles. And every society adjusts to its own communicative prescriptions.

In ancient India a caste system became established which was at least as significant rhetorically as it was socially and economically. It constituted a rhetoric by which even the most ignorant, the most illiterate, and the most stupid were governed. Yet not even the most learned and the most intelligent and sophisticated could transcend its regulations. Caste in old India was a system of rhetoric that was both illimitable and implacable.

From earliest times India has been a land of tremendous diversities —of race, religion, language, social customs, politics—yet also a country of indubitable unity. Hinduism placed its stamp indelibly upon the culture and in the personalities of the people—so much so that to be Indian is essentially different from being Persian, or Afghan, or Burmese, though all these peoples are close and ancient neighbors and among them there have been intimate relationships. An essential difference is this: at the heart of Hinduism is caste.

31

Only in very general terms does caste compare with the social classes that exist in other parts of the world. Not even in countries having serfdom or even slavery at one extreme and a hereditary aristocracy at the other is class membership inviolable. A slave may be liberated and might under unusual circumstances even be elevated to the aristocracy. An aristocrat might be punished by being made a slave. By simple choice he could renounce his titles and enter the middle class. But ancient India's caste system identified every individual inexorably and finally as a member of the caste into which he was born. A bird is a bird; a fish is a fish; an elephant is an elephant. Just so, an Indian was a member of his caste until released from it by death.

The origin of the caste system is lost in prehistory. The oldest extant reference to it is in the tenth book of the *Rig-Veda*. However, it was in the "Code of Manu," which dates from the early years of the Christian era, that caste rules were first formally described. This code identified the origin of the four castes, or Varnas, as having been created respectively from the mouth, arms, thighs, and feet of Brahmā.

The Brahmin caste, created from the mouth, were to be the teachers and priests. They were both the speakers to and the spokesmen for the people. The other three castes, comprising the warriors, merchants, and farmers, were also important to the society, and theoretically the castes were equal. In ancient days the warrior caste seems to have had the highest prestige, simply because it represented the greatest power. Gradually however, by the Vedic Period, the Brahmins, controlling both education and religion, persuaded the others to yield more and more property and power to them. Thus, through intellectual dominance they imposed on the population an acceptance of their superiority. The farmers, meanwhile, sank in the social scale to the lowest level, and from their ranks descended the most abject group of all: the unfortunate Untouchables.

The Varnas were divisions of mankind based upon the presumed innate nature of the individuals as indicated by their birth into specific families. For the legal, social, and political necessities of making and maintaining viable distinctions among individuals in the population, some three thousand subdivisions known as Jatis were designated.[1] Each Jati had characteristics of rigidity making it comparable to a sub-caste in its social effects. Everyone was born into a specific Jati, could marry only within its confines, was bound by its peculiar vocational and other behavioral rules, and generally could leave it only through death.[2]

The literature descriptive of India's caste system is enormous, comprising, in a count made in 1945, over five thousand separate works.

Many of them were written by Indian apologists who wanted to make caste meaningfully acceptable to Westerners; some were written by casual observers of India who were impressed by whatever seemed to be sensational or quaint. Indian historians were sometimes induced by an unsophisticated and partial Westernization to renounce the traditional values of their country; and others were fiercely defensive. In recent years anthropologists have made their own reexamination of caste and its effects. What all these divergent inquirers agree upon is the importance of caste and its pervasiveness in Indian life.

A major effect of caste was to keep united into one culture a people heterogeneous in race, language, occupation, tribal origin, customs, and political organizations. What they had in common was their religion and particularly their belief in transmigration of souls. Caste worked in India precisely because everyone believed that a given life-span is but an insignificant stage in a journey that persists for countless generations, and that what happens during that life-span is both a result of prior experiences and a determinant of future status. "Thus even the most wretched man with his most degrading occupation remains satisfied with the belief that the miseries of his present life are the result of sins in his previous life, and that if he submissively performs his caste duties in this life he will be born in a high caste in the next life."[3] Whatever dissatisfaction was felt was directed not against society but against oneself; whatever aspirations a person might have tended to take the form not of social-improvement plans but of greater personal moral and spiritual striving. To believing Hindus this society was one within which every individual could seek to the ultimate of his abilites for advancement in the progression through the generations toward the blessed goal of nirvāna.

Meanwhile, the rhetorical function had to be achieved of adjusting ideas to people, people to ideas, and people to people. In the area of free decision-making, the legislative assemblies debated and groped for consensus. In the multiple relations of everyday living, caste regulations either prescribed or influenced behavior. Far less than in most Western societies the individual was left to discover or to contrive solutions of his own.

The communicative functions of the caste system pointed in two directions: to the relations of individuals within a particular caste and to relations between members of different castes. In both instances some latitude of choice existed, but the prescriptions were both detailed and strictly enforced.

As a general principle it might be said that within a caste members were required to treat one another with fairness under difficult circumstances of continuous intimacy; and that individuals of different castes were enjoined to maintain strictly a social distance that forbade intimacy and that prescribed clearly the gradations of respect and of privilege arising from the respective status of the castes involved.

This principle proved to be exceedingly complex, for it incorporated the lifelong and day-by-day minutiae of activities within the family and the community, at work, at play, and in civic and personal affairs. Caste influence was so pervasive that the individual was never free from it—neither in the most impersonal of his civic and vocational duties nor in the most intimate acts of his boudoir and toilet. The family bedroom was governed as surely as was the public forum.

One of the early English studies of caste fairly summarized its scope, though the author seems to have been somewhat naive in his addiction to the quaint and the curious. Caste, he averred,

> . . . gives its directions for recognition, acceptance, consecration, and sacramental dedication, and vice versa, of a human being on his appearance in the world. It has for infancy, pupilage, and manhood its ordained methods of sucking, sipping, drinking, eating and voiding; of washing, rinsing, anointing and smearing; of clothing, dressing and ornamenting; of sitting, rising and reclining; of moving, visiting and travelling; of speaking, reading, listening and reciting; and of meditating, singing, working, playing and fighting. It has its laws for social and religious rights, privileges and occupations; for instructing, training and educating; . . . for intercommunion, avoidance and excommunication.[4]

And the list goes on and on. Hutton, a later and more sober student of caste, points out that caste membership determines social status, vocation, marriage, education, friendships, civic duties and privileges, intellectual interests, health, burial, and the respect paid by the living to the dead.[5] An anthropologist who made a detailed study of caste operations in a particular Indian village agreed that the influence of caste is pervasive, though he noted there are somewhat elusive and ill-defined differences in the nature and extent of restrictions operative in different castes.[6] The laws in ancient India, it may be inferred, bore more heavily upon some than upon others.

Nevertheless, there were significant elements of commonality applying alike to all caste groups. The first and perhaps most important was the influence of localism. Individuals were much aware of relations with their own caste members in their own village, and with members of other castes whom they encountered directly. Beyond this narrow range, personal contacts were infrequent. Every caste was shaped in part by the character of the locality in which its members lived. The nature of the rural community or urban center in which they dwelt helped to shape their behavior in conjunction (rarely in opposition) with their caste responsibilities. Similarly, the influence of family and caste was interwoven, for, especially in smaller villages, most caste members would be blood relatives—a situation created by restriction of marriage to members of one's own caste.

Hence, caste, community, and family exerted intertwined influences. Generally these effects were complementary; seldom were they competitive. In short, the dwellers of ancient India were not likely to be torn by conflicting loyalties. In most instances the demands of family, community, and clan reinforced one another. This was especially true of the lower castes, but to a high degree for all of them.

Another important general principle was that at least in theory all the castes were equal. This did not mean that members of different castes had equal status in a specific community, but it did mean that a caste superior to others in one locality might have only medium or even low status in another. The changing status of castes could be effected by variations in the wealth or political power or religious connections of its influential members, but there was no dependable formula for such a generalization. A caste member might find in traveling that he either rose or fell in the social scale as he went from place to place. This posed no special problems except for the few who occupied positions of wealth or power, since most ancient Indians seldom strayed far from home.

The rhetorical significance of caste can be clarified only by viewing individuals in their personal and communal life. The two questions of moment are: how did they communicate with one another within their own caste, and how did they communicate across caste lines. These are the questions to be examined as we look more closely at the lowest and the highest caste groups in early India—the Harijans and the Brahmins.

As we turn to an examinattion of particular castes, one difficulty that must be accepted is that any particularized descriptions of caste behavior have to be from our own time. No such records come down from ancient times. However, by citing only particular descriptions that conform to generalized comments about caste influences in early India, we shall probably get a rather dependable picture of how caste governed personal and community life some twenty-five hundred years and more ago.

Rhetoric and Untouchability

If the shadow of an Untouchable fell upon the cooking pot of a member of any of the other castes, the food became polluted and had to be thrown away. In a land where famine was endemic and hunger a daily experience, a taboo of such stringency indicates how great was the gulf between members of the lowest caste and their village neighbors. But this restriction was not the ultimate; even a glance from a man of low caste falling upon the food required that it be discarded.[7]

The carefulness taken to stress the social distance between the Harijans, or low-caste Untouchables, and members of the respectable castes indicates how contaminating personal contact was thought to be. A Harijan, for example, could never use the pronoun *I* in speaking to a neighbor of a higher caste, but always had to say instead, "Your slave." He dared not refer to his food grain as rice but must call it "dirty gruel." His children he must call "monkeys" or "calves," and if he got a piece of silver he had to call it copper. When referring to parts of his own body, he was required to use the prefix "old," so that he spoke of his "old eye," "old ear," "old hand." Moreover, while speaking to a higher caste member, he had to hold his hand over his mouth, in order that his breath would not contaminate the listener; and, of course, his eyes must be fixed upon the ground.[8] Social relations between the Untouchables and the remainder of India's population were sharply limited, and when they proved to be necessary they were patterned in ways that emphasized the great inferiority of the low-caste individuals.

It should be emphasized that such restrictions were not imposed upon the lower castes by the higher ones. They were rooted in religious belief, crystallized in tradition, and were accepted without question and apparently without a sense of injustice.[9] Generally, members of the low castes were more rigorous even in the enforcement of caste barriers than were the higher-caste members. For instance, if a Brahmin should for any reason enter the house of a low-caste Kuricchan, the latter would seek to eliminate the pollution by plastering his walls with cow dung.[10] The lowest castes were even more conscientious than were their more fortunate neighbors in punishing with utmost severity any violation of their caste rules. Perhaps the reason lay in the religious basis of caste. Since low-caste membership was thought to be a punishment for sins committed in prior incarnations, and since only through virtuous living could an individual hope for rebirth in a higher caste, there was strong motivation for puristic observance of all moral and behavioral regulations.

Throughout southern India, the communication barriers between members of different castes were rendered more complex by the observance of what was known as "distance pollution." Depending upon the relative social status of particular castes, members of the lower castes would pollute higher-caste members if they came within a specified distance of them. A Harijan must, of course, remain far away from all other caste members. In villages where distance pollution as such was not practiced, a low-caste member might nevertheless be required to walk around a village rather than through it, lest his shadow pollute food. Commonly, low-caste members were forbidden to use water from the village well. They were restrained from pasturing their work animals in the shared pasture lands, and they could not drive their carts on village streets. In the words of a leading Indian anthropologist, "The Chamar [Untouchables] are, all the time, forced to lead a life of humiliation and degradation."[11]

Restrictions such as those imposed by caste might be expected to result in considerable frustration, and this is precisely what observers of life in contemporary Indian communities do report. According to Majumdar, the children tell outrageous lies, and at play they quarrel violently and abuse one another with filthy language. Adults, too, he says, are quarrelsome and abusive in their relations with one another. In all social relations not covered by caste rules, behavior is likely to be undisciplined and inconsiderate. In other words, what might be expected apparently became the rule: a people bound by iron-clad and oppressive regulations were quick to manifest license in speech and behavior whenever they could.[12]

Carstairs, in his study of a high-caste Indian community, found that this same frustration was a marked feature even of the members of the privileged social levels. Generally they behaved toward one another with great formality and civility, even when their real feelings were antagonistic. "On the surface," he found, "there was a deceptive show of cordiality and esteem." However, "When feelings of ill-will *did* find open expression, as happened in a number of explosive quarrels during my stay in the village, two features were especially remarkable. Firstly, the utter collapse of self-control, all the more remarkable for its contrast with the formality of normal exchanges. During a quarrel, the participants' faces were contorted with hatred, their eyes bloodshot, their whole bodies quivering. They abandoned themselves to anger with a completeness which previously had been familiar to me only in the temper-tantrums of young children." Then he added: "The second consistent feature of village quarrels was the presence of peacemakers, who inter-vened between the disputants, reminding them how wrong it was to give way to anger, urging self-control and compromise."[13]

As might be expected, quarrelsomeness was even more evident among the members of low castes. Stephen Fuchs, in his monumental study of a community of Untouchables known as Balahis, found there were "endless quarrels among the women," and that "caste meetings are indeed frequently the scenes of violent quarrels,"[14] even though the Ba-lahi people were generally meek, unassertive, and timid. Majumdar, confirming this view that Indian society tended to be violently quarrel-some on occasion, reported that "sobriety in language is unknown to the children when they quarrel, and even when they play, they use abusive language. Even when talking to elders, they speak rudely. When a child is checked for any fault, there flows a torrent of filthy words from his mouth. . . . Parents and elders do not give much thought to this. They let the children talk as they will." Then he adds, "brought up in this way the children grow up into men and women whose first thought is about themselves, and not of others. This selfishness makes family life often unpleasant, for the people often have difficulty in adjusting to one another's way of life."[15] Fuchs points out that the principal function of the *panchayat,* or village council, was to settle disputes between caste members.[16]

One of the frustrating restrictions which hampered free communica-tion between members of different castes was the custom of giving to every individual a name which served as a continuous reminder to him-self and to others of his caste status. According to the primitive rules governing the Varnas, the name of a Brahmin should be selected to in-dicate something auspicious; a warrior's child should be given a name that signified power; a merchant should select for his sons names that were indicative of wealth; and, in contrast, the low-caste children would all receive names designating something contemptible.[17] Perhaps, as Sharma insisted, this practice was not always followed. Certainly it served as a general pattern, so that deviations from it would be observed as something odd. Examples from primitive times include the tendency to name high-caste boys for the god Krishna—a practice still followed in the naming of the twentieth-century Brahmin diplomat Krishna Menon. Among the Untouchables, on the other hand, names were se-lected to signify "the lame one," "the one-eyed," "the poor cripple," and the like. Such distinctions of names served several communication functions: to discourage discourse across caste lines, to enhance feelings of unity within a caste, and to signal clearly the relative status of individuals when they chanced to converse, even if they met as strangers.

Sociability was highly developed in Indian society. Along with the outbreaks of quarrels which have been noted, there was also a gregarious enjoyment of social talk. Majumdar indicates that fluency and liveliness of speech were considered to be favorable personality traits and helped to create a circle of friends for a man.[18] Fuchs described with zest a village council meeting which he observed:

> It was a pleasure to watch these simple villagers talk. In the cool, calm starlit night every sound could be heard; the men spoke with an eloquence and volubility, with a variety of superb gestures and suggestive change of voice, now pleading and imploring, then stern and firm, all of a sudden sarcastic and ironical, so that I could not but admire their oratorical talents. The assembled community responded splendidly to the down-pour of words. . . . Many spoke at the same time without listening to what the others said. Some intervened and tried to calm the excited speakers, but failed and after fruitless endeavours to pacify the others, got angry themselves and started shouting louder than the rest. . . . Then the whole crowd dissolved into several groups, discussing the case among themselves.[19]

This description is fully in accord with Eliot's observation that "the love of Hindus for every form of argument and philosophizing is well known."[20]

In contrast with this picture of communal garrulity is the brute fact of innumerable restrictions against communication, especially between the members of lower and higher castes. A particularly unfortunate group of Untouchables were called Unseeables, because the mere sight of one of them would pollute other people. As a result, they were allowed to move about only at night, and then must drag a palm branch behind them—partly so that the rustling would warn others of their approach and partly to erase their footprints, to obviate this form of pollution of the landscape. These Unseeables earned their living as sorcerers, who visited evil upon individuals for a fee.[21] The only communication they could have with the rest of the community was of a particularly ghoulish nature, concerned with murder and the payment for it.

In some of the primitive castes in central India, parents were forbidden to jest with their children; but there could be a joking relationship between grandparents and grandchildren.[22] A wife was considered immodest if she called her husband by his name, and husbands were reluctant to use the names of their wives.[23] A jocularly intimate communion existed between a man and his wife's younger sisters and also between a wife and her husband's younger brothers. In both instances, jestful conversation was encouraged and often the relationships were "very much more intimate than mere jocularity or even romping."[24] These regulations and licenses were applied to members not only of one caste but also of one family. When the question was one of communication across caste lines, the barriers were formidable—especially for the Untouchables, yet members of the highest castes also suffered from the restrictions and taboos.

In the Buddhist literary work, *The Matanga Jātaka,* it is related that sixteen thousand Brahmins lost their privileged caste status because all unknowingly they ate a meal which had been contaminated by contact with the leavings from the lunch of a single Chandala—an Untouchable. In another *Jātaka* narrative it is related that a merchant's daughter washed her eyes with scented water because inadvertently she had seen two Chandalas. *The Chitta-sambhuta Jātaka* points out that the Untouchables were distinguished from the rest of society by their speech.[25] In another of the tales, a Brahmin who accidentally ate food left by a Chandala tried to expiate his sin by committing suicide. Such were the barriers between the top caste and the bottom, and they were inviolable from either side.

The fullest study of the Untouchables is Stephen Fuchs's report of his ten-year residence among the Balahis of central India, who call themselves "children of Hari," meaning direct descendents of God. Their pride in themselves and in their traditions is thus very real, despite the fact that they constitute the extreme bottom layer of the society to which they are loosely connected. In his final summation, Fuchs describes them as "mean, ignorant, fatalistic, dirty, dull, . . . the tragic products of an execrable fate, of a heart-breaking past."[26] Their home life is largely a condition of self-inflicted misery, with the young wife subjected to the cruelties of her mother-in-law, forbidden to speak to men outside the family, and never addressed directly even by her own husband.[27] The children receive no education at all, except for home training in the tasks they are expected to perform. Nevertheless, their lives have many ameliorative features. They have frequent holidays, marked by gay festivals and fairs. They are warmly attached to their religion and feel especially favored by Bhagwan, who is the chief of the many deities that keep intervening in their daily lives.

Among such a people, sociability took variable forms. They had, according to Fuchs, at least three distinct patterns of social talk. "In their conversation with their equals the Balahis are rather garrulous and talkative, and on the whole they are affable and polite. Towards people of superior rank they often assume an attitude of abject humility. They overdo their professions of submission and devotedness, try to humour and flatter in every possible way, and agree to everything that is said or demanded from them. Towards people inferior to them, the Balahis can be as haughty and arrogant as the high-caste people often are to them."[28] The "inferior people" toward whom they express their own resentments, incidentally, are commonly the most unfortunate of their own communities, along with the occasional hapless outcasts who venture into their midst. Such is the way of life of the sixty million Untouchables who currently inhabit India; and so, much like this, it must have been, even back in the earliest of times.

RHETORIC AMONG THE BRAHMINS

In sharp contrast with the degradation of the Untouchables was the privileged position of the Brahmin caste. Unlike the hereditary aristocracy of Europe, they did not possess special titles or grants of landed estates. Unlike the leading financial and political families of the United States, their status did not depend specifically upon acquired wealth or power. According to the Hindu tradition, the Brahmins were originally created from the mouth of Purusha, the creator of the world. Their function explicitly became that of serving as guardians and exemplars of all that had to do with oral communication. They were the only members of the Hindu community who were allowed to memorize the unwritten scriptures and literary classics and thus to transmit them from generation to generation by word of mouth. They were the priests and the teachers; and they became the lawyers and politicians. Whenever speech was to be used to guide and direct the affairs of the people, the Brahmins had the right and the responsibility of undertaking the task.

Far more definitively than has been true elsewhere in the world, India assigned the role of speaker to a specific class. In many primitive communities, the essential roles of priest, teacher, prophet, and lawgiver have been combined in one individual official, who has generally been known as the priest, or the medicine-man, or sometimes simply as the chief. But in India these functions were lodged not in a selected person but in a special caste. Whoever was born a Brahmin was born to live by the skills of oral communication. This was his destiny from birth, not to be neglected or avoided whatever his preferences might be. And equally true, no one not born a Brahmin could intrude into these functions.

The dictum of the ancient Romans that an orator is made, not born, was explicitly denied by the ancient Hindus, who viewed the matter very differently than it was conceived in Rome. To the Latins, as to the Greeks, eloquence was an art that could be taught and learned, with some individuals attaining superiority in its mastery. To the Hindus, mastery of the arts of oral discourse was a way of life which must be exercised fully just because communal existence depended upon it. Whether, or to what extent, it should be done well was a secondary question. The essential consideration is that it must be done, whether well or ill, and the welfare of the society required that it be accomplished dependably.

Superiority of eloquence would be a merely accidental factor, like the particular beauty of some individual women. A woman was needed to be a wife and mother, whether beautiful or not. Speakers were needed to transmit the heritage and to guide the society, whether eloquent or not. Oratory was neither a decorative art nor a means to personal advancement. It was a fundamental instrument of organized society. Such being the case, it made good sense to insure its practice by allotting its function to a special class of people. So, the Brahmins were the mouth of Purusha. Their destiny was to speak to and for the community. The problem was genuine and the solution was neat.

The Brahmins emerged in the topmost level of Indian society, principally because they were the custodians of both religion and education. Moreover, as was pointed out by Will Durant, they possessed "a monopoly of knowledge. They were the custodians and remakers of tradition, the educators of children, the composers or editors of literature, the experts versed in the inspired and infallible *Vedas*."[29] Stringent laws forbade any competition in their prescribed functions. If a member of another caste listened to the recitation of the sacred literature by any but a Brahmin, his ears should be filled with molten lead. If he himself ventured to commit the texts to memory or to recite them, his tongue should be split in two. Such were the laws, and so implicit was the acceptance of their justice that the penalties seldom needed to be invoked. The transcendence of the Brahmins in the realm of oral discourse was accepted as immutable and as divinely ordained. The only way to become a Brahmin was to be born one. The great oral professions were strictly hereditary.

In a dramatic historical demonstration of the power of speech, this class which monopolized the oral professions maintained its dominance in Hindu society virtually unquestioned. Conquerors came and went; empires rose and fell. Wealth came now to one profession, now to another, as social needs and opportunities changed. But always the Brahmins remained the social leaders of Indian society. They might and often did beg for their livelihood. Many of them wandered the roads from community to community, without the shelter of a settled abode or the protection of their families. In other instances, Brahmins lived in luxury on great estates, risking calumny, theft and high taxes. From all these diverse evils the Brahmin caste appeared immune. Only they could perform the great essential tasks which through speech nourished the minds and the spirits of the people. In this favored position lay their power. It proved to be an unshakable bastion.

CHAPTER 4

Hinduism and Other Pre-Buddhistic
Rhetorical Theories

THE UPANISHADS

IN THE SEVENTH AND SIXTH CENTURIES B.C. an exuberance of change
was sweeping through India's intellectual community. The Brahmins
were on the ascendant, basing their claims to dominance upon their
monopoly of the sacred scriptures, including especially the Vedic hymns
and the Upanishadic writings. But their status was not yet so firmly
fixed that it went unchallenged. Various heretical doctrines were widely
held and ably promulgated, and many conflicting ideas were vigorously
debated. The basic stability of the society was underscored by the storms
which beat upon and around the main philosophical concepts and the
social structure, without fundamentally affecting them. Nevertheless,
highly interesting ideas were stated and tested in the forum of contentious advocacy.

In this chapter consideration will be given to the Upanishadic orthodoxy, to the dramatic developments in debate, and to the challenges presented respectively by the skeptics, the Ajīvikas, and the Jains. These
forces joined together in active contention, causing an intellectual and
social ferment that helped to instigate and make acceptable the new
insights of Buddhism that were shortly to follow.

Among the great seminal works of the world, the Upanishads must
be included for the vision they present and illuminate of the soul of man
as an integral part of an inseparable universe. Their essence was well
stated by Edmond Holmes: "They are dominated by one paramount
conception, that of the ideal oneness of the soul of man with the soul
of the universe."[1] The lesson they teach is that mankind is not bound
together by love, or by moral responsibility, or by devotion to a father-
god, but by the unshakable fact of indissoluble and essential unity. More
than loving our neighbor as we love ourselves, we actually are one with
our neighbor—blood of his blood, spirit of his spirit. The destiny of all

is so intertwined that there can be no separate salvation or separate damnation. Whoever scorns or harms or loves or helps another, so he also does to himself. This is the light that shines through those gospels which the Indians call Upanishads. It is an illumination of a particular kind, with a message of its own—a message with strong rhetorical implications.

No one can say how many Upanishads there are, for the number is indeterminate. The term may be defined as "sitting for instructions" or, simply, as "teachings." The spirit of the Upanishads may be represented in a quotation from one of the greatest of them, the *Chhāndogya Upanishad,* which asserts (in its seventh section, sixteenth paragraph): "When a man speaks words of truth he speaks words of greatness; know the nature of truth." A French version of fifty of them, translated by Antequil Duperon from a Persian edition in 1802, was read by the German philosopher Schopenhauer, who enthusiastically introduced them to European readers. It is of interest that the Persian collection was authorized by the son of the emperor who built the fabled Taj Mahal. Those who travel to Agra to view the Taj are enthralled by its majestic beauty; but millions who remain at home may have their lives enriched by the treasures of the Upanishads.

Since there is no canon establishing the text of the Upanishads, there is no way by which their number can be definitively determined. Theoretically, new Upanishads may be composed even today. The body of traditional writings given this general title number about one hundred and twelve, all dating from around 1000 to about 300 B.C. Some authorities include the *Bhagavad Gita* among the Upanishads; generally, however, it is accounted so great a work that it is simply listed by itself, as a classic *sui generis.* The character of the Upanishads varies considerably, for some are essays, some poems, some narratives—either sustained or anecdotal—and some are dialogues. In length they vary from the *Isa Upanishad,* which consists of only eighteen verses or sentences to others that consist of at least one hundred pages. The length of the one hundred and twelve traditional Upanishads is about the same as that of the Bible. The authorship of the various works is completely unknown. For centuries they were repeated verbatim, from memory, not being committed to writing until the third or fourth century A.D.

The long oral tradition of the Upanishads was not accidental but deliberate since the ancient Indians had a far deeper confidence in living speech than in the more impersonal and derivative written communication. When words issued from the mouth of a sayer, they carried a personal endorsement. As a student of the Upanishads wrote: "It is a truism that ideas or thoughts are expressed by words or speech. Human thought first found vent, or burst forth, by means of articulate sound. For that reason, in the eyes of the primitive peoples, words or speech came to possess, from the very beginning, an important significance. . . . Accordingly, we find that Brahman, in the Upanishads, was at first identified with speech. It may therefore be taken that Brahman at first meant speech or word."[2]

Neither is it accidental that the Upanishads contain no internal evidence as to when, where, or by whom they were composed. Their very thesis is that we dwell in the midst of a timeless eternity, with everything so indissolubly united that particular areas or places are of no concern. Who might be the author of an idea or of a way of communicating it must be of no importance whatsoever, since truth is truth. All that matters is the degree to which an utterance might reveal the common treasure of insightful knowledge which is the rightful heritage of us all. As Chakravarti says, "The old thinkers of India, likewise, did not attach much importance to dates, when dealing with ultimate ideas, for the reason that, according to them, they belonged to no particular time, but were meant for all time."[3] Confirming this judgment, Radhakrishnan, in his germinal history of Indian philosophy, avers that "the problem of determining the exact dates of early Indian systems is as fascinating as it is insoluble, and it has furnished a field for the wildest hypotheses, wonderful reconstructions and bold romance."[4] What we can learn about the Upanishads must be learned from a study of them as discourses; there is no external aid in the form of biographical and historical context.

In the prestigious opinion of Max Müller, the Upanishads consist of vast heaps of rubbish, from the midst of which solitary fragments of gold may be extracted.[5] This would seem to be a preliminary opinion that was based upon initial examination of them. Considered evaluation must accord them a far higher status. Few would question the judgment of Ranade that "the Upanishads occupy a unique place in the development of Indian thought. All the later systems of Indian philosophy . . . have been rooted in the Upanishads."[6] Radhakrishnan agrees that "the Upanisads [his spelling] are the highest and purest expression of the speculative thought of India."[7] If on a casual reading they may seem in long stretches to be barren, the best counsel is that which Dr. Johnson in somewhat different circumstances gave to Boswell: "Sir, read it again."

Actually, the neophyte gaining his first acquaintance with this body of Indian classics is less likely to think them barren than to consider them excessively repetitive. This reaction has justification, for the central theme of the Upanishads is simple and their unifying characteristic is their faithful adherence to this theme. The theme is simple precisely because it is vital. Time after time the Upanishads examine the question, "What is the meaning of life?" Ultimately, finally, underlying all the din and confusion of transitory troubles and desires, what is life all about? From whence did life come and toward what goal does it proceed? What relationship does one segment of life have to the others? Is there meaning in suffering, in sin, in seeming reward for ill-doing? Is the universe just? Is existence justified? The questions may appear to multiply, but actually, as the Upanishadic seers well understood, they all have common root. And the answer they gave is one: "Who sees variety and not the unity wanders on from death to death."[8] Or, as it is restated in the *Bhagavad Gita:* "When one sees eternity in things that pass away and Infinity in finite things, then one has pure knowledge."[9] What the Upanishads endeavor to teach is what this knowledge truly is, and how it may be attained. Its message is the simplicity that lies in sheer essence.

UPANISHADIC RHETORIC

According to one of the greatest students of Indian philosophy, the purpose of the Upanishads is the pragmatic aim of serving psychological needs, rather than the disinterested search for truth. In his words, "The aim of the Upanisads is not so much to reach philosophical truth as to bring peace and freedom to the anxious human spirit."[10] In this view, the tracts are sermonic rather than philosophical, therapeutic rather than investigative. This same scholar again emphasizes their psychological (rather than philosophical) character when he notes that in the various Upanishadic writings "the soul of man is the keyhole to the landscape of the entire universe . . . the limpid lake which mirrors the truth."[11] In this sense, these writings are motivational—an effort to explain why human beings feel, believe, and act as they do. In practical usage they are rhetorical, embodying an explanation of how individuals must be perceived and dealt with in order to motivate effectively their thoughts, attitudes, convictions, and actions.

The *Svetāsvatara Upanishad,*[12] which many consider to be the most basic, asks the fundamental questions: Is Brahman the original cause, the first mover? From whence are we born? How should we live? What happens to us when we die? The answer given is that God is innate in His qualities, which are the particles of the universe. He is the One in whom all originates, by whom all is directed, and toward which all is headed. As long as the human soul believes that it is individual and thereby separate from Brahman, it must continue in the cycle of rebirths. When it comes to know that it is a part of Brahman, it may come to rest in him. Its teaching is: "Know Him who only is to be known, so that death may not grieve thee."

The retorical significance is inherent in its philosophy. In communicating with one another, we should stress the unity of interests and of views rather than to try to shift the listener from his premise to that of the speaker. We should seek to discover and to disclose universal truth, rather than the partial truth of particular propositions. Rather than seeking to give persuasive support to statements that are *probably* true (which to Aristotle constituted the true province of rhetoric) we should simply explicate theses that are *certainly* true. The emphasis is clearly upon the message rather than upon the means by which it should be organized, supported, illustrated, and presented. As the *Svetāsvatara Upanishad* insists: "God is concealed within His own qualities." The function of the teacher, the seer, the knower is to provide guidance that will help the uninitiate to penetrate through the external superficialities to the underlying reality.

The *Mundaka Upanishad,* which is the most popular and most often quoted, aims to show how errors may be avoided. Immortality is not to be attained by good deeds, it declares, for they themselves are mortal. Knowledge of the things of this world cannot suffice, for it is of secondary significance. The infinite, which is primary, can be known by self-examination, for the individual is part of the infinite. Hence, individuals must be impelled to surrender the interests and desires which bind them to this world, in order that they may attain oneness with the essential unity. To any question that may arise, the meaningful answer is: "Know thyself." This same theme is pursued in the *Isa Upanishad,* which warns that whoever pursues good deeds enters into blind darkness; and whoever worships knowledge enters an even blacker darkness. The key verse reads: "He who sees all creatures in himself and himself in all creatures, no longer remains concealed (or separated or ignorant)." Identification, which is emergent from meditation on oneself, constitutes the only avenue to true communication.

The *Kena Upanishad* emphasizes that no speaker or doer can actually pursue a purpose of his own, since purpose itself is a function of the unified universe. All the individual can do, if he is to be true to himself, is to unveil the hidden meanings. Or, as the *Kena* phrases it, in the form of a series of suggestive questions in its opening verse: "At whose wish does the mind sent forth proceed on its errand? At whose command does the first breath go forth, at whose wish do we utter this speech? What god directs the eye or the ear?"

The speaker, it is clear, is in fact a spokesman. His aim is not to originate propositions, much less to defend them or to urge their acceptance. The only legitimate speech is that which reveals a truth that belongs as much to hearer as to speaker and, ultimately, to neither of them, but to the basic nature of the universe.

Somewhat more detailed examination is merited by the *Brihadāranyaka* and the *Chhāngdogya Upanishads,* which are among the longest of the group and are believed to be also the oldest. Each of them not only indicates a philosophic concept within which rhetoric must operate but also illustrates the prevalent rhetorical methods, which consisted of dialogue with question-explanation-challenge-and-definitive explication, of explanation based on analogy, and of authority based on demonstrated insight.

The *Brihadāranyaka* opens (Book 1) with forthright ridicule of the sophistic Brahmins. A Brahmin named Balaki appears in the court of King Kshatriya and, for the price of one thousand cows, offers to explain the true nature of Brahman (or of ultimate reality). The king accepts the offer and listens as Balaki parades his extensive knowledge of the classics. Ultimately, through a series of probing questions, the king forces Balaki to recognize that truth may only be discerned through insight into one's own nature—since the perception of all else depends upon the senses, and these are undependable. The remainder of this Upanishad relates the adventures and views of a ruler named Yājnavalkya, who abandons all possessions and leaves home to become a hermit, after explaining to his favorite wife, Maitreyi, that only self matters, since it contains the essence of all else.

The third book of this Upanishad is of special rhetorical interest, since it relates how Yājnavalkya vanquishes all the Brahmins in a court debate, for which the prize consists of a thousand cows, each one with a bag of gold attached to each horn. It is obvious that oral argument was highly valued, and it is clear that high prestige attached to the ability to win prevalence for one's own view of truth. Yājnavalkya won this debate by elaborating the same theme he had explained to his wife. He maintained successfully that the self is the true ruler of the universe, since it incorporates the essence of all that exists. The king was so completely convinced that he showered Yājnavalkya with gifts. Finally, he offered Yājnavalkya his kingdom when the sage pointed out to him that man attains understanding and also happiness—which derives from illumination or true insight—when he frees himself from desires, evil, fear, and sorrow. Then never more is he father, husband, thief, or caste member, for he transcends all limited responsibilities and characteristics.

Yājnavalkya proceeded to show that man becomes outwardly whatever he innately is: a man of good deeds becomes good, of evil deeds evil. To whatever a man's mind is attached, he is drawn. Hence, through pursuit of desire he is reborn again and again into the world of sensations, where desires may be pursued. Only when an individual surrenders desire can he transcend the need to be reborn and may then rejoin Brahman (or original essence). As part of this exhortative interpretation, Yājnavalkya explains (in Book 4, section 4, verse 6) what rebirth involves: "Then his knowledge and his works and his previous experience take him by his hand. As a caterpillar which has wriggled to the top of a blade of grass draws itself over to a new blade, so does a man after he has put aside his body draw himself over to a new existence."

It is clear that the moral standard incorporated in this philosophy was of the highest and that its sanction was of the utmost severity. Everything has inevitable consequence for the individual himself—if not in this incarnation, in the next. Whatever a man is, he becomes. It is impossible to be a louse in secret, for one is thereby making himself into a louse in fact. Likewise, it is unnecessary to try to herald one's good qualities, for inevitably they will be apparent. No light can be hidden in a basket underneath a hill. Nothing can be hidden—neither bad nor good. Of course the unveiling of a man's true character may require a full generation of time. It may not emerge until after his rebirth in a new incarnation. But why should the search for the truth be hurried? Eons of time pass, age succeeds age, and still the individual soul continues its hegira through birth after birth, death after death, until a continuing succession of good deeds will eventually permit the final incarnation into nirvāna.

Within the context of such a philosophy, the rhetorical function appears vastly different than in non-Indian realms, where birth is a beginning and death an end, with all that matters to be accomplished between the two. In ancient India the rhetorical end could be only a common search by speaker and listener for enlightenment, through penetration into a unified truth which encompasses them both and all else besides. This the *Brihadāranyaka* implies, and the same theme is reinforced in the *Chhāndogya*.

The *Chhāndogya Upanishad* consists of eight parts, of which Part VI renders concrete the general message of them all. It consists of a dialogue between a father, A'runi, and his twenty-four-year-old son, Svetaketu, who has just returned home after completing his education, swollen with the pride of knowledge. A'runi asks him if he has learned how it is that what cannot be heard is audible, what cannot be seen is perceived, and what cannot be known is nevertheless understood? When Svetaketu confesses ignorance of this knowledge, A'runi demonstrates that by knowing the properties of a small handful of clay, one comprehends the nature of all clay. Then he explains that the universe consists of a unified essence; therefore, all that exists anywhere and in any manner must also be comprised within one's own self; hence, the surest route to all knowledge is not through the learning of masses of facts but through meditative insight into one's own nature. The same point is then reemphasized by A'runi's illustration that the essential life-property of a banyan tree is contained in the invisible kernel of its seed—and that salt, though dissolved in water, is nevertheless incorporated into every part of the water.

The following two parts make clearly explicit the point that understanding will be misled if the inquirer turns to the world about him, hunting for specific facts. The more he knows, the more confused he will become. True understanding may be found solely through insight into one's own nature. As part seven concludes: "Meditation is in truth higher than thought." And the way of meditation is to free oneself from all desire—from all interest in externals such as food, drink, women, and friends. Then, finally, from concentration upon the nature of reality, when the voice speaks, it is the spirit that speaks—the spirit not alone of the speaker but of the universe of which he is a part. This is the ultimate truth to which all must bow.[13]

In reviewing the unified message which emerges from the Upanishads, it is clear that the fundamental psychology which they represent is virtually directly contrary to that which has prevailed in Western culture. The West has consistently through the centuries stressed the value of individuality, of ego-consciousness, of personal identity, and personal responsibility. In this psychological context what is of utmost value is the identification of an "I" which confronts other "I's" and seeks on tenable terms to deal with them. In the orthodox philosophy of India, precisely the opposite has been the underlying theme. The stress is upon the negation of the "I"—upon the identification of the ego with all being. Ego-consciousness is renounced as the great sin, for it is precisely the barrier which prevents the individual from finding its haven and its goal in reunion with the monistic universe.[14]

Rhetorically, this means that whereas the West has emphasized purpose and persuasion, in the form of an eternal conflict between a speaker who seeks to dominate and a listener who seeks to defend his own conceptions, in orthodox India the emphasis has been upon avoidance of both purpose and persuasion, thereby renouncing the concept of conflict. The only tenable aim of speaker and of listener is to try to comprehend the unity which encompasses them. Differences become illusions. Identity is taken for granted, and whatever appears to deny it is accounted by both speaker and listener to be a sin resulting from their limitations of character and of understanding. This, at least, is the philosophy of the Upanishads. It is a rhetorical point of view which has exerted continuing influence upon Indian society and the Indian mind.

Forms of Debate in Ancient India

During the century or so preceding the birth of Gautama Buddha, the unity characteristic of the intellectual community in India, as summarized in the Upanishads, was rent by disputes. Old certainties had come into question, and no fewer than fifty-eight contending schools flourished, each professing to represent orthodox Hinduism. Because of the contradictions of the philosophers' contentions, a suspicion arose in the minds of many students that perhaps none of them knew the real truth. Sīlānka, a ninth-century A.D. Indian scholar who specialized in the study of pre-Buddhistic skepticism, divided the proponents of these schools into three groups: (1) those who taught out of ignorance; (2) those who were skeptics because they realized the imperfection of existing knowledge; and (3) those who considered themselves extraordinarily wise.[15] A school of skepticism arose in which it was contended that whatever an individual might apprehend has in reality three parts: near, middle, and far. What is near to him he perceives relatively clearly, but it is only a part of the whole and moreover is a prejudicial part, being selected for attention simply because of its nearness. The middle may be perceived only dimly and the far not at all. Since different individuals stand in differing relations to any object, they necessarily see it differently. One consequence is that disputes arise, and knowledge might be clarified if the disputes could be properly regulated and interpreted.

As a result of these observations, debating became for a time in the immediate pre-Buddhistic period a major feature of Indian intellectualism. Elaborate rules governing these verbal contests were established. Great crowds gathered to listen to the contestants and to judge the effectiveness of their argumentation. Perhaps nowhere else at any period in history has debating skill been held in higher regard.

Basically, debates were divided into two broad categories: friendly, and unfriendly. A friendly debate occurred when two rivals attempted to correct one another's views of a matter concerning which they agreed on the basic premise and in which they respected one another's expertise. In an unfriendly debate, the effort was to destroy the credibility of the opponent, perhaps because each felt the other to be utterly wrong in his fundamental assumptions, or in which the debaters lacked mutual respect for one another's character or scholarship.

The effectiveness of the debaters was judged by their audiences, which were not necessarily unprejudiced. The *Caraka Samhita* described debates held for audience decision and pointed out that it was an unwise debater who permitted himself to be drawn into a contest before listeners who were partisans of his opponent. The *Atharva-Veda*, describing such debates, contended that an audience ought not to be impartial in any of three circumstances: (1) when an unrighteous theory was being defeated by the skilled presentation of another unrighteous theory; (2) when a righteous theory was being undermined by an unrighteous one; (3) when a theory that was partly right and partly wrong was attacked with unrighteous arguments. Naturally the custom of appealing to audience decision led to development of "hair-splitting" and "eel-wriggling" persuasion. So prevalent did such word-juggling become that in the time of the Buddha the *Majjhima Nikāya* was composed to appeal for well-reasoned and fair-minded argumentation.

Perhaps the historical analogy from which these debates developed was the question-and-answer dialogues or discussions that were featured in the primitivistic hymns of the *Rig-Veda*. These discussions (*brāhmodyas*) were in the form of religious charades, in which simple concepts were explained by cryptic answers to brief questions. Gradually, however, the desire to outwit a rival began to characterize the verbal exchanges. Sharp phrases began to be introduced, such as "not superior in knowledge art thou to me." In the *Mahābhārata* the debates had largely ceased to be teaching devices and had become avowed contests, held in public assemblies principally as entertainment for the listeners. In these accounts it was represented that "eloquent reasoners put forth many theories with the intention of defeating one another." In the *Chhāndogya Upanishad*, "the study of discussion and debate" was indicated as one of the principal studies for Brahmins. Jayatilleke indicates that this is a unique comment and that references in Indian literature were generally to the study of dialectics or of logic rather than of argumentation and persuasion. He went on, however, to indicate that in some

contexts, at least, the participants in the frequent discussions were prac-
ticing the arts of casuistry rather than of logical inquiry.[16]

By the sixth century B.C. the prevalence of skepticism had led to
the formalization of a list of some thirty approved debating propositions,
which were to be either defended or attacked, such as: everything is
created, or nothing is created; everything is impermanent, or everything
is permanent; the world is monistic, or the world is pluralistic; everything is (or is not) subject to causation; everything is (or is not) ex-
plicable.

Just as the topics became standardized, so did the arguments; thus,
what remained as bases for decision as to victor and vanquished was
skill in persuasion. So far as the records show, nothing was said about
ability in delivery, but there was careful consideration of the quality of
argumentation. The *Caraka Samhita,* in particular, identified five "faults
of speech" which the skillful debater should avoid. These were: (1)
saying too little, which occurred when supporting reasons were omitted,
or examples were not given, or application of an argument to the central thesis was lacking; (2) saying too much, which might consist of
irrelevancies or of needless repetition; (3) meaninglessness, when the
words seemed jumbled and the speaker perhaps meant to impress rather
than to enlighten; (4) incoherence, when the categories or definitions
used by the speaker were overlapping or vague; and (5) contradictions,
which might consist of contrary verbal assertions or of opposition between examples cited and the over-all context of the speaker's remarks.

It is clear that the debating of the time was highly sophisticated and
that speakers were expected to adhere to established rules. It is also evident that audiences hugely enjoyed the debates and that the debating
processes were debased into entertainment, rather than maintained as
intellectual inquiries or contests. These were faults which, as will be
seen, Gautama Buddha deliberately undertook to eradicate when he
proposed his own program of debate and discussion.

The kinds of arguments which were recommended appear to have
been tricky rather than logical. The *reductio ad absurdum* was approved,
in such an example as: the offering of food at ancestral graves would
be like expecting those standing on housetops to be gratified by food
placed below; or, the dead can no more be gratified by offerings than
could distant travelers be satisfied with food which one eats in his home.
Similarly, arguers are advised to puncture false analogies. For example,
if a speaker likens the dead to travelers, it should be pointed out that
travelers return to their homes, as the dead do not.[17]

A worthy called Payasi, whose exploits are recorded in the *Dīgha*

Nikāya, undertook to substitute "scientific experimentation" for the spu-
rious reasoning which was prevalent in those days. In an effort to determine whether or not a soul issues from the body at death, he bound a
thief in a heavy clay jar, closed the jar securely, and placed it over a
fire, where he kept it until he judged the thief must be dead. Then he
carefully uncorked the jar, watching closely to observe whether the soul
emerged. In another experiment, even more gruesome, he killed a man
by gradually stripping off his skin, flesh, cuticle, bones, and marrow,
seeking at each stage to determine whether or not a soul managed to
escape from the diminishing body. In still another endeavor, he weighed
a man before and after death, to see whether a diminution of weight
might indicate the escape of a soul. However unsatisfactory these experiments may seem, nevertheless they indicated a dissatisfaction with
the kinds of reasoning which they sought to displace; also, in the judgment of one earnest student of the subject, they show "that he had a
fundamentally unbiased and scientific outlook to the study of a problem."[18] Weak as the logic of the debaters had been, the Indians of that
time no doubt preferred it to the crass practicality of Payasi's experiments. In any event, the reasoning prevalent in India continued to be
metaphysical rather than empirical.

THE SKEPTICS, THE AJIVIKAS, AND THE JAINS

The settlement of issues through reasoning, which the debaters popularized, rather than through appeal to the authority of the sacred scriptures, led to a wide diversity of both beliefs and methods. Three principal modes of attaining clarity of understanding were by now developed.
The one, which was the most ancient and was held tenaciously by the
orthodox Brahmins, was that truth was contained in the Vedas, which
had been transmitted by direct revelation from the gods to the primitive
rishis, or seers, who first received and preserved them. Subsequently, no
one except the Brahmins was allowed to memorize and recite the Vedas; hence they and they alone were the sources of dependable truth.
It was a tradition which, naturally, the Brahmins cherished and promulgated.

The second mode of ascertaining truth, which was taught in the
Upanishads, was that insight into the genuine nature of the monistic
universe was to be sought through meditative concentration upon the
self. The pitfalls in this method were many, for concentration upon the
real self is obstructed by a host of insistent secondary or external inter-

ests and needs and desires. The method of *yoga* gradually evolved, comprising a complicated series of stages through which an individual may win himself away from attachment to the misleading enticements of the flesh and thereby free his faculties for complete self-immersion into the original well of unsullied truth. So fascinating did this search prove that it has been continued down to the present in India and has many proponents elsewhere in the world as well.

The third method of seeking understanding was through argumentation and debate, through which various alternative ideas were subjected to challenge and examination. As was noted in the preceding section, this method for a time gained considerable popularity—presumably because it alone directly involved the listeners in the process by requiring the exercise of their judgment. Besides, this method was fun. A public contest was entertainment, and at that time entertainment was hard to come by.

The debating, however, had the confusing result that a variety of opposing views were constantly being proposed and defended. A school of skeptics arose, who contended that truth was smothered by the contradictory arguments, just as vegetables might be choked out by a profusion of weeds. Since so many clever speakers were advocating so many incompatible ideas, who could know what to believe?

Those who claimed knowledge, speaking with positive assurance and supporting their claims with facts and arguments, could not in fact be wise; for they in turn were denounced by opponents who in method and in skill were much like themselves. Where there was so much to be said for contrasting viewpoints which could not possibly all be true, the natural presumption was that none of them was true. Such confusion was compounded by the fact that the sincerity of the speakers in an argumentative situation must always be in doubt, for they were observed to shift the grounds of their arguments if not their very assumptions when they encountered unanswerable refutation. Moreover, the skeptics held that the inner mind of the speaker could not confidently be apprehended by observation of his features, gestures, gait, movements, voice, or changes in his eyes or facial expressions.

In addition to these objections to the argumentative mode of seeking truth, the skeptics noted that debates often involved bickering, personal attacks, the misery of defeat, and an unlovely rejoicing in personal victory. Lasting enmity and quarrels between participants sometimes resulted. The net result of the debates, then, was that they enhanced confusion rather than knowledge and that they caused unhappiness rather than joy.

Since debate thus interfered with the clarification of truth and the cultivation of bliss—which should be the two principal goals of human endeavor—debating was to be deprecated. It was better to maintain a skepticism that maintained placidly: "What you assert I do not know how to judge; and what I believe I do not know." Through this stance both conflict and confusion could be avoided. So the skeptics believed, and for a brief time (until their influence was undermined by the teachings of Gautama) they constituted a serious anti-rhetorical influence in India.[19]

Another movement which challenged the reigning orthodoxy along lines similar to but distinct from the attacks levied by the skeptics was led by a wandering seer named Makkhali Gosāla (died 485 B.C.), whose followers took the name Ajīvikas.[20] For some two thousand years this sect flourished, unified by its fatalistic view that nothing an individual might do, either good or evil, could possibly affect the predestined course of his successive transmigrations. "There is no deed performed either by oneself or by others, no human action, no strength, no courage, no human endurance or human prowess which can affect one's destiny in this life. . . . Just as a ball of thread will, when thrown, unwind to its full length, so fool and wise alike will take their course, and make an end of sorrow."[21]

Obviously a conviction of the futility of human purposiveness was definitely anti-rhetorical. But the views of the Ajīvikas were not wholly negative. They also made a striking contribution to the psychology of cognition, which had strong rhetorical effects.

The cognitive contribution of the Ajīvikas was their insistence that the mind does not conceive of reality in either monistic or dualistic terms. On the contrary, our normal thought processes, they asserted, are triadic. As the leading student of Ajīvikism declares: "The distinctive characteristic of the Ajīvika system of epistemology . . . was the division of propositions into three categories."[22] Their logic did not divide reality into "A" and "non-A" but into "A," "non-A," and "both A and non-A." They were the first major advocates of the concept of truth as a continuum, with contrary properties being contained in greater or lesser degree in any depiction of reality.

The rhetorical significance of this continuum theory was illustrated by Jayatilleke, when he pointed out that something might have the characteristic of "q" from one standpoint, the characteristic of "non-q" from another and, when both standpoints are taken into account, the characteristics of both "q" and "non-q."[23] This mode of thinking encouraged the viewpoint that a given act might be considered to be just by one observer, to be unjust by another, and by yet others to be both just and unjust or even to be neither just nor unjust but, for example, simply true or not true, or avoidable or inevitable.

In sum, the principal rhetorical contribution of the Ajīvikas was in transcending the orthodox Hindu emphasis upon speaking clear and simple truth by insisting that truth is relative and depends upon the stance from which a given item is observed. They incorporated into Indian psychology the notions of uncertainty and of individual preference.[24] This would have opened the way for a rhetoric which, like that of Aristotle, should deal with the choices to be made within the realm of probability—except for the Ajīvikas' belief in fatalistic predetermination.

Actually their net contribution was the viewpoint that endless discussion of a subject is possible, since it may be viewed with equal pertinence from varied points of view, each of which justifies a different conclusion—but that the discussion ultimately can have no valid effects, for the matter has already been settled through predestination. Thus their rhetoric accorded exceedingly well with the Hindu penchant for synthesizing contraries into functional paradoxes. There was encouragement for endless discussion combined with an insistence that nothing that might be said could possibly affect the outcome.

For six years during his early maturity Makkhali Gosāla had attached himself to another wandering seer whose reputation both at that time and during the subsequent centuries far surpassed his own. This man was Nigantha Nataputta (who lived from about 599 B.C. to about 527 B.C.), better known as Vardhamāna Mahāvīra, founder of the sect that proudly calls itself Jaina, from the Sanskrit term meaning "Conquerors." Mahāvīra was strictly orthodox in his acceptance of the literal authenticity of the Upanishads, but he developed a special interpretation of Hinduism that has been fiercely defended and maintained by the Jaina sect through all the succeeding centuries.

Mahāvīra accepted the Hindu view of the monistic basis of the universe, which makes all living things kin, according so much emphasis to it that *ahimsa,* or "non-killing," became a particular mark of the Jains. He also accepted wholeheartedly the Upanishadic view that ultimate reality is best apprehended through meditative insight into the nature of one's own self. Hence, introspective meditation became the other predominant mark of the Jains.

Mahāvīra's principal rhetorical significance lies in his view of the means by which truth is to be apprehended. The pain-filled and repetitive cycle of rebirths can only be ended for an individual, in his opinion, through the attainment of a right view of truth, for everyone is born to proceed through life-experiences again and again until finally he can see clearly his own essential connection with the monistic universe. Whatever way the mind operates in order to attain to this understanding is primordial and therefore must be the correct kind of mental process. The test of cognition (or of logic), then, is whether or not it leads the individual to a wholesome and satisfying sense of unity with all being. Whatever induces in an individual this sense of incorporation within the ultimate wholeness of the universe is logical or sound thinking; whatever leads him to regard himself as being apart, different, or in opposition to other elements of being must be illogical or unsound thinking. The test of the quality of thought is the result it effects. And the end result which is the goal of all human endeavor is the engagement of one's own consciousness into the totality of existence.[25]

Jayatilleke outlines in the following chart[26] the means by which Mahāvīra and his followers sought to determine the truth of a given matter:

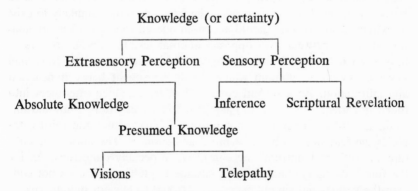

The avenue of sensory perception, in the view of Mahāvīra, has obvious weaknesses. Specific items of experience are perceived differently by different individuals and by the same individual at different times. The scriptures, which are also apprehended through the senses, as they might be seen or heard, also are subject to various and often contradictory interpretations. Whatever leads to diversity of understandings and therefore to conflicting interpretations cannot be sound cognition, for the results are conflict and confusion rather than clarity and harmony. Therefore, the inevitable conclusion is that sensory perception is a weak and undependable means by which to seek certainty of knowledge.

The avenue of extrasensory perception was more promising, he felt, but far from certain. Just as sensory perception often is wrong, so is the claim of insight. Individuals who insist upon their own introspective judgment often disagree among themselves; and what seems to a person to be sure insight on one occasion may seem dubious to him at another time.

There is, however, Mahāvīra felt, a kind of insight which is so clear and unequivocal that it may be deemed "absolute knowledge." This is the realm of self-evident truth. An example might be the understanding that it is wrong to cause pain, injury, or death to another living creature. The more one meditates upon such an introspective conclusion, the more certain he becomes of its rightness. In contrast, there are such forms of introspective conclusions as visions or telepathic communications. These, he felt, are by no means to be dismissed categorically; but they are nevertheless unsure and hence should not be accepted without other substantiating support.

Aside from his ideas on how truth is to be perceived, Mahāvīra's rhetorical views concerned principally ways in which knowledge is to be communicated. In the first place, he felt that truth is unlikely to exist at extremes, so that one should accustom oneself to looking for explanations that lie between two opposite alternatives. In this he appears to have been influenced by the insistence of his early associate, Makkhali Gosāla, upon a continuum which should be sought between negation and affirmation. As a second contribution, he classified utterances into four categories: (1) truth, (2) untruth, (3) a mixture of truth and untruth, and (4) neither truth nor untruth.[27] The second and third categories, he felt, were to be condemned and avoided. The third—the mixture of truth and untruth—he considered especially dangerous. As for the fourth category, there is wide latitude for talk which does not concern the verities but simply expresses personal feelings or preferences.

In concluding this discussion of the various rhetorical theories which existed in India at the time of Gautama, it is evident that there was considerable emphasis upon the unanswerable assertiveness of personal insight, which led to the two extremes of skepticism and sophistical debating. The society was much inclined to be talkative, and ill-prepared to judge and evaluate the cogency or dependability of the talk. This was the situation which confronted Gautama as he undertook his life's mission. And these circumstances no doubt exercised considerable influence upon the careful and detailed program with which he undertook to regulate the social relationships which depend upon speech.

CHAPTER 5

The Rhetorical Influence of
Gautama Buddha

THE KNOWN AND THE UNKNOWN

THE ORIGINS OF BUDDHISM are a curious mixture of the known and the unknown. E. Zürcher, one of the soundest scholars of its early development, notes that its beginnings are "shrouded in almost impenetrable darkness."[1] He finds variations of at least five hundred years in avowedly reputable estimates of the birth date of Gautama. As for most major religions, the origins of Buddhism were obscure. To both devout believers and inquiring scholars the mysteries and unanswered questions are tantalizing. But much also is known. What is certain is that in about the sixth century B.C. in India there lived a powerful personality whose influence precipitated one of the great spiritualizing movements in the history of the world. In this chapter we shall seek to indicate what it meant rhetorically.

The sixth century was no less a time of ferment in India than it was in the China of Confucius, the Persia of Zarathustra, and the Greece of Aeschylus and Pericles. For Indians it proved to be a period of spreading prosperity because of the invention of the plough, the discovery of new mineral deposits, and the growth of trade. It was also a time of disruption because of sporadic warfare among the country's four major kingdoms and its many small princely states and city republics. Intellectually, it was an age characterized by the breakdown of traditional orthodoxies and exploration of new ideas. The basic concepts of the unity of being and the transmigration of individual life remained unchallenged. But widespread skepticism existed concerning orthodox tradition that had sought to provide detailed interpretations of these phenomena.

Nevertheless, until the advent of Gautama, who came to be recognized as Buddha, there was no clear and convincing alternative around which the rejecters of old doctrine could rally. When he commenced

61

preaching, the results were immediate and overwhelming. The impact of his life and ideas was similar to the effect Confucius was having at about the same time in China. In significant ways these two sages were alike.

Like Confucius, Gautama's concern was with the humanistic problem of how to live in this world, without worrying about the unanswerable questions of metaphysics. Like Confucius, Gautama believed that the kind of behavior which best satisfies one's associates will also best satisfy oneself. In short, he saw no conflict between the needs of the self and duty to society. Again like Confucius, Gautama was intent upon identifying means by which the wisdom of the past could be brought to bear in solving problems of the present. And even more than Confucius, Gautama came quickly to be revered by followers who accepted his humanism yet virtually deified him through their acceptance of his every thought and command. Both men lived long in quiet byways, creating broadening spheres of influence through the strength of their intellects and personalities. And through the centuries both have been subjects of enormous quantities of interpretative scholarship.

It is true of Gautama, as of Confucius, that though details of his life are scanty the record of his words and characteristics is so suggestive that he is one of the great historical personages with whom it is easy to feel acquainted. We know what he liked and disliked, how he responded to new and unexpected situations, how his mind worked—quizzically, humorously, and with sharp cogency—in confronting new challenges. Despite the differences that made these two great seers contrasting figures—differences as great as those between China and India—the two would feel at home with one another.

Their rhetorical ideas start with similar premises but extend in quite different directions to encompass differing principles aimed toward divergent results. Each brought into focus the principles of communication and social relationship which were already evident in their countries before their advent and which (shaped by their examples and teaching) have subsequently influenced enormous numbers of their followers.

In contrast to the brevity of the Confucian *Analects,* the basic writings of Buddhism, consisting of sayings and sermons attributed to Gautama, together with interminable explications by his early disciples, are staggeringly extensive. The Pali Canon, representative of the many sects of Theravada Buddhism, consists of forty-five lengthy volumes, exclusive of its commentaries. The Chinese Buddhist scriptures comprise one hundred volumes of a thousand pages each; the Tibetan texts fill three hundred and twenty-five huge volumes.[2]

Despite the enormous outpouring of Buddhist literature in the East, it was not until the end of the seventeenth century that the first Buddhist writings were made available to Europeans.[3] The principal missionaries in India at the close of the eighteenth century confused Buddha with an obscure Hindu or Egyptian deity.[4] It was not until the mid-nineteenth century that the first significant translations of Buddhist scriptures were made by a Hungarian scholar, Alexander Csoma de Koroa, and by two English diplomats, Brian Houghton Hodgson and George Turnour. Hermann Oldenberg, with his edition of the *Vinaya*[5] (1879–83) and Thomas William Rhys Davids, with his founding of the Pali Text Society (1881), laid the foundations for the scholarly investigations that led to publication of *The Sacred Books of the East* series and the continuing research initiated by The Royal Asiatic Society.

A Westerner who is not an Orientalist or Indologist can only enter this domain fortified with the warning that Edward Conze wrote in the Introduction to his selection of Buddhist writings: "The baffled reader is advised to read on without bothering overmuch about their exact meaning."[6] The ambiguities are troublesome. Surely the history of human ideas offers few if any other body of writings which persist so consistently in eluding precise understanding by their readers. Moreover, such difficulties are compounded when the attempt is made to discern in this literature a pattern of rhetorical influence that is only indirectly suggested.

Nevertheless, the search is not hopeless. The basic factors at least are clear. "The fundamental truths on which Buddhism is founded are not metaphysical or theological, but rather psychological."[7] Gautama was always concerned with the nature of human motivation and its effects. Moreover, he himself did a great deal of evangelistic speaking. Hence, his rhetorical influence was substantial. What he meant by effective speech and the means by which to achieve it emerges relatively clearly from his teachings and his practice. What he meant to communicate about the significance, the nature, and the methods of rhetoric is part of his enormous heritage. It deserves to be interpreted, and it does have its own special meaning to impart.

THE MAN AND HIS MESSAGE

The founder of Buddhism was born to wealth, power, and privilege, as a prince and heir-apparent in the small kingdom of Sakya, located on the southern slope of the Himalayas, in Nepal, near the northeastern border of what is modern India. His family name was Gautama, and he was given the boyhood name of Siddattha. During his maturity he was often known as Sākyamuni, the "Sage of the Sakyas." He also was called Tathāgata, a title meaning "One Who Has Attained Perfection." Finally he came to be Buddha, "The Enlightened One"—or, to much of the world, the Buddha. Actually he was but one among many, for Buddhas are born into the world from time to time; in this select company Gautama was but the first among equals. It was he, however, who formulated the principles of Buddhism, and it is in his name that they are taught.

The birthdate of Prince Siddattha that is most commonly accepted is 563 B.C., and he is said to have died perhaps about 483 B.C., at the age of eighty.[8] During twenty-four previous incarnations Gautama had been a Bodhisattva: which means that after attaining full wisdom or enlightenment he voluntarily refrained from entry into nirvāna. Instead he sacrificially subjected himself to continuing the round of rebirths because of his compassionate desire to continue to share the fate of living creatures. The insight which he attained and passed on was not a philosophical explanation of the universe but a method of attaining individual salvation, by which he meant emancipation from all pain and suffering.[9]

The experiences of Gautama during the preparatory and purifying series of prior lives are recounted in the *Jātaka,* a remarkable series of narratives intended to illustrate the philanthropic aspect of the Buddhist ideal in which morality is equated with compassion. Typical of the whole is the story relating how the Bodhisattva found a tigress who was so weakened from having given birth to seven cubs that she lay near death from starvation. Thinking that he should give his own body to the tigress to preserve her and her seven cubs, the Bodhisattva reasoned: "For a long time I have served this putrid body and given it beds and clothes, food and drink, and conveyances of all kinds. Yet it is doomed to perish and fall down, and in the end it will break up and be destroyed. How much better to leave this ungrateful body of one's own accord and in good time! It cannot subsist forever, because it is like urine which must come out. Today I will use it for a sublime deed. Then it will act for me as a boat which helps me to cross the ocean of birth and death." Thereupon he lay down beside the tigress; and when she was too weak to slay him, he stabbed his own throat with a piece of bamboo so that she might lick the blood and thereby gain strength sufficient to devour his carcass.

Still another of the *Jātaka* stories represents Gautama in an earlier incarnation as an ascetic who had left his home to live in the woods as a preaching hermit. "He had understood that life in the home is indeed attended by a great many faults and calamities; that it is governed by a perpetual concern with material gain and sensual pleasure, and in consequence is not conducive to tranquility; that it is constantly assailed by the dust and dirt of passions, such as greed, hate, delusion, impatience, anger, self-intoxication, conceit, and niggardliness." Because of his calm wisdom, crowds of people came to listen to his sermons; and in discourses which "gladdened their ears as well as their hearts, . . . [he] talked to them in terms which womenfolk can easily grasp, careful to illustrate his meaning by examples and similes."[10] This was a mode of speaking which Gautama never forsook.

The boy Gautama, born into his father's palace, was reared in princely luxury and given an aristocratic education. At the age of sixteen his father selected a wife for him, and a decade later a son was born. For years Gautama's father took care to prevent his son from learning about the miseries of life; but eventually, on expeditions out of the palace, when he was twenty-nine years old, Gautama observed an old man, a sick man, and a corpse lying beside the road. The contrast between the luxuries of the palace and the unavoidable facts of sickness, old age, and death struck Gautama with shattering force. He determined to leave his home, for, as he later explained to his disciples: "Not easy is it for him who dwells in a house to practice a completely full, completely pure, and perfect religious life."[11]

For a brief time Gautama studied successively under two religious teachers, but he found their doctrines unsatisfactory. Then he turned to the old Hindu method of asceticism, associating himself with five devout hermits. For a period of six years Gautama lived with them in the wilderness, eating only enough to maintain life, dressed in rags, and sleeping on the bare ground. In the *Majjhima Nikāya,* spoken years later, in a passage which well illustrates the vividness of his style, he recalled this experience:

> My body became extremely lean. . . . The mark of my seat was like a camel's footprint through the little food. The bones of my spine when bent and straightened were like a row of spindles through the little food. As the beams of an old shed stick out, so did my ribs stick out through the little food. . . . And as a bitter gourd cut off raw is cracked and withered through wind and sun, so was the skin of my head withered through the little food. When I thought I would touch the skin of my stomach, I actually took hold of my spine, and when I thought I would touch my spine, I

took hold of the skin of my stomach, so much did the skin of my stomach cling to my spine through the little food.

Severe and sustained though these austerities were, Gautama found to his disappointment that he did not seem thereby to attain any clearer or truer insight into the nature and meaning of life. Such suffering as he daily endured might be worthwhile if it led to enlightenment; but he perceived that the actual result was that it kept his attention focused upon his pains and his hunger and the cold and weariness of his body. This, he told himself, cannot be the route to salvation. He thought then, that he would try eating solid food to see whether with the renewal of his strength he might find enlightenment. At this the five recluses left him in disgust, saying, "The ascetic Gautama lives in abundance; he has given up striving and lives in abundance." Meanwhile, Gautama found that with his bodily health and strength regained he did indeed find an increase in pleasure but had no special increase of insight into the nature of life.

Once again Gautama set upon his wanderings until he came to the district of Magadhas. "There I saw a delightful spot, with a pleasant grove, a river flowing delightfully with clear water and good fords, and round about a place for seeking alms." This, he told himself, was "surely a fit place for the striving," and he sat down under a Bodhi tree, determined to go no further until enlightenment should come to him. While he sat under the tree meditating, Māra, the Hindu devil, appeared in his visions and tempted him to leave his introspective search and start upon a new life of doing good among the poor and distressed. But Gautama rejected this temptation, replying that not good deeds but faith, heroism, and wisdom were what were demanded of him. This resistance by Gautama to a temptation to "do good" is perhaps the principal barrier that stands between his views and the Western mind; for, as Conze has pointed out, "a show of benevolence is so much more welcome to the contemporary mind than a profound insight into reality."[12] Gautama, however, clung stubbornly to his own destined mission, which was to seek out the nature of the good life.

Then to Gautama came the great insight which so yearningly and for so long, amidst hardships beyond imagining, he had earnestly sought: *when desire ceases life becomes whole.* With this realization he was suffused with a great joy. The joy of the pleasures of this world and the vast joy of heaven, all combined, were not, he thought, the sixteenth part of the total joy that comes from renouncing craving. When he rose from his seat under the Bodhi tree, he was ready to commence his life's work. The message he sought had been found. Continuing the narrative of his enlightenment in the *Majjhima,* he explained: "Then I thought, now I have gained the doctrine, profound, hard to know, tranquil, transcendent, beyond the sphere of reasoning, subtle, to be known by the wise. Mankind is intent on its attachments, and takes delight and pleasure in them. For mankind, intent on its attachments . . . it is hard to see the principle of causality, origination by way of cause. Hard to see is the principle of cessation of all compound things, the renunciation of clinging to rebirth, the extinction of all craving, absence of passion, cessation, nirvāna."

The doctrine, then, which does not lead to salvation but which in itself is salvation, was now clear to Gautama; and so, too, was the fact that it is a doctrine easy to formulate but hard for people either to understand or to accept. At this point he took upon himself the role of evangelist, with the responsibility of presenting his message in a form so clear and so persuasive that it would be perceived and activated. His personal problem became one of mastering the arts of persuasion. For, he declared, "if I were to teach the doctrine, and others did not understand it, it would be a weariness to me, a vexation."

For his first project in evangelism, Gautama undertook an especially interesting challenge. The five hermits with whom he had shared six years of austerity, and who had turned against him when he abandoned asceticism, were the ones he would attempt to win as his first converts. He found they had taken temporary quarters in the Deer Park, at Benares, and it was there that he sought them. The hermits, seeing him approaching, said to one another that this was the man who had first joined them, then deserted them to seek a life of ease and abundance. They determined to ignore him. However, old friendship proved too strong, and as he arrived they arose, called him by name, took his robe, and offered him a seat, with water to bathe his feet. Gautama, however, spurned their friendliness and spoke sternly to them, saying he was no more their friend but, instead, had become a Tathāgata, fully enlightened. He had come not for comradeship, but to instruct them. Taken aback, the five hermits quite naturally retorted coldly that he never had displayed special enlightenment while sharing their life of deprivation and dedication, and they could not believe he had improved his insight by surrendering to the lust for abundance and a life of ease. Gautama replied that he did not live in ease and abundance and that he was indeed enlightened. Then, with the quizzical humor which was so deeply a part of his personality, he asked them: "Have I ever talked this way to you before?"

The record shows that the crash method of overwhelming assertiveness which Gautama chose to use as his first method in evangelism was successful. The five hermits, no doubt with a large fund of affection for him, perhaps with guilt for their renunciation of him, and impressed by the calm confidence he now exuded, accepted his claims, abandoned their own asceticism, and agreed to receive his teachings. Then, with these five converts gathered around him, Gautama preached to an assembled crowd his first recorded discourse—the famous sermon in the Deer Park, in which his message of enlightenment was first set forth.[13]

Mindful of his primary audience, Gautama commenced by declaring that there were two false ways of searching for the truth. The first way was the pursuit of pleasure by satisfying the passions—which he characterized as "low, vulgar, common, ignoble, and useless." The other was the method of self-torture through asceticism and self-denial, which he called "painful, ignoble, and useless." What lay between these two extremes was a middle path of calm insight. The insight which undistraught meditation revealed was that there are four noble truths. The first of these is that suffering exists: "birth is painful, old age is painful, sickness is painful, death is painful, sorrow, lamentation, dejection, and despair are painful. Contact with unpleasant things is painful, not getting what one wishes is painful. In short the five groups of grasping are painful." The second truth is that suffering is caused by craving—by the lust for "finding pleasure here and there; namely, the craving for passion, the craving for existence, the craving for non-existence." The third truth is that suffering can be ended when craving is renounced. And the fourth truth is that renunciation of all desires must be sought by following the eightfold path of right views, right intention, right speech, right action, right livelihood, right effort, right mindfulness, right concentration.

In this one brief sermon, Gautama set forth the basic principles which constituted his teachings; what followed during the remaining forty-five years of his life was largely the establishment and elaboration of his concepts. Never afterward did he change them or add significantly to them, though in his preaching he made them wonderfully vivid and warmly appealing. This is the essence of Buddhism: four basic truths— that men suffer, that suffering is caused, that suffering ends when the cause is removed, and that the means of eliminating the cause are available and manageable; and the eightfold path of right living, by means of which the cause of suffering is eradicated.

Many call Buddhism a religion, but Gautama did not concern himself with metaphysics much more than did Confucius. Both men sought an answer to the question of how individuals may live in a way that is satisfying to themselves and to their fellow beings. Gautama did not speculate on how life, or the universe, began; he was content to accept the fact that *here we are,* and to confine himself to considering *what we shall do about it.*[14] His answers were religious in the sense that any consideration of fundamental and eternal values is religious. His answers were rhetorical in the sense that how an individual should live inevitably for Gautama involved significantly the problem of how he should live with his associates. The nature of the rhetorical influences derived from his teachings and his speaking are considered next.

GAUTAMA AS PREACHER AND TEACHER

For the last forty-five years of his life Gautama was primarily a preacher and a teacher, engaged in the widest possible dissemination of his ideas. Many of his sermons, narratives and sayings were preserved, at least in substance. The actual writing down of his speeches did not take place until long after his death,[15] but these discourses nevertheless are as much his own as, for example, the Sermon on the Mount is veritably a discourse by Jesus or the *Analects* are the product of Confucius. Perhaps more so, for in accordance with the firmly established Indian practice, ardent disciples memorized word for word the sayings of their master and repeated them not only to general audiences but to one another, doing their best to preserve the wording intact. As T. W. Rhys Davids, the first general translator of the sermons, explains it: "The Buddha, like other Indian teachers of his time, taught by conversation. A highly educated man (according to the education current at the time), speaking constantly to men of similar education, he followed the literary habit of his time by embodying his ideas in set phrases, sutras, on which he enlarged on different occasions in different ways. . . . When the Buddha died these sayings were collected together by his disciples into the Four Great Nikāyas. They cannot have reached their final form until about fifty years afterwards."[16]

Davids details how carefully the sermons were composed by Gautama, and no doubt paraphrased by his disciples, into "memorial sentences intended to be learnt by heart; and the whole style, and method of arrangement, is entirely subordinated to this primary necessity."[17] Other aids to memory consisted of the liberal use of numbered groups of ideas, the use of frequent word-for-word repetition, the phrasing of ideas in successive sentences having identical grammatical form, and the elimination of elaborations and qualifications of concepts. Inasmuch as Gautama was intent not only upon converting immediate hearers but also upon providing materials which his disciples might use in their own evangelism, it is highly probable that he himself followed the stylistic forms which he knew conduced to literal memorization. This was, after all, precisely the tradition within which his own education had been conducted; it was the only communicative method he knew.

The approximate authenticity of the texts ascribed to Gautama seems to be reasonable. In the first place, his numerous disciples, who actually heard him, were in quite close agreement concerning his wording, as is indicated by the lack of substantial variations in the different texts which survive. In the second place, the discourses contain various materials which would naturally have been obliterated or revised if the texts had been tampered with—such as the record, for example, of Gautama's marriage, since the Buddhist monks generally discouraged marriage for members of their order. But beyond such considerations is the fact of the genuine originality of the discourses attributed to Gautama. He did indeed present a new insight; a fresh interpretation of the nature of the good life and the means of attaining it. And he did this solely on his own authority and on the strength of the reasoning he presented. He did not follow the orthodox method of basing his ideas upon the authority of ancient Hindu literature. He did not claim any special revelation. He did not even assert that his views derived from intuitive insight. On the contrary, he set them forth as clearly and persuasively as he could, and let them stand on their merits. His was a new personality on the Indian scene. The best proof of the general authenticity of the sayings attributed to Gautama is that no one else would have said what he said, either in substance or in style. He was an original. On this point the discourses themselves provide the safest testimony.

The parable was one of Gautama's effective means of rendering his ideas persuasive. On one occasion a woman whose son had died came to him to ask that her child be restored to life. "Seeing that she was ripe for conversion," Gautama welcomed her, then said: "Go enter the city, make the rounds of the entire city, beginning at the beginning, and in whatever house no one has ever died, from that house fetch tiny grains of mustard seed." Eagerly the mother commenced her rounds, but in house after house she found that some member of the family had died. Soon she learned the lesson Gautama wished to teach and, taking her son in her arms to the burial ground, she caressed his body, saying: "Dear little son, I thought that you alone had been overtaken by this thing which men call death. But you are not the only one death has overtaken. This is a law common to all mankind."[18]

Another mode of persuasion which was often used by Gautama was an air of gentle humor which took a point of the utmost seriousness and developed it with such subtlety of wit or irony that it aroused no laughter nor even so much as a smile, yet created a pleasing aura that made the point more palatable and memorable. An example is from his sermon on sacrifice, in which he undertook to renounce the age-old method of trying to appease the gods with sacrificial offerings and recommended instead the living of a moral life. To illustrate his point, he told of two kings who tried to learn of their own faults but could not because they were surrounded by flatterers. Each one gave up the throne, dressed in common clothes, and traveled out through the country, seeking understanding. Eventually they drove their chariots, from opposite directions, into a narrow defile, meeting half-way through it, with no room by which to pass. Each one haughtily demanded that the other back out since, as each pointed out, he was a king. But since both enjoyed the same distinction, their claims were canceled out. They then tried to settle the matter by granting precedence to the elder; but they turned out to be the same age. After this, in turn, they sought to establish priority in terms of their wealth, the strength of their armies, the extent of their realms, and the distinction of their castes and families— but to no avail, since in all these respects they were equal. At last one of them became angry at the continuance of the impasse; and then, as both agreed, the angered one had lost the contest and must retreat, since anger is conquered by calmness.[19]

On another occasion, when a disciple offered Gautama fulsome adulation, declaring him to be greater and wiser than any other who had ever lived or who would live in the future, Gautama reproved him gently, saying: "Grand and bold are the words of thy mouth, Sariputta; verily, thou hast burst forth into a song of ecstasy! Of course, then, thou hast known all the Blessed Ones who in the long ages past have been Arahat Buddhas, comprehending their minds with yours, and aware what their conduct was, what their doctrine, what their wisdom, what their mode of life, and what salvation they attained to?" The reprimand was effective.[20]

Ridiculing the notion that one could worship within a religion which he did not understand, Gautama likened it to an extravagant claim of wanting to love the most beautiful woman in the land. People would say to such a yearning lover: "Well! Good friend! This most beautiful woman in all the land, whom you so love and long for, do you know what the name of that most beautiful woman is, or what is her family name, whether she be tall or short, dark or of medium complexion, black or fair, or in what village or town she dwells?" Since the man would know none of these things, the people must rightly conclude that his vain assertion was foolish talk.[21] By such pithy, humorous, and concrete applications Gautama drove home his points that religion is more concerned with right living than with right rituals, and that it is necessary to understand a faith in order to practice it.

In the final sermon which he preached to his disciples just before his death, at the age of eighty—sometimes called the Sermon of the Great Decease—Gautama used autobiographical reminiscence as a means of emphasizing his injunction that they carry forward unceasingly the work of evangelism. Now he was more teacher than preacher, trying to convey to them understandings that would make their own evangelism effective. He explained to them that they would encounter eight different types of assemblies, and that they would often be fearful of their ability to convince the people gathered there. "Now I call to mind," he said, "how when I used to enter into an assembly of many hundred nobles, before I had seated myself there or talked to them or started a conversation with them, I used to become in colour like unto their colour, and in voice like unto their voice. Then with religious discourse I used to instruct, incite, and quicken them, and fill them with gladness. But they knew me not when I spoke, and would say, 'Who may this be who thus speaks—a man or a god?' Then having instructed, incited, quickened, and gladdened them with religious discourse, I would vanish away. But they knew me not even when I vanished away; and would say, 'Who may this be who has vanished away? A man or a god?' "[22] By such means Gautama dramatized his point that it did not matter who did the speaking—what mattered was that it be done effectively.

In the same discourse, and reinforcing his same point, he reminded them that he was old: "I have reached my sum of days, I am turning eighty years of age; and just as a worn-out cart can only with much additional care be made to move along, some think the body of the Tathāgata can only be kept going with much additional care." Then he drew his conclusion—that they no longer could depend upon his leadership, but only upon their own strength and resolution. "Therefore, be ye lamps unto yourselves. Be ye a refuge unto yourselves. Betake yourselves to no external refuge. Hold fast to the truth as a lamp. Hold fast as a refuge to the truth. Look not for refuge to anyone besides yourselves."[23]

The principal rhetorical canon which Gautama emphasized again and again was that of holding fast to the truth. In one of his early sermons he declared to his disciples the chief duty that devolved upon one who became his follower: "He speaks truth; from the truth he never swerves; faithful and trustworthy, he breaks not his word to the world." Beyond this, he stressed the social functions of proper discourse. The true disciple should speak "as a binder together of those who are divided, an encourager to those who are friends, a peacemaker, a lover of peace, impassioned for peace, a speaker of words that make for peace." And he also advised the development of skills to make their discourse effective; for the good disciple "speaks, and at the right time, words worthy to be laid up in one's heart, fitly illustrated, clearly divided, to the point."[24]

Gautama's own speaking was praised for precisely these very characteristics: that he spoke truth and spoke it effectively. As one of his contemporaries said of him: "Most excellent, O Gautama, are the words of your mouth, most excellent! Just as if a man were to set up that which has been thrown down, or were to reveal that which has been hidden away, or were to point out the right road to him who has gone astray, or were to bring a light into the darkness so that those who had eyes could see external forms—just even so has the truth been made known to me, in many a figure, by the venerable Gautama."[25]

In one of his discourses Gautama utilized his skill in irony to relate how he had been criticized by an ascetic named Nigrodha, who had warned an inquirer against the teachings of Gautama, telling him:

> . . . know you with whom the Samana [Ascetic] Gautama talks; with whom he holds conversation; by intercourse with whom does he attain to lucidity in wisdom? The Samana Gautama's insight is ruined by his habit of seclusion. He is not at home in conducting an assembly. He is not ready in conversation. He is occupied only with the fringes of things. Even as a one-eyed cow that, walking in a circle, follows ever the outskirts, so is this Samana Gautama. Why, forsooth, if the Samana Gautama were to come to this assembly, with a single question only could we settle him; yea, methinks we could roll him over like an empty pot.

When Gautama was told of this diatribe, he confronted Nigrodha who "sat silent and annoyed, with hunched back and drooping head, brooding and dumbfounded." Then Gautama reminded him that the speech he was accustomed to hearing consisted of "talk with loud voices, with noise and clamour, carrying on childish talk of various kinds, to wit, talk of kings, robbers, and the like, or speculative talk about existence and non-existence, as you and your teacher do now." Nigrodha, thus challenged, was quick to admit that his comments were stupid, foolish, and wrong; and Gautama forgave him. Then he addressed himself to Nigrodha and his fellow ascetics, saying: "Let a man of intelligence come to me, who is honest, candid, straightforward—I will instruct him."[26]

This is an example of the persuasive method which led Davids to conclude that Gautama's procedure was "not to argue about anything; to accept the opponents' position throughout, and simply to outflank it."[27] Davids was right in noting that Gautama avoided direct refutation and sought instead a common ground of agreement. "Outflanking" must not, however, be interpreted as avoidance of an opposing point. Coomaraswamy, in his study of Buddhism, makes precisely the right point when he says: "Gautama is not . . . a poet and a mystic, but a psychologist; he does not speak to uneducated fishermen, but to practiced metaphysicians, and in an atmosphere of controversy: he makes no personal appeal, he speaks with well-considered purpose rather than enthusiasm or fervour, and he is concerned to leave no loophole for possible or deliberate misunderstandings."[28] It would be fair to characterize Gautama's manner as non-argumentative but patiently and minutely explanatory.

Gautama himself made it clear that he recognized different kinds of auditors and used methods suited to each type. Coomaraswamy notes that he spoke in one manner to a group of disciples, who had already been familiar with his ideas, and in quite another way to an audience of eighty thousand laymen who were sent to him to seek instruction. In this latter situation, according to Coomaraswamy, he spoke in a "much more popular style—milk for babes."[29]

Gautama himself explained to his disciples that before commencing his evangelism he gave careful thought concerning the types of people to whom he might address his message: "I saw beings of little impurity, of much impurity, of keen or dull faculties, of good or bad conditions, easy or hard to teach, and some too I saw who perceived the danger and faults affecting a future life."[30]

With this need for audience analysis in mind, Gautama said that he finally decided to direct his preaching first to the five ascetics who had been his companions for six years—on the grounds that they would most quickly comprehend what he had to say and that their conversion would impress others and thus make his evangelistic mission easier. It is obvious that he did not set upon his life's work fortified by nothing but zeal; he also had considerable skill as a rhetorician, with a sound understanding of problems to be dealt with in persuasion. He was not only an effective preacher but also a skilled and thoughtful theorist and teacher of the art of rhetoric.

GAUTAMA AS RHETORICIAN

The rhetoric of Gautama Buddha derives directly from his generalized system of life values. Depart from the insignificant, he urged, in order to concentrate upon the significant. This was his basic message.

In the collection of lengthy dialogues called the *Dīgha Nikāya*, Gautama applied this principle directly to speech. To his disciples he said: "Brethren, if outsiders should speak against me, or against the Doctrine, or against the Order, you should not on that account either bear malice, or suffer heart-burning, or feel ill-will. . . . But also, Brethren, if outsiders should speak in praise of me, in praise of the Doctrine, or in praise of the Order, you should not on that account, be filled with pleasure, or gladness, or be lifted up in heart."[31] Continuing, he warned his disciples also against self-pride, which might lead a man to avoid stating his own opinion from fear that he might not be able to defend it. "Thus fearing and abhorring the being wrong in an expressed opinion," Gautama said, "he will neither declare anything to be good, nor to be bad; but on a question being put to him on this or that, he resorts to eel-wriggling, to equivocation, and says: 'I don't take it thus. I don't take it the other way. But I advance no different opinion. And I don't deny your position. And I don't say it is neither the one nor the other.' "[32] He concluded with the reminder that a man "stands in the truth" only when he has learned to desire nothing—neither bodily sensations, nor fame, nor happiness, nor surcease from unhappiness. Then he has attained a sureness which reveals itself in perfect serenity and his word will be received and believed.[33]

The fundamental rhetorical questions to which Gautama addressed his attention derived directly from his determination to concentrate wholly upon consequentials. To unravel his rhetoric it is necessary to consider the following problems: First, what is the purpose of inquiry? What is it that we seek to understand—and why? Second, what is the nature of truth? How do we judge in a given instance between truth and falsity? Third, what is the nature of man? What are the wellsprings of human motivation? By what means may men be led to or diverted from truth? Fourth, in terms of the foregoing questions, what kinds of discourse are effective? What are the responsibilities of speakers? Of listeners? What are the proper uses of speech?

According to the philosophy in the Upanishads, the answer to the first question very clearly is to seek for the absolute unity which underlies all seeming diversity. In this view, truth could be only the understanding that apparent differences are illusory. Such a concept renounces rhetoric in favor of dialectic—though there always remains the need of persuading individuals who persist in believing that, for example, decorum is preferable to justice, or poverty is less desirable than wealth. Gautama was deeply influenced in his own thinking by this Hindu monistic theory. But for him the purpose of inquiry was more personal: to attain understanding of the unity of the self with the inclusive tendencies of the universe, to the end that craving or desire might be destroyed through identification of the personal with the impersonal and of the transient with the permanent.

Like all abstractions, this one—which seems precise and unalterable —turns out upon pragmatic examination to be ambiguous. The individual is part of the immutable and unchanging totality; but how should this unity of all being manifest itself? Or should this same goal of universality be sought through an active and philanthropic ministry of service?

Gautama himself appears not to have settled this issue, for he recommended in turn introspective withdrawal from the world and a life of compassionate service. A. Foucher, a leading European interpreter of Buddhism, finds this same bifurcation to lie at the heart of the historic development of Buddhism: "So there arose the great schism that still divides the Buddhist Church into two camps. One has put the emphasis on compassion, universal good will, selfless devotion, and love of one's fellow man extended to all living beings to the point of forgetting oneself completely. The other advocates, above all, the withdrawal into the self, concentration of spirit, constant vigilance over acts and words and thoughts, solitary meditation, and the complete suppression of all emotion."[34]

Yet underlying both these tendencies, and more fundamental than either since it encompasses both, is the inescapable truth of *dharma:* that whatever is thought or said or done by a man becomes his heritage. Nothing is lost; nothing can be avoided; nothing is forgotten or forgiven. The law of *dharma* operates with complete inexorability: as you do, so shall you be. There is no escaping this ultimate responsibility.

The purpose of inquiry, then, is always the discernment of truth. For an individual can have no other destiny than to align himself with the absolute. The effect of this view is that ethics and rhetoric become all but indistinguishable. In the view of Buddha, there is not an ethic *for* rhetoric but an ethic *of* rhetoric. Whatever may be said has direct consequence not alone (not even especially) for the hearer, but most explicitly and inevitably for the speaker himself. This is vastly different from the Western ethic which insists that you may fool some of the people all the time and all the people some of the time, but not all the people all the time. Gautama's view was that utterance is its own monitor. Truth must be the object of discourse, for what is true governs what we are and will be.

One informed interpretation of the nature of truth, as Buddhism represents it, is that all human experience shares three characteristics: all that we know is transient, impermanent, and therefore of only temporary value; all that we know is partial, incomplete, and therefore unsatisfactory if not actually hurtful and disagreeable; and all that we know is separated from ourself, since we could not observe it except as we view it outside of the vantage point of the perceiving self.[35]

With this negativistic philosophy,[36] Buddhism represents a profoundly pessimistic interpretation of the visible, physical, sentient experiences which we normally interpret as being life itself; but this is merely to reject and cast off the impediments which stand between us and genuine reality. Or, as Gautama phrased it, we must learn to repudiate craving, clinging, grasping. We must free our inner and central life core (he refused to call it a soul) from the limitations and demands of temporal and sensuous experience, in order that we might attain the release of not needing to be reborn.

As in all other cultures, Buddhist India was inevitably concerned with the next question—how truth is to be discerned. Falsity often presents so plausible an appearance and truth may seem so uncouth that man's judgment between the two is prone to error. Aristotle for this reason posited the necessity of persuasion, in order that the seer may lead the blind from non-sense to sense. Gautama was particularly impressed by the danger that man's experience with day-by-day particulars would obscure his vision of the generalized principles which underlie them. This philosophy, in the view of F. S. C. Northrop, "tends to produce a people who find peace of mind and equanimity of the spirit by facing realistically and with aesthetic sensitivity the transitoriness, the attendant suffering, and the undeniable relativity of sensed things, thereby fitting one to accept circumstances as they are, rather than to transform them in ways other than those which a cultivation of one's intuitive fellow-feeling for all creatures elicits."[37] The test of truth, in other words, is the ability to see the essential unity that inheres amidst all manner of contradictories, and the ability to see permanent good in whatever may appear to be transitory evil.

This view of the means by which essential truth is discernible has two major rhetorical implications. The first is that attention should be directed away from the externals of physical problems and social ills to the internal realities of the spiritual nature and unity of all being. In other words, the goal should be to try to adjust people to circumstances, rather than to try to adjust circumstances to people. The result was to divert human endeavor away from the physical and social sciences and toward rhetoric. It became less important to do something active about a situation than to engage in discourse which led toward understanding of it. "Let's be up and doing" was a sentiment far less admirable, under this philosophy, than "I see; I understand—and therefore I accept." And the second of the rhetorical effects of the Buddhist idea system was that it encouraged expository discourse while discouraging persuasion. The constant contradiction between essential truth and its apparent contradictions demanded continual and exhaustive efforts at elucidation. As Gautama advised: "Let the wise put questions one to another, ask for reasons, talk the matter over, with or to their teacher, with or to their fellow disciples."[38]

The nature of man (the third of the Buddhist rhetorical questions)—which determines how ultimately he may be governed or directed—was conceived by Gautama quite differently than it was by either the Aristotelian or the Judeo-Christian traditions of the West. Aristotle concluded that man is prone to self-seeking emotionalism but that finally he is a rational being who can be brought to perceive and accept objective truth when it is logically expounded. The Judeo-Christian theology represents man as having an individual soul which will be either rewarded or condemned for all eternity depending upon whether it accepts or rejects subjection to the will of a just God. Aristotle represents man as standing outside of and apart from the world around him, so that he is capable of evaluating it objectively and separately from personal involvement. The Judeo-Christian view emphasizes the importance of the individual, wholly different from the nonhuman universe, and destined for eternal and self-conscious continuity. In contrast with both these views, Gautama viewed man as being a part of the monistic totality of all being— unable eventually to perceive either the world or himself logically, for he cannot separate himself as observer from what it is that he seeks to observe.

Hence, the proper method of inquiry is not logical—not even mental

—but intuitive. The individual cannot think his way to understanding; he must feel his way toward it. The end sought is not objective clarification but subjective insight. Tennyson sought to portray one aspect of the Buddhist method with his "Flower in a Crannied Wall"; Walt Whitman depicted another in his "Song of Myself." Emerson perhaps came even closer in his lyrical "Brahma."

Gautama was keenly aware that individuals exemplify temporality as well as timelessness and are prone to crave the transitory pleasures of the world around them. Blinded to their own genuine welfare, men renounce the peace which leads toward nirvāna because of the temptations of worldly sensation. Far from seeking naturally their own welfare through agreeable discourse, they are prone to quarrelsomeness—engaged "in mutual strife and conflict," as he said, "quarrelling and wounding each other with wordy weapons."[39] In such a case, however, Gautama told his disciples, it is not the mistaken individuals who are to blame but those who have been ineffective in teaching them. The trouble is that "the teacher is not supremely enlightened; his Norm (message) is badly set forth, badly imparted, ineffectual for guidance, not conducive to peace, not imparted by one supremely enlightened."[40]

What the speaker should do is appeal not to the mistakenly transitory interests of his listeners, but to their unrecognized timeless qualities. In short, the motivation should consist of an appeal not *to* man's selfishness but *from* it. Speakers will attain their greatest effectiveness when they show their listeners that they ought not to seek satisfaction of their desires but should instead seek to transcend desire itself.

The very question of how one should speak to men who need to be converted from their mistaken notions or wrong feelings was proposed by some of Gautama's opponents, in the form of a dilemma, after he had consigned one of them (Devadatta) to a cycle in hell for having rebelled against him. Was such a mode of speaking compatible with the gentleness Buddha advocated? This is the dilemma they projected: "Go to the ascetic Gautama and ask if he would utter that speech which is unpleasant and disagreeable to others. If he says yes, then ask how he differs from the common people, for the common people utter speech that is unpleasant and disagreeable to others. But if he denies, then ask why he said of Devadatta that he was destined to states of punishment, to hell . . . for at that speech Devadatta was angry and displeased."[41] To the critics of Gautama this seemed to be a neat dilemma. "If the ascetic Gautama is asked this question," they chortled, "he will be able to swallow neither up nor down."

When the question was put to Buddha by Prince Abhaya, who happened to be holding a child on his knee at the time, Gautama replied by rephrasing the challenge:

> "What do you think, prince? If this boy through the carelessness of you or his nurse were to get a stick or a pebble in his mouth, what would you do?"
>
> "I should take it from him, Lord, and if I could not get it at once, I should seize his head with my left hand, and, bending my finger, get it with my right hand, even if I drew blood. And why? Because I have compassion on the boy."

Gautama must have smiled as the solution of the presumed dilemma was rendered so clear by the very man who posed it:

> Even so, prince, speech that the Tathāgata knows to be untrue, false, and useless, and also unpleasant and disagreeable to others, he does not speak; that which he knows to be true, real, and useful, but also unpleasant and disagreeable to others, in that case he knows the right time to express it. Speech that he knows to be untrue, false, and useless, and also pleasant and agreeable to others, he does not speak; that which is true, real, but useless, and also pleasant and agreeable to others, that, too, he does not speak; but that which is true, real, and useful, and also pleasant and agreeable to others, in that case he knows the right time to express it.

With the identification of the three functions of speech—that it be true, real (in terms of the attendant circumstances), and useful—and with the reminder that what is said must be adjusted to the feelings of the listener through proper timing, Gautama herewith laid down at least the beginnings of a rhetoric. Frequently he spoke of the characteristics of effective speech, which he recommended to the monks whom he recruited as missionaries. An initial consideration which he impressed upon them was the responsibility they bore for whatever they might say: "If a man speaks or acts with an evil thought, pain follows him as the wheel follows the foot of the ox that draws the carriage."[42] Concurrently, he assured them it is also true that speaking from a basis of good thoughts gives effectiveness to their discourse, for: "If a man makes himself as he teaches others to be, then, being himself well-subdued, he may subdue others; for oneself is difficult to subdue."[43] How a monk might subdue himself and attain effectiveness as a preacher, Gautama stated explicitly:

> Abandoning falsehood, he speaks the truth, is truthful, faithful, trustworthy, and breaks not his word to his people.

Abandoning slander, he does not tell what he has heard in one place to cause dissension elsewhere. He heals divisions and encourages friendships, delighting in concord and speaking what produces it.

Abandoning harsh language, his speech is blameless, pleasant to the ear, reaching the heart, urbane, and attractive to the multitude.

Abandoning frivolous language, he speaks duly and in accordance with the doctrine and discipline, and his speech is such as to be remembered, elegant, clear and to the point.[44]

Another time, Gautama came to the door of a lecture hall in which one of his principal followers, Nandaka, was giving a lengthy discourse to an audience of monks, on the meaning of the good life. Apparently the speech was a good one, for it is recorded that it "taught them, roused them, incited them, and gladdened them"—a series of well-coordinated results. Gautama must have been in a mischievous mood, for, when he entered the hall, he indulged fully in his penchant for ironic humor. "Surely, Nandaka," he called out, "this *dharma* discourse, which you preached to the monks, was a long one! My back ached as I stood outside the doorway, waiting for the discourse to end." Then, seeing that Nandaka was genuinely embarrassed, Gautama hastily assured him that the speech had been a good one, that it was well adapted to the listeners, and that with such a subject the only choice was between saying nothing at all or speaking at length.[45]

Gautama on another occasion explained to his monks four ways by which they might deal with listeners who were skeptical concerning their message. The first way was to ask questions which would unveil the basis for the doubts, so that they could be resolved through suitable answers. The next method was to proceed directly to a concise statement of the merits of the message that was to be presented. The third method was to divide the matter into separate categories, through questioning the listeners to determine reasons for their doubt, then to deal with each category in turn. But if none of these methods looked suitable for a particular occasion, the fourth recourse was simply to ignore the skepticism. Speakers should be alert to determine which method would best suit the needs of each particular audience.[46]

Continuing his instructions, Gautama advised that an evangelistic sermon should commence with topics already familiar to the audience, and concerning which they would be in agreement—such as the value of alms-giving, the rewards of moral living, and the virtues of retirement.

In proceeding beyond this point, careful attention should be earned by a compassionate concern for the welfare of the listeners. Thirdly, irrelevant matters should be avoided. And, finally, the speakers should avoid any caustic comments or attacks against opposing views or individuals. The pattern clearly was one calling for audience adaptation, conciliation, and use of the "yes-technique." This same advice he repeated when asked by a disciple how to respond to verbal attacks: "Issue has been joined against you, you are defeated, set to work to clear your views, disentangle yourself if you can."[47]

In another discourse, Gautama warned the monks not to be misled by empty expressions of support and friendship. A man who had not actually been converted, he warned them, might nevertheless be sufficiently influenced as to act superficially like a convert. Such a one, he said, "is to be reckoned as a foe in the likeness of a friend: he makes friendly professions as regards the past; he makes friendly professions as regards the future; he tries to gain your favour by empty sayings; when the opportunity for service has arisen, he avows his disability."[48] This is about as explicit a formula for determining the actual effectiveness of a persuasive discourse as may be found in any rhetoric.

So important was effective speech for the spreading of the doctrine that Gautama did not overlook even the mechanics of delivery. It was said of him that "Gautama hath a pleasant voice, and pleasing delivery, he is gifted with polite address, distinct, not husky, suitable for making clear the matter in hand."[49] In his depiction of the ideal religious devotee, Gautama identified him as "he who controls his speech," for "good is restraint in tongue, . . . good is restraint in speech. . . . The Bhikshu (monk) who controls his mouth, who speaks wisely and calmly, who teaches the meaning and the law, his word is sweet."[50]

But always Gautama taught more through example than through precept. His rhetoric emerges most surely from the methods he employed in his own preaching. As a concluding instance, the means by which he replied to a heckler who interrupted his sermon with a torrent of personal abuse is cited as exemplifying his own calm wisdom, his method of turning an argument about so that it reflects upon his opponent, and his use of gentle humor and conciliation to win agreement:

> When the man had finished his abuse, the Buddha asked him, saying: "Son, if a man refused to accept a present made to him, to whom would it belong?" And he answered: "In that case, it would belong to the man who offered it."
>
> "My son," said the Buddha, "thou hast railed at me, but I de-

cline to accept thy abuse, and request thee to keep it to thyself.
Will it not be a source of misery to thee? As the echo belongs to
the sound, and the shadow to the substance, so misery will overtake the evil-doer without fail."[51]

The rhetorical influence of Gautama, in sum, proved to be similar to
that of orthodox Hinduism: seek for the unity that underlies seeming
diversity; turn aside wrath with a gentle response; clarify and seek acceptance of your ideas by phrasing them in terms of the predilections
and understanding of your listener; try to find premises so acceptable
to the listener that he will himself argue for your conclusion; and keep
your discourse pleasing through use of humor and homely illustrations
rather than indulging in denunciation and assertive argumentation. Perhaps an even more significant rhetorical influence stemming from Gautama's lifework lies in the example he set of tireless and patient evangelism. He manifested great faith that men may be won by oral discourse.
From the time he first entered into full enlightenment so that he attained
unshakable confidence in his own message, he not only spoke widely
and frequently himself, but he tirelessly organized great numbers of disciples and patiently taught them the values and the methods of evangelistic speech. He should be remembered as one who sought to revolutionize men and society not with a sword but with a gentle and
sympathetic persuasion. His faith in what words well spoken could accomplish was high. As one student of his lifework has found, he left as
his heritage a fourfold guide which not only advocates attainment of
the good through skillful speech but also indicates how speech may be
made effective:

> The goodly word calm men proclaim supreme;
> And second, speaking *dharma,* not elsewise;
> Third, speaking kindly, not unkindly words;
> And speaking truth, not speaking false, is fourth.[52]

CHAPTER 6

China: The Rhetorical Milieu

THE SOCIAL SETTING

ANCIENT CHINA was separated from India not only by the Himalayan Mountains but also by deep-seated differences in customs and culture. Nevertheless, in China as in India (though in quite different ways) speech was important and the manner of speaking was a subject of considerable attention. Not less than in India, talk in China was the primary medium for the exchange of ideas. Eloquent speakers were influential in the moulding of social ideas, ideals, and institutions. There were various kinds of speakers who served specific needs of the society.

One of these was the "talker of books," who preserved and propagated the history of earlier times. Book-reciters were of two kinds—scholars who memorized and thus preserved ancient classics, as well as adding their own commentaries; and public entertainers, who dramatized legends, myths, and historical narratives for crowds of illiterates who gathered around them on street corners or under spreading trees on hot summer days. Another class of speakers included professional mediators of disputes, somewhat like modern lawyers, performing their functions at the feudal courts, where their verbal skill provided entertainment while they were meanwhile also fulfilling the more important function of guiding the kings and ministers in their formulation of governing policies and in their modes of administration. Diplomatic agents were yet another class of speakers, often utilized by quarreling kings who sent them on missions to one another's courts—sometimes to avoid wars and sometimes to intrigue for delays while preparations for fighting were carried on in secret.

Disputations and debates were practiced at court by skilled dialecticians and rhetoricians, as a kind of entertainment, especially during the long winter evenings. There was also a class of practical-minded scholars who sometimes flattered and sometimes dared to criticize the kings in an effort to guide policy and to advance their own political fortunes. Often these scholar-counsellors engaged in debates with one another on crucial questions, with the lives of the losers liable to forfeiture and with wealth and power to be gained by the winners.[1] It is significant that the earliest of the Chinese classics is a collection of speeches, set orations, and harangues (which will be discussed in Chapter 7).

The historical and the critical discussion of the speech of a period or of a people offers problems distinctly different from those confronted by the student of literature. Literature aims to be timeless, speaking to be timely. The province of rhetoric is the consideration of how discourse may be rendered effective within the set of particular circumstances in which it occurs.[2]

A speaker confronts an audience that has certain preconceptions because of its culture. Communication takes place in a setting which in many ways vitally affects what is said and the manner of the saying and the responding. Motivational patterns differ in different cultures and are always deeply affected by specific circumstances.

In order to evaluate any specimen of oral discourse one needs to know by whom it was spoken, what problem he was seeking to solve, what goal he hoped to attain, what the listeners felt and believed concerning the speaker and his subject, and how the speaker interpreted the receptive potential of his audience. For such reasons it is hopeless to try to understand the nature and role of speaking in a society without penetrating substantially inside the value system and behavioral relationships of the people. A poem may and perhaps should be judged by and for itself, independent of the circumstances of its composition. Who cares whether its author was old or young, rich or poor, harassed or at peace? But a speech is different. It reflects and incorporates the circumstances that led to and attended its presentation.

A speech is far more than the printed or even orally preserved transcript of what was said. It involves the speaker's problem which led him to decide to try to solve it by giving a speech. It requires consideration of how he decided upon the selection, arrangement, support, and adaptation of his materials in ways that he thought would result in making his speech effective. A poet, like a philosopher or an artist, aims at universality; whereas, a speaker aims toward specificity of effect.

From the point of view of the speech critic, this means that every utterance being studied must be interpreted in terms of its social and psychological setting. For the rhetorician it means also that every culture has its own rhetorical residue or effects. Every society makes its own rhetorical requirements, based on its own set of presumptions. Determination, then, of the rhetoric of ancient China is dependent upon extrapolation of rhetorical *factors,* using the word in its generic sense of *making* or *forming,* found in the culture of the time. The rhetoric must be found and interpreted within its social context.

In examining Chinese culture, one notable fact about it is that, like the ancient culture of India, it was remarkably stable. There were veritable whirlwinds of surface conflicts, but however much they changed specific political attachments, they affected the basic structure and value system of the people very little. It was not progress, dynamism, and change that characterized early Chinese civilization but continuity, stability and dependability.

Quite properly China is studied more as a civilization than as a nation. The early Chinese people were both too provincial and too cosmopolitan to be highly nationalistic. It seemed natural and proper for them to feel loyalty and commonality both toward their immediate associates, family, and community, and with mankind as a whole. They also felt a high sense of responsibility to accept and support their king, who stood for them as a sort of enlarged father-figure. But when they thought of themselves as "Chinese" it was largely in the sense of sharing a cultural heritage rather than a set of political identities. Geographically China was too large and socially it was too diverse for individuals in one section of the country to feel close unity with those in other parts.

The Chinese who lived around 500 B.C. belonged to what they thought of as the Middle Kingdom. This designation was significant in two very different ways. For one thing, it signallized the Chinese view that their land was the center of the known universe. Whatever else existed was simply peripheral. Civilization was surrounded by barbarians. This conviction was so deep-seated that it persisted through many centuries, down to modern times. When England's George III sent an embassy to China late in the eighteenth century, the Manchu Emperor haughtily rejected the offer to establish trade and diplomatic relations, saying: "Our celestial empire possesses all things in prolific abundance and lacks no product within its own borders. There is therefore no need to import the manufactures of outside barbarians."[3] It was this same impulse that led to the building of the Great Wall across the northern boundary of China by the great Ch'in Emperor Shih Huang Ti. China lay at the center, and what lay outside might be dangerous or disagreeable but could have little value. This was one meaning of the Middle Kingdom.

The other meaning, never so clearly stated but always strongly felt, was that the people of China (and people generally) occupied a middle position in the scheme of creation between a supernatural and a naturalistic set of beings on either side. In this respect the Chinese were very unlike the Indians. The Chinese did not envision all creation as one entity; nor did they see themselves as akin to all other forms of life. Deeply and fully, they were humanists. They conceived mankind to be a special form of life, unlike all others. They sought a clearer understanding of the nature of humanity—of how it differed from all other creatures, of how so to live as to most truly realize the potentiality of being man. This was a second meaning of the Middle Kingdom.

The earliest primitive explanations by the Chinese of the nature of the universe attempted to picture a harmonious order that fitted what they observed as they looked about themselves and meditated upon their own inner feelings. It was natural for the Chinese then, as they have since, to start with the here and now, with the observed and the experienced. Far more than most peoples, and far more than the Indians, the Chinese were pragmatists and in that sense realists. What they could not know and did not understand they had to imagine, but they kept their imaginings as close to observed reality as possible.

From this stance, they concluded that the creation of the world occurred through a heaving and surging of original chaos, until it coalesced into two harmonious and coordinate primal entities which they called the *Yin* and the *Yang*. These were complements which, working together and supporting one another, formed a unity. *Yin* and *Yang* comprised male and female, right and wrong, up and down, dark and light, life and death, yes and no, being and nonbeing. The image which represented them showed two tadpole-like figures curling together to form a circle, thus indicating that they were separate and distinct yet also coordinate, and that together they constitute the completeness and the unity of the universe.

The process of creation envisioned by the Chinese was mysterious but did not stress the supernatural idea of a *deus ex machina*. From the union of *Yin* and *Yang* was born a man-god P'an-Ku, who labored eighteen thousand years to make the earth, moon, sun, and stars. Then he sacrificed himself to compose the substance of earth: his head the mountains, his breath the clouds, his veins the rivers, his voice the thunder, his hairs the trees; and the insects which crawled upon his body became human beings and peopled the earth.

Following P'an-Ku came twelve Emperors of Heaven, each of whom reigned for eighteen thousand years. Then nine Emperors of Mankind ruled for a cumulative total of forty-five thousand and six hundred years. As in the mythology of other ancient regions, specific names stand out: Sui Jen, who produced fire; Fu Hsi, who taught the arts of hunting, fishing, and the domestication of animals; Shen Nung, the father of agriculture; Huang Ti, inventor of boats, carts, utensils, and the calendar; and Queen Su Ling, who discovered how to spin and weave silk. There is much that is fanciful but little that is abstractly metaphysical in this cluster of legends. The Chinese looked about them and invented orderly and speciously rational explanations of their origins.

Following these legendary myth-heroes came two model Emperors, Yao and Shun, whose reigns Confucius depicted as the Golden Age. After them began the first semi-historical period, the reign of King Yu, who founded the Hsia dynasty in 1989 B.C. Two hundred and twenty-three years later, in 1766 B.C., Hsia was replaced by the Shang dynasty, whose kings ruled until 1122 B.C. In that year the authentically historical Chou dynasty was founded. Even so, systematic historical records go back no further than 841 B.C. China, unlike Egypt, for example, had weather that was damp and that varied from hot to cold; such records as were made were not carved in stone but were written on perishable bamboo sticks. Hence, there is no chronicle of the beginnings of orderly society in China.

It is significant that the very earliest references indicate the importance which the ancient Chinese attached to the practice of free speech. The ninth of the Chou emperors, a King Li, who was represented as miserly, cruel, and arrogant, boasted to his prime minister, the Duke of Shao, that: "I have suppressed all criticism, for people no longer dare to speak." To this the Duke courageously replied: "You have made a barrier. But to close the mouths of the people is more difficult than to dam up the waters. When the course of water is stopped up, it overflows elsewhere and victims of the floods are many. It is the same with the mouths of the people."[4]

The compilers of this history drew a clear moral from the experience of King Li. He was overthrown shortly thereafter, and China commenced a six-hundred-year period of feudalism and decentralized power. The people, it was made plain, could be ruled effectively only while discussion was free, for public criticism identified faults while there was still time to correct them. Bad rule that went uncriticized built up a floodtide of resentment that eventually burst all barriers and swept the government away. Again and again this lesson has been reiterated in Chinese history.

As was true for India, in order to visualize the social circumstances of ancient China it is necessary to look at the historical scene which is available for examination. Like the Indians, the Chinese have been ultra-conservative. Changes naturally occurred; but to a high degree the Chinese felt themselves to be united with their past and future, as well as with one another. It has been "a fundamental assumption of the whole Chinese people . . . that antiquity was the prototype of modernity."[5] It was a tenet of their education that the ancient sages had attained to ultimate understanding.[6] Hence, with a penchant for looking to the past, "they read the same books [as did their forebears]; they perform practically the same ceremonials; they affect the same religion; they think the same thoughts."[7]

The qualities both of society and of personality which were fostered in ancient China were such as seemed appropriate for rural villages and crowded towns. The people lived close together and depended intimately upon one another. The cities were crowded, and even farmers lived in tightly packed villages. They could not abide unnecessary conflict for it was too disruptive. They developed a high regard for tolerance. Their political ideal was less justice and equality than harmony. To them, justice was so complicated that the very effort to define it often led to disputes and conflict; and they thought that equality manifestly was not observable among human beings. The ancient Chinese did not question that mankind is divided into higher and lower classes, with field laborers at the bottom and scholars at the top. Eventually they devised a fourfold class system, with soldiers at the lowest level, then merchants, next farmers, and the scholarly officials in the highest category. Then they sought to avoid the evil of societal rigidity by devising an examination system which opened the way for even the poorest peasant's son to win his way by ability and study to the highest ranks. Thus they reached a compromise: a hierarchical social structure that provided for individual mobility within it.

Another result of their pragmatic concern with how people may best live when they must always be crowded close together was that they came to value commonality and representativeness as principal personality attributes. Uniqueness and individuality were regarded as eccentric, to be condemned not admired. The personality type favored by the Chinese was not that which attracted attention to itself by being different but that which manifested the wisdom of conformity to the social norm.

It also was a cardinal characteristic of traditional Chinese culture that no one person could possibly be intelligent enough or experienced enough to develop a particularized insight that could be equal to the understanding clarified through the multiplied intelligence and experience of past generations. The authority of a venerated past, as distilled in the words and acts of great sages and revered historic personages, came to exercise a dominant role in Chinese culture. The authority of tradition

came, thus, to have a more convincing effect than even direct observation and personal experience. It was more likely that a person would
be wrong about what he thought he saw or felt than that the condensed
and evaluated wisdom of the past could be misleading. Hence, proverbial sayings were often quoted and were heard with respect.

Ancient Chinese society presented a series of contrasts between the
bright and the dark. There was the light of brilliant minds setting a high
standard of insight into humanistic values, and the darkness of widespread illiteracy resulting in rustic ignorance. There was the light of
meticulous courtesy, decorum, and propriety in social conduct, and the
darkness of customary and cynically accepted official corruption, cruelty,
and indifference to the welfare of the masses. There was the light of
unusual boldness and freedom of inquiry among the aristocratic and
educated minority, and the darkness of abject acceptance of inequality
by the uninformed and deprived majority. One of the darkest aspects
of ancient Chinese society was the autocracy of its rulers. And one of
the brightest factors was the courage and frankness of the scholarly
counsellors who dared to analyze the rulers' faults and failures and to
prescribe persuasively a set of principles and programs of reform.

The Chinese masses suffered less direct exploitation, however, than
such an abbreviated summary might suggest. Politically, ancient China
did indeed manifest tyranny at the court, but it also fostered a kind of
laissez-faire democracy in its farming and fishing villages. The aristocrats
crowded around the court enjoyed leisure and luxuries, but they also
lived in dread of possible destruction at the capricious whim of the ruler
or his favorite ministers or concubines. Han Fei-Tzu, for example, cited
many instances of purely adventitious cruelty—as when a king's favorite
concubine falsely whispered to him that "the new court ladies disliked
the smell of his majesty's breath," and in consequence, "the newcomers
had their noses cut off."[8] The masses, meanwhile, were neglected, could
safely be robbed, and were subject to unpredictable outbursts of governmental oppression. Generally, however, they were left free from ex-
cessive governmental exactions—for example, wars typically were confined to midwinter or midsummer, so that soldiers could go home to
plant and harvest crops—and they were rich in the dignity of ordering
their own lives according to the traditions and standards of their communities.

Even in its intimate relationships, the old Chinese traditional society
was a curious patchwork of lights and shadows. Within the family, in
the guilds through which most vocations and basic functions (such as
marriages and funerals) were managed cooperatively, and in the gen-

eral affairs of the community, each individual had roles that were carefully defined and fully protected. Every Chinese could count confidently upon a set of stabilized and dependable relations with his parents, his brothers and sisters, his children, and his friends. The kinds of obligations existing among them were not only enforced by affection but were fully prescribed in the detailed injunctions of traditions that were beyond question. Outside the restricted sphere of such intimate relationships, all whom he might encounter were strangers. Between him and them there were no bonds that mattered. A stranger at best was a nuisance to be lightly brushed aside, at worst an enemy to be hunted or avoided.

The picture of ancient Chinese society emerges clearly even through the mist of time and in the absence of detailed daily records. The closeness of the bonds of intimacy was counter-matched by a lack of cohesiveness in the broad society. China was more a culture than a nation. The strength of the people lay in their unbreakable stability—in their family life, in their devotion to tradition, in their disciplined decorum. Their weakness derived from this same conservatism, resulting in stagnation and decay. They were taught to make the most of what they had, rather than to seek more.

TRADITIONAL USES OF SPEECH

Individuality was suppressed rather than encouraged in the traditionalist society of ancient China. Insurmountable dfficulties confronted anyone who should dare to try to stand alone. The great social skills which the ancient Chinese developed were the arts of compromise, adjustment, and etiquette. As a result, daily life in all its complexities was guided less by personal preference than by an intricate system of prescribed ritual. The scope and significance of the prescribed etiquette will be considered for its rhetorical implications in Chapter 8. But it cannot be neglected here in view of its pervasiveness and significance in shaping the behavior of individuals in their social relationships.

For example, the etiquette governing "The Mode of Speaking and the Direction of the Eyes" in various social situations was detailed and precise:

(a) Whoever comes to speak with the Prince, first of all puts himself at his ease, thus settling his mind, and then speaks. This does not apply to one answering the Prince's questions.

(b) In speaking with the Prince, one talks of one's official business; with an official, of one's service to his Prince; with older men, of the control of children; with young people, of their filial and brotherly duties; with the common man, of geniality and goodness; with those in minor offices, of loyalty and sincerity.

(c) In speaking to an official, one begins by looking him in the face to gauge one's chances of a favorable reception; towards the middle of the interview one looks at his breast as an indication of one's trust in him, and also respect, indicated by the lowering of the eyes; and at the end of the interview, one's eyes are again directed to his face, to see how he is impressed. The order is never changed and is used in all cases.

(d) In the case of a father, the son's eyes are allowed to wander, but not higher than the face, so as not to seem too proud, nor lower than the girdle.

(e) If one is not speaking, then, when the other is standing, one looks at his feet, and, if he sits, at his knees, in sign of humility.[9]

In a discussion of how to conduct diplomatic missions, the envoy is advised: "(a) There is no set form prescribed for the speeches, but it is essential that they shall be in a style of formality suitable for governmental utterances, and pleasant. (b) If the speeches are too long, they sound artificial. If they are too short, they fail to convey the speaker's meaning. The perfection of the speaking art is to make speeches that convey the speaker's meaning and no more."[10]

One of the distinctive social achievements of ancient China was development of the principles of *li,* or of decorum, in the five basic relationships which concern everyone: "The duties are those between sovereign and minister, between father and son, between husband and wife, between elder brother and younger, and those belonging to the intercourse of friends. Those five are the duties of universal obligation."[11] Through careful management of these relationships, the primary goal of harmony could be maintained; for all would know what to expect, and the natural anticipations of conduct would be fulfilled.

The classic text in which these regulations are set forth, *The Doctrine of the Mean,* is somewhat ambiguous in describing the sanctions by which the regulations are enforced. It forthrightly insists that the rules of right conduct must be practiced because such behavior is *right,* not because it is correct or expedient or enforced. "Sincerity," it insists, "is that whereby self-completion is effected, and *its* way is that by which man must direct himself. Sincerity is the end and beginning of things; without sincerity there would be nothing."[12] But the classic also argues that what matters is that behavior in each of the five categories must be correct and traditional. The motive is of less import. "Some practice them with a natural ease; some from a desire for their advantages; and some by strenuous effort. But the achievement being made, it comes to the same thing."[13]

The goal of all the *li* regulations is not only to assure harmony among the classes by prescribing behavior but also to teach unquestioning acceptance of the lot into which one is born:

> The superior man does what is proper to the station in which he is; he does not desire to go beyond this.
>
> In a position of wealth and honour, he does what is proper to a position of wealth and honour. In a poor and low position, he does what is proper to a poor and low position. . . . In a position of sorrow and difficulty, he does what is proper for a position of sorrow and difficulty. The superior man can find himself in no situation in which he is not himself.[14]

The "superior man," it should be noted, is not one who holds a position of superior wealth or power, but one who contains within himself an inviolable regard for virtue and for the observance of *li*. A peasant who behaves as a peasant should is as much a "superior man" as a prince who behaves like a prince. And when things do not turn out as one would wish, the blame is not placed upon others or upon unfavorable circumstances. For it is in life as it is in archery: "When the archer misses the center of the target, he turns round and seeks for the cause of his failure in himself."[15]

Western predilections should not lead us to think that the Chinese rejection of individuality meant a denial of the importance of the individual. Again and again the ancient Chinese classics insist that the prosperity or the destruction of the whole society may depend upon the right conduct of a key individual. And who is this key individual? It may be the emperor, because all eyes are upon him. It may be the father, because he is the keystone of the family. But it may be the wife, the elder brother, a younger brother, sister, friend, or fellow villager or a stranger. For every person, everywhere, has his own prescribed niche and duties, neglect of which may cause dissension or catastrophe. A social problem is like an infectious disease: once it starts, there is no telling how far or in what directions it may spread. Responsibility for all rests upon each one.

Much as the Chinese valued harmony, quarrels among them were far from infrequent. As V. R. Burkhardt, a close student of Chinese traditionalism, has observed: "Living as they do, in such close proximity to one another, it would be a miracle if tempers were not sometimes frayed, and hasty words did not lead to temporary estrangements."[16] Somewhat ungallantly, the classical *Book of Odes* stigmatized women for bringing discord into the courts:

> Clever men build cities,
> Clever women topple them.
> Beautiful, these clever women,
> But they are owls, they are kites.
> Women have long tongues,
> Stairways to ruin.
> Disorder is not sent down from Heaven,
> But bred by these women.
> Impossible to teach, impossible to instruct,
> Such are women and eunuchs.[17]

Charles K. Parker, an American who spent many years in China, sought to reconcile the two seemingly contradictory ideas that the Chinese value harmony yet frequently quarrel. In a chapter entitled, "China Talks," he depicted the modern Chinese (who in this respect may not be very different from their ancient forebears) as being reasonable, in that they would rather talk out their problems than fight over them. They may seem to be quarrelsome, he says: "Yet, because the disputants try to win by debate, instead of by an exchange of blows, you can see that Chinese social custom puts a premium on discussion and reason as opposed to blows and bloodshed."[18]

However much quarrelsomeness existed, it was heartily deprecated. Du Halde, a French Jesuit whose description of China did much to form the eighteenth-century impressions of the Orient held by Europeans and Englishmen, reported the Chinese expressing sentiments that must have been common among them for centuries: "There are some people whose character is to be impudent, even to brutality; who observe measures with nobody, but tell a man of honour to his face what they know is most capable to make him uneasy; who rip up the disgrace of families, and the most concealed irregularities of the fair." Since such people are about, one should guard his listening carefully: "There are three sorts of discourse which we ought not to hear. First, those which mention intrigues or unlawful engagements; such is the talk of a woman who has forgotten that which forms the glory of her sex. Secondly, those which propose an advantage which can only be obtained by injustice; such is the discourse of the vulgar. Thirdly, the discourse which proceeds from a double heart and dissembling lips; such is the discourse of rascally people."[19]

Du Halde pointed out that a proverbial saying ascribed to Tzu-Ssu, the grandson of Confucius, was spoken often in the villages: "A stab with the tongue is often more dangerous than a wound with a sword."[20]

Aside from the city-dwellers, the ancient Chinese farmers lived in small villages that typically numbered about twenty-five families. Both in the family and in the villages their lives were closely knit. Individuals seldom had problems which were not shared by their associates. Men did not try to live apart or alone. Neighborliness was an essential characteristic of their way of life. This is why social harmony was so highly valued—and why slanderers and fomentors of discord were so sharply censored:

> There are people who, finding themselves possessed of some degree of wit, have an inclination to be talking upon every subject; but their harangues have generally no other tendency than to raise their own reputation by depressing the characters of other men. Their mouth is a kind of monument with two faces, one of which gives you an encomium on themselves, the other exhibits the faults of their neighbors. Their tongues are daggers unsheathed, lifted up, and ready to strike, for which reason they are dreaded and avoided by the whole world; yet it must be confessed that they generally prejudice none so much as themselves; for as they pour out their invectives to the first comers, without reserve, they are very frequently betrayed, and even those on whom they have at other times conferred benefits are made their enemies. Thus they involve themselves in a thousand perplexities and are soon stripped of all they have to lose.[21]

Even talk that was constructive and to the point should be guarded, for loquaciousness is tiresome. Howevermuch one enjoys the melody of a songbird, for example, "if he sings all day long, his voice ceases to be agreeable. The roar of a tiger strikes the hearer with horror; but if he roars all the day, custom reconciles us to it, and we are no longer affrighted. However important your discourse may be," the moralist concluded, "let it not be too frequent or too long."[22]

Finally, after a lengthy chapter on the moral philosophy of the Chinese, Du Halde devoted a chapter to summary accounts of their "other sciences," of which rhetoric was one. After describing their logic as reflecting "the natural light of reason," he added:

Their Rhetoric is, in like manner, entirely natural, they being acquainted with very few Rules proper to adorn and embellish a Discourse; however, they are not absolutely without any. But Imitation serves them almost continually instead of Precepts; they content themselves with reading the most eloquent Compositions, therein observing the Turns that are most likely to affect the Mind, and make such an Impression as they aim at: 'tis after these Precedents that they copy in framing any set Discourse. Their Eloquence does not consist in a certain Arrangement of Periods, but in lively Phrases, and noble Metaphors, as well as bold Comparisons, and chiefly in Maxims and Sentences taken from the ancient Sages; which, being expressed in a spritely, concise, and mysterious Style, contain a great deal of Sense, and Variety of Thoughts in a very few Words.[23]

The emphasis here is exactly upon the right point: for in speech, as in all else, the ancient Chinese were distinctly traditionalistic. What was established they did not mean to upset. What was practiced, they meant to follow. And the speech patterns which they found most firmly fixed were those that Du Halde perceptively noted: a liberal use of metaphor, analogy, and sententious phrasing, including a frequent quotation of proverbs and maxims from their sages. Moreover, he also was correct in saying they did not devote much attention to formulating theories and precepts of rhetoric. What they taught was implicit in their practice; and beyond this the rhetorical principles were suggested by pertinent tenets of their philosophy and social regulations. In a way quite different from caste in India—far less systematic and indirect—the ancient Chinese, too, had a *rhetoric in being:* a rhetoric that was talked rather than talked about.

SPEECH AND SOCIETY: SAVING FACE

No society anywhere ever surpassed that of ancient China in its care to protect and preserve human dignity. Both in its structure and in its operative rules and customs, the role of each individual was carefully defined. No one could undermine the established character of a person except as he himself might do so—either carelessly or willfully. And detailed provision was made to protect his dignity both from attacks by others and from his own misjudgment.

As has been noted, ancient Chinese society was strictly hierarchal. There were two major social divisions: the aristocratic elite and the illiterate laboring and farming class. Between the two there was seldom need for any very intimate two-way communication. It was a maxim among the scholars that "The masses may be led but cannot be made to comprehend."[24] Hsün-tze, a principal exponent of Confucianism during its early stages, explained the class structure as follows: "Different grades of men live together with similar likings but different moral standards, with similar desires but different amounts of knowledge—this is nature. Their original capacities are alike in wisdom and stupidity. But their developed abilities are different. . . . If there were no prince to rule the subjects, if there were no superior to rule the inferior, the country would be injured and people would give rein to their desire."[25] Here is an approach to societal needs that is directly contrary to the tenets of Lockean democracy. John Locke, like Hsün-tze, concluded that individuals are equal at birth and become unequal because of differing conditions and education. Locke thereupon defended democratic equalitarianism, demanding that states equalize opportunities so that all men might be equal in fact as they are potentially. Hsün-tze, being concerned more with the over-all welfare of the community than with individuals, pointed out that society requires services varying from unskilled labor upward to the complex demands of governing.

Confucius agreed with the view that social needs must take priority over individual preferences. This was the basis for the Confucian political philosophy of subordination and respect for established authority. It also led the great sage to advise the people of his time: "Do not talk of policies when you are not in a position to make them."[26]

The examination system, which was inaugurated early in the Han dynasty, theoretically provided a practical means both of revitalizing the ruling class by infusions from below and of assuring opportunity for upward mobility of the capable poor, thus reducing the pressures of discontent in the lower echelons. Generally speaking, however, the kind of education that fitted candidates to pass the examinations was available only to the aristocracy. Even so, the examination system was wholly compatible with the Confucian view that the welfare of the community was more important than individuals. Government was not administered by a hereditary aristocracy, which should claim the right to rule by accident of birth; instead, an effort was made to select those able to rule on the basis of intellectual achievements and proven capacity. The method of selection based on knowledge of the classics may have seemed unrealistic. Nevertheless, it led to humanistic values being stressed rather than slighted. And verbal skills were emphasized.

The principle on which the system rested was that human behavior remains predictably uniform under stable conditions, so that what has proved to be efficacious in the tested experience of past generations is a better guide for present policies than the limited insight attainable through individual reason and experimentation. Even in the everyday relationships of ordinary village life, the ancient Chinese peasantry was not left to spur-of-the-moment inspiration but was guided by some three thousand detailed approved modes of conduct.

Arthur Smith, an observer of the Chinese scene in the nineteenth century, found conditions that probably had not changed much in their basic social relationships since the time of Confucius. He noted that "there are few Chinese who do not know the proper thing to be done at a given time, incomparably better than the most cultivated foreigner." The ritualistic etiquette which every child learned as he grew up had as a major function to "serve as lubricating fluids to smooth human intercourse." Like rhetoric, its purpose was to "adjust people to people." And however "unnatural" this formalized behavior might seem from the Western viewpoint, it constituted a sort of air-cushion, which "eases the jolts wonderfully."[27]

"Easing the jolts" was a major purpose of ancient Chinese rhetoric, so much so that their social processes had as one of their principal functions the avoidance of embarrassment—or "saving face," as it came to be known. Kenneth Latourette, a lifelong student of Chinese society, concluded that this emphasis arose precisely because of the stability which we have noted as a prime characteristic of the culture. In a fluid society, one who failed could simply move on and try his fortune again elsewhere. But in China the ties that bound individuals to their family and community were too tight to be broken. Whatever happened, the individual had to remain and deal with it. Any festering discontent that was needlessly introduced proved a lasting problem not only for the individual but for the community.[28] Thus, saving face was well worth the trouble.

To the ancient Chinese, dignity was not only a mark of gentility but also an innate right. It was not to be jeopardized, whether the individual was of high or low status. A household servant should not be reprimanded directly; a better method would be to remind him that only "vulgar fellows" behave in such-and-such a manner. Usually a hint would suffice, without leaving scars of conflict or of denunciation. Loud talk and abusive language were considered poor behavior. Instead, disapproval could be indicated by a bland expression and an inconspicuous gesture. Suggestions, innuendoes, and analogical comments were preferred to direct assertions concerning personal behavior. To deliberately render communication indirect might seem to blunt its effectiveness, but the ancient Chinese preferred the problem of interpreting minor cues to the greater problem of dealing with conflict, blame, guilt, and resentment.

No people have learned better than did the ancient Chinese how to deliver unpalatable truth in palatable form. The preservation of face was among their highest social goals. However widely opinions might differ, propriety and decorum were to be preserved. For in the long run the maintenance of general harmony was of greater value than the achievement of any particular result in an individual dispute. This was the atmosphere in which the various rhetorical practices and views of the ancient Chinese were nourished. It gave to their thinking about rhetoric a special Chinese cast. For its detailed developments we must look from the generalized society to particular examples of the speaking and of reasoning about the nature and uses of discourse.

CHAPTER 7

The Book of History: An Anthology of Speeches

SPEECHES AS HISTORY

IT IS NOT ACCIDENTAL that the earliest histories of ancient China were primarily concerned with speeches and speech-making. It was Lord Macaulay in nineteenth-century England who observed that "Government is two-thirds talk." In ancient China speech was the principal means by which the ruler and his people mutually influenced one another. This was because government operated without a vast structure of bureaucracy. Laws did not penetrate into every aspect of personal life. Government existed basically to preserve a viable social harmony. If the people were content with their ruler and he with their behavior, the reign was successful. Mutual satisfaction was a prerequisite. How to represent events so that they would be pleasing and thus avoid arousing criticism was a social and political skill greatly valued. Hence, the first historical writings in ancient China were anthologies of speeches by kings and their counsellors, with brief commentaries about them.

Two of these works became minor classics. One, the *Commentary* by Tso Ch'iu-ming on the volume said to have been composed by Confucius, *The Spring and Autumn Annals,* details the history of the state of Lu from 722 to 481 B.C.; and the other, with the intriguing title *Conversations of the States,* consists of speeches and discussions representing about the same epoch.

The *Commentary*—somewhat in the manner of Thucydides' *History of the Peloponnesian Wars*—presented numerous fictional speeches by imaginary statesmen and rulers as vehicles for offering indirect advice concerning virtuous and socially correct conduct.[1] The discourses contained in the *Commentary* are clear evidence that the ancient Chinese regarded oral discourse as an important rhetorical form; but, being fictional, they indicate little about the style actually used by speakers of that time. The *Annals* themselves are a mere chronology of successive reigns. But one sentence from them exercised deep and continuing influence on the style of many generations of Chinese. Its high prestige arose because it was presumably written by Confucius himself. But aside from the authorship, the style was noted as being most unusual and proved to have lasting influence. The sentence as translated reads: "Stones fell in Sung five." Many later Chinese teachers and critics have pointed out that the sentence did not read, "Five stones fell in Sung." Instead, they have taught, Confucius wisely directed initial attention to the strange fact that stones (meteorites) fell—a most unusual happening. The fact of secondary importance was that they fell in a particular location, Sung. Only incidentally did he add the less important information that the meteorites numbered five.

The *Conversations of the States* at least purports to present relatively authentic speech texts. Their authenticity, however, is not the crucial fact about them. As Watson properly concluded, "However true the picture may be to historical reality we shall probably never know, but it is a picture which has had a powerful influence upon the Chinese imagination."[2] The compiler apparently intended to illustrate, repeatedly, his thesis that bad government leads to revolution. As one example, he presents a discussion by Prime Minister Kuo, who is giving counsel to his king: "When the state is about to perish, its ruler is greedy, reckless, depraved and perverted. He is lewd, indolent, negligent and lazy. He is vulgar and cruel. . . . And because his punishments are imposed on the basis of treachery and slander, his people desert him and divert their loyalty elsewhere."[3] The lesson was clearly taught.

Such preachments as this indicate the importance of the collections of speeches, regardless of their authenticity. They demonstrate the cardinal role ascribed by the ancient Chinese to oral discourse. They also illustrate the mode of persuasion by indirection and the high value placed upon the citation of specific incidents from earlier times. There is no doubt that the ancient Chinese considered effective speech to be a valid and vital instrument of government. The importance attributed to it becomes very evident as we turn to the short shelf housing the greatest of the Chinese classics. Four of these are the *Analects* of Confucius, the *Great Learning,* the *Doctrine of the Mean,* and the *Book of Odes.* And the fifth is another history that, like the two cited, consists largely of a collection of speeches. It is called simply the *Book of History.* "From the time of Confucius down to our own days," Ch'ên Shou-Yi, a historian of Chinese literature, avers, it "has exerted an uninterrupted influence upon the literary style and taste of the Chinese people."[4] The speech texts included in the book indicate a great deal concerning the rhetorical standards and practices of China during the fifteen hundred years from 2255 B.C. to 628 B.C., the period covered by the compilation.

SPEECH AS GOVERNMENT: CHARGES AND INSTRUCTIONS

The *Book of History* has a clear theme which was supported and enforced in the precepts and practices of the great prototype emperors and their chief ministers. This theme is that *to rule well meant to communicate honestly, intelligently, and effectively*. Such communication must flow unimpeded in two directions: from the throne to the people and from the people to the throne. Ministers must be courageous in speaking with utmost frankness to their monarchs; and kings must make unmistakably clear what responsibilities and duties they expect their ministers, generals, and officials to exercise. Social harmony and individual dignity were clearly the major *desiderata* of the society; but they could not be attained by evasive speaking, by false flattery, or by curbing of honest criticism. The kind of speech repeatedly recommended was that which aimed to achieve the speaker's goal through means that would enhance rather than undermine communal contentment. Disruptive personal attack or appeal to self-interest in persuasive appeals was always to be condemned. What was good for the individual, if he could but fully understand it, was what was good for the entire community. The best of speaking was that which showed that the good of each one inhered within what was good for all.

The definitive text of the *Book of History* finally took form, after various alterations, toward the end of the Chou dynasty in the sixth century B.C. Tradition holds that Confucius himself edited the final version of it. The most prestigious western translator of the work, James Legge, concluded that "There were no doubt mutilations and transpositions, as well as alterations of the ancient text, but they were not so great as to affect the substantial integrity of the book."[5] Naturally, the oldest of the documents, which date back to the twenty-third century B.C., are not as well authenticated as are the more recent ones.

The book opens with an account of the first of the model emperors, King Yaou, who set an example of great devotion to the welfare of his people. As he neared death, he married two of his daughters to his favorite minister, a noble named Shun, in order that in the intimacy of marriage the daughters might discover for him whether he was correct in his judgment that Shun was worthy of becoming his successor. Their report was favorable, and Shun became the second of the model emperors. He also was the first to make manifest the relationship between government and effective speech.

Shun's first stated policy upon ascending the throne was "to throw open the doors of communication between the court and the empire," for he "sought to see with the eyes and hear with the ears of all." As might be expected, when free communication was established, the king learned that there was much dissatisfaction among his people. Understandably, he placed the blame upon them rather than upon the condition of the kingdom. Hence he charged his newly appointed Minister of Education as follows: "The people continue unfriendly with one another, and do not observe docilely the five orders of relationship [li]. It is yours, as the Minister of Instruction, reverently to set forth the lessons of duty belonging to the five orders. Do so with gentleness." The complaints continued and King Shun finally decided upon the rigorous step of trying to close the doors of communication which at the start of his reign he had opened. He appointed a General Regulator, or Censor, telling him: "I abominate slanderous speakers, and destroyers of right ways, who agitate and alarm my people. I appoint you to be the Minister of Communication. Early and late give forth my orders and report to me, seeing that everything is true."[6]

Like many another ruler, King Shun felt convinced that if everyone did his duty and understood the real problems of government, then affairs "will be well ordered, and the people will sedulously seek to be virtuous." If only this state of frankness, honesty, and goodwill could be established, then censorship would be abolished; then "good words will nowhere lie hidden." However, he realized that "The mind of man is restless, prone to err; its affinity for the right way is small." He knew, too, that selfish and unscrupulous counsellors would bring to the throne advice that was aimed not so much to advance the welfare of the realm as to give advantage to themselves. Hence, he warned his favorite minister (a nobleman named Yu, whom Shun was educating to become his successor): "Do not listen to unsubstantiated words; do not follow undeliberated plans."[7]

Three kinds of speeches are represented in the *Book of History*. The first type are "charges," which were exhortations delivered by kings or generals to their troops on the eve of battle, to incite them to fight better. The second type are "instructions," which may be either advice given by ministers to rulers or guidance presented by kings to newly appointed ministers. Third were "announcements," actually major policy speeches, often highly charged with persuasion, delivered by kings to assemblages in their courts. In general they dealt with matters of major policy for which the support of public opinion was needed. These were the kinds of occasions for speeches which the early historians accounted of principal importance.

The Charges

The earliest recorded charge was delivered by Prince Yu, Minister of Justice, after King Shun ordered him to conquer the neighboring country of Meaou:

> Ye multitudes here arrayed (said Yu), listen all of you to my orders. Stupid is this prince of Meaou, ignorant, erring and disrespectful. Despiteful and insolent to others, he thinks that all ability and virtue are with himself. A rebel to the right, he destroys all the obligations of virtue. Superior men are kept by him in obscurity, and mean men fill all the offices. The people reject and will not protect him. Heaven is sending calamities down upon him. On this account I have assembled you, my multitude of gallant men, and bear the instructions of the emperor to punish his crimes. Do you proceed with united heart and strength, so shall our enterprise be crowned with success.[8]

The basic pattern that Yu established of first justifying the war, and then of calling on the soldiers to fight bravely for success, was followed by his successors. Soon, however, they added yet a third element: a threat of dire punishment if the soldiers should slacken in doing their duty. The first of the charges to add this new aspect was given by King K'e, the son of Yu, when in the first year of his reign he marshaled his armies to lead them against a prince (named Hoo) who had rebelled against his rule. After the usual depiction of the causes of the war and the appeal for support in the cause, King K'e added an ominous note: "If you left-side men do not do your work on the left, it will be a disregard of my orders. If you right-side men do not do your work on the right, it will be a disregard of my orders. If you charioteers do not observe the rules for the management of your horses, it will be a disregard of my orders. You who obey my orders shall be rewarded before my ancestors; and you who disobey my orders shall be put to death before the spirits of the land; and I shall also put your children to death."[9] This kind of incitement, offering a reward with one hand and punishment with the other, must have been effective, for it became the customary manner of concluding the charges.

Nevertheless, the charges never became merely ritualistic. Despite the similarity in their basic patterns of organization and motivation, they possessed about as much individuality of style and content as the nature of the occasion permitted. After all, a general seated on horseback before battle-arrayed troops does not have much latitude in what to say or how to say it. There must be an inspirational reference to the justice of their cause and an exhortation to do their full duty. If the speech is to be heard and comprehended, it must be brief, the sentences short, the tone positive. Even so, generals, like everyone else, have differing temperaments, and such differences were fully indicated in the charges preserved in the *Book of History*.

When the prince of Yin was commanded to lead the six armies of the empire against two recalcitrant provincial governors, He and Ho, Yin discreetly failed to mention to the troops that the rebels were suspected of being in league with a claimant to the throne—for he did not wish to arouse any fears that the throne might change hands. Instead, Yin merely said that He and Ho were drunken and irresponsible in the conduct of their official duties. Yin then added a promise of clemency for all among their foes who might surrender, saying: "I will so destroy only the chief criminals and not punish their forced followers, while those who have long been stained by their filthy manners will be allowed to renovate themselves." Then, in keeping with his compassion for the enemy troops, he forebore to threaten the usual punishment in case his own soldiers should fight poorly, and instead concluded: "All ye, my warriors, exert yourselves, and be cautious."[10] Even without any fuller historical details, it is easy to infer an especially cordial relationship between Prince Yin and his troops.

In contrast with Yin's speech is one made by General T'ang, founder of a dynasty that would rule China for six hundred and forty-four years. The time was 1765 B.C., and T'ang was leading a rebellion against the king. He was a hard man, and although he made a strong effort to appear virtuous and patriotic in the body of his speech, his ruthless temper shows clearly in his conclusion:

> Come, ye multitudes of the people, listen all to my words. It is not I, the little child, who dares to undertake what may seem to be a rebellious enterprise; but, for the many crimes of the sovereign of Hea, Heaven has given the charge to destroy him.
>
> Now, ye multitudes, you are saying, "Our prince does not compassionate us, but is calling us away from our husbandry to attack and punish the ruler of Hea." I have indeed heard these words of

you all: but the sovereign of Hea is an offender, and, as I fear God, I dare not but punish him.

Now you are saying, "What are the crimes of Hea to us?" The king of Hea does nothing but exhaust the strength of his people, and exercise oppression in the cities of Hea. His people have all become idle in his service and will not assist him. They are saying, "When will this sun expire? We will all perish with thee." Such is the course of the sovereign of Hea, and I must go and punish him.

Assist, I pray you, me, the one man, to carry out the punishment appointed by Heaven. I will greatly reward you. On no account disbelieve me; I will not eat my words. If you do not obey the words which I have spoken to you, I will put your children to death; you will find no forgiveness.

The anonymous chronicler recorded that after T'ang's victory, "he had a feeling of shame on account of his rebellion, and said, 'I am afraid that in future ages men will fill their mouths with me' "—that is, "will speak contemptuously of me." Whereupon, we encounter an example of the second type of speeches—the instructions.

The Instructions

T'ang's expression of shame presented an opportunity which one of his principal ministers, Chung-Hwuy, was quick to seize: "When a sovereign's virtue is daily being renewed, he is cherished throughout the myriad States; when he is full of his own will, he is abandoned by the nine classes of his kindred. . . . Order your affairs by righteousness; order your heart by propriety; so shall you transmit a grand example to posterity. I have heard the saying: 'He who finds instructors for himself comes to the supreme dominion; he who says that others are not equal to himself comes to ruin. He who likes to ask becomes enlarged; he who uses only himself becomes small.' "[12] Such sentiments, addressed to a brusque and willful general who had just won a kingdom for himself on the battlefield, took courage indeed.

Little is known of Chung-Hwuy beyond the bare record of this single speech. Ssu-Ma Ch'ien, the great Han historian,[13] did not even mention him. Later Chinese historians have searched the records assiduously and have come up with very little. Legge summarized what is known: that Chung seized the opportunity offered by T'ang's off-hand expression of repentance to read him a lesson in good government, after first building a foundation of confidence by assuring him that his rebellion had been justified.[14] Giles, who prepared a biographical dictionary of ancient China, noted only that he was of noble ancestry, being "descended from Hsi Chung, who was Master of the Equipage under the Hsia dynasty."[15] Actually this fact emphasizes the courage of Chung-Hwuy, since he criticized the victorious T'ang while the new king recognized him as the son of a functionary of the very sovereign who had been overthrown.

Mencius, who lived some seven hundred years after the event, gives us by far the most tantalizing account. He cited Chung-Hwuy as a model ministerial counsellor, and hinted that he ended his life in disgrace and exile, though with no abatement of his courage or dignity:

> Hwuy of Lew-hea was not ashamed to serve an impure prince, nor did he think it low to be an inferior officer. When advanced to employment, he did not conceal his virtue, but made it a point to carry out his principles. When dismissed and left without office, he yet did not murmur. When straitened by poverty, he yet did not grieve. When thrown into the company of village people, he was quite at ease, and could not bear to leave them. He had a saying, "You are you, and I am I. Although you stand by my side with breast and arms bare, or with your body naked, how can you defile me?" Therefore, when men now hear the character of Hwuy of Lew-hea, the mean become generous and the niggardly become liberal.[16]

This eulogy by Mencius is as fine as a man could hope for; and because of it Chung-Hwuy's name has been honored in Chinese history. His life supports the conclusion of his famous instructions to T'ang: "Oh! he who would take care for his end must be attentive to his beginning. There is acceptance for the observers of propriety, and overthrow for the blinded and wantonly indifferent. To revere and honor the way of Heaven is the way to preserve the favouring regard of Heaven."[17]

Chung's instructions to Emperor T'ang illustrate the principal characteristics of this form of speaking: that it be conciliatory in the sense that it was clearly intended to aid the king to carry out his heavy responsibilities; that it be forthrightly honest and frank; and that it should consist of broadly ethical generalizations supported by historic examples. The pattern for such instructions was first established by the model emperor, King Shun, when he assembled his ministers and courtiers around him and advised them as follows:

My ministers constitute my legs and arms, my ears and eyes. I wish to help and support my people; you give effect to my wishes. I wish to spread the influence of my government through the four quarters [of the kingdom]; you are my agents. . . . When I am doing wrong, it is yours to correct me; do not follow me to my face and when you have retired have other remarks to make. Be reverent, ye who stand before and behind and on each side of me. As to all the obstinately stupid and calumniating talkers, who are not to be found doing what is right, there is the target to exhibit their true character;* the scourge to make them remember; and the book of remembrance! . . . If they become reformed, they are to be received and employed; if they do not, let the terrors of punishment overtake them.[18]

It is significant that following this instruction by the king, Minister Yu boldly responded, admonishing the king to do his own duty, and reminding him that his ministers had rendered him services well beyond the required norm. After this exchange of injunctions, the court turned to music and entertainment, indicative of the pleasure they had in one another's company. Forthright speaking was possible because they dwelt in harmony. They liked and trusted one another; they shared similar principles and goals; and they were guided by their commonly accepted ethical principles. Public opinion was their major sanction, controlling and guiding their conduct—along with the example of their forebears and the judgment of posterity. Their ethics were based on humanistic rather than supernatural grounds, and perhaps for this reason they felt a close unity in their sense of duty.

The greatest of the ministerial counsellors, both in his own era and in the view of China's long history, was a countryman named I Yin, who served both Emperor T'ang and his grandson-successor, T'ae Kea. So grandly did he live and so reverently was he remembered that tradition accorded him an extraordinary origin: "he was born in a hollow mulberry-tree."[19]

When Emperor T'ang heard of his remarkable learning and sent an

---

* The reference, as would readily be recognized by Shun's hearers, was to archery—a common imagery in the speech of ancient China. Whether or not the arrows (or the words) flew true to the target provided an instant and dependable test of the quality of the archer (or speaker). In other words, if a speaker made promises or prophecies, were they fulfilled?

envoy to fetch him to court, I Yin refused three times, thus proclaiming his independence. However, when he arrived in court, he was astute enough to ingratiate the emperor. Knowing that King T'ang prided himself on his cookery, I Yin took care to talk with him about unusual and appealing recipes. A personal relationship was established that enabled the minister to exercise a high degree of influence in public policies.

Among the high services I Yin rendered to King T'ang was to unveil to him the rebelliousness of his grandson and heir—whom I Yin courageously sent into exile. Mencius praised him for exemplifying "that they who are first informed should instruct those who are later in being informed, and they who first apprehend principles should instruct those who are slower in doing so." So keen was I Yin's sense of responsibility, Mencius continued, that when he saw the masses of people suffering deprivation, "it was as if he himself pushed them into a ditch; for he took upon himself the heavy charge of the empire."[20] This was the character of the man who dared to come out of the obscurity of the back country, armed only with his intelligence, learning, and courage, to give bold and unvarnished counsel to the victorious founder of a new dynasty.

The grandson of T'ang, T'ae Kea, was often admonished in his childhood by the doughty minister. In order to win King T'ang's endorsement as his successor, T'ae Kea was forced to accept a rigorous discipline that he found exceedingly distasteful. Yet so powerful was the influence of I Yin that even after he was elevated to the throne, he called his courtiers around him to apologize in their presence to the aged counsellor. "Heretofore I turned my back on the instructions of you, my Tutor and Guardian," he said; "my beginning has been marked by incompetency. May I still rely on your correcting and improving virtue, keeping this in view that my end may be good!"

How sternly I Yin dealt with the unstable young king is illustrated in a speech presented by the aged counsellor to officials of the court and nobles who had assembled from all the provinces, on the occasion of a memorial service for the late Emperor T'ang. After a brief eulogy to the departed emperor, I Yin turned toward T'ae Kea and said: "Now your Majesty is entering on the inheritance of his virtue; everything depends on how you commence your reign." Then, with all the court listening attentively, he gave the king hard-headed advice: "Oh! the former king began with careful attention to the bonds that held men together: he listened to expostulation and did not seek to resist it; he conformed to the wisdom of former people; occupying the highest position, he displayed intelligence; occupying an inferior position [before ascending to the throne], he displayed his loyalty; he allowed the good qualities of others, and did not seek that they should have every talent; in the government of himself, he seemed to think he could never sufficiently attain. It was thus he arrived at the possession of the myriad regions." In such fashion I Yin continued on and on, until at last, carried away by his own sense of power and righteousness, he concluded in a rush: "Revere these instructions in your person. Think of them! Sacred counsels of vast importance, admirable words forcibly displayed."[21]

In the months ahead, however, the young king dared to disregard I Yin's ministrations, and neglected his duties to engage in licentious revels. I Yin thereupon placed him in an easy sort of confinement, near the grave of T'ang, during the three years of prescribed mourning for the old emperor. Then, seeing that the young king was penitent and determined to be more virtuous, he restored him to the throne. As he did so, he warned T'ae Kea that the expressions of joy by his courtiers and subjects upon his restoration were not trustworthy. For, I Yin admonished him, "The people are not constant to those whom they cherish; they cherish only him who is benevolent." In other words, watch your step.

Now, grown old, tiring of the cares of office, and eager for retirement, I Yin resigned his office with a farewell address compact of advice:

> Oh! It is difficult to rely on Heaven; its appointments are not constant. But if the sovereign sees to it that his virtue be constant, he will preserve his throne; if his virtue be not constant, the nine provinces will be lost by him. . . .
>
> Your course must be as when ascending high you begin from where it is low, and when travelling far you begin from where it is near. Do not slight the occupations of the people; think of their difficulties; do not yield to a feeling of repose on your throne; think of its perils. Be careful for the end at the beginning. When you hear words against which your mind sets itself, you must inquire whether they be not right; when you hear words which accord with your own mind, you must inquire whether they be not contrary to what is right. Oh! what attainment can be made without serious thought? What achievement can be made without earnest effort?

In the course of this farewell address, I Yin interspersed moral maxims somewhat resembling those of Benjamin Franklin's Poor Richard or the homilies in the Book of Proverbs. In their combination of hard-headed practicality and idealistic ethics they provided a legacy of guidance for China which, enforced by the approval Confucius later gave them, exercised a considerable effect for centuries:

> Good and evil do not wrongly befall men, because Heaven sends down misery or happiness according to their conduct. . . .
>
> Virtue has no invariable model; a supreme regard to what is good gives the model of it. What is good has no invariable characteristic to be supremely regarded; it is found where there is a conformity to the uniform consciousness in regard to what is good. . . .
>
> Do not think yourself so large as to deem others small. If ordinary men and women do not find the opportunity to give full development to their ability, the people's lord will be without the proper aids to complete his merit.[22]

How much T'ae Kea profited from all this advice, history does not reveal. He ruled for thirty-three years, until his death in 1720 B.C. I Yin survived the young king by eight years. It is uncertain whether he accomplished his wish for retirement or was prevailed upon to remain as counsellor at the court. He was buried with the honors usually reserved for emperors. A biography of him was prepared by one of his fellow ministers; but unfortunately it did not survive. I Yin's memory, however, is revered. He is considered to have been the best of the ministerial counsellors in pre-Confucian China.

ANNOUNCEMENTS: SPEECHES OF POLICY

The third class of addresses contained in the *Book of History* are those which we would most readily call public speeches. It is significant that the anonymous compilers called them announcements. These were speeches by a king to his assembled officials and courtiers. Their purpose was to gain support for crucial policies.

They must have been prepared with great care, for the throne always depended upon the support of the influential classes. The king ruled "by the mandate of heaven," but this did not mean by divine right. It meant by public approval. When the conduct of a king fell under widespread disapproval, the mandate was presumed to have been withdrawn. Rebellion then became not only a right but also a duty. It was, accordingly, of great importance to the kings to have their policies sympathetically understood and favorably received.

The circumstances clearly called for persuasion. Yet, as the name "announcements" suggests, the tone was generally expository rather than argumentative. The mood was not conciliatory but authoritative. Those who listened must be led to understand; and once they understood, their acceptance could either be taken for granted or commanded by the king as his right. If a time came when this relationship between monarch and subjects no longer obtained, rebelliousness would have proceeded beyond the reach of persuasion.

How public speaking was regarded by the ancient Chinese is clearly indicated in many references. One such occurs in poem 46 in "The Airs of Yung," a portion of the classical *Book of Odes*. It reads:

> Words in the chamber
> Must not be rehearsed.
> What could be rehearsed
> Would be the most shameful tale.[23]

Lu Chi, writing in the third century A.D., sought to refute those scholars who contended that substance rather than style is what mattered. "Reason supplied substance to erect the trunk," he said, "and rhetoric multiplied the branches to consummate the fruits and flowers."[24] This same idea was developed more explicitly by Ssu-ma Chi-chu, a diviner, who lectured two visiting scholars on the proper behavior of learned men:

> Surely, gentlemen, you have observed the rhetoricians and orators. All their plans and schemes are simply the products of their own minds. But if they merely blurted out their own ideas they could never capture the imagination of the ruler. Therefore they always begin their speeches by discussing the kings of antiquity and open their orations with a description of ancient times. In setting forth their schemes and plans they make up elaborate tales about the successes of the former kings or tell about their failures, in order to move the ruler to admiration or fear and thereby achieve their objective. When it comes to talking exaggerated and imposing nonsense, as you put it, no one can match them. Yet if one wishes to strengthen the state, insure the success of the ruler, and fulfill his duty as a loyal minister, he must resort to such means or his words will never be heeded.[25]

It is obvious that the scholars of early China approached the challenges of speech-making with considerable sophistication, well aware of the value of what might be accomplished and of the dangers of empty elegance or pretentious pomposity. Nor did the kings with their reigns at stake speak lightly.

The best examples of rhetorical skill in the announcements are in a series of speeches by King Pwan-kang, a descendant of T'ang and T'ae Kea, who reigned from 1401 to 1374 B.C., some three hundred years after the great counsellor I Yin. This king and this minister are linked not only by their common possession of the gift of eloquence, but also by the curious coincidence that the new dynasty Pwan-kang established was given the name of Yin. Pwan-kang did not become the head of a new dynasty by revolution, for he was a legitimate successor in the line started by Emperor T'ang. Pwan-kang's great contribution to Chinese history was that he removed the capital to the southern bank of the Hwang Ho, or Yellow River.

The immediate occasion of the move was the fear of floods which periodically inundated the northern bank of the river. In the long view of history the move was particularly significant because it placed the Yellow River between the new capital and the restless tribes of the northern and western borderlands. In the relative safety of the southern bank, the first great Chinese artistry developed. The written script was improved, and art pieces in bronze, jade, stone, and ivory appeared.[26] China owes much to the courage and foresight of King Pwan-kang.

Like most innovators, he encountered serious opposition. When he proposed the move, there was no flood or imminent threat of one. There were no attacks by barbarians. The shift of the city across the river would mean the abandonment of established homes and farmlands; much worse, it meant desertion of the hallowed ancestral graves.

It is no wonder that his decree of removal aroused a storm of rebelliousness. So serious was the discontent that Pwan-kang devoted a series of three speeches to try to allay it. He commanded the leading citizens to gather in his Great Hall, where they stood crowded together to hear him.

King Pwan-kang made his first speech when he became aware of the depth of defiance his announcement of the move had aroused.[27] He was unsparing in his denunciation of his courtiers and the leading citizens, whom he held to be responsible for the unrest. Nevertheless, he cannily sought to "save their faces" by finally assessing the basic blame against himself.

It was their duty, he reminded them, to advise him in private if they felt he had made a wrong decision, and not to "exceed the truth in their communications with the people." But they had done precisely the op-

posite. "Now, however, you keep clamoring and get the confidence of
the people by alarming and shallow speeches. I do not know what you
are wrangling about." Then, abruptly he changed his tone from anger
to conciliation: "I see you as clearly as one sees fire," he warned; he
quickly added: "but by my undecided plans I have produced your
error."

He went on with a mixture of admonishment and appeal. "If you
can put away your selfish thoughts, you will bestow real good upon the
people, reaching to your relatives and friends." He reminded them of his
power of patronage and that this power could be extended through them
to advance the welfare of those they might wish to favor. Then he
launched the claim many another chief of state has also used—that he
understood, as they did not, the great issue that confronted them: "You
do not fear the great evils which are far and near. You are like the hus-
bandman who yields himself to ease, and is not strong to toil and labor
on his acres, and who in such a case cannot have either rice or millet."
Following this, he concluded at some length with a crescendo of denunciation:

> You do not use friendly and good words to the people, and are
> only producing suffering for yourselves. As destroyers and calami-
> ties, villains and traitors, the punishment shall come on your per-
> sons. You set the example of evil, and must feel its smart, what
> will it avail you then to repent? Look at the poor people; they can
> still consult together about remonstrances which they wish to ad-
> dress to me, but when they begin to speak, you are ready with
> your extravagant talk: how much more ought you to have me be-
> fore your eyes, with whom it is to make your lives long or short!
> Why do you not report their words to me, but go about to excite
> one another by empty speeches, frightening and involving the mul-
> titudes in misery? When a fire is blazing in the plains, so that it
> cannot be approached, can it still be beaten out? Thus for you to
> cause dispeace in this way: it is not I who am to blame.

Thus far Pwan-kang had spoken strictly according to tradition, min-
gling commands and threats as had the monarchs in times past. In his
conclusion he introduced a note of conciliation, seeking to win a willing
cooperation. He spoke of the value of having counsellors from old, established families and reassured his hearers that "for generations the
toils of your families have been approved." His last word, however, was
another reminder that his will was unshakable, buttressed with another

warning: "bring your mouths under the rule of law—lest punishment come upon you, when repentance will be of no avail."

No doubt Pwan-kang felt that his anger and frustration were righteous. It was his right and duty to make the ultimate decisions concerning the good of the kingdom and it was the responsibility of his court circle to support him publicly, even while they might remonstrate with him to seek to change his mind. If it were true that his courtiers were going about among the masses deliberately encouraging their resentment, the king had cause both for anger and for worry. Traditionally, when the court rejected their monarch, the populace would rise against him.

Not unnaturally, in the following weeks resentment among the populace swelled to new heights. Under orders by the king, the people were clearing their possessions out of their homes, preparing to demolish them. They were leaving the fields cultivated by their families for generations. They were making farewell obeisances at the ancestral graves, preparing to abandon them to strangers.

So far as the general populace could see, the decision to move the capital was an arbitrary and capricious example of monarchal tyranny. No floods threatened. No hordes of barbarians were approaching the city gates. No urgent reason whatever could be found for the move. Yet the royal orders were to load what they could on barges and push out across the great river. There on the other side they would have to seek and break out new home sites from the raw earth. Those who held privileged sites on the north bank might fare worse on the south. Even the poorest peasants were being forced away from homes that were hallowed and warmed by familiarity.

For the people it was a sad time. For King Pwan-kang it was a time of danger. Once again he sought to meet the emergency with a speech. In an effort to stem the rebellious complaints and to induce sincere acquiescence in the move, he once more called an assembly. This time the meeting must have been held in the open courtyard, for his speech indicates that he spoke not only to the nobles and the courtiers, as he had the first time, but also to the populace.

This time his speech was more conciliatory, though it, too, ended with a threat. "When great calamities came down on Yin," he reminded them—already using the new name he had selected for the dynasty— "the former kings did not fondly remain in their places. What they did was with a view to the people's advantage, and therefore they moved their capital." Then gently he assured them, "It is not that any guilt attaches to you, so that this movement should be like a punishment. . . . My present undertaking to remove with you is to give repose and stability to the State." His tone now became sterner: "You only exhaust and distress yourselves. The case is like that of sailing in a boat; if you do not cross the stream at the proper time, you will destroy all its cargo. Your sincerity does not respond to mine, and we are in danger of going together to destruction." He proceeded then to lecture them on the theme that governing should be left to those who understand its complexities: "You do not consult for a distant day, or think of the calamity that must befall you. You greatly encourage one another in what must prove your sorrow. Now you have the present, but you may not have the future. What deliverance can you look for from above? Now I charge you to have but one mind. Do not let wicked thoughts arise to ruin yourselves. I am afraid that men bend your persons, and pervert your minds."

He then asked them sharply, "Do I force you by my majesty? My object is to support and nourish you all." He reminded them that he himself would be punished by the spirits of his ancestors if he neglected to do his duty to the realm. In a rush of emotion he concluded:

Ah! I have now announced to you my unchangeable purpose: do you perpetually respect my great anxiety; let us not get alienated and removed from one another; share in my plans and thoughts, and be prepared to obey me; let every one of you set up the true rule of conduct in his heart. If there be bad and unprincipled men, precipitously or carelessly disrespectful of my orders, and taking advantage of this brief season to play the part of villains or traitors, I will cut off their noses, or utterly exterminate them. I will leave none of their children. I will not let them perpetuate their seed in this new city.

With a gesture of dismissal, and with his self-control somewhat restored, he added, still sternly but seeking cooperation: "Go! preserve and continue your lives. I will now transfer you to the new capital, and there forever establish your families."

The new move was accomplished and the people accepted it in better spirits than their defiant protests had indicated. But then a new trouble arose. Having completed the crossing, the people indulged themselves in revelry and games instead of settling down to the hard work of clearing fields for cultivation, establishing homes, and erecting public buildings.

Once more King Pwan-kang called the whole populace together. His third speech opened scornfully: "Now I have disclosed my heart and belly, my veins and my bowels, and have fully declared to you, my people, all my mind." What more could he, should he, say? Somewhat wearily he repeated to them what he had told them before concerning the move.

The tone of this speech, however, was different from the others—more conciliatory, less candid, even less self-assured. He promised that no one would be punished for earlier opposition, and urged them to stop their present complaints. Somewhat speciously he told them that the crossing of the river had been undertaken "with the sincere and respectful advice" of his ministers. All had been done, he insisted, with "a reverent care for the lives of the people." His conclusion was on a sly note. Turning toward the officers of the realm who were lined up in serried ranks, first the high ministers, then their subordinates, and behind them the lower officials, he said: "Ah! ye chiefs of regions, ye heads of departments, all ye, the hundreds of officers, would that ye were animated by a true sympathy! I will exert myself in the selection and guidance of you; do ye think reverently of my multitudes."

Obviously there had been some reshuffling of appointments, and he made it clear that still more changes were being contemplated. "I will not employ those who are fond of wealth," he continued, "but those who are rigorously yet reverently laboring for the lives and increase of the people, nourishing them and planning for their enduring settlement, I will use and respect." His last words were an appeal for cooperation: "in fostering the life of the people seek to find your merit. Reverently display your virtue in behalf of the people. Forever maintain this one heart."

Few details have been preserved concerning the later reign of King Pwan-kang, following the removal of the capital. It is related that he revived the strength of the government and that a new prosperity was enjoyed by the people. He ruled for twenty-eight years, dying in 1373 B.C.

The end of the Yin dynasty came two hundred and fifty years later. In 1122 B.C., the kingdom was in disarray and the reigning king was mentally unbalanced. The Viscount of Wei called together other high officers of the court and delivered to them an old-fashioned charge:

> The great deeds of our founder were displayed in former ages, but by our being lost and maddened with wine, we have destroyed the effects of this virtue in these after times. The people of Yin, small and great, are given to highway robberies, villainies and treachery. The nobles and officers imitate one another in violating the laws; and for criminals there is no certainty that they will be apprehended. The lesser people consequently rise up and make

violent outrages on one another. The dynasty of Yin is now sink-
ing in ruin; its condition is like that of one crossing a large stream,
who can find neither ford nor bank.[28]

This was indeed the end. But it was also a beginning. For in that year
King Woo founded the Chou dynasty, one of China's greatest, which
continued from 1121 to 221 B.C., a fruitful period of some nine hundred
years. It was to include the period of the great philosophers. It was in
the time of Chou that ancient Chinese rhetoric achieved its culmination.

The beginnings may be found in the thirteenth year of King Woo's
reign. At this time he sought out his wisest counsellor, Viscount Ka,
and asked him to devise a "great plan" whereby the new dynasty might
bring China prosperity and happiness. Ka presented a plan in which
he identified the five fundamental human concerns: "first, demeanour;
the second, speech; the third, seeing; the fourth, hearing; and the fifth,
thinking. The virtue of demeanour is called respectfulness; of speech,
accordance with reason; of seeing, clearness; of hearing, distinctness;
and of thinking, perspicaciousness. The respectfulness becomes manifest in gravity; accordance with reason, in orderliness; the clearness, in
wisdom; the distinctness, in deliberation; and the perspicaciousness, in
sageness."

The rhetorical implications are that people should manifest a respectful, grave bearing; should speak in an orderly, reasonable manner
designed to win agreement; should see and hear clearly and distinctly,
in order to understand properly; and should govern their thinking by a
balanced consideration of all relevant factors. Viscount Ka further elaborated his rhetorical ideas when he said: "If you have doubts about
any great matter, consult your own heart; consult with your nobles and
officers; consult with the masses of the people; consult the tortoise and
the milfoil [for divinations]."[29] In other words: try to determine your
own feelings, get expert advice, consider what the popular reaction
might be, and seek to penetrate into the truth of the matter.

This advice on how to formulate policies was comprehensive, but
not always easy to follow. Like other monarchs before and since, the
kings of the Chou dynasty were much concerned about the responsibilities which rested upon them as absolute monarchs. There was no
way by which they could evade the duty of making ultimate decisions.
This awesome difficulty was much on the conscience of King Mu, who
reigned from 1001 to 947 B.C., a century after the dynasty was founded.
When he assumed the throne, he attested that "the trembling anxiety of
my mind makes me feel as if I were treading on a tiger's tail, or walking
on spring ice."[30] If he had been a younger son, he would have welcomed

escape from official life, for being a scholarly recluse would have suited his temperament better.

The turbulence of the time permitted him no such luxury. The Chou dynasty had not been able to correct quickly the dissoluteness that marred the last decades of Yin. Indeed, so great was the disorder that King Mu's father was unable to punish a murderer who had flagrantly killed a rival in the open court; instead he had helplessly to permit him to assume high office. Internal law and order had virtually broken down. Meanwhile, external affairs also were difficult. Despite King Mu's desire for a quiet retreat, he was forced to lead an expedition to fight off incursions by the northern barbarians. According to the historian Ssu-ma Ch'ien, the power of the throne had perilously declined. Then he added a touching note. When King Mu took to the field to drive back the invaders, he captured and brought back with him four white wolves and four white deer. Obviously he was a man who longed for the pleasantries of peace. As a militarist, he was inadequate. From the time of Mu's reign, the barbarians no longer sent annual tributaries to the throne.[31] King Mu needed all the help he could get. When he appointed a new Minister of Instruction, he said to him: "I now give you charge to assist me; be as my limbs to me, as my heart and backbone."[32]

But if he was weak, he was also gentle. In his instructions to his new minister, he said: "In the heat and rains of summer, the inferior people may be described as murmuring and sighing. And so it is with them in the great cold of winter. How great are their hardships!" His own shortcomings were much on his mind. In appointing a new Chamberlain, he exclaimed: "I am fearful and conscious of the peril of my position. I rise at midnight and think how I can avoid falling into faults." But King Mu was also clear-visioned, a man of intelligence. He warned the Chamberlain: "Be careful in selecting your officers. Do not employ men of artful speech and insinuating looks, men whose likes and dislikes are ruled by mine: one-sided men and flatterers; but employ good men. When these household officers are correct, the sovereign will be correct; when they are flatterers, the sovereign will consider himself a sage."[33] For personnel guidance, the advice was sound.

In ancient China it was felt that not only right living but also right speaking was of cardinal importance. Bad deeds could be misrepresented by misleading speech; for "persons of artful tongue" might not be "good persons." Persuasion might be accomplished not only by the example of virtue (which was "good" persuasion), but also by "men of quibbles, skillful at cunning words, and able to make the good man change his purposes" (which was "bad" persuasion).[34]

The arts of speech were to be well used, for when they were abused the king might be misled, the people would lose confidence, and the state might fall into disorder or rebellion, or be conquered by invaders. A heavy and inescapable responsibility rested upon the individual—every individual, no matter who or where he might be. "The State may be as a tree without branches because of one man. Or it may resemble a plant in the glory of its leaves and flowers because of the excellence of one man."

It is with this theme, in a somber speech by Duke Muh of Ts'in, that the *Book of History* concludes. To enforce the statement quoted above, the Duke said to his court officials:

> Ah! my officers, listen to me without any noise. I solemnly announce to you the most important of all sayings. . . .
>
> I have deeply thought and concluded; Let me have but one resolute minister, plain and sincere, without other abilities, but having a simple complacent mind, and possessed of generosity, regarding the talents of others as if he possessed them; and when he finds accomplished and sage-like men, loving them in his heart more than his mouth expresses, really showing himself able to bear them: such a minister would be able to preserve my descendants and my people, and would indeed be a giver of benefits.
>
> But if the minister, when he finds men of ability, be jealous and hates them; if, when he finds accomplished and sage-like men, he opposes them and does not allow their accomplishment, showing himself really not able to bear them; such a man will not be able to protect my descendants and people; and will there not indeed be dangers from him?[35]

The *Book of History* was closed. The year was 628 B.C. The theme by which Chinese culture was to be evaluated was clearly set forth: words and deeds alike were to serve responsibly the needs of the people, as indicated in the experience of history. This was a charge placed alike on every individual. In these terms each man was to be judged. A century more was to pass, and then in China appeared another man who made this message so vivid the world has taken note of it. His name as known around the world was Confucius. In him was the culmination of what the ancient history of China sought to teach.

CHAPTER 8

Confucius: The Authority of Tradition

THE CONFUCIAN TRADITION

THERE WAS Confucius, and there was Confucianism. The latter imposed its rigidities upon China for many centuries. Confucius himself had a message for his own time that remains ever fresh. Its rhetorical significance has been influential all through the East and has a value that should not be overlooked for the different cultures of the rest of the world.

For centuries, the "Confucian industry" of China has matched the "Shakespeare industry" of Anglo-American scholarship in its production of books, lectures, and educational programs. Nowhere has any political apparatus been more influential than the dominance of Chinese life and politics by the prescriptions of Confucianism. No other culture has been so strongly marked by the characteristics of so unsystematic a philosophical system. In no other part of the world except where the Hindu-Buddhist idea system flourishes has there been a comparable experience of encompassing authority vested in a humanistic, non-metaphysical set of doctrines. The man Confucius resolutely kept his attention devoted to the practical problems of the world as he observed it. The Confucian tradition that developed was partly an explication of his views, partly a system devised to serve those who promulgated it.

This man whose personality became imprinted upon the whole history of China was a wispy, wistful, shy yet confident schoolmaster named Kung Ch'iu, who lived in the small state of Lu during the sixth century B.C. He was poor, untitled, without official position, and had fewer students in his lifetime than a popular modern professor might assemble in a single class. Yet the goal he deliberately set for himself was to change the nature of Chinese civilization with a bloodless revolution. Unimpressive and unpretentious though he was, the vitality of his personality and his ideas proved to be unsurpassed.

In the latter years of his life this schoolmaster was given the honorific designation of Tzu, meaning Master. Accordingly, his students called him Kung Ch'iu-Tzu. In Europe he came first to be known as Confucius through a Jesuit translation into Latin of the *Analects,* in 1622, under the title *Sapientia Sinica*—the wisdom of China. In 1696, Louis Le Comte's *Memoires de la Chine* was condemned by the faculty of the Sorbonne for its declaration that China had "for two thousand years . . . practiced the purest moral code while Europe was yet steeped in error and corruption." The very next year Leibniz emphasized the humanistic character of Confucianism by suggesting in his *Novissima Sinaica* that China should send missionaries to Europe to teach "natural religion" even while European missionaries went there to teach "revealed religion." Tremendous interest in Chinese culture was stimulated in the early eighteenth century by the widespread popularity of Jean Baptiste du Halde's *Description of the Empire of China.* The Marquis d'Argens, Horace Walpole, and Oliver Goldsmith popularized the device of criticizing European civilization through letters supposedly written by a Chinese observer.

A Chinese fad swept through Europe, affecting literature, household furnishings, food, dress, and gardens. In politics the Chinese ideals of tolerance and social harmony began to be cited as precedents. Western philosophers began to use Confucianism as proof that ethics and brotherhood could be championed without need for supernatural authority.[1] Voltaire, in his *Essai sur les Moeurs* (1756), based his rationalized Unitarianism on the example of Confucianism. François Quesnay was proud to be known as "The Confucius of Europe." The growth of rationalistic deism in France and England was aided by the example of Confucianism.

Even democracy, a political philosophy alien to ancient Chinese thought, drew support from Confucianism in presenting an idea too daring to stand alone: "I have observed that in *China* no man is a *Gentleman* by his *Birth,* but that the Mandarines, or Gentlemen, become such by their own *Parts* and *Learning.* These Mandarines, by a fundamental Law of the *Chinese* Empire, are allowed to tell the Emperor, in respectful yet plain terms, whatever they think is amiss in his Conduct; and we are assured, that whenever they think the *Honour* of their Prince, or the *Good* of their *Country,* makes it necessary, they never fail to make use of their Privilege."[2]

Even while Rousseau, espousing the virtues of primitivism, was arousing throughout the West an enthusiasm for the Noble Savage, concurrently this fresh introduction of Europeans to the culture of ancient

China was leading them to no less an interest in the Noble Sage. The latter had an influence perhaps no less profound than the former. For intellectualism in Europe was quickly responsive to the discovery that China had developed a genteel culture of humanistic values even earlier than the presumptive date of the creation of Adam and Eve in the Garden of Eden.[3]

More influential, however, than all the philosophers, scholars, and writers who helped to popularize Confucianism in the West, was an Aberdeen missionary named James Legge, who sailed for China in 1839. Finding the country newly closed to missionaries, he settled in Hong Kong. There during a span of thirty years he worked on his monumental translation and annotation of *The Chinese Classics*. Through these translations the writings of Confucius and other classics were for the first time made available in English, illuminated by lucid commentaries on their historicity and significance. Oxford University rewarded Legge by establishing for him a chair of Chinese Language and Literature, which he occupied from 1876 until his death in 1897. James Legge may well be considered the father of Western Confucianism. Every translator and interpreter of the Confucian tradition remains indebted to his work.

No other civilization has been so dominated by the personality and precepts of one man as has been China by Confucius. It is a part of the quality of his genius that its influence extended backward in time as well as forward. This was because he was the first great teacher and the first great editor. He selected out of the past what was worth knowing. Whether or not he actually edited the great classics is dubious; but unquestionably his interpretation of them became the Chinese standard by which they were read. Moreover, he made antiquity a living force, projected forward into the present and future.

To Arnold Toynbee it appeared that a "disintegrating" Chinese civilization was characterized by "the moralized ritualism and the ritualized morality of Confucius."[4] This did not happen automatically, however. Confucius held no mortgage on Chinese intellectualism which he was entitled to foreclose. For a time the Utopian insights of Mohism and the pragmatic discipline of Legalism held a greater appeal for the Chinese aristocrats than did Confucianism. The otherworldiness of Taoism and, later, of Buddhism posed direct challenges to the humanistic practicality taught by Confucius. In later centuries occasional geniuses have been able to impose their own variant interpretations on the basic Confucian teachings. The most outstanding of these re-interpreters of Confucianism have been Chu Hsi (1130–1200), Lu Hsiang-shan (1139–92)

and Wang Yang-ming (1472–1529). Confucianism not only has enjoyed unrivalled prestige but it also has often been misinterpreted and
misused in both public and private realms.

Nevertheless, its insistence upon example and precedent, upon filial
duty and family loyalty, and upon subordination as the best practical
means for reconciling the needs of individual dignity and social harmony, all combined to make this philosophy well suited to a stable,
village-centered civilization. For such reasons Confucianism proved so
satisfactory that its status was made official.

Early in the Han dynasty, in 136 B.C., the scholar-counsellor Tung
Chung-shu persuaded King Wu to establish an educational and examination system through which government officials would be trained and
selected, based on the Confucian canon of classics. For two thousand
years the Confucian examination system determined who should admin-
ister, who should prosper, whose sons should advance, whose families
ripened into prominence. The education taught unquestioning acceptance
and detailed knowledge of the books designated as classics by Confucius,
together with his own *Analects* and a few later classics derived from his
influence. The examinations required not a critical evaluation of these
works but a literal mastery of them.

The theory supporting this system was that what is worth knowing
is what has been most dependably known. New knowledge, new insight,
and new understandings were stamped as suspect. "It was the nature of
Chinese thought, historically oriented, to sanctify practice in terms of
precedent."[5] Nor was there any need to try to adapt old wisdom to the
circumstances of succeeding generations, for humanity was considered
to be all of a piece. Only confusion would result from emphasizing
merely transient and unimportant differences. Hence, simplicity was the
key to wisdom. People should look always for what is eternally true,
judging the immediate and the particular in general terms. When one
trusts in immutable principles one's mind need not be disturbed by specific facts and daily perplexities. This, with its virtues and its faults, the
Confucian educational system taught and the examination system enforced.

Such a philosophy discouraged innovation and individualism. It un-
dervalued initiative, insight, and fresh experience. It rationalized avoidance of personal responsibility for failures of policy. But it also established a staunch and demanding standard of moral behavior by which
the conduct of affairs should always be evaluated.

The central theme of Confucianism was that ethical conduct creates
conditions that result in just and harmonious human relations. The way

to judge ethics was to compare words and acts with the record left by the model emperors and the sages of earlier times. The selection of governmental officials by examinations based on such records provided a means by which merit could flow upward, avoiding the sterility of automatic succession to power based merely on heredity. These were the arguments by which the Confucian tradition became entrenched in ancient China.

Germinal Influences upon Confucius

The sixth century B.C. into which Confucius was born was a time of troubles for China. The Spring and Autumn Era (722–481 B.C.) was drawing toward its close. The monarchy had lost most of its power; small kingdoms and dukedoms were contending over the bits and pieces of the old empire. The Period of the Warring States (481–221 B.C.) was commencing. Together these two periods constituted China's five hundred years of feudalism. It proved to be a political system that served the people ill.

Banditry was rampant. Drunkenness, adultery, incest, and murder were commonplace and often went unpunished. Misgovernment left the people helpless against the rapacity of corrupt officials. In the judgment of a contemporary, "The world is one seething torrent, and who can change it?"[6] Feudal states broke down into a growing number of smaller and smaller fiefs. Every nobleman had one or perhaps several wives, together with as many concubines as he could afford to support. And the sons of all of them had to be maintained.

The multiplicity of sons became a serious problem. Each could not inherit the family domain. They were too aristocratic to be allowed to live in poverty; they were too noble to do useful work; they were too well educated to be content in idleness; and some of them possessed superior talents that festered in frustration when they were unemployed. Some hired out as mercenaries. Some turned to banditry. Others became *You-schwei*—wandering philosophers and scholarly adventurers: dilettants and intellectual rebels.

In this time of disruption and disorder, old loyalties were breaking down. Questions were being asked that old answers did not fit. China was not only rife with misery but also alive with the fresh vigor of unleashed intellectual inquiry. "What does it all mean?" became a relevant question.

The *You-schwei* wandered from court to court, seeking employment as counsellors. Some of them began to devise their own theoretical systems of human behavior and government. Significantly, they did not turn to speculation about the essence or the laws of nature. They had no interest in scientific analysis, or logic, or the abstractions of mathematics. Their concern was not to determine what was *verifiable,* but what was *realizable*—what could be rendered useful. Their interests related to what was humanistic, not naturalistic or supernatural. Their concern was to determine how people could live together more satisfactorily.

The result was a hodgepodge of ethics, political science, and rhetoric. The ideas of the *You-schwei* were generally unsystematic—perhaps because as wanderers they lacked libraries, leisure, and any incentive to develop well-rounded and inclusive philosophical systems. But they were intensely interested in the problems of human relations.

Of course they were also, in some degree, rhetoricians. "Adept in persuasion, quick of wit, owing no allegiance to anything beyond their own aggrandizement,"[7] this was a class of men who lived on their eloquence. These wandering scholar-rhetoricians made jobs for themselves by convincing kings that their counsel was needed. Persuasion was their stock in trade. The skill they sought to attain was mastery of the strategy of influencing human behavior.

The conditions encouraging the development of persuasive theory and practice were especially important in the district where Confucius was born. His homeland was the small state of Lu, which stretched along the southern shore of the lower reaches of the Yellow River—encompassing the region in which, some nine hundred years earlier, King Pwan-kang had built his new capital.

Although small and weak, the importance of Lu was well recognized throughout China. It had been founded by the Duke of Chou, whose brother was founder of the Chou dynasty. Nowhere were the old traditions more zealously guarded than in Lu, and thus for centuries Lu was known as the citadel of traditional Chinese culture. Being both weak and wealthy, Lu was often invaded and ravaged. Nevertheless, its reputation as the great culture center safeguarded it from utter destruction. Other states could and did conquer and ravish Lu—especially the powerful state of Ch'i, on the North, and the large, barbaric state of Ch'u, in the Southwest.

During the Spring and Autumn Era Lu was invaded twenty-one times, an average of once every fifteen years. Still further adding to its miseries, it was beset internally by a continuing struggle for power among its three principal families. Disrupted by both attacks from without and disunity within, Lu was atrociously misgoverned. Local officials often refused to remit taxes to the Duke of Lu; but they never failed to collect them from the people. Luxury flourished in the midst of impoverishment. Corruption, bribery, nepotism, and favoritism were everyday characteristics of the bureaucracy. Licentiousness and uncontrolled sexuality led to violent quarrels. The common people were taxed, robbed, kidnapped, scourged, and, when they sought to rebel, tortured without mercy. Occasional acts of heroism or of patriotism were noted almost with awe, they were so rare. The traditions of gentility which Lu cherished were in stark contrast with the harshness and cruelty of its actual conditions.

This was the society in which Confucius grew up. It is little wonder that he looked back with yearning upon the fancied glories of a vanished past. What is of great importance is that courageously and with single-minded tenacity he set about teaching the hopeful lesson that the merits of the idealized past could be translated into the practice of the present and thus could be made to shape a great destiny for the future. What he clearly realized and taught was that the nobility of historic example could inspire people to try to elevate their own thoughts and conduct. This message was his heritage to China and to the world.

THE MAN, HIS PERSONALITY, AND HIS CHARACTER

Confucius' own life was beset by difficulties and disappointments. What is reliably known about him is scanty. He was born in 551 B.C. into a family that had neither money nor social position. Apparently he was orphaned in early childhood. Of his family, all that is known with certainty is that he had an elder brother and a niece. He married a woman of whom nothing is known, and he fathered one or two daughters as well as one son, all of whom preceded him in death. These are the ascertained facts. But the myth-makers more than compensated for the scantiness of the record.

The legendary stories that accumulated around the Confucian tradition are interestingly related by Carl Crow in his book, *The Story of Confucius: Master Kung* (New York: Harper, 1937). According to these legends, Confucius' father was a heroic warrior eight feet tall, who divorced his first wife after she bore him nine daughters but no son. His second wife, a young girl, became the mother of the sage. When Confucius was born—in a cave—the trees held up their leaves in adoration. A unicorn and two dragons attended the birthing. The superstitious credulity of succeeding generations added yet more miracles to the story. But the real miracle of Confucius was that penetrating and surpassing the mindless adulation which enshrouded his memory there shone the clear light of his fundamental reasonableness, to illuminate and guide the conduct of his followers.

Somehow Confucius gained a scanty education, perhaps serving as an apprentice to a minor official. For a time he was in charge of a government granary, and he served briefly as overseer of some pasture lands. He read such books as he could find, which were not many. Undoubtedly he memorized the whole of the classical *Book of Poetry*. His favorite reading was the *Book of Changes,* a strange discussion of moral philosophy, which will be examined in the following chapter. This work Confucius read until he wore out three sets of leather thongs with which it was bound; and he wrote several appendices for it.[8] He told his disciples that if fifty years were added to his life, he would spend them in studying this *Book of Changes*—"and might then escape falling into great errors."[9]

Uncommonly bright and with a winsome personality, Confucius received enough praise during his childhood to awaken ambition. Accidentally and almost casually he discovered his true vocation as a teacher. Neither public nor private schools were known in his time. Apparently, he gathered together a few friends to form a debating society; then, because of the obvious superiority of his mind and knowledge, they turned to him for instruction. Soon the group expanded to twenty-five or thirty. At times as many as seventy students gathered around Confucius, coming not only from Lu but also from neighboring states. Cumulatively, through the years, he may have taught as many as three thousand students. This was the foundation from which his influence spread.

Confucius himself gave his disciples a thumbnail summary of his life: "At fifteen, my attention turned to learning; at thirty, my purpose in life got set; at forty, I was free of temptation; at fifty, I learned how to resign myself to providence; at sixty, what came through the ear could not disturb my inner peace; at seventy, I did what my heart listed and yet never went wrong" (*Analects,* II, 4).

His philosophy of resigned acceptance came hard, for the ambitions he early set for himself were not realized. Ten or more of his disciples were appointed to high governmental positions. But, despite their best efforts on his behalf, the most they could get for him was a nominal office, without power, which he held briefly. He lived on gifts presented by his students in lieu of tuition; and he resolutely rejected offers of sinecures which were intended to bribe him to forebear criticism of the ruling princes.[10] Gradually, as the years passed, Confucius came more and more to desire a post of authority in which he could put into practice the reforms he felt would rectify society. The chance did not come.

At the age of sixty he put pride aside and started on a several years' journey from court to court, seeking employment. Ssu-ma Ch'ien, his earliest biographer, reports that "although he sought employment with over seventy different rulers, he could not find a welcome anywhere."[11] Then he "did what his heart listed," settling down at home in peaceful composure. His students found this spirit of resignation hard to accept. One of his favorites, Tzu-kung, a counsellor famed for his eloquence, who for some thirty years figured importantly in interstate diplomacy, reproached him for his aloofness, saying: "Suppose I have a beautiful gem here; should I just keep it stored away in a case, or should I get a good price and sell it?" Confucius startled him with the rejoinder: "Sell it, sell it by all means. I, you see, am just waiting for the price" (*Analects,* IX, 12). The price that Confucius demanded for his services was power to revolutionize the government; and this no prince would grant him. Tzu-kung and the other disciples felt Confucius' lack of success deeply; and Tzu-kung especially referred often to the pain he felt that the merits of the great Sage were so little recognized. Confucius turned aside such dubious compliments, declaring: "The good man does not grieve that other people do not recognize his merits. His only anxiety is lest he should fail to recognize theirs" (*Analects,* I, 16).

Although there were other disciples whom Confucius admired more than he did Tzu-kung (Yen-Hui, for example), with no other was he as intimate. Confucius was proud of Tzu-kung's outstanding success and of his ability to marshal all his quick inventiveness as an orator in dealing with unexpected situations. Tzu-kung had good reason to realize the perils of public life, where one word wisely and appropriately spoken could win a reputation for wisdom but one word imprudently uttered could tag a man as a fool. Time after time, Tzu-kung badgered Confucius for advice on how to be a success as an official; and time after time Confucius chastised him for rashness or misunderstanding.[12]

It was Tzu-kung who was praised at court for having greater wisdom than Confucius himself. In reply, Tzu-kung not only revealed a modest awareness of his own inferiority to his master but also gave a plausible explanation of why Confucius remained unrewarded while he himself was consistently honored: "Let us take as our comparison the wall round a building. My wall only reaches to the height of a man's shoulder, and it is easy enough to peep over it and see the good points of the house on the other side. But our master's wall rises many times a man's height, and no one who is not let in by the gate can know the beauty and wealth of the palace that, with its ancestral temple, its hundred ministrants, lies hidden within. But it must be admitted that those who are let in by the gate are few; so that it is small wonder His Excellency [the Prince] had spoken as he did" (*Analects*, XIX, 23).

Despite the paucity of details of Confucius' life, Pyun Yung Tai was right when he insisted that "no other immortal teacher of mankind . . . is nearly so well preserved in record as Confucius is in the *Analects*. In fact, few of our celebrated contemporaries are made so familiar to us as Confucius has been, or rather can be, through this book. If he were still alive and invited to our homes, we should not be at a loss as to how to set him at ease, thanks to the complete knowledge of him and his taste embalmed there."[13]

What we know of Confucius, while not considerable, is often variably interpreted. For instance, Creel thought that "Confucius condemned eloquence so frequently that we cannot but suspect that he unconsciously envied those who possessed it."[14] In Pyun's judgment it was never eloquence Confucius objected to but hypocritical glibness.[15] The record itself seems to be ambiguous.

When Confucius was told that Jan Yung, one of his disciples, was a good man but a poor talker, he responded: "What need has he to be a good talker? Those who down others with clap-trap are seldom popular. Whether he is Good, I do not know. But I see no need for him to be a good talker" (*Analects*, V, 4). He once commented sharply that "A man of sweet words and ingratiating manners is seldom good" (*Analects*, I, 3). In his view, "A gentleman covets the reputation of being slow in word but swift in deed" (*Analects*, IV, 24), meaning that promises should not outrun performance. When he heard an official arguing persuasively against the value of book learning, he exclaimed: "There! That is why I hate a man with an artful tongue!" (*Analects*, XI, 23).

The fact that Confucius himself was eloquently persuasive is manifest in the tremendous power he exercised over the minds and behavior of his capable and skeptical students. When a critic compared Confucius unfavorably with the eloquent scholars who drifted from court to court, a disciple contrasted their oratory of display and the unobtrusive persuasiveness of Confucius: "Mild, meek, pious, and plain, the Master gets by yielding" (*Analects*, I, 10). Another pointed out, "The Master has a way of instructing people gradually and by stages" (*Analects*, IX, 10). Still another insisted: "My Master speaks only at an appropriate moment and nobody is tired of hearing him" (*Analects*, XIV, 14).

Confucius himself explained why he might seem eloquent to some and inarticulate to others: "I do not teach those who show no passion for learning, nor do I prompt those who are not anxious to speak up. Suppose I raise a corner of a subject, so to speak, and no response is shown by the learner concerning the other three, I drop the subject" (*Analects*, VII, 8). Why bother to talk with those who would not or could not show a discriminating interest in the question? But when he had an acute and knowing listener—his favorite, Yen Hui, for example—he exercised every skill in leading him deeper and deeper into the insight he was trying to develop. "The deeper I bore down into it," Yen Hui sighed, "the harder it becomes. I see it in front, but suddenly it is behind. Step by step the Master skillfully lures me on. When he has broadened me with culture, he restrains me with ritual. Even if I wanted to stop, I could not. Just when I feel that I have exhausted every resource, something seems to rise, standing out sharp and clear" (*Analects*, IX, 10). No speaker could ask for higher praise from an astute listener.

Mencius quoted Confucius as having said, "In the matter of speeches I am not competent."[16] The record shows that he was being unduly modest. His students, who comprised virtually his entire audience, found him irresistibly appealing. Chuang-Tzu, perhaps his most virulent opponent, in a savage attack upon Confucius, accused him of not too little but too much eloquence, uttered with irresponsibility: "Agitating your lips and flapping your tongue, you presume to say what is right and what is wrong to the point that you confuse the leaders of the world and keep students from their basic occupation."[17] It was much the way the solid patricians of Athens were at about that same time speaking of Socrates. The similarity was not inappropriate, for both philosophers were seeking to shake society out of its existing errors into a dependable stability.

THE CONFUCIAN PHILOSOPHY

A troublemaker Confucius undoubtedly was, both for his own time and for later generations. He was profoundly dissatisfied with things as they were. He was the quintessence of a revolutionist. His aim was no less than the complete remaking of society. What he sought to destroy was the whole panoply of organized society, including its laws, its armies, and its authority. As he said: "In hearing a litigation case, I am no better than others. But my aim is rather to enable the people to dispense with litigation altogether" (*Analects*, XII, 13). And the methods he advocated were always rhetorical, dependent on persuasion and reason.

Recurrently, throughout his long life of teaching, he repeated his basic lesson that government should be by example rather than by force. "The essence of statecraft is justice," he insisted. "If you lead with justice, who can dare to be unjust? . . . If you cease to be covetous yourself, the people will not steal, even if encouraged." Then he added: "Why must you kill in order to rule a country? If you wish to be kind, the people will be kind, too. Excellence in the prince may be compared to wind; excellence in the people to grass. When the wind blows, the grass bends" (*Analects,* XII, 16–19). So much superior is example to authority that, "If a great man carry himself with rectitude, he will prevail without giving orders, but if he fails to do so, the people will not obey even if expressly commanded" (*Analects,* XIII, 6). Concerning his eloquent disciple Tzu-kung, who sought to belabor people into doing what he considered good for them, Confucius commented wryly: "He must be very wise to find so many faults in others. As for me, I just do not have that much leisure" (*Analects,* XIV, 30).

This was the essence of Confucian philosophy. It was not rhetoric, for it turned attention inward, inviting people to examine themselves, rather than outward, to seek to influence others. But it was conducive to the rhetorical views which, as will appear in the next section, developed naturally from his philosophic goals.

What Confucius sought above all was a society in which harmony would prevail because propriety and loyalty would be practiced by the rulers and the people. The method by which he sought this goal was through self-purification by individuals. The way by which individuals should perfect themselves was through increased knowledge; for, like Socrates, Confucius believed profoundly that one could not renounce what he knew to be right. He abjured force because he believed it to be self-defeating. Force is used in an effort to rectify the conduct of someone else through external restraints, whereas conduct by its very nature develops from inner impulses.

Confucius concentrated his attention upon individuals because a man who cannot rectify himself, over whom he has full control, surely cannot improve others, over whom he has at most only partial control. His concern above all was with individuals as they lived within the family. The highest virtue he knew was filial loyalty. The reason was that, when harmony is the goal, what is most important is how individuals behave toward one another. This behavior has its greatest significance in the family, for it is here that human relations are most intimate and also most vital.

This philosophy was cogent, clear, consistent, and practical. Moreover, it was wholly humanistic and therefore self-contained and self-enforcing. It could withstand the sharpest scrutiny and rebuff the most skeptical of challenges. It required of its believers no commitment either to supernaturalism or to perfectionism. It asked only that they bring to its testing a sincere and clear-sighted interpretation of their own experience, enlarged and supported by the cumulative historical experience of the ancient sage-kings.

Confucius did not expect either immediate or full success for his reform program. When a disciple asked why he labored on behalf of people who did not appreciate his merit, Confucius patiently replied: "If the world were already on the right path, I would not have to think of changing it" (*Analects,* XVIII, 6). When he was told that his doctrines were being rejected even though they were right, he responded: "Let a man hear the truth in the morning and he may die in the evening without regret" (*Analects,* IV, 8). When it was pointed out to him that princes often were mistakenly praised for errors that were misinterpreted as virtues, he retorted: "I myself am more fortunate. When I am in the wrong people all know it" (*Analects,* VII, 30).

In one conversation with his disciples, Confucius was reminded of an old saying that, "Only if the right sort of people had charge of a country for a hundred years would it become really possible to stop cruelty and do away with slaughter." His first impulse was to agree. But he quickly corrected himself, saying that if a "kingly man" were to appear, benevolence would spread across the country, from the force of his example, within a single generation. He then permitted himself a rare expression of disappointment at his own lack of recognition: "If only someone were to make use of me, even for a single year, I could do a great deal; and in three years I could finish off the whole work." Then, regaining his self-control, he generalized: "Once a man has contrived to put himself aright, he will find no difficulty at all in filling any governmental post. But if he cannot put himself aright, how can he hope to succeed in putting others right?" (*Analects,* XIII, 10–13). Here was the point at which his philosophy merged with and became rhetoric: influence derives from probity.

His union of rhetoric with philosophy emerged most fully in a work called *The Great Learning,* in which his disciples, perhaps including his grandson Tzu Ssu, sought to preserve his educational theories. A brief essay of only some seventeen hundred and fifty words, it came to exercise an enormous influence throughout China. In this essay Confucius committed himself solidly to the principle of *causation:* "Things have their root and their branches. Affairs have their end and their beginning." Nothing can be done without resultant consequences. Nothing eventuates from itself alone. When a given result is sought, the proper method is to trace back to an inescapable cause from which it must evolve. Then he illustrated how this might be done:

> The ancients who wished to illustrate illustrious virtue throughout the kingdom, first ordered well their own States. Wishing to order well their States, they first regulated their families. Wishing to regulate their families, they first cultivated their persons. Wishing to cultivate their persons, they first rectified their hearts. Wishing to rectify their hearts, they first sought to be sincere in their thoughts. Wishing to be sincere in their thoughts, they first extended to the utmost their knowledge. Such extension of knowledge lay in the investigation of things.

> Things being investigated, knowledge became complete. Their knowledge being complete, their thoughts were sincere. Their thoughts being sincere, their hearts were then rectified. Their hearts being rectified, their persons were cultivated. Their persons being cultivated, their families were regulated. Their families being regulated, their States were rightly governed. Their States being rightly governed, the whole kingdom was made tranquil and happy.[18]

It is in the light of this exposition of the centrality of the search for understanding that we see the significance of the highest claim Confucius ever made for himself. "In a hamlet of ten houses," he once told his disciples, "you may be sure of finding someone quite as loyal and true to his word as I. But I doubt if you would find anyone with such a love of learning" (*Analects,* V, 27). And once he wryly berated a disciple who had failed to respond adequately to an inquiry as to what manner of man his Master really was. "Why did you not say to him," Confucius asked, "this is the character of the man: so intent upon enlightening the eager learner that he forgets his hunger, and so happy in doing so that he forgets the bitterness of his lot and does not realize that old age is at hand?" (*Analects,* VII, 18).

Old age found Confucius ready when it came. In terms of his own youthful ambitions and judged also by the standards of society, his life was a failure. The several minor positions he held for brief periods were far inferior to his abilities. He never mastered the arts of flattery and of compliance through which success was won in a government career. In all his lifetime he attained neither fortune nor fame. Neither did he leave behind him anything consequential that might be said to have been his own creation. In the opening of Book VII of the *Analects* he is quoted as saying: "I have transmitted what was taught to me without creating anything of my own." Despite these limitations, what he achieved was astounding.

He was the founder in China of organized education. He established both the principle of charging tuition and the practice of awarding scholarships to students who were both capable and poor: as he said, "I never refused to teach anyone who wanted to learn, even if he could bring no more than a bundle of dried meat" (*Analects*, VII, 7). He impressed his personality on the best minds of his own time. And he left a legacy of moral philosophy which has been honored for twenty-five hundred years, even though it proved too rigorous to be put into practice. More than most of the world's great value systems, however, Confucianism actually has impressed itself into the lives of its professed followers. This is partly because of the prescribed examination system which made its study mandatory for all who wished advancement in China. But even more it was because its humanistic common sense made it available to the understanding of even the unlearned; and because its precepts proved to be practical and effective when they were tried.

Even so, his philosophy also permitted a rationalistic misuse of his cardinal precepts. In the name of Confucian harmony, evils were tolerated to avoid strife. Nepotism flourished in the name of filial loyalty. Autocracy was sheltered by such precepts as, "Do not talk of policies when you are not in a position to make them," and "The masses may be led but cannot be made to comprehend" (*Analects*, VIII, 15, 10). Governmental inefficiency, laziness, and inability were difficult to eradicate when officialdom was sheltered by the Confucian tradition demanding uncomplaining loyalty from the populace. In the name of Confucianism, individuals too often have evaded responsibility on the ground that individualism itself is of less value to society than conformity and subservience to tradition. In the name of family solidarity, youth has too often been condemned to endure paternal tyranny. As has proved true also of other value systems in other parts of the world, the heritage Confucius left has been twisted and distorted to serve selfish privilege, as well as, in other ways, serving as a beacon light of reason and justice.

Confucius died in 479 B.C., at the age of seventy-three. He had resisted the temptation to serve the princes of this world on their terms. He had not violated or betrayed his own high standards. He had endured the agony of seeing the persistence of social evils for which he believed an effective remedy was instantly at hand if only it would be accepted and applied. He suffered both from rejection by rulers and from adulation by followers. By both groups his teachings were distorted and misapplied. The wonder is that even so through all the mist of antiquity and the self-serving misrepresentation by others which overlie his life and message, the precepts that he taught were so clear and simple, so strong and self-evident, that they flourished and survived.

THE ELEMENTS OF CONFUCIAN RHETORIC

The rhetorical ideas of Confucius are found principally in the *Analects,* the sayings and anecdotes put together after his death by his disciples; in "The Doctrine of the Mean" and "The Great Learning," two essays written by his grandson and other disciples as summaries of his philosophy; and in *The Spring and Autumn Annals* and the "Appendices" to the *Book of Changes,* which presumably were written by Confucius himself. Other sources are the biographical anecdotes and references concerning him which abound in the *Book of Rites* and in the works of Mencius, Hsüntze, Mo-Tze and Chuang-Tzu.

Confucius' concern for rhetoric derived directly from his political philosophy. As has been seen, his social goal was harmony, to be achieved through a recognition of the underlying identity of interests of all members of society, regardless of how diversified or how competitive they might appear to be. His rhetorical ideas were comprehensive and clearly defined.

The purposes of speaking, as he stated them in the *Analects,* were sevenfold: to "communicate ideas clearly" (XV, 39); to "captivate the will" of those whose loyalty must be won (IX, 24); to maintain social functions, for, as he said: "Human relations not rectified, speech would grate; speech grating, activities would not carry on" (XIII, 3); to reform the conduct of a prince or of a friend, for, "How can one help . . . rectifying, through persuasion, the one to whom he is loyal?" (XIV, 7); to win personal advancement, since experience shows that "Unless gifted with the artful tongue of Ceremony-Master T'o and the handsomeness of Prince Ts'ao of Sung, one can hardly get on these days" (VI, 15); to gain a truer understanding of other people, since "He who does not know the value of words will never come to understand his fellow-men" (XX, 3); and to represent clearly and accurately the true nature of the speaker, for: "There are three facets to a gentleman. Looked at from a distance he seems stern; at close range he is pleasant; as we listen to his words, they are clear-cut" (XIX, 9). Such purposes all help to preserve harmony.

To accomplish these purposes, Confucius recommended at least fourteen persuasive methods—all found in the *Analects* except as otherwise noted.

First, the speaker should pursue goals that are as helpful to the listeners as they are to the speaker. This seems to have been basic in his rhetoric. When Confucius was asked, "Is there one word that will keep us on the path to the end of our days?" he replied: "Yes. Reciprocity! What you do not wish for yourself, do not do unto others" (XV, 24). On another occasion he said, "A good man, you know, wishing to stand himself, helps others to stand, and wishing to prosper himself, helps others to prosper. Thus, to make oneself the criterion to decide what to do to others may be called the means of being good" (VI, 29).

Second, to be lastingly persuasive one should support his contentions with the authority of tradition rather than with one's own individual ideas. Describing his own method, he declared: "I transmit, but I do not create" (VII, 1). And when a disciple questioned whether it was always best to try to adhere to the pathways of the past, Confucius replied: "The path may not be left for an instant. If it could be left, it would not be the path. On this account, the superior man does not wait till he sees things to be cautious, nor till he hears things to be apprehensive" ("Doctrine of the Mean," I, 2). However dimly one may himself apprehend matters, the truest light is cast upon them by the cumulative experience of the race, as crystallized in tradition.

Third, the truth which one is presenting should be supported by simple insights that are the fruit of prolonged and thoughtful study. Such statements are always simple, uncomplicated, and direct, for "He who possesses sincerity is he who without an effort hits what is right and apprehends without the exercise of thought. . . . To this attainment there are requisite the extensive study of what is good, accurate inquiry about it, careful reflection upon it, the clear discrimination of it, and the earnest practice of it" ("Doctrine of the Mean," XX, 18–19). In other words, like Jesus, Confucius recommended for persuasion that one should speak with authority; and he took pains to make clear how authoritative certainty could be attained.

Fourth, persuasion rests always on a foundation of sincerity, for "Sincerity is the end and the beginning of things; without sincerity there would be nothing. On this account, the superior man regards the attainment of sincerity as the most excellent thing" ("Doctrine of the Mean," XXV, 2). Such sincerity is akin to reciprocity, since, "When one cultivates to the utmost the principles of his nature, and exercises them on the principle of reciprocity, he is not far from the path. What you do not like when done to yourself, do not do unto others" ("Doctrine of the Mean," XIII, 3).

Fifth, persuasive words must be supported by appropriate deeds. Indeed, "A virtuous man tends to underdo in words and over-do in deeds" (XIV, 28). Meanwhile, speakers should bear in mind that "He whose language is unrestrained will have difficulty in living up to his assertions" (XIV, 20).

Sixth, persuasion is conciliatory, both in words and in manner. "The superior man does not impose burdens on a people until he has won their confidence; otherwise, they will feel he is severe with them. He does not remonstrate with his own superior until he has won his trust; otherwise, the prince will feel that he has been maligned" (XIX, 10).

Seventh, to be truly persuasive, one should take care not to speak overmuch and to fit his speech appropriately to the time and the occasion. As a disciple said in praise of Confucius, "My master speaks when it is time to speak, and so men do not get tired of his speaking" (XIV, 14). On the other hand, when an occasion does call for speech, it must not be avoided, for: "To lead an uninstructed people to war is to throw them away" (XIII, 30).

Eighth, persuasive effectiveness requires of speaker and listener that they understand the prejudicial power of emotion, both in distorting truth and in reinforcing it. "Men are partial where they feel affection and love; partial where they despise and dislike; partial where they stand in awe and reverence; partial where they feel sorrow and compassion; partial where they are arrogant and rude. Thus it is that there are few men in the world who love and at the same time know the true qualities of the object of their love, or who hate and yet know the excellencies of the object of their hatred" ("The Great Learning," VII, 1).

Ninth, like Aristotle, Confucius recognized *ethos* as basic to persuasion. "Build up your character so as to inspire the people with assurance," he advised (XIV, 44). Again he said: "If a great man carries himself with rectitude, he will prevail without giving orders; but if he fails to do so, the people will not follow even if expressly commanded" (XIII, 6). In speaking one should keep in mind that his listeners are bound to consider: "Is earnestness in discourse a mark of a virtuous man or of a pretender to virtue?" (XI, 19). When they decide he is indeed virtuous, his words carry great weight. "If a man is sincere and reliable in speech and considerate and respectful in conduct, he would get acceptance even in a barbarian community. If he is, on the other hand, insincere and unreliable in speech and inconsiderate and disrespectful in conduct, would he be accepted even by his own country folk?" (XV, 4).

Tenth, speech should have a practical objective that is attainable. "It is of no use to criticize a thing already done or try to dissuade from what is already set or blame what is past" (III, 21).

Eleventh, avoid talking about matters that lie outside your own sphere of responsibility. A rather obscure passage on this theme is translated variously as: "Do not talk of policies when you are not in a position to make them" and "Let the other man do his job without your interference" (VIII, 14). The general meaning at least is clear. Persuasion depends in part upon minding one's own business.

Twelfth, when trying to persuade those who are in authority, the speaker should combine conciliation with firm adherence to his own purpose. For example, "In serving his parents, a son may remonstrate with them, but gently; when he sees they do not incline to follow his advice, he shows an increased degree of reverence but does not abandon his purpose; and should they punish him, he does not allow himself to murmur" (IV, 18).

Thirteenth, effective persuasian requires that the discourse be adapted to the nature of the listeners. On one occasion Confucius bewildered his disciples by giving two diametrically opposite answers to the same question when it was asked him in succession by two different men. Smilingly, Confucius explained: "As Ch'iu is timid, I wanted to encourage him; as Yu is foolhardy, I wanted to discourage him" (XI, 20).

Fourteenth, both for immediate and lasting effect, it is essential that the persuasion be presented with utmost clarity, using terms accurately. "If the designations are not accurate, language will not be clear. If language is not clear, duties will not be carried out. If duties are not carried out, the proprieties will not be observed. If the proprieties are not observed, punishments will not be uniformly applied. If punishments are not applied uniformly, the people will not know how to act without getting into trouble. Therefore, the superior man takes care that his terms be stated accurately, so that what he says may be carried into effect appropriately. He never uses language carelessly or incorrectly" (XIII, 3).

Confucius was no less strong in his condemnation of wrong uses of persuasive speech than in his recommendation of right goals and methods. Sharply, he pointed out, "A man with sweet words and ingratiating manners is seldom good" (I, 3). "A clever talker," he warned, "upsets states and homes" (XVII, 17). "A man of virtue," he told his disciples, "hates those who, when they have a dirty motive, gloss it over with words" (XVI, 1). Similarly, "A gentleman dislikes those who point out the faults in others. He dislikes those who, being of low estate, villify their superiors . . . . and those who mistake tale-bearing for honesty" (XVII, 24).

Speech is a mirror which reveals the true character of the speaker; nevertheless, there is a heavy responsibility upon the listener to discriminate carefully, for first impressions may be quite wrong. "The man of perfect virtue is cautious and slow in his speech" (XII, 3). "A virtuous man is bound to speak good words, but one who speaks good words does not necessarily possess virtue" (XIV, 5). Accordingly, "The superior man does not accept a man for his words alone; neither does he reject a suggestion because of the man alone" (XV, 23). Still and all, despite the difficulties of interpretation, "one cannot know people without knowing their words" (XX, 3). This conclusion is so important that it stands as the final statement of the *Analects*.

The manner of speech was always important to Confucius, and again and again he reverted to it, seeking to impress upon his disciples the overwhelming importance of speaking with carefulness, insight, knowledge, and sincerity—always aiming to accomplish a socially helpful goal. "A gentleman uses only such language as is proper for speech," he asserted, "and only speaks what it would be proper to carry into effect. A gentleman is never careless in stating what he means" (XIII, 3). Responsibility was a characteristic Confucius regarded very highly, as he sought time and again to impress on his followers. "If a man blames himself more and others less, he will avoid resentment," he told his disciples (XV, 13). Perhaps it was this same saying that was recalled years later in another form: "In archery we have something like the way of the superior man. When the archer misses the center of the target, he turns round and seeks for the cause of the failure in himself" (*Doctrine of the Mean*, XIV, 5).

When his disciples asked him, as they often did, to explain how to be successful at court, Confucius would answer variably, depending on the occasion and the nature of the questioner. On one occasion his response was cryptic: "It is the highest wisdom to avoid political life altogether; next best, to move from a disordered state to one that is well-governed; next, to be alert to a ruler's facial expressions, which indicate his displeasure; finally, be quick to interpret the meaning of what is said" (XVI, 6). Inevitably, however, he would finally insist that to speak wisely and considerately is the best guarantee of success at court. There was no lasting refuge in silence, even though to speak one's mind is always dangerous. Speech is too important to be ignored. "Not to talk to a man who is amenable to persuasion is to lose a man. To talk with those who will not listen is to waste one's words. The truly wise adjust their speaking to occasions, so that they will lose neither men nor words" (XV, 7).

Isolated extracts from Confucius cannot properly represent his rhetoric, no matter how carefully they may be fitted together. His rhetorical views are implicit in his philosophy, which is finally consistent and coherent. Hence, to complete and round out the summary that has been presented, it is necessary to engage in an overview of his writings, seeking to identify their general rhetorical qualities.

As a rhetorician, Confucius recognized that speech may be used to influence listeners only if the means employed are variable, since every circumstance in which oral discourse is used is unique. Consequently, principles may be adduced but rules are misleading. His rhetorical aim was to guide his students in their independent and individual development. He sought to teach them to think for themselves in confronting problems of communication. What he sought was to instill in his disciples a confidence in their own abilities, together with a humble awareness of the need for continuing study. Every honestly inquiring mind, he believed, is too sturdy to be confined within artificial limits and too narrowly encompassed by natural limitations to be permitted to trust wholly in its own unaided intuition. To his youthful followers he said: "The younger generation is to be regarded with awe. Who dares say that they will be inferior to the people of today? But those who fail to achieve reputation by the age of forty or fifty are no longer worthy of respect" (*Analects,* IX, 22). Urging that the study of established principles must be combined with thoughtful consideration of emergent conditions, Confucius pointed out that to qualify as a teacher demands both "mastery of the old and receptivity to the new" (*Analects,* II, 3).

In renouncing rules, however, Confucius did not mean to question the sanctity of principles founded on tradition and experience. He was certain that there are eternal and unchanging truths to which men should always adhere, regardless of specific circumstances. "The path," he warned, "may not be left for an instant. If it could be left it would not be the path" (*Doctrine of the Mean,* I, 2). He was equally sure that "it is indeed harmful to come under the sway of utterly new and strange doctrines" (*Analects,* II, 16). There is a universal principle, he believed, by which all conduct should be measured as meticulously as a carpenter governs his woodworking with a ruler: "What a man dislikes in his superiors, let him not display in the treatment of his inferiors;

what he dislikes in his inferiors, let him not display in his service to his superiors; . . . what he hates to receive, . . . let him not bestow" (*The Great Learning,* X, 2).

In a word, the dependably immutable principle is *reciprocity.* Do as you would be done by—but Confucius stated it negatively, do not do to others what you would not want them to do to you (*Analects,* XV, 22). It is often exceedingly difficult to know what can be done to help another person; it is seldom difficult to know how to avoid harming him. But on another occasion Confucius stated the same principle in an affirmative form: "A good man, you know, wishing to stand himself, helps others stand, and wishing to prosper himself, helps others prosper" (*Analects,* VI, 29). Beyond this principle of reciprocity he recognized two others that are also indispensable guides to effective communication. These lie at the heart of his rhetoric. The first was to know what is right and therefore might be done with propriety. And the second was to understand the need always to adapt to immediate circumstances.

These two indispensable guides Confucius called *jen* and *li. Jen* has been variously translated as gentility, benevolence, or goodness. It is behavior characteristic of a superior man. It is good taste governing judgment, thus providing an individualizing variability in meeting well whatever new situations may not seem to be wholly covered by tradition. Achievement of *jen* is the ultimate attainment of self-improvement and has been called the keystone of Confucianism.[19] It is the foundation on which his rhetoric rests.

What he meant by *li* may be translated as propriety, appropriateness of behavior, or conformity to the best social traditions. This is the operational aspect of his rhetoric. The basic prescriptions of *li* were fivefold: "The duties are those between sovereign and minister, between father and son, between husband and wife, between elder brother and younger, and those belonging to the intercourse of friends" (*Doctrine of the Mean,* XX, 8). In *The Book of Etiquette and Ceremonial,* these *li* principles were spelled out in great detail, amounting to several thousand explicit patterns of behavior that must be memorized and adhered to under appropriate circumstances. Merely ritualistic correctness, however, was not enough. Confucius was emphatic in his view that whatever is done must be done from the heart, with understanding and single-mindedness.

Jen prescribed that one should, with sincerity and insight, behave according to the highest standards. *Li* provided a comprehensive reminder of what the standards were and of how to observe them. As has been noted earlier, Confucius taught that "without sincerity there would be nothing."

The Confucian *jen* was similar to the Aristotelian *ethos,* with special emphasis upon benevolence and sincerity. Not more than a few men in any society could be expected to attain *jen.* These few were the *chun-ju,* or gentlemen—aristocrats who possessed power over people and were to exercise that power paternalistically, in a spirit of *noblesse oblige. Li,* akin to the Western code of etiquette, held that there is a right way of doing whatever must be done. Confucius felt that harmony would be best safeguarded when individuals adhered to expected patterns of behavior.

Conduct, indeed, was what principally concerned Confucius. He gave less attention to what men should say and how they should say it than to what men should do, and how they should do it. Thus the province of *li* constituted a peculiarly Chinese type of rhetoric of behavior, to be examined in the following chapter. The basic tenet was that everyone should behave always in a predictable and traditional manner. Everyone accordingly knew what to expect of himself and of others. Even quarrels were to be conducted ritualistically. When meeting strangers, when introduced at court, even when dining within the family— for any and all occasions there was a prescribed mode of behavior.

Confucius did not invent the social code. He felt strongly that such patterning of behavior was a function of historic tradition rather than a choice to be left to individuals. He endorsed strongly the code as he found it established. And he made clear his conviction that through decorum, propriety, and politeness feelings would be protected, dignity preserved, and harmony enhanced. These were rhetorical goals. And the code of *li* was a rhetorical instrument designed to help individuals to attain them.

Perhaps the rhetorical injunctions of Confucius might have been more affirmative and less negative if he had had a higher confidence in the integrity and wisdom of ordinary human beings. He was an optimist in his view that acceptable behavior could be taught to people; but he was a pessimist in his belief that if left to their own devices individuals would be quarrelsome and selfishly aggressive. This is why persuasion is necessary; facts do not speak for themselves. "I have yet to meet a man," he observed sadly, "as fond of Excellence as he is of outward appearances." Then he went on to explain how he tried to deal with human nature as he encountered it: "My teaching may be compared to the building of a mound of earth. If a man stops before the last load is placed, I stop. It may be compared to leveling land. Even though a man deposit but one load, there is progress. I go to him" (*Analects*, IX, 18, 19).

The kind of speaking with which Confucius was concerned was that which he observed to be the most important in the society he knew. This included the speaking of counsellors to princes and the intimate talk within the family and inside a small community—talk through which harmonious relationships were maintained. He knew nothing of such circumstances as abound in modern society, in which a man because of his skill in speaking seeks out audiences to address. If it had occurred to him to imagine such a situation, he would have been scornful of it. He knew nothing of the social custom of organizing clubs or forums for the purpose of bringing speakers before audiences. If he had known of such organizations, he would have wondered whether their purpose was entertainment, or sociability, or the rationalization of existing convictions, or the fostering of attacks on public policies, or the stimulation of the minds of the members with new information and ideas. Only the last purpose could have had his full approval, although he would never have underestimated the value of sociability as an end in itself.

Without ever consciously undertaking to be a rhetorician, Confucius was nevertheless deeply and in detail concerned with basic rhetorical considerations. He could not avoid such concern; for he devoted his life to the problem of how people could live together in harmony and with justice. He abjured violence. As Creel has emphasized, his social philosophy was that persuasion must replace force in the guidance of human relations.[20] The last statement by Confucius which his disciples put down in the *Analects* was: "One cannot know people without knowing their words." They must have known what he considered of final importance.

He could not avoid being a rhetorician because his entire moral philosophy was rhetorical. The focus of his inquiry was upon effective means of adjusting people to ideas, ideas to people, and people to people, This was the humanist way, as he conceived it. This was his philosophy. This was his rhetoric.

CHAPTER 9

The Rhetoric of Behavior: Ceremony, Etiquette, and Methodology

MANNERS AND ETHICS

THE MOST TYPICALLY Chinese operative rhetoric in ancient times was the prescribed formalism by which individual behavior was governed under all foreseeable conditions. This was a civilization that placed high value on conformity to social expectations. The chief sanction an individual sought for his conduct was social approval based on the prescriptions of tradition.

Individualism in the culture of ancient China was considered a kind of eccentricity. Originality, initiative, and inventiveness were restricted and generally disapproved. From birth to death, and in both public and private life, there were few circumstances in which an individual should try to devise his own special mode of behavior. Instead, detailed and precise instructions were available indicating what he should do and how he should do it. The culture viewed human relationships as being too important and also too difficult to be left to the whim, insight, or the variable judgment of the moment.

Rhetoric in Chinese society thus came to be very much akin to sheer propriety. The utility which rhetoric was to serve was the maintenance of harmony. The way to this goal was through ceremony, etiquette, and methodology. There was a right way of doing things—a way that was established and accepted. When behavior conformed to this pattern of expectation, the individual's relations with his fellows would be predictable and dependable. Accordingly, the community would have a decent and decorous stability.

Such was the rhetorical aim. Of course it did not work out that way. Strife and instability, as we have seen, characterized the age. Human selfishness and willfulness were no more eradicated nor more successfully curbed in ancient China by its rhetoric than they have been in the West by ours. But the problem as it was identified in the East was

145

different than as seen in the West. The Chinese traditionalists thought the solution lay in the suppression of the individual. The purpose of this chapter is to examine the means by which this goal was pursued.

The sources to be considered are the *I-Li* or *The Book of Etiquette and Ceremonies,* a technical treatise studied chiefly by scholars; the *Li Chi* or *The Book of Rites,* a very lively book containing many anecdotes about Confucius as well as prescriptions for social guidance; and the *I Ching* or *The Book of Changes,* which, according to one of its editors, for three thousand years "has served as a principal guide in China on how to govern a country, organize an enterprise, deal with people, conduct oneself under difficult conditions, and contemplate the future."[1]

Even the peasants, most of them illiterate, came under the influence of these classics, for ceremonial forms of behavior were taught to them from their earliest childhood. A nineteenth-century observer in China found that "there are very few Chinese who do not know the proper thing to be done at a given time, incomparably better than the most cultivated foreigner."[2] The formal politeness of the common people was also emphasized by Du Halde, who wrote: "It is not only among Persons of Distinction that these polite and humane Manners prevail; they are even communicated to all Ranks: Workmen, Domestics, and Peasants themselves treat one another with Civility, making their compliments, placing themselves upon their Knees before each other when they are taking leave, and omitting none of the Punctilies prescribed by the Chinese Politeness."[3]

The aim and the effect of these books have primarily been to enhance harmony by curbing individuality. Self-expression and self-assertion tend to generate strife. When the choice had to be made, the ancient Chinese chose conformity in preference to conflict. And when they made the choice, they worked assiduously to support it. As Liu Wu-chi, a Chinese historian, said: "In the course of centuries there had been built up a large body of moral treatises, exhortations, and admonitions, and though modern critics tend to disparage them, their sway over the Chinese mind and conduct was great and lasting."[4]

The social role of an individual was of more consequence than the special characteristics of his personality.[5] A father was to be obeyed because he was the father, not because he might exemplify unusual wisdom or benevolence or insight. An elder son was dominant over his siblings because of his priority of birth, regardless of his temperament or character or behavior. Friendships once formed were deemed unbreakable, even if later differences in education or fortune should lead to growing incompatibility. Marriages were arranged by parents or professional "go-betweens," not by youthful passion or preference. The ancient Chinese of course noted differences of ability, appearance, and temperament. But their practice was to stress the similarities among people, which, they felt, were fundamental; the differences were largely trivial.

Such views of personality and of social relationships resulted in a strong emphasis upon ritualistic politeness. Instead of "doing what comes naturally," the injunction was to "do what is approved traditionally." A rhetorical effect of this point of view was to discourage inventive originality in ideas and in manner of speaking, or in style. The aim of speakers was not to originate fresh points of view or to devise new ways of supporting arguments, but to draw upon a common source of accepted understanding. "This is the way it should be done because this is the way it always has been done." Such an approach lends to social intercourse a confident dependability. What custom decrees is what ought to be and what will be done. Mere cleverness had little leeway for winning special rewards. The chief contribution an individual could make toward influencing the result of a social encounter was to know instantly and precisely what should be done. To be socially correct was an end in itself, needing no further justification and sanctioning no exceptions.

It did not follow, however, that the formalism which governed behavior was empty, hypocritical, or meaningless. Far from it. The ethical requirements of the ancient Chinese social code were fully as high as the etiquette was explicit. The spirit was well expressed in the *Book of Rites:* "When the heart is deeply moved, expression is given to it by ceremonies."[6] Ralph Waldo Emerson, in his essay on "Behavior," explained a relationship between manners and ethics which is strictly applicable to the traditional Chinese view:

> Bad behavior the laws cannot reach. Society is infested with crude, cynical, restless and frivolous persons, who prey upon the rest, and whom a public opinion concentrated into good manners— forms accepted by the sense of all—can reach: the contradictors and railers at public and private tables, who are like terriers, who conceive it the duty of a dog of honor to growl at any passer-by and do the honors of the house by barking him out of sight. I have seen men who neigh like a horse when you contradict them or say something which they do not understand: then the overbold, who make their own invitation to your hearth; the persevering talker, who gives you his society in large saturating doses; the pitiers of themselves, a perilous class; the frivolous Asmodeus, who relies on you to find him ropes of sand to twist; the monotones; in short,

every stripe of absurdity; these are social inflictions which the magistrate cannot cure or defend you from, and which must be entrusted to the restraining force of custom and proverbs and familiar rules of behavior.[7]

In this passage Emerson precisely indicated the needs which the ancient Chinese sought to serve through "the restraining force of custom" and "familiar rules of behavior." In the several classics on ceremony, ritual, and etiquette, it is taken for granted that manners and ethics are relatively similar in nature and overlapping in their functions. For both etiquette and ethics, a primary function of good social conduct is to ease feelings at points of possible friction, to avoid causing embarrassment, to prevent awkwardness, and to preserve good will. Even when an individual feels no positive impulsion to treat another person with special thoughtfulness or courtesy, the mere fact that he does behave "correctly" preserves the social amenities and enhances the pleasantness of relations. A youth need not ask himself what reason there is for him to respect an elder in order to make meaningful and socially helpful the fact of addressing him as "Sir."

The uses of etiquette are desirable regardless of the feelings of the social participants. Whether or not food is eaten with fingers has nothing to do with sincerity but a great deal to do with social acceptability. For a wide range of behaviors, formalized etiquette simply provides an impersonal guide to conduct that helps people adjust to one another. As it is stated in the *Li Chi,* such established modes of conduct are "things advantageous to man." If a man should boorishly "neglect the rules of propriety, how shall he succeed?"[8] To *mean well* may be heartwarming, but what society requires is that its members *do well.* The fulfillment of social expectation relaxes tension and assures confidence in the stability of relationships. Violating expectations would arouse bewilderment and cause resentment.

It should be noted that the elaborate Chinese code of etiquette resembles the Hindu caste system in providing a socially accepted, readily understood, and prevailingly dominant rhetoric in being or rhetoric of behavior. Beyond this the two codes are in sharp contrast. The caste system was designed to recognize and perpetuate the fact of human inequality; Chinese ceremonialism was devised to harmonize social relationships regardless of the differing status of the individuals. In India the question was: how should men comport themselves in view of the inevitability of their being members of groups that were separated sharply from one another? In China the question was: since individuals inevitably live in close and interlocking relationships, how can the points of friction best be lubricated? As Confucius expressed it, "In the application of rules of manners, harmony is to be valued. . . . all had harmony as their key" (*Analects,* I, 12).

In both India and China a significant body of rhetoric was enshrined in social customs that served as immutable controls over conduct. As always happens, what started as social patterns, when they were fully accepted in the culture, became etched deeply into the personalities of the people. In time it became almost pointless to try to distinguish between external "regulators" of conduct and internal "adjustments" which led the individuals to want to do what society insisted they must do. Social preferences and individual preferences merged and became one.[9]

The Book of Etiquette

The *I-Li, The Book of Etiquette and Ceremonial,* was first rendered into English by John Steele in 1913.[10] The tradition was that it had been composed by Chou Kung, founder of the Chou dynasty, in the twelfth century B.C. Whatever its origin, *The Book of Etiquette* comports with the ancient saying that "The Hsia dynasty valued loyalty, the Yun dynasty reality, and the Chou dynasty ornament." The twenty-two chapters, comprising nine sections which remain from its original text, are thought to be no more than fragmentary survivals from the great bulk of its primitive form. The aphoristic style of its precepts, somewhat reminiscent of the Book of Proverbs in the Old Testament, suggests that it may have been derived from folk sayings. Without question, its teachings lay close to the heart of the beliefs and practices of Confucian China.

These teachings were far from being merely formal or traditional. The very concept of ceremonialism was cardinal in the life of the ancient Chinese. "It was meant to inculcate the habit of self-control and ordered actions which were the expression of a mind fully instructed in the inner meaning of things, and sensitive to every impression of honour and nobility that came to it in its contact with truth of whatever kind. That at least was the ideal."[11] In short, *politesse* was only secondarily a way of doing; primarily, it was a way of feeling and understanding. Etiquette was enshrined as a way of life.

A major function of *The Book of Etiquette* was to prescribe what should be said and how to say it in a wide variety of social situations. For example, when a marriage was being arranged, the father of the prospective groom should send a messenger to the home of the intended bride to consummate the arrangements. After preliminary details were completed, the host should say to the messenger:

> "Since your honour has come on business to my house, I use the custom of ancient time, and ask to be allowed as an assistant to offer you a glass of new wine."
>
> To which the reply is: "Since the business which I have come upon is already finished, I venture to decline the honour."
>
> To this the host replies: "According to the custom of the ancients, I venture to press my invitation."
>
> And the guest answers: "Since I cannot secure permission to decline, dare I do other than obey?"[12]

The rhetorical pattern is clear and precise. Whatever is to be said and done derives not from the individualistic peculiarities of the participants but from the "custom of ancient time." The method is also prescribed: first refuse, then accept. Whether or not one likes the discourse of his fellow thus becomes of little consequence; for it is not the speaker who is responsible but the whole impressive weight of ancient culture. To this one can but bow, regardless of his personal likes or dislikes.

The import is enormously consequential rhetorically. It shifts the accountability both for what is said and for the manner of speaking from the speaker to the impersonal and uncontradictable authority of tradition. The pleasant quirks and ego-satisfactions of individuality are renounced; but acceptability without the pains of responsibility is assured. Once a train of discourse is commenced, its outcome is assured.

What the individual speaker must master is twofold. First, he must learn a huge and complex set of prescribed modes of speech, mastering them so thoroughly that he will instantly be able to bring to mind for his use the words and the manner appropriate to the circumstance. And second, he must attain skill in initiating the specific situations in which the ceremonial discourse that suits his wishes will be prescribed.

As the *I-Li* is read, both its copiousness and its ingenuity in providing for all manner of social situations become evident. There was little need for individual inventiveness when tradition supplied effective discourse for every normally encountered occasion. Moreover, the traditional norms were carefully designed to provide the optimum of satisfaction for all participating.

For example, when one medium-ranking official visits another of equal rank, great care is taken to preserve the dignity of each and to insure against any presumption that either the visitor or the host has a superior status. The elaborateness of the provisions for emphasizing equality of prestige may seem pretentious; but an examination of the locutions employed indicates how well the dignity of both officials is protected:

> The visitor says: "I have desired an interview for some time, but have had no justification for asking for it; but now his honour So-and-So orders me to an interview."
>
> The host replies: "The gentleman who introduced us has ordered me to grant you an interview. But you, Sir, are demeaning yourself by coming. I pray your honour to return home, and I shall hasten to present myself before you."
>
> The guest replies: "I cannot bring disgrace on you by obeying this command. Be good enough to end by granting me this interview."
>
> The host replies: "I do not dare to set an example as to how a reception of this kind should be conducted, and so I persist in asking your honour to return home, and I shall call on you without delay."
>
> The guest answers: "It is I who do not dare to show the example, and so I persist in asking you for an interview."
>
> The host replies: "As for me, as I have failed to receive permission to decline this honour, I shall not press it further; but I hear that your honour is offering me a present, and this I venture to decline."
>
> To this the guest replies: "Without a present I cannot venture to come into your presence."
>
> The host replies: "I am not sufficient for the conduct of these ceremonies, and so I venture to persist in declining."
>
> The guest answers: "If I cannot have the support of my gift, I dare not pay you this visit, so I persist in my request."
>
> The host replies: "I also am decided in declining; but as I cannot secure your consent that I should go to your house as aforesaid, how dare I not respectfully obey?"[13]

The fact that such interchanges were completely prescribed and therefore wholly predictable gave them a certain monotony and artificiality. Nevertheless, they had decided value. What they accomplished was an effortless and dependable harmonization of human relations. They eliminated anxious concern over how a delicate interview should be conducted. What the participants lost was the excitement of unpredictability and perhaps the pleasure of fresh experimentation—possibly also a brashness or rashness of personal assertiveness. What they gained was an assurance of dignity and peace of mind. Communication, under their system, was rendered comfortable for both speaker and listener. The end both sought was assured. The results were good enough to enshrine the practice.

The remainder of the *I-Li* detailed carefully prescribed instructions to both host and guests for a private dinner party and for a state banquet; for participants in an archery contest, indicating the proper behavior for both winner and losers; for the conduct of a diplomatic mission and for its reception;[14] and for conducting various types of funerals, depending on the status of the deceased and his family.

In depicting the conduct of a diplomatic mission, it is significant that the only important portion not prescribed was the content of the speeches to be exchanged between the diplomat and the monarch whose court he would visit. These speeches were to be left to the invention of the speakers, but it was stressed that "it is essential that they be statesmanlike and pleasant." Warning was given against making the speeches either too long or too short. Then it was added: "The perfection of the speaking art is to make speeches that convey the speaker's meaning and no more."[15]

THE BOOK OF RITES

The *Li Chi* or *Book of Rites* has "engaged the universal attention of students," according to Ch'ên Shou-Yi, a historian of Chinese literature.[16] The richest and most suggestive of the ceremonial volumes, it contains many anecdotes concerning Confucius. It also contains two essays already noted in Chapter 8, *The Great Learning* and *The Doctrine of the Mean*.

Various collections of works on rites were referred to by Confucius and Mencius, but it was not until 164 B.C. that the *Li Chi* as presently constituted was compiled. By the time the Imperial edition was published in 1748, the commentaries of two hundred and forty-four scholars were appended to it. J. M. Calley, translating a portion of the work in 1853, declared in his introduction that "Le cérémonial résume l'esprit Chinois": ceremonialism manifests the Chinese spirit. The discussion of ceremonialism in his book has so intrigued the Chinese mind that it has "echoed and re-echoed in subsequent literature."[17]

James Legge made the first English translation of it in 1885, calling it "A Collection of Treatises on Propriety and Ceremonial Usages."[18]

It is a rhetorically rich compendium of advice on the right uses of speech and on the means of effective speaking. The spirit of the work is well illustrated in a quotation it offers from Confucius: "In the service of a ruler, when great words are spoken to and accepted by him, great advantages may be expected from them; and when words of small importance are presented to him, only small advantages are to be looked for. Therefore, a superior man will not for words of small importance receive great emoluments, nor for words of great importance small emoluments" (II, 334). In short, the worth of a message is equivalent to its weight.

The *Li Chi* opens with an exhortation to use speech well for the benefit of the state. "Speech composed and definite," readers are told, "will make the people tranquil." On the other hand, contentiousness, especially about trivial matters, disturbs the populace. Accordingly: "Do not seek for victory in small contentions; do not seek for more than your proper share. Do not positively affirm what you have doubts about; and when you have no doubts, do not let what you have to say appear simply as your own view." There are rules of propriety designating what is proper to be done for each time and circumstance. "According to those rules, one should not seek to please others in an improper way, nor be lavish of his words" (I, 62–63).

Then came a significant caveat: "The rules of propriety do not go down to the common people. The penal statutes do not go up to great officers" (I, 90). The meaning is clear: the uneducated masses should not be condemned if their manners were uncouth; and high officials were to be considered above the law. Less license was granted to both groups, however, than we might assume. The commonality could always be loyal and respectful, if not polished in their manners; and the aristocracy was enjoined to live by a code of morality and service even more rigorous than the letter of the law. The greater the privileges and attainments of an individual, the higher were the standards by which his behavior should be evaluated. Even in bearing, the rank of a person should be reflected in differing ways: "The demeanor of the Son of Heaven should be characterized by majesty; of the princes, by gravity; of the great officers, by a regulated composure; of inferior officers, by an easy alertness; and of the common people, by simplicity and humility" (I, 112). Wealth and power were not to be refuges for either corruption or arrogance.

The principle of personal responsibility is carried to its ultimate conclusion: "He who has given counsel to another about his army should die with it when it is defeated. He who has given counsel about the country or its capital should perish with it when it comes into peril" (I, 145).

The ends to be sought in speaking were declared to be the maintaining of "correct relations" between a ruler and his ministers; "generous regard" between father and son; "harmony" between elder and younger brothers; and a "community of sentiment" between husband and wife (I, 366). The rules of propriety in discourse must be observed because they are "the embodied expression of what is right" (I, 390), and they "serve as instruments to form men's characters" (I, 394). Moreover, their social consequences are momentous. "In the right government of a state, the rules of propriety serve the same purpose as the steelyard [balance or scales] in determining what is light and what is heavy; or as the carpenter's line in determining what is crooked and what is straight; or as the circle and square in determining what is square and what is round" (II, 257). The conclusion is inevitable. "Therefore, let the ceremonial rules be observed: in the country life at home, and there will be the right distinction between young and old; inside the door of the female apartments, and there will be harmony among the three branches of kin; at court, and there will be the right ordering of rank and office" (II, 272).

The rules of propriety were far too important to be either neglected or experimented with. Individual idiosyncrasies were not to be tolerated. Personal innovations were too dangerous to be permitted. "The path should not be left for an instant; if it could be left, it would not be the path" (II, 300). Even to the pettiest of details, the ceremonial rules were essential; for, without them, an individual in a social situation "would not know how to dispose of his hands and feet, or how to apply his ears and eyes; and his advancing and retiring, his bowings and giving place would be without any definite rules" (II, 272). To the ancient Chinese propriety encompassed not only the niceties of external behavior but also the vitality of moral principle. "Common men and women, however ignorant, may intermeddle with the knowledge of it; but in its utmost reaches, there is that which even the sage cannot attain to" (II, 304).

Thus the wheel came full circle: individualism that ignored social rules was merely eccentric and disturbed the harmony which was the great goal of ancient Chinese culture. But the full understanding and interpretation of ceremony and propriety were beyond normal ability. The individual was governed not by arbitrary restraints but by the qualities of his own nature. As was noted earlier, the *Li Chi* emphasized that ceremonialism without feeling is dead. "Of all the methods for the good ordering of men, there is none more urgent than ceremonialism." For this "is not a thing coming to a man from without; it issues from within him, and has its birth in his heart" (II, 236). Sincerity is not smothered by ceremony and formalism. The desire to do what is right is not lessened by being instructed in what is right. Instruction helps to fulfill natural intent.

Instruction in effective speech was conducted by the ancient Chinese with considerable sophistication. The instruction commenced in the nursery. As soon as infants were able to speak, differential education was given to boys and to girls, each fitted to the role they would be expected to play in society. "A boy was taught to respond boldly and clearly; a girl, submissively and low" (I, 477). At the age of ten boys were taken from their homes to a school, where they were taught to read aloud and to master the forms of polite conversation. Girls were kept at home, to be taught by a governess to develop "pleasing speech and manners" and "to be docile and obedient" (I, 478). The son was taught to address his parents respectfully: never to refer to them as being old, and to avoid "reckless, reviling or derisive laughter" (I, 28, 69). The son was also instructed that when he should be sent on a mission to a person of rank, "Do not listen with the head inclined to one side, nor answer with a loud, sharp voice, nor look with a dissolute leer, nor keep the body in a slouching position" (I, 76). As the boy became old enough to assume more serious missions, he was told: "At court the conversation should be according to the rules of propriety; every question should be so proposed, and every answer so returned" (I, 118–19). Further, the boy was taught, "The style prized in conversation required that it should be grave and distinct. The demeanor prized in the court required that it should be well regulated and urbane; that at sacrifices was to be grave, with an appearance of anxiety" (II, 73–74).

The instructions were far from mechanical; neither was the student taught to be an obedient robot. Voice training, for example, was considered important. And the voice was to be improved in precisely the right way—by directing the boy's attention to his own thoughts and feelings while speaking. "All the modulations of the voice," it was explained, "arise from the mind and are produced by things external to it. The affections thus produced are manifested in the sounds that are uttered." Then, with more knowledge of phonemes than might be expected, the *Li Chi* continued: "Changes are produced by the way in which those sounds respond to one another; and those changes constitute what we call the modulations of the voice" (II, 92).

Careful attention was given also to the methods of both teaching and learning. The good teacher was described as follows: "Thus in his teaching, he leads and does not drag; he strengthens and does not discourage; he opens the way but does not conduct to the end, leaving this to the learner's own efforts. Leading and not dragging produces harmony. Strengthening and not discouraging makes attainment easy. Opening the way and not conducting to the end makes the learner thoughtful. He who produces such harmony, easy attainment, and thoughtfulness may be pronounced a skillful teacher" (II, 87).

When, however, the students entered into advanced studies, the whole atmosphere became sterner, more demanding, and less personalized. A cane was prominently displayed, for students were to be reminded of the punishment they would receive if inattentive to their studies. Examinations were given once a year. Students were watched carefully, but the masters did not talk with them personally. The young men listened to the lectures but could not ask questions; they were expected to follow the course of study without deviations (II, 84–85).

Nevertheless, the instruction was far from mere rote memorization. The skillful learner, the Li Chi insisted, even if his teacher appears indifferent, will make twice the progress of an inattentive student; and in retrospect he will realize that his attainment was owing to the ability of his teacher. The inept student, on the other hand, will not profit even from the diligent pains of a conscientious teacher, and he will blame his failure on his instructor. Teacher and student, it was pointed out, must cooperate, each probing the mind of the other. "The skillful questioner is like a workman addressing himself to deal with a hard tree. First he attacks the easy parts, then the knotty. After a long time, the pupil and master talk together, and the subject is explained. The unskillful questioner takes the opposite course. The master who skillfully waits to be questioned may be compared to a bell when it is struck. Struck with a small hammer, it gives a small sound. Struck with a great one, it gives a great sound. But let it be struck leisurely and properly, and it gives off the sound of which it is capable. He who is not skillful in replying to questions is the opposite of this. This all describes the method of making progress in learning" (II, 89).

The forms of speech that were taught were those of which students had the greatest need: conversation, the presentation of counsel at court, leadership in the conducting of formal ceremonies, and personal behavior in times of grief and stress. The prescriptions were always precise. When, for example, a young man should meet an older acquaintance on the road, he must hasten to him and stand respectfully, with head bowed and hands clasped across his breast. If the elder spoke to him he should reply; if not, he should quickly retire (I, 70). The careful attention to diction is indicated in directions on how to speak of death. Of a dead king it should be said that he has fallen; of a prince that he has crashed; of a high official, that his life has ended; but of an inferior official's death it may be observed that he now is unsalaried (I, 117). In giving advice to a superior officer, the counsellor should phrase his suggestions indirectly; and if his advice was rejected three times, he should resign. On the other hand, he must always expect that sometimes his counsel would go unheeded (I, 114).

The rhetoric of the *Li Chi* was unabashedly practical. It was not designed to encourage individual inventiveness but to assure fulfillment of social patterns of expectation. Speakers were not told how to win acclaim for personal brilliance, but how to avoid the pain of failure. The rhetoric taught: do thus-and-so and avoid turmoil and trouble. By this means harmony most surely could be preserved.

THE BOOK OF CHANGES

The *I Ching* or *Book of Changes* was concerned not with external behavior but with the methodology of thinking. Its rhetorical significance is therefore internal, not external. More than either the *I-Li* or the *Li Chi,* it encouraged individual thought—but always in accordance with rules and tradition. Like the works on etiquette, it sought dependability through tradition. Its rhetorical guidance is limited in extent but profound, for though it had little to say about speech, whatever it did say had enormous influence.

Chinese and foreign scholars specializing in the intellectual history of China testify to "the overwhelming importance of the Book within the history and the system of Chinese thought."[19] It was, as was pointed out in Chapter 8, Confucius' favorite book. More than three thousand years after its composition, it found renewed popularity in the United States, with the sale of a translation soaring to over fifty thousand copies a year.[20] The book consists of sixty-four brief moral essays on social and political themes, each illustrated by a set of broken and unbroken lines that are arranged in patterns. Each pattern, or figure, composed of varied groupings of the broken and unbroken lines, is explained in a brief essay, supplemented by a set of seven appendices. To the Chinese, however, what was important about the figures was not only what the commentaries found them to mean but what individual readers might deduce concerning particular meaning for themselves. Traditionally, the patterns were utilized in divination. But as Ch'ên Shou-Yi insists, "the basic recommendations [in the linear patterns] for the charting of action to seek security and avoid disaster rested squarely on logic and ethics."[21]

The intelligentsia found in them virtually any explanation of being or becoming. The great virtue of the varied combinations of lines derived from their possessing at one and the same time two contrary attributes: that is, they represented an enormous variety and range of meanings, yet all the meanings were comprised within a closely restricted set of cultural values and all were to be explicated by clearly defined rules. On the one hand, then, they indicated that much meaning is contained in small compass; on the other hand, they show that however restricted a source may be, it may give rise to multiple and extensive meanings.

The original author of *The Book of Changes* is thought to have been Fu-hsi, who was born in 3322 B.C. Looking about him at the sky and the earth, and examining his own feelings, he observed a variety of qualities which he thought could be represented by arranging broken and unbroken lines into eight trigrams, which all together would "classify the qualities of the myriad of things." As R. G. H. Siu explains it: "At any given moment, everything fits into the particular pattern of the moment. The fate of the seeker is thus inextricably bound with the cosmic interplay of the yin and the yang."[22] Some two thousand two hundred years later, King Wan, founder of the Kua dynasty, and his son, the Duke of Kua, revised Fu-hsi's ideas into what came to be accepted as the standard form of *The Book of Changes*. Thus it took form in the twelfth century B.C., contemporaneously with the writing of the Pentateuch in the Old Testament.

The imperial edition of the *I Ching*, published in 1715, contained quotations from the commentaries of two hundred and eighteen Chinese scholars. Perhaps ten times that number have devoted their lives to its interpretation during the long centuries after the editing by King Wan. The first European translation was a Latin version by a Jesuit priest, P. Regis, in the early eighteenth century. It was put into English first by McClatchie, in 1876, then by James Legge, who spent twenty years at the task. Its most famous editor was Confucius, who is reputed to have been the author of several of its seven classical appendices.

The unbroken line used in the figures is the concept of *Yin*, the broken line of *Yang*: the two ancient concepts of the complementary qualities that comprise all being—positive and negative, male and female, right and wrong, here and there, now and then, down and up, and so on.

The type of rhetorical significance suggested in the *I Ching* is illustrated in the Phi hexagram, which consists of three broken lines topped by three unbroken lines. The meaning is that men are divided into two classes, the weak and the strong; yet, paradoxically, the weak, uneducated, and unskilled are closer to nature and thus have a stronger survival potential. King Wan interpreted this to mean that the upper and lower classes are not in sympathetic communication, with the result that no state is well regulated. He warned that "the way of the small man appears to be increasing, that of the superior man to be decreasing."[23] Better communication would surely rectify conditions and thereby would strengthen the position of the ruling class.

The kind of communication to be sought is suggested in the Sung hexagram, an intermixture of two broken lines and four solid lines, which warns that differences of viewpoint cannot be overcome by contention. The utmost sincerity, if expressed argumentatively, simply arouses increased opposition. Convictions should be set forth with "apprehensive caution." It is advantageous to seek opportunities to present one's view to those in authority, but it is disadvantageous to urge ardently acceptance of one's views. "Contention is not a thing to be carried on to extremity."[24]

A similar idea is presented through the Khien hexagram, comprised of five broken and one solid line, which warns that pride and assertiveness arouse resentment, whereas humility induces friendliness. The Fang hexagram, of three broken and three solid lines, enforces the point metaphorically: "When the sun has reached the meridian height, it begins to decline. When the moon has become full, it begins to wane. . . . How much more must it be with the operations of men!"

Appendix III has been especially valued because of all the seven appendices it most generally has been thought to have been the work of Confucius. Both Legge and Creel discount the theory that Confucius wrote it, but the legend of his authorship has given it increased authority. In any event, it has considerable intrinsic value. Confucius valued the hexagrams because they suggested a wide range of meanings without prescribing any. The wisdom of the sages was contained within them, but every inquirer would have to use his own ingenuity to understand their import. Through their great variety, they suggested the breadth of human problems which need to be interpreted and solved. The ambiguity of the symbols gave to Confucianism a foil for the ambiguity of Taoism and thus helped to maintain its preeminence. More importantly, the book gained its influence through its representation that an enormous and amorphous totality of causeless, hit-or-miss bits and pieces of reality swirl continuously around us and that every moment must be interpreted in terms of this patternless immensity. Whereas the Western mind traditionally has sought to penetrate through the surrounding maze of impressions by a process of selection, analysis, definition, and classification, the Chinese sought to intuit an impression that accepted the undefinability and relatedness of every element in the undifferentiated mass.[25]

In the hexagrams of *The Book of Changes* the full contents of the minds of the sages cannot possibly be represented. No words can make meanings wholly clear. All communication must forever be partial. The great need is to realize that a message is no more than a cue from which each listener (reader) may devise for himself a meaning suitable to the immediate circumstances.

This awareness of a lack of certainty must not result in anxiety, for anxious men are ineffective. "The superior man in a high place composes himself before he tries to move others; makes his mind restful and easy before he speaks; settles the principles of his intercourse with others before he seeks anything from them."[26] When he does speak, he should neither flatter his superiors nor speak rudely to his inferiors.[27] Care must always be taken, for: "When disorder arises, it will be found that ill-advised speech was the stepping stone to it."[28]

The influence of speech for both good and ill is stressed in Appendix III of the *I Ching,* where it is written: "The superior man occupies his apartment and sends forth his words. If they be good they will be responded to at a distance of more than a thousand *li;* how much more will they be in the nearer circle! He occupies his apartment and sends forth his words. If they be evil, they will awaken opposition at a distance of more than a thousand *li;* how much more will they do so in the nearer circle! Words issue from one's person and proceed to influence the people." These are the forces which (together with actions) determine a man's "glory or disgrace" and "move heaven and earth."[29]

If the speaker be a man of wisdom, much good flows from his words. "The sages influence the minds of men, and the result is harmony and peace all under the sky."[30] The function of constructive persuasion could scarcely be more highly honored.

CHAPTER 10

Mencius: The Bold Prophet

THE ASSURANCE OF RIGHTEOUSNESS

IN THE JUDGMENT of D. T. Suzuki, a notable Japanese philosopher, the Confucian dominance of Chinese thought through twenty centuries was a direct result of the courageous and persistent advocacy of Mencius.[1]

The triumph of Confucianism over rival systems was by no means assured. During the hundred and fifty years of internecine struggle which followed the death of Confucius, men of learning sought their personal safety by pandering to the wishes and the vices of princes—a most un-Confucian behavior. The Hundred Schools of Philosophy which arose during that distraught era presented challenging alternatives. Taoism, Mohism, Rationalism, and Legalism each attained a popularity that, for a time, made them active competitors with the teachings of the great sage. Then Buddhism, introduced from India, became another formidable rival. Confucianism might have been driven out of public notice, as was Mohism; or it might have been converted to a popularized system of superstitions, as was Taoism. Perhaps the inherent appeal of the practical, political, moral, and humanist teachings of Confucius might have been enough to insure their survival as the keystone of Chinese culture. Such a possibility was not put to the test, because the dominance of the doctrines was established through the crusading zeal and skill of Mencius, who overwhelmed opposition with his brilliant defense of the proposition that "Never since the creation of the world was there a person equal to Confucius."[2]

Because of Mencius' manly vigor and realistic optimism, his name and teachings have been respected and admired in China second only to Confucius and Confucianism. The altars of Confucian temples inscribe the name of Confucius as "The Most Saintly Ancient Teacher," and next to his the name of Mencius as "The Almost as Saintly." Chinese scholars acclaim him as the founder of the peculiarly Chinese concept of democracy—a theory that the emperor rules with absolute power but

161

only so long as he enjoys the favor of the people.[3] Leonard A. Lyall, an English orientalist, accords him primacy because of his staunch defense of the worth of human nature.[4] H. G. Creel, an American sinologist, declares that his "fame overshadows that of all the other Chinese of his day," and praises his writings as "undoubtedly one of the great books of the world's literature."[5]

Specifically, Mencius made considerable contributions to the theory of rhetoric. In some respects he reinforced and clarified certain rhetorical views that had been set forth by Confucius. He also made original contributions. A principal one is that individuals may be motivated most lastingly and even most surely by appeals directed to their innate goodness of character.

More than Confucius, Mencius was explicit and definitive in his rhetorical views, for it was a cardinal point of his philosophy that men of insight have a primary duty to exercise the full weight of their influence in directing rulers into policies that will serve the needs of the masses of the people. It is as a rhetorician that Mencius assumes his greatest significance—yet, curiously, his rhetorical principles have not heretofore been identified and evaluated.

The *Book of Mencius* was first systematically edited and analyzed by a scholar named Chao Ch'i, who lived in the second century A.D., suffering imprisonment, persecution, and poverty until his death at the age of ninety. Concerning his editorial labors he wrote: "I wished to set my mind on some literary work by which I might be assisted to the government of my thoughts, and forget the approach of old age." He chose Mencius for his studies, for he found him to be "wide and deep, minute and exquisite, yet obscure at times and hard to see through"; and the ideas of Mencius, he found, "deserve to be properly ordered and digested."[6] Chu Hsi, in the twelfth century, wrote three commentaries on Mencius, which established the orthodox interpretation of his philosophy.

Unlike the *Analects,* the *Book of Mencius* is a continuous and connected discourse. Its value has been compared by I. A. Richards to the contribution of Plato.[7] The book may have been composed by Mencius himself in his later years, or perhaps it was put together by a group of his disciples working in close collaboration. The first Western-language translation, in Latin, was publishsed in Paris in 1824–29. The second translation, in English, was made by the indefatigable James Legge. Succeeding English versions have been rendered by Leonard A. Lyall, Lionel Giles, and James R. Ware.[8] Unfortunately, they have not been widely read, and Mencius remains far less known in the West than his worth merits.

Meng-k'o, to give him his Chinese name, was born about 372 B.C., in the same state of Lu in which Confucius had lived nearly two hundred years earlier; he died about 289 B.C. There is little dependable information concerning his life, except the considerable autobiographical details in his book. In his later years he lived in retirement, greatly honored and surrounded by a small group of his disciples. Of his childhood, it is difficult to renounce the attractive anecdotes that have been preserved.

His parentage was aristocratic, but had fallen into obscurity before Mencius' birth. His father died when Meng-k'o was a child. His mother became a byword in Chinese history because of her wisdom and sense of duty.

The family home was near a cemetery, and as a small boy Mencius began to amuse himself by imitating the funeral rituals which he often observed. To remove her son from such influences, his mother moved to a house in a market area. She soon realized this was a mistake, for the boy commenced to play at salesmanship. Her next move was to the vicinity of a school, with the result she desired; Mencius began to imitate the ceremonial politeness of scholars and developed a taste for books. Her understanding of developmental psychology is further illustrated in a domestic incident. Seeing a butcher shop, Mencius inquired why pigs were killed. His mother made the natural reply that it was to provide food for them. Then, fearing that he might think she was not being truthful, and thus learn to be deceptive, she promptly purchased a piece of pork for his supper. Still another anecdote relates that upon his return from school one day she asked him how he was doing and got an indifferent reply. Instantly she picked up a knife and cut the threads in the cloth she was weaving. When he showed surprise, she pointed out that her cutting the threads was like his neglecting his studies. The admonition is said to have been effective.

One further incident, from the time of Mencius' early manhood, illustrates the continuing influence exerted by his mother. Mencius told her one day that he planned to divorce his wife because he had entered her chamber and found her squatting in a most indelicate posture, indicative of her lack of taste. "It is you who have violated propriety," she told him, "for the *Li-Chi* plainly says that 'when approaching a room you should raise your voice, and when entering you should lower your eyes,' in order to protect the privacy of whoever is there." Thereupon Mencius turned his reproaches upon himself and absolved his wife of blame.

These stories, told in China to illuminate the qualities of mother-hood, give at least some indication of the personality and character of Mencius. According to Ssu-ma Ch'ien, the great Han historian, Mencius studied under disciples of Confucius' grandson. Apparently the first forty years of his life were spent in study, during which time he familiarized himself with China's history and literature. More importantly, he developed his own system of thought and a boldness of character that must have been founded on complete self-confidence. Like Confucius, he became a teacher around whom disciples gathered to hear his lectures. He never attained a permanent place as chief counsellor to a king, but he traveled from place to place, offering advice to such princes as would receive it.

MENCIUS AS SPEAKER

The *Book of Mencius* describes his entry into public life and demon-strates his skill and boldness as a state counsellor. He went to the court of King Hui of Liang, where the king received him and observed that since he had come from afar he must feel that he had counsel to offer that would be of profit and advantage to the kingdom. The comment was no doubt intended to be gracious to the unknown scholar; and the king probably leaned back to listen with some skepticism to what he antici-pated would be a pandering effort to win a position on his staff. Instead, Mencius brushed his comment aside imperiously. "Why speak of profit?" Mencius asked coldly. "What I am provided with are counsels to benev-olence and righteousness, and these are my only topics."[9]

Mencius went on to say that if the king thought only of profit for his kingdom, his officials would think of profit for themselves, and so would the people. To get profit they would try to take advantage of one another, and soon the kingdom would be endangered. In a profit-seeking society, the most successful brigands would be the most honored citizens and eventually the greatest robber would seize the throne itself. This, Mencius concluded, is the natural result to be expected from thinking of profit. Better to think of benevolence and righteousness, and to set these virtues as models for the people.

King Hui insisted that he himself was a benevolent ruler, who did his best to help his people through such tribulations as years of famine; yet to his regret he did not gain popularity. Mencius asked him: "Is there any difference between killing a man with a stick and with a sword?" When the king replied that he saw no difference, Mencius then asked him: "Is there a difference between doing it with a sword and with the style of government?" Driving his point home, Mencius continued: "In your kitchen there is fat meat; in your stables there are fat horses. But your people have the look of hunger."

When the king protested that his heart was uncommonly tender and cited, in proof, his unwillingness to see an ox slaughtered for the state sacrifices, Mencius asked him: suppose one of your subjects claimed he could lift a heavy weight but not a feather, or that he could see a single hair but not a wagonload of wood; could you accept his distinctions? When the king agreed that this would be foolish, Mencius made his point inescapably clear: "Now here is kindness sufficient to reach to animals, and no benefits are extended from it to the people. How is this? Is an exception to be made here? The truth is, the feather is not lifted because strength is not used; the wagonload of firewood is not seen because the eyesight is not used; and the people are not loved and protected because kindness is not employed. Therefore, your Majesty's not exercising the royal sway is because you do not do it, not because you are unable to do it."

This was by far the boldest talk King Hui—or any other of the lords and princes of his time—had ever heard. The king must have been as attracted as he was shocked by the unprecedented boldness of this young and unknown scholar who had come uninvited to his court and proceeded to hurl challenges and denunciations in his teeth. But Hui was a patient man and apparently recognized unusual merit when he encountered it. Instead of dismissing Mencius as an ill-natured country lout, he continued the colloquy in a spirit of good humor.

"When you charge that I do not advance the welfare of my people," the king asked, "how do you know it is because I will not do it? How do you distinguish between not doing a thing and being unable to do it?"

Mencius replied with a vividness of analogy and a use of familiar items in his illustrative comparisons which were to be hallmarks of his style: "In such a thing as taking the T'ai mountain under your arm and leaping over the north sea with it, if you say to the people—'I am not able to do it,' that is a real case of not being able. In such a matter as breaking a branch from a tree at the order of a superior, if you say to the people—'I am not able to do it,' that is a case of not doing it; it is not a case of not being able to do it. Your Majesty's not exercising the royal sway is not such a case as taking the T'ai mountain under your arm. . . . It is such a case as not breaking the branch off the tree."

Mencius then pointed out that all things may be measured by using the right kinds of measurement; and that it would be possible by examining the king's mind to determine what he really wanted most to accomplish. Was it to be kind? Scarcely, since his kindness reached only to animals and not to people. Examine your own mind, Mencius went on. "I beg your Majesty to measure it. You collect your equipments of war, endanger your soldiers and officers, and excite the resentment of the other princes." Gently, then, Mencius chided him, pointing out that he was living in luxury and had no need of further territories. But even if he did wish to rule over the surrounding states he was going about it very unwisely. "Doing what you do to seek for what you desire is like climbing a tree to seek for fish." When the king, interested now by the prospect of getting advice that might help him in his ambitions, exclaimed, "Is it as bad as that?" Mencius retorted: "It is even worse. If you climb a tree to seek for fish, although you do not get the fish, you will not suffer any subsequent calamity. But doing what you do to seek for what you desire, doing it moreover with all your heart, you will assuredly afterwards meet with calamities."

The king brusquely asked him, "May I hear the proof of that?" Mencius replied by asking him whether a small state attacking a large one would suffer defeat, and the king agreed it would. Then Mencius pointed out that all the surrounding territories if they were combined would be eight times the size of King Hui's domain and suggested that an attack upon any of them might unite them all in a pact of mutual defense. "Now if your Majesty will institute a government whose action shall be benevolent," Mencius explained, in a distinctly Confucian spirit, "this will cause all the officers in the kingdom to wish to stand in your Majesty's court, and all the farmers to wish to plough in your Majesty's fields, and all the merchants, both travelling and stationary, to wish to store their goods in your Majesty's market-places, and all travelling strangers to wish to make their tours on your Majesty's roads, and all throughout the country who feel aggrieved by their rulers to wish to come and complain to your Majesty. And when they are so bent, who will be able to keep them back?" Thereupon, the king was sufficiently impressed to invite further advice, and Mencius outlined for him a plan designed to enhance the welfare and contentment of the people by sponsoring education and agriculture.

The second of the speeches by Mencius, recorded in Part 2 of Book I, reveals his cleverness in utilizing whatever topic is suggested as a means of getting to the point he cherished: namely, the responsibility of rulers to enhance the welfare of their subjects. King Hsuan, of Ch'i, was a notable pleasure-lover who neglected the needs of his people. In a colloquy with him, Mencius convinced him that in pursuing his own pleasure he antagonized his people and thereby aroused rebellion; whereas, if he would make it a point to provide the same pleasures for his people that he himself enjoyed, his own satisfaction would increase and he would in addition become popular.

King Hsuan, prior to his talk with Mencius, had blamed the disorders of the kingdom on the bad character of the people and the low moral standards of the time. In proof of this view, he observed that his people hated him for having a hunting park, although they had loved King Wan, of an earlier period, who had had a park almost twice as large. True, Mencius replied, "but the grass-cutters and fuel-gatherers had the privilege of entering into it; so also had the catchers of pheasants and hares." Then he added: "When I first arrived at the borders of your kingdom, I inquired about the great prohibitory regulations before I would venture to enter it; and I heard that inside the barrier gate there was a park of forty square *li,* and that he who killed a deer in it was held guilty of the same crime as if he had killed a man."

There is no harm, Mencius said, in loving pleasure; for so do all men. What is needful is to share it. "When a ruler rejoices in the joy of his people, they also rejoice in his joy; when he grieves at the sorrow of his people, they also grieve at his sorrow." The effectiveness of Mencius' arguments to the king was impressive: "From that time he began to open his granaries to supply the wants of the people." Moreover, he kept Mencius at his court and sought his continuing guidance.

King Hsuan was not only pleasure-loving but was also greedy for wealth and sensuality. To govern with benevolence was difficult. In order to confirm him in high standards of righteous government, Mencius led him into many illuminating discussions, of which the following is typical:

> Mencius said to the King, "Suppose that one of your Majesty's ministers were to entrust his wife and children to the care of his friend, while he himself went into Ch'u to travel, and that, on his return, he should find that the friend had let his wife and children suffer from cold and hunger; how ought he to deal with him?" The King said, "He should cast him off."

> Mencius proceeded, "Suppose that the chief criminal judge could not regulate the officers under him, how would you deal with him?" The King said, "Dismiss him."

> Mencius again said, "If within the four borders of your kingdom there is not good government, what is to be done?" The King looked to the right and left, and spoke of other matters.

In another passage with King Hsuan which has become famous in Chinese history for its justification of rebellion against a wicked monarch, the king referred to an uprising in a neighboring kingdom, in which King Chau had been killed by one of his own ministers. "May a minister, then, put his sovereign to death?" the King asked, no doubt sharply. Mencius in reply said: "He who outrages the benevolence proper to his nature is called a robber; he who outrages righteousness is called a ruffian. The robber and ruffian we call a mere fellow. I have heard of the cutting off of the fellow Chau, but I have not heard in this case of putting a sovereign to death."

In still another notable passage, King Hsuan sought approval from Mencius for conquering a neighboring country called Yen, on the ground that the people in it were ill-governed and needed to be rescued. Mencius replied that if the king went to them with baskets of food to relieve their distress, they would turn to him in gratitude; but if, in the name of liberation, he went among them with swords and chariots and slew their fathers and elder brothers in combat, they would regard him as a scourge, not as a liberator.

Despite his insistence upon benevolence in preference to force, Mencius was not a pacifist. When a Duke whose territory lay between two warring kingdoms asked him what to do, Mencius replied: "Dig deeper your moats; build higher your walls; guard them as well as your people. In case of attack, be prepared to die in your defense, and treat the people so that they will not leave you; this is a proper course."[10] When the Duke persisted, saying it appeared his enemies were strong enough to overrun his domain, Mencius advised him to choose between two courses: to leave for a distant unoccupied territory, letting such of his subjects follow him as wished to do so; or to remain and die in defense of his homeland. This was a choice no advisor could make for him; but in either case there should be no surrender, even to superior force.

Mencius was a man of extraordinary common sense, as well as of insight and courage. When a court favorite turned the ruler against him, and Mencius was informed of this by a gossipy friend, he retorted indifferently that a man's advancement might indeed be affected by the intervention of friends or enemies. But what really mattered was whether the king trusted him sufficiently to follow his counsels. If the king did not trust him fully, his ministry would be ineffective even without the intervention of a rival or enemy.[11]

As a philosopher, Mencius accepted the importance of the two Confucian principles of *jen* and *li*, gentlemanliness and propriety, and to them he added *yih*, or righteousness. The good man, he insisted, must not only act rightly, he must also maintain inner purity. Only thus can he have an unperturbed mind. To a disciple, Mencius explained: "If, on self-examination, I find that I am upright, I will go forward against thousands and tens of thousands."[12] This principle of the unperturbed mind based on a confidence in one's own integrity lay at the heart of Mencius' rhetoric. A man who knows he is right need have no concern, whatever the situation.

Mencius not only taught this principle but exemplified it. He knew well the power of example, especially when it comes from on high. To him *ethos* was central in persuasion. "What the superior loves, his inferiors will be found to love exceedingly. The relation between superiors and inferiors is like that between wind and grass. The grass must bend when the wind blows upon it."[13] Likewise, "If a man himself does not walk in the right path, it will not be walked in even by his wife and children."[14] When a disciple urged that he pander to the court in order that he might retain his influence for good, Mencius retorted: "If I were to bend my principles and follow those princes, of what kind would my conduct be? And you are wrong. Never has a man who has bent himself been able to make others straight."[15]

Mencius was capable of going to extreme lengths to emphasize his own integrity and the importance which he attached to self-confident independence. On one occasion, after Mencius had attained fame as a sound counsellor, when he was visiting in the state of Ts'e, the king of that state courteously sent him a message, saying, "I was wishing to come and see you. But I have got a cold and may not expose myself to the wind. In the morning I will hold my court. I do not know whether you will give me the opportunity of seeing you then." Mencius sent the messenger back with this reply: "Unfortunately, I am unwell and unable to go to the court." The next day he ostentatiously went about the town. The king, meanwhile, sent his own physician to treat the honored scholar. A friend sent the physician back to the court with a message for the king saying Mencius was feeling a bit better and had left for the court; then he sent several men to find Mencius, urging him to hasten to the court before the king should learn of his impertinence. Mencius, instead, went openly to a friend's home to visit. This friend berated him, saying, "I have seen the respect of the king to you, sir, but I have not seen in what way you show respect to him." Mencius replied that he respected the king far too highly to talk to him as though he thought he were vain and proud; he could advise him only to practice benevolence and righteousness. "There is therefore no man in Ts'e who respects the king so much as I do." Then he explained that he could be useful to the king only if there were absolute trust in his integrity and independence of mind; if it were suspected that he might say things only to please, his counsel would be ignored. By a proud show of utter independence, therefore, he established the only kind of relationship that would make his words effective.[16]

The basis of his self-confidence was his sense of assurance that he knew what was right and that he adhered to it. "The way of truth is like a great road," he said. "It is not difficult to know it. The evil is only that men will not seek it."[17] What seemed to Mencius to be difficult was not how to ascertain the right modes of behavior but how to understand why men did not follow them. In small things, he pointed out, men are assiduous to conform to common norms. It is only in significant matters that men seem intent upon deviating from the "great road" of obvious truth.

"Here is a man," he told his disciples, "whose fourth finger is bent and cannot be stretched out straight. It is not painful, nor does it incommode his business; and yet if there be any who can make it straight, he will not think the way from Ts'in to Ts'oo too far to go to him; because his finger is not like the finger of other people. . . . But if his mind be not like that of other people, he does not know dissatisfaction. This should be called—'Ignorance of the relative importance of things.' "[18] The meaning and the value of conformity in modes of thinking and behaving could scarcely be better exhibited. No supporting argument was needed, for Mencius made his truth self-evident by his manner of presenting it.

THE PATTERNS OF MENCIAN RHETORIC

Book VI of the *Book of Mencius,* from which the two preceding quotations have been drawn, is by far the most important part of his work. "For his views of human nature as here developed," in Legge's judgment, "Mencius is mainly indebted for his place among the sages of his country."[19] More sweepingly, I. A. Richards considers this book "one of the most important arguments in the history of thought."[20] It is precisely because of this book that Mencius became more than a bold and brilliant expositor of Confucianism and a vivid and moving speaker. In it he assumed an independent posture as a significant philosophical rhetorician.

In Book VI Mencius posited two basic propositions. The first is that human nature is basically good. The second is that through persuasive instruction individuals may be reclaimed from erroneous behavior which they have learned or been induced to follow and may be set again upon the path of righteousness which is in accord with their nature. Part I of this book is in the form of a dialogue between Mencius and Kao Pu-hai, a philosopher who sought to reconcile the views of Confucius and Mo-Tze.

Both Confucius and Mo-Tze had avoided consideration of the fundamental nature of man, though the reasonable inference from their teaching is that man is inherently fallible and must be induced to transcend his own failings. Mencius was entirely clear in his own belief that this could not be. Basic nature—including human nature—cannot be changed. Whatever man is, he is. Just as water seeks its own level, so will man behave in the long run in a manner consistent with what he most truly is. The beginning of rhetorical speculation, therefore, is to determine the genuine nature of man. And Mencius was confident that he had found the answer: namely, that innately human nature is good.

Book VI opens with Kao presenting a condensed analogy which he doubtless believed to represent orthodox Confucianism: that man's nature is like a piece of willow wood, which may be fashioned into a bowl, representing righteousness. In reply Mencius pointed out that workmen must change the nature of a piece of wood in order to make a bowl of it. If, then, in order to attain to benevolence and righteousness it is necessary to alter the basic nature of man, these presumed virtues must be reckoned as calamities.

Kao tried again, using a different analogy: water may be induced to flow East or West, depending upon where it may be dammed, or where channels are opened. Mencius retorted: "Water indeed will flow indifferently to the east or west, but will it flow indifferently up or down? The tendency of man's nature to good is like the tendency of water to flow downwards. There are none but have this tendency to good, just as all water flows downwards." Then he added that of course water might be made to leap upward if it is struck and may even be dammed in a fashion to make it rise up the side of a hill; but this is not natural to water; it is the result of external force applied to it.

After a lengthy discussion aimed to ascertain whether behavior is motivated internally, by natural feelings, or externally, by custom and rules of propriety, a disciple points out that some believe man's nature is such that it may be induced toward good or evil, and some think that innately some men are good and others evil. On what basis, he asks, does Mencius disagree with both of these common views? Why does he insist that all men are good? Mencius agreed that "In good years the children of the people are most of them good, while in bad years the most of them abandon themselves to evil." But, he said, the difference occurs because of circumstances rather than because of differences in their nature. Then he reminds the listeners that barley will produce a good or bad crop depending on cultivation, soil, and rainfall; yet the seed is the same.

When evil behavior is widespread and persistent, Mencius went on, it is as though men were viewing a mountainside which once had been beautifully covered with forests but now is ugly and barren since the trees were cut down and the ground eroded. "But is this the nature of the mountain?" Then he added: "The way in which a man loses his proper goodness of mind is like the way in which the trees are denuded by axes and billhooks." Since evil behavior is readily observable on every side, Mencius felt constrained to illustrate still further his contention that such actions are not in accord with nature.

"Suppose," he said, "the case of the most easily growing thing in the world; if you let it have one day's genial heat, and then expose it for ten days to cold, it will not be able to grow." Or assume, he said, that a master chess player is attempting to teach skill in chess to two men of equal intelligence—one of whom pays close attention, the other of whom lets his mind wander to the hunting of swans. The fact that one will learn chess and the other not is no indication of their difference in intelligence. The wide variance in human behavior may be illustrated, he went on, by the fact that a beggar may be so proud that he would refuse an offered plate of rice, though he were starving, if it were offered in an insulting manner, whereas a fawning courtier might accept a gift of lands and mansions from the king, even though he already were wealthy and had no need of them. The difference, however, does not prove that their basic natures are different. It simply indicates that the courtier had lost his natural mind.

How lamentable it is, Mencius exclaimed, that men lose their natural minds and do not seek them again. When a dog is lost, or a fowl, the owner instantly searches for them. But when a man loses his own nature, he does not know enough to search it out. "The great end of learning is nothing else but to seek for the lost mind."[21] The problem is not only to learn what to seek but also to learn the means of seeking it. Men think they value life and dread death; yet, "There are cases when men by a certain course might preserve life, and they do not employ it; when by certain things they might avoid danger, and they will not do them." There is no part of a man which he himself does not love, Mencius continued, so we try to preserve every inch of our skin from harm. Yet what shall we say of a man who is so fond of eating and drinking that he neglects the cultivation of what is more important to him?

This trend of argument proved confusing to the disciples, one of whom observed: you have said all men are alike in their basic nature; yet now you indicate that some do what is proper, some not; how can this be? "Those who follow that part of themselves which is great are great men," Mencius replied; "those who follow that part which is little are little men."

"Benevolence is man's mind," he insisted, "and righteousness is man's path." But why, then, a disciple asked, do some men depart from this path by following that in themselves which is small? "The senses of hearing and seeing do not think," Mencius replied, "and are obscured by external things. When one thing comes in contact with another, as a matter of course it leads it away. To the mind belongs the office of thinking. By thinking, it gets the right view of things; by neglecting to think, it fails to do this. . . . Let a man first stand fast in the supremacy of the nobler part of his constitution, and the inferior part will not be able to take it from him. It is simply this which makes the great man."

To be truly benevolent is the natural way of man, he went on; but the easy way—following the smaller part—is to practice just so much benevolence as may be observed by others, or as may seem to be required. Benevolence subdues evil, he observed, just as water subdues fire. But if men practice benevolence with restraint, it is like trying to put out a large fire with a cup of water. Such a practice must fail, and this failure discourages those who are of small benevolence. The result is that those with small benevolence give it up altogether. To clarify his point further, Mencius added: the best of grain will not grow unless the seed is matured. "So, the value of benevolence depends entirely upon its being brought to maturity."

The rhetorical significance of Book VI seems clear: believe in your own goodness, do good with all your might, and all men will respond by themselves being good. In this way you become a great leader. On the contrary, usually you distrust your own goodness, for the reason that you do not observe goodness in the behavior of others. Hence you try to attain your ends either by small measures of benevolence or by altogether pursuing selfish goals. The result is that your example encourages the evil behavior of others. In a popular but perverted sense, you may then be considered to be a leader, inasmuch as you are contributing to shape the conduct of the group. Nevertheless, with everyone, under these circumstances, intent upon seeking his own individual goal, men are leaderless; their acts are not unified but diverse—not working together, but each for himself. Those who seem to be leading and guiding the group are actually disrupting and corrupting those whom they influence.

This pseudo-leadership, which Mencius condemned by indirection, had been condemned directly by Confucius, during his brief tenure as Minister of Justice, when he sentenced a demagogue to death, on the grounds that "his arguments could easily appeal to the mob and make perversity appear respectable; and that his sophistry was sufficiently recalcitrant to take a stand against the accepted judgments of right."[22] On this ground Mencius trod where Confucius had mapped the way.

In the second part of Book VI, Mencius dealt with various objections and counter-proposals raised by his disciples. They, no less than the general public, found it difficult to believe that men could be persuaded to act in accordance with the goodness presumed innate in their own natures. A disciple, for example, declared that if the kings of Ts'in and Ts'ee were about to go to war with one another, he would go first to one, then to the other, to try to dissuade them from fighting. To Mencius' question of what persuasive appeal he would use, the disciple replied that he would tell them how unprofitable their proposed warfare would be to them. No one, he would point out to them, really wins a war.

"Master," Mencius courteously replied to him, "your aim is great, but your argument is not good." He explained: if you get them to stop the war in order to gain greater profit for themselves, they, their generals, and their soldiers will gladly forgo the war to seek their own advantage. "Ministers will serve their sovereign for the profit of which they cherish the thought; sons will serve their fathers, and younger brothers will serve their elder brothers, for the same consideration: and the issue will be that, abandoning benevolence and righteousness, sovereign and minister, father and son, younger brother and elder, will carry on all their intercourse with the thought of profit cherished in their breasts. But never has there been such a state of society without ruin being the result of it." No, Mencius counselled, do not advise peace because it is profitable; urge it because such is the way of benevolence and righteousness. The result of such a plea, he admitted, was indeterminate. The appeal might not prevail. But if it did, only good and not additional evil would result.

Later in the colloquy, still attempting to mould his disciples into wise ministers who would serve truly the genuine needs of the state, Mencius dramatically told them that evil men who aid the king in pursuing an established train of wickedness have only minor guilt; greatly guilty are those who advise him in ways that lead toward the commencement of wicked behavior. Those who counsel kings in ways designed to fill the royal treasuries and granaries are helping them to become robbers of the people. "The way in which a superior man serves his prince contemplates simply the leading him in the right path, and directing his mind to benevolence."

The confusions which beset men's minds, Mencius believed, derive from the failure to understand genuine meanings. And this failure derives not from an ambiguity or complexity in data, but from the mind of man being misled away from true insight. The misleading occurs because men depart from their normal nature to pursue goals which do not truly satisfy their needs. This departure may be caused by external circumstances, including natural calamities, or by force exerted by others, or from sophistic persuasion through which one person seeks to derive selfish advantage from others. The remedy is to help men to free their minds from mistaken notions; to direct their attention away from the superficialities which clamor for notice, back to the clear and simple realization that they themselves harbor benevolence toward men and cherish righteousness and that others, being creatures like themselves, must feel similarly. Then and only then will men deal toward one another with true propriety in a spirit of gentlemanliness, so that the Confucian goal of harmony may be attained.

THE ELEMENTS OF MENCIAN RHETORIC

As has been indicated, Mencius' principal rhetorical concept was that listeners may be induced to return to the original benevolence of their nature if the speaker clearly and convincingly leads them to understand the truth concerning the matter being discussed. No man, he believed, can see truth and turn away from it. The problem for the speaker, then, is primarily one of establishing a persuasive definition. Indeed, as will be shown later, he had a remarkable understanding of the complications of definition and worked out a thoroughly rhetorical way of solving the problem.

His rhetoric, however, dealt not only with a comprehensive problem to be solved but also with the specific methods for solving it. The rhetorical ideas which are dispersed throughout his book may be summarized in terms of the purposes of speech, the ethical problem of persuasion, the methods of persuasion, the abuses of persuasion to promote self-interest, and the need for evaluative and critical listening.

In his view, speech has three primary purposes. The first is to rectify human behavior through clarifying the understanding of the listeners. "Men for the most part err," he declared, "and are afterwards able to reform. They are distressed in their mind and perplexed in their thoughts, and then they arise to vigorous reformation. When things have been evidenced in men's [speakers'] looks, and set forth in their words, then they [the listeners] understand them."[23] The second purpose is to induce individuals to attain their own highest potentiality. "Those who follow that part of themselves which is great," he said, "are great men; those who follow that part which is little are little men. . . . Let a man first stand fast in the supremacy of the noblest part of his constitution, and the inferior part will not be able to take it from him. It is simply this which makes the great man."[24] And the third purpose is to defend sound doctrine against heretical attacks. He warned that "perverse" and "corrupt" teachings of "each for himself" on the one hand, and "to love all equally" on the other, both cause "delusions to spring up in men's minds and do injury to their practice of affairs." Therefore, Mencius explained, a principal goal of speech was "to put an end to those perverse doctrines, to oppose their one-sided actions and banish away their licentious expressions."[25]

The principal ethical problem of persuasion, in Mencius' view, is that in order to accomplish a goal that is immediately desirable, a speaker may be tempted to use motivational appeals which in the long run will induce greater evils than those he is attempting to avert. This view emerges with great clarity in his own practice—for example, in his long colloquies with King Hui and King Hsuan and in his brusque treatment of the King of Ts'e. To seek for immediate success in terms that insure eventual failure is not only a violation of ethics, as Mencius sought to demonstrate, but also a sacrifice of one's own essential purpose. To be ethical meant, to him, to be sincere—supported by his insistence that sincerity depends upon completeness and clarity of understanding.

The methods of persuasion that Mencius advocated are: first, to induce listeners by indirect suggestion to arrive for themselves at the right conclusions. To explain why he sometimes restrained the natural forthrightness of his speech, Mencius said: "There are many arts in teaching. I refuse, as inconsistent with my character, to teach a man, but I am only thereby still teaching him."[26] The second method is to make the listeners realize the sincerity of the speaker. Third, Mencius advocated emotional appeals to support the speaker's purpose. Like many another theorist both before and after him, Mencius frankly confessed that it was difficult to explain what he meant by emotions. Nevertheless, he insisted, men are governed more by their wants, fears, and hopes than by their minds, and if one is skillful with words he will be able to make listeners understand how the speaker's goals will serve the listeners' "flowing passion nature." His appeal to emotion was far more compelling than was Aristotle's reluctant awareness of emotional effects. For Mencius' conviction that men are basically benevolent led him to conclude that "The passion nature . . . is the mate and assistant of righteousness and reason. Without it, man is in a state of starvation." Follow your emotions where they lead you, he urged, for they develop as healthfully and naturally as growing grain. What the "passion nature" most strongly wants is precisely what the mind, when used properly, will rightly recommend. The argument is complicated, and Mencius himself was fully aware of its vagueness—as the discussion in Book II, Part 1, chapter 2, makes evident. But he was also staunchly convinced that unless an argument is supported by emotional force, it will probably be wrong and will surely be ineffective.

Fourth, like all the Chinese rhetoricians, Mencius believed that example is by far more powerful than argument. The people will respond in terms of their leader's behavior: "As the wind blows, the grass bends." Fifth, if the speaker is truly superior in his knowledge and understanding, the listeners will unfailingly note this fact and will be influenced accordingly to accept his counsel. Throughout his book, Mencius insists that rightness, as well as righteousness, will always prevail. Akin to this method is his sixth: persuasion depends on integrity. "Never," he said, "has a man who has bent himself been able to make others straight."[27] Finally, as seventh and eighth methods, he recommended reasoning by analogy—as he himself did repeatedly—and, like Confucius, appeal to authority as enshrined in the rules of propriety. To those who insist on their own individuality, he retorted that every man's truest nature is the common nature of the race. This is the path clearly defined by tradition, and to leave this path in the fanciful pursuit of what seems at the moment to be more natural or honest or appealing is to wander through the wilderness and be lost.

When speakers did wander from the right path and sought what appeared in a narrow and perverted view to be their own self-interests, they were misusing persuasion, and Mencius condemned them unsparingly. Actually, as has been seen, they were not only trying to mislead their listeners but were also undermining their own welfare. "If you look at their countenances," he said, "they are full of blushes. I do not desire to know such persons."[28] On this matter he was very explicit. "When a scholar speaks what he ought not to speak, by guile of speech seeking to gain some end; and when he does not speak what he ought to speak, by guile of silence seeking to gain some end, both these cases are of a piece with breaking through a neighbor's wall."[29]

Responsibility for ethical discourse, Mencius felt, was not borne wholly by speakers but must be shared also by listeners. When a disciple asked him to identify his own strongest quality, Mencius replied: "I know the significance of what is being said." Asked for further elucidation, he went on: "Inexact speech shows that something is being concealed; unrestrained speech, that something is being ensnared; evil speech, that discord is being created; evasive speech, that something is being omitted."[30]

These principal elements of the Mencian rhetoric are supplemented by many other indications of his general view of the importance of speech, both as it reveals true traits of the speaker and as it affects, for good or ill, social relationships. Insincerity in speech, he felt, can scarcely be concealed for it is evident to anyone who watches the speaker's eyes.[31] The style employed in speaking should be simple and direct, for "Words which are simple, while their meaning is far-reaching, are good words."[32] And if speakers violate sound practices, they can be taught to do better, since "Glibness arises simply from the speaker's not having been reproved."[33] Such are the random observations of one who never tired of exploring the problems of rhetoric.

Underlying these rhetorical elements were some general and deeply held convictions. One of them was that sincerity was the foundation of personal character and effectiveness. To Mencius sincerity was akin to righteousness. Western rhetoricians appear to consider sincerity a quality dependent on the perception of listeners. Listeners perceive the sincere speaker as one who believes what he is saying. Secondly, sincerity is valued as a means of fortifying the spirit of the speaker; if he truly means what he says, he can say it with greater confidence and can pursue his cause with more assiduity. These factors were also of importance to Mencius, as is evidenced in his declaration: "Never has there been one possessed of complete sincerity who did not move others. Never has there been one who had not sincerity who was able to move others."[34] On another occasion he warned against even the most careful and meticulous observance of the proprieties if this were done only in an effort to please, rather than because the speaker understood why they were requisite and felt the respect for others which they were intended to signal.[35]

But in Mencius' view, the persuasive effects of sincerity were directly derivative from and secondary to its effects upon the character of the sincere speaker. What was essential was that a man be sincere not for the effect this would have in influencing others but for the resultant peace and tranquility in his own mind and spirit.[36] The one person whom each of us most has to please is himself. Beyond this, he who attains equanimity of spirit is effective in dealing with others.

Sincerity becomes more than an undivided intensity of conviction. It is this plus a valid insight into the truth and righteousness of what is believed. In Western rhetoric it is far from inconceivable that a man may be sincere and wrong; indeed, sincerity is often cited as an excuse for wrong-headedness. In Mencian terms, this judgment would be inconceivable, because sincerity and validity are two inseparable qualities.

There is indeed, in the thought of Mencius, a distinction between being right and saying what seems to the speaker to be right or appropriate or demanded by the circumstances. But he was unsparing in his insistence that the requirements of rightness and righteousness are always the primary considerations. As was seen in Mencius' discourses with various rulers, he insisted upon telling them precisely what he thought to be true, even though the demands of propriety itself could readily have been interpreted to excuse him for telling them what they wanted to hear. The point is made with even greater insistence in his account of his public refusal to go to the king's court to tender counsel. As he explained to his friend, it was imperative to dramatize the fact that he decidedly would not please the king at the expense of his own feelings. And the nature of sincerity, in his view, was further clarified when he advised a disciple against the plan of arguing kings Ts'ee and Ts'in out of going to war on the plea that war is inevitably unprofitable to winner as well as loser. This plea might be effective and it is true so far as it goes; furthermore, the disciple could plead this case with utter conviction. The trouble was that ultimately that kind of argument would cause more evil than it would prevent and thus righteousness would be undermined rather than upheld.

Sincerity demands far more in the Mencian view than it does in Western terms: it demands ultimate responsibility for being right. And this was, finally, a demand Mencius could make with good grace, whereas it would be untenable in the West. For while Westerners generally consider truth to be ultimately inscrutable, to Mencius it was a broad pathway easily seen and not missed except when men chose not to follow it.

Why men of good will and intelligence differ—and thus why persuasion is needed to lead one to accept the views of another—may best be understood in terms of what I. A. Richards calls the "principle of Multiple Definition."[37] Every definition, he explains, is really multiple, involving subjective as well as objective elements. Every definition is composed from a particular point of view, and it is correct only from that stance. In order to view a subject truly it must be seen in terms of multiple definitions. This fact needs to be understood by both the speaker and his respondents for genuine communication to occur.

Like all Chinese philosophers, Mencius was no logician. He depended upon "chains of reasoning" which met no test more rigorous than mere coherence. He made free use of analogy, assuming it to be a form of proof. The syllogism was unknown to him and his countrymen. He did not try to interpret the effects of intention and attitude upon the perception of the nature and form of whatever might be spoken about. His definitions were purposely vague. To Mencius, meaning included the purpose or intent of the speaker, the attitude of the speaker toward both his subject and his listeners, and also the objective character of the subject matter. This view of meaning often renders it vague, for it comprehensively and indiscriminatively combines unknown and even unknowable components. But in a psychological sense, it may be the only way meaning can be interpreted.

When human beings communicate, their purpose and their attitudes are fully as realistically and truly involved as is the referent which their words presumably define. Both the speaker and the listeners are incorporated within the meaning, rather than passively observing it from outside. What Mencius sacrificed in clarity and definiteness, he regained in comprehensiveness and in socio-psychological realism. The truth he sought to encompass was not an ultimate reality known only in abstract meditation severed from human circumstances; his truth was a broad road readily seen by men, since its route lay through their experience and feelings.

He defined not what is true, but what is true to us, considering all the factors that will be taken into account by the participants, regardless of their logical relevance. He placed his faith not in any of the usually classified forms of definition—operational, literal, descriptive, or prescriptive—but in what may properly be called *rhetorical definition,* since its essential characteristic is its effort to encompass all the elements that would be accounted significant by speaker and listeners.

Naturally, a characteristic of such discourse is that the understanding resulting from it would be variable. Purposes of speakers and of listeners need not be identical; their attitudes may differ toward the subject and toward one another; and each may view the referent differently. Nevertheless, the subject matter is depicted in such inclusive terms that each may comfortably see within it his own meanings and may feel an extensive latitude for diverse meanings entertained by the other. It is precisely because of such nonlogical qualities that the analogy and the example are held in Western tradition to be extra-logical contrivances. But precisely because of such qualities, they are considered in Chinese practice, including the practice of Mencius, to be rationally valid. It is not logic but the principle of coherence that governs the natural sequence of ordinary discourse, and it is when this natural sequence is violated that men's minds begin to devise objections to what is being said.

This is not precisely the point made by Hu Shih in his *Development of the Logical Method*. But it seems to be descriptive of the methods of the reasoning-to-a-conclusion used by Mencius, and also by Confucius—and, as will be seen, by Mo-Tze and others of the early Chinese rhetorical philosophers.

In this interpretative summary of the rhetorical ideas of Mencius, it appears that he was a valiant and brilliant defender of Confucian principles. He was more than that. He was an independent and constructive thinker in his own right. Confucius clearly saw the value of bringing one's own sharpest independent judgment to the test of comparison with the best that has been thought and said and done in purer primitive times. Mencius agreed, but he felt there was also another criterion that was even more valid: the truth. This was a criterion not easily avoided, he believed, because the truth can be sensed intuitively by anyone who cultivates the clarity of vision which is truly innate.

No rhetorician has ever demanded of his disciples that they be bolder in adhering to the truth as they see it. None has been more adamant in his insistence that whatever ought to be done because it is right can be done because the rightness is wholly available to observation and understanding. Mencian rhetoric offers no defense for those who thoughtlessly or ignorantly offer wrong counsel to their listeners. More even than Confucius, Mencius posed the challenge to every speaker to rise to his own highest moral and intellectual potential. The heart of his rhetoric was in his refusal to accept the dictum succinctly phrased by Ralph Waldo Emerson: "Men's minds descend to meet." Men's minds most surely meet, Mencius observed, when they rise up to the altitude of a selfless vision of truth. For the one thing on which all men may finally agree is their acceptance of the truth when it is clearly and truly stated.

CHAPTER 11

Theorists of Human Motivation

CONFUCIUS AND MENCIUS were concerned with the nature of the good life, which they enjoined well-meaning individuals to follow. Like all rhetoricians, they speculated about what motives might induce desired action, and how these motives might be activated. Still other philosophers, roughly contemporaneous with them, gave much more explicit consideration to the fundamentals of human motivation. As has remained true of motivational theorists through succeeding centuries, their conceptions were basically philosophical and hence were broadly various. Motivational speculation necessarily is founded upon personality theory. How people may be induced to behave in prescribed ways inevitably depends upon the characteristics of their human nature. Hence students of human motivation are first of all students of personality structure. Their motivational systems depend directly on their diverse views of human personality.[1]

No rhetorician could possibly avoid consideration of what people basically are like and of how they may be persuaded through appeals based on their innate and acquired characteristics. But to some rhetoricians these considerations are unexamined or little examined prior assumptions—preliminary determinations made or accepted from the cogitations of others before the rhetorical problems of application to discourse are explicitly confronted. It is as though they say to the philosophers or the psychologists: "You tell us what man is like and we shall undertake to consider how such men may communicate effectively." Other rhetoricians consider the two types of insight to be inextricably interrelated. To them the application of motive depends directly upon the analysis of personality. When the nature of the person is understood, they feel, the means of inducing his reactions will be derived inevitably. The rhetorician of this type is fundamentally a motivational theorist.

In this chapter are brought together Mo-Tze the Utopian, Hui Shih

182

and Kung-Sun Lung the rationalists, and Hsüntze the Confucianist—men who had little in common except their focal interest in personality theory as the essential guide to motivational conclusions. They were pioneers among the rhetoricians who insist that nothing is more practical than sound theory—that insight into the nature of man must precede consideration of how persuasion may become effective.

An even more significant rhetorical contribution by the men grouped in this chapter is that they very considerably broadened the social range of rhetoric. In the *Book of History,* in the several works on etiquette and ritual, and in the speculations of Confucius and of Mencius there was little specific consideration for any social group except that of the court. It was the considered view of Confucius and of Mencius that if the king behaved well his nobles would do likewise, and if the nobles set good examples, the people would conform to them. Mo-Tze, however, took all mankind as his province and laid down precepts that were to govern the behavior of the peasants as well as of the courtiers. The pseudo-logicians believed they had penetrated to an understanding of the basic operations of the human mind—not just of the kingly and aristocratic mind, but of mental processes wherever and whenever noted. And Hsüntze set himself the formidable task of redeeming Confucianism from what he considered to be a major heresy by Mencius and of demonstrating its utility at all levels of society and for all circumstances. Under their influence, Chinese rhetoric became a social instrument applicable in the rice-paddy villages and in the bargaining among merchants fully as much as in the courtly circles where wary (and sometimes wise) ministers gingerly offered advice to autocratic (and often fickle) monarchs.

Mo-Tze the Utopian

For a hundred and fifty years, during the fifth and fourth centuries B.C., after the death of Confucius and before the maturation of Mencius, Mohism—the teachings of Mo-Tze—was a formidable adversary of Confucianism in China. Then, principally because of the effectiveness of Mencius and of Hsüntze, which led to the establishment of the Confucian canon as the basis for education, Mohism virtually disappeared from the history of Chinese thought, not to be revived again until the twentieth century. True, during the eighteenth century, when the Manchu invaders were attempting to consolidate the support of the influential scholars for their imposed regime by sponsoring the publication of critical editions of all the ancient classics,[2] a definitive edition of the long-neglected *Book of Mo-Tze* was issued at Peiping, in 1784, with the text edited by Pi-Yuan. Concurrently, however, the regime's emphasis upon rigid adherence to formal Confucianism prevented any public interest in Mohism.

It was not until a group of French Catholic scholars (notably Maurice Courant in 1900 and Mme. Alexander David in 1907) commenced to reinforce their contention of the universality of the Roman Catholic religious concepts by citing Mo-Tze as a presumed exemplar of similar doctrines, that studies of his views and influence began to multiply.[3] Even then, such studies were far more concerned to use his authority in support of their authors' religious, social, or political views than to note the original and valid ideas which Mo-Tze presented. The religionist use of Mo-Tze culminated in a doctoral dissertation presented at Loyola University, Chicago, in 1945, and published in Taipei twenty years later: *The Moral Philosophy of Mo-Tze,* by Augustinus A. Tseu, in which Mo-Tze is virtually reinterpreted as a proto-Christian. Social philosophers began to cite Mo-Tze to support their pacifistic and egalitarian ideas.[4] Chiang Kai-shek and Madame Chiang utilized the teachings of Mo-Tze as a basis for their "New Life Movement" in the 1930's.[5]

It was not until 1929 that there appeared the first translation of Mo-Tze's works into English. It was through this edition that the Mohist ideas began to be considered in modern times in terms of their own worth, rather than in terms of what support they might offer for other causes. This book was the edition prepared by Mei Yi-Pao, *Moral and Political Works of Motse,* now, unfortunately, out of print. For such reasons Mo-Tze is not widely known, and his influence has not been significant except in recent years in China.

The *Book of Mo-tze* consisted originally of seventy-one chapters, which were in the form of popular lectures, probably addressed to his three hundred disciples, and preserved from their notes. Ten chapters were wholly lost, and eight are known only by their titles. Of the remainder, some forty chapters (8 through 39 and 47 through 61) are considered to be authentically compiled from the notes kept by Mo-Tze's immediate disciples. The rest were apparently added by later followers, consisting of their interpretation of what they thought their master probably had believed.[6]

Concerning Mo-Tze's life, little is known. Even the dates of his birth and death are lost. It is presumed that he was born in the state of Lu— the same province that nurtured Confucius and Mencius—shortly after the death of Confucius, and that he died shortly before the birth of Mencius. The dates, "somewhat arbitrary and certainly approximate," which his biographer Yi-Pao Mei assigned for him are from 470 B.C. to 391 B.C.[7] He is believed to have served for a time as a high official in the state of Sung. His disciples described him as being of dark complexion and negligent in his dress. He ate and drank frugally and led a very simple life.[8] Chuang-Tzu, writing a few years after the death of Mo-Tze, declared that he and his disciples wore short worsted jackets and straw sandals—and that they toiled day and night without rest, making self-mortification their goal. "Not to set the future an example of extravagance nor be wasteful of anything in nature; not to glory in quantities; to restrain oneself with a plumb line, as it were"—such was Chuang-Tzu's summation of the teachings and example of Mo-Tze. Then he added sourly: "When one teaches people such things I fear there is no love for others; and when one practices such things, certainly there is no love for oneself." In his view, this was "the zenith of disorder and the nadir of good order." Even so he considered Mo-Tze a genuine humanitarian and concluded, "He was certainly a talented man."[9]

From his lectures, it is evident that Mo-Tze was highly practical and very active. His disciples declared that he never warmed a seat, for he sat still so little. His aim was to reform society and his goal was always to attain practical results. In addition to being a theorist, he was also an assiduous inventor and promoter of defensive weapons of war, which he frequently urged rulers to acquire as a means of discouraging aggression. He is remembered as a pragmatic Utopian idealist; the ideal he most persistently pursued was that of practical action that might lead to social justice for all.

The ideas with which he is most closely identified are universal love and the doctrine of human equality. These ideas he persistently advocated in public addresses noted for their "simplicity of style, clarity of exposition, depth of conviction, and directness of appeal."[10] No one believes that there are any precise extant texts remaining, or even that it is known when or to whom Mo-Tze spoke. But the record of his discourses in the book put together by his disciples provides convincing internal evidence that an eloquent man was pressing home to intent listeners convictions which he felt they must embrace for their own good and for the preservation of society. In the following passage, translated by Hu Shih, the living tones of Mo-Tze's voice may almost be heard as he employed vivid analogies, questions, comparisons, reiteration, cumulation, vituperative scorn, and personal appeal in condemning aggressive war:

> Here is a man who enters his neighbor's orchard and steals some peaches and plums therefrom. When this is known, he is con-

demned by the public, and, when caught, will be fined by the government. Wherefore? Because he has injured his neighbor to profit himself.

And if he steals from his neighbor a dog, a pig, or a chicken, he commits a wrong greater than the stealing of peaches and plums. Why? Because he has done a greater injury to another man; and the greater the injury he does, the greater is the wrong, and the severer shall be his punishment.

And if he steals his neighbor's horse or cow, he commits a wrong still greater than stealing a dog, a pig, or a chicken. Why? Because he does a greater injury to another; and the more he injures another, the greater is the wrong, and the severer shall be his punishment.

And if he goes as far as to waylay an innocent man, take away his fur cloak, and stab him with his sword, then his crime is still greater than that of stealing a horse or a cow. Why? Because he has done thereby a still greater injury. And the greater the injury a man does to another, the greater is his crime, and the severer shall be his punishment.

In all these cases the gentlemen of the world agree to condemn this man and declare, "He is wrong!"

Now here is the greatest of all crimes—the invasion of one nation by another. But the gentlemen of the world not only refuse to condemn it, but even praise it, and declare, "It is right!"

Shall we say that these gentlemen know the distinction between right and wrong? . . .

Here is a man who sees a few black things and calls them black, but who, after seeing many black things, calls them white. We must all say that this man does not know the distinction between black and white.

Here is another man who tastes a few bitter things and calls them bitter, but who, after having tasted many bitter things, calls them sweet. We must all say that this man knows not the distinction between bitter and sweet.

Here is the world which condemns a petty wrong and praises the greatest of all wrongs—the attack of one nation upon another—and calls it right. Can we say that the world knows the distinction between right and wrong?[11]

This is surely an eloquent and vivid use of rhetoric to condemn aggression. Living as Mo-Tze did, while the turmoil amid the Warring

States was causing death, suffering, and disruption in the cities and villages of all China, he saw many reasons around him for hating war. But in a cardinal respect his speaking belied his own rounded understanding. His rhetorical skill in this instance undermined the clarity of his judgment. The summation of his remarks preserved by his disciples suggests that to Mo-Tze the ethical problem posed by war is inevitably clear and simple. War is bad, peace is good. However, his lifetime behavior indicates that he realized full well the complexity of conflict. He was, as has been pointed out, an inventor of defensive weapons and was assiduous in promoting their adoption and use. Moreover, he well knew that in the tangled affairs of states, with the succession to the throne often in doubt, and with many injuries inflicted in many ways by one state upon another, it often is wholly impossible to determine which state is the aggressor and which one the defender. As has been true of many speakers throughout history, he permitted himself, in this passage, to let persuasive ability and his love of influencing listeners dominate his own understanding of the subject he was discussing.

On some matters Mo-Tze was unmistakably clear. Most fundamentally, he utterly rejected the Confucian-Mencian principle of selective love. The fivefold obligations of exclusively loving and serving one's sovereign, parents, spouse, children, and friends, which the Confucian sages advocated, could only lead to conflict and to injustice in relations with all other people, Mo-Tze believed. If love is circumscribed to a designated few, the indifference felt for the many will inevitably lead to disregard for their rights or their feelings, thereby arousing antagonisms that lead to oppression and struggle. In his view, love which is not extended universally is self-defeating. Not to love the strangers beyond one's own family or clan means to exclude them from beneficial behavior. This in turn arouses their resentment. And resentment readily expresses itself in detrimental actions that injure the circle of those who are loved. Thus the restriction of love to a few results in injury to those very ones who are the exclusive objects of one's devotion. To Mo-Tze the principle seemed clear that love is truly love only when it extends to all mankind.

From this reasoning flowed a concurrent idea that all men are essentially equal. If they are unequal, there would be reason for preferring (hence loving) some more than others. If all are to be loved alike, all are to be valued alike; all in effect are to be considered alike. He never questioned the social and political stratification which constituted the only society he knew. But he did challenge directly the view that those who held higher positions were indeed superior. To manifest his belief in equality, he lived as simply as did the peasants and, like them, worked in the fields with his hands. The dignity of labor was another necessary conclusion from his basic teachings.

In still another important respect Mo-Tze's teachings differed widely from those of the Confucianists. To the Confucianists the good that was to derive from decorously proper behavior was social harmony. The reason for behaving toward others with justice and courtesy was that the nature of human beings is such that we respond harmoniously to one another only when we treat one another with mutual respect and in accepted ways. But to Mo-Tze righteousness was of value for its own sake. Without having any clear conception of a divine essence in the universe, he nevertheless had a distinct idea that there is a natural law, or a natural state of being, which is inviolate. And, to him, righteousness was an implicit aspect of natural order. An individual should love all mankind not because this would lead to harmony, but because it was right to do so. All men should be treated with equal consideration and justice not as a social expedient but as a recognition of similarity in their innate nature. The ultimate test to which he brought his philosophy was not, after all, social effects, but adherence to reality.[12]

Actually, Mo-Tze was neither a religionist, a materialist, a pragmatist, nor, strictly, a humanist. Like all his Chinese predecessors, he believed deeply in harmony as the greatest good. The difference is that whereas Confucius and Mencius (as well as most of the other theorists, named or anonymous) centered their thinking upon the harmony of man's social relations, Mo-Tze insisted upon adherence by man to an underlying harmony of nature. In this respect his views were so much like those of the Hindu-Buddhist tradition that some scholars have suspected he must somehow have been influenced from India. Much more probably, he was influenced by the distinctly Chinese philosophy of Taoism—though, as will be seen, its passivism was in sharp contrast to his activism.

From the foregoing considerations, several significant conclusions emerge concerning Mo-Tze's theories of rhetorical motivation. First, his basic aim was to teach the means of living individually and socially in harmony with the innate and unalterable nature of the universe. Second, this aim, he believed, could not be attained by adhering passively to primitivistic tendencies but by seeking actively to eradicate unrighteous behavior. Third, the principal motivational inducement to desirably harmonious behavior is universal love. Universal love is natural to man because it is in accord with the ultimate basic harmony of all nature. Universal love can be taught to erring men by showing them that only through loving all mankind can they, their family, their state, and their friends hope to benefit. Fourth, through universal love, it is apparent that all men are equal. Among equals, changes of behavior must be sought through persuasion, not through force or appeal to authority. Among equals, whatever motivational appeals are used must be such as comport with feelings of self-respect and of regard for the dignity and personal worth of the one to be influenced. Fifth, there is no means of avoiding personal responsibility for one's words and acts, and for the results flowing from them. Responsibility cannot be shifted to a superior, for, morally, no man has superiors. Responsibility cannot be shifted to fate, or circumstances, or nature, for each man should act in accordance with the fundamental harmony of nature. And sixth, the principal persuasive method, then, is to assist listeners to comprehend the means of behaving harmoniously—that is, lovingly. To understand what is truly right includes the understanding that to behave righteously is to live in accordance with one's own nature. Such understanding induces right conduct as the only means of being true to oneself and thereby of accomplishing one's own wellbeing. By this reasoning, conflict between selfishness and unselfishness is eliminated by the claim that they are essentially the same: whatever truly helps oneself helps mankind, and whatever truly helps mankind helps oneself. The individual is interpreted as being an integral portion of the totality of nature.

In Mo-Tze's view, his basic insight—that all nature is one integral and hence harmonious whole—was self evident when examined and therefore irrefutable. When opponents urged him to reconsider this concept, in view of the many apparent disharmonies and conflicts, he replied loftily: "My principle is sufficient. To abandon my principle and exercise thought is like abandoning the crop and trying to pick up grains. To refute my principle with one's own principles is like throwing an egg against a boulder. The eggs in the world would be exhausted without doing any harm to the boulder."[13] When a disciple questioned the wisdom of his continual recommendation of righteousness, in view of the general indifference to moral considerations, Mo-Tze replied: "Suppose a man has ten sons. Only one attends to the farm, while the other nine stay home. Then the one who does the farming must work all the more vigorously. Why? Because many eat while few work. Now, none in the world practices righteousness. Then you should all the more encourage me to continue my teachings."[14]

Despite Mo-Tze's faith in the self-evident truth of his insight, he did not advocate unthinking adherence to it. Men and communities deviate from the right in many ways; hence, the rectification of their conduct must rest upon analysis of the nature of their deviation. When a disciple sought to gain from him a simple categorical statement of what should be taught, Mo-Tze retorted with the insistence of a true rhetorician upon audience adaptation: "Upon entering a country one should locate the need and work on that. If the country is upset and in confusion, teach them with the Exaltation of the Virtuous and Identification with the [political and social] Superior. If the country is in poverty, teach them with Economy of Expenditures and Simplicity of Funerals. If the country is indulging in music and wine, teach them with Condemnation of Music and Antifatalism. If the country is insolent and without propriety, teach them to reverence heaven and worship the spirits. If the country is engaged in conquest and oppression, teach them with Universal Love and Condemnation of Offensive War. Hence we say one should locate the need and work on that."[15] Whatever the situation, the speakers should always aim at results, never at impressiveness, or mere entertainment. "Any principle that can modify conduct," Mo-Tze advised, "expound much; any principle that cannot modify conduct, do not expound much. To expound much that which can not modify conduct is just to wear out one's mouth."[16]

To enforce his insistence that choices should be made on the basis of practicality for achieving specified goals, Mo-Tze used the following analogy: "Suppose that your parents met with disaster thirty-five miles away. And there was just a single day within which they must be reached if their lives were to be saved. Here are a strong wagon and an excellent horse, and also a bad horse and a square-wheeled cart. If you were allowed to choose, which one would you take?"[17]

The primary authority to which Mo-Tze appealed when his own reasoning was not deemed (by his listeners or by himself) to be sufficient was the precepts or the example of ancient sages. Because he forebore references to contemporary events and preferred (like Christian preachers who use illustrations from the Bible) to cite incidents from the remote past, he was occasionally likened by his critics to "the carpenter who knows only the decaying lumber but not the living tree."[18] His defense, however, was much like that with which Confucius defended his own similar practice: "We are to rely upon what many have jointly seen and many have jointly heard."[19]

However, in his reliance upon antiquity, Mo-Tze was Confucian with a difference. Confucius relied heavily on antecedents drawn from the Chou dynasty, and from events related in the *Book of History*. As a principal editor of the classics, Confucius was sensitive to historical specificity and accuracy. Mo-Tze, on the other hand, drew his historical authority mainly from the Hsia dynasty, which flourished a thousand years earlier than the Chou. Because the events to which he referred were only dimly known and hazily interpreted, he could and did imbue them with his own sense of what was significant. In effect, he presented his own views but enforced them with such a vague phrase as, "as was known (or done) in ancient times." By these means he maintained the utmost freedom for innovation while aiming also for the authoritarian support of traditionalism.

Mo-Tze, however, also had a secondary court of appeal which he used for authoritarian support, with more originality. He would submit on assertion to the test of congruent observation. "The way to find out whether anything exists or not," he argued, "is to depend on the testimony of the ears and eyes of the multitude. If some have heard it or some have seen it then we have to say it exists. If no one has heard it and no one has seen it then we have to say it does not exist. So, then, why not go to some village or some district and inquire?"[20] This attitude depends heavily on social concurrence, on everyday experience, and on harmony of opinion, rather than, as often in the West, upon objective measurement which is indifferent to popular beliefs.

The view that what people believe is what must be believed is a pseudo-logical tool to be used with extreme caution. Mo-Tze was far too keenly aware that men may be led into errors of belief and conduct to accept any such principle carelessly. What he meant was that the basic understanding of people provides a court of appeal. He well realized that a speaker might have to drive through clusters of misunderstandings in order to bring his listeners to an awareness of what constituted even their own genuine beliefs. Both his insight into how people normally act in contradiction to their own understandings, and his methodology in penetrating through the false façade to the underlying certainties, are well illustrated in the following passage from one of his lectures:

> Gentlemen of the world today know small things and do not know great things. How do we know? We know from their conduct at home. If in their conduct at home they offend their elders, there are still the homes of neighbors to which to flee. Yet relatives, brothers, and acquaintances all warn and admonish them, saying, "You must be cautious. You must be careful. How can it be to offend elders in one's conduct at home?" Not only is this true of conduct at home. It is also true of conduct in the state. If in one's conduct in the state one should offend the ruler, there are still the

neighboring states to which to flee. Yet relatives, brothers, and acquaintances all warn and caution him, saying, "You must be cautious. You must be careful. How can it be to offend the ruler by one's conduct in the state?" These are people who have places to which to flee. Yet the warning and caution to them are strong like this. Should the warning and caution not be much stronger for those who have no place to flee? There is a saying: "If one commits a sin in daylight, where can he flee?" I say: There is no place to flee. For heaven should not be regarded as a forest, a valley, or an obscure gate, where no one is present. It will surely see the evil action clearly. But with regard to heaven, gentlemen of the world today are all negligent and do not warn and caution one another. This is how we know that the gentlemen of the world know small things but do not know great things.[21]

For "heaven" in this passage, we might properly read "universe," for Mo-Tze meant no more than to reassert the basic unity and harmony of nature. Whatever one may do must be done within the intermeshing unity of all being. There is no hiding a thought, a word, or an act, since every individual item is an indissoluble part of the whole, and if a word, thought, or act violates the harmony (or the ethic) of the whole, the disharmony which results will be apparent. As Mo-Tze points out, this all men know, even when they act in ways that are selfish, or base, as if they somehow felt their own particular deeds could be hidden. He felt that the motivational appeal which works best is to remind his hearers of their own genuine insight, which has become concealed from their own notice by their temporary concentration upon some limited and selfish goal.

This same method of appeal through and beyond false ideas, which act as a screen to the vital insights underlying them, was also used by Mo-Tze in a speech on the redeeming quality of universal love, preserved in Chapter 15 of his book. To his vivid depiction of the glories of a world in which calamities, usurpation, hatred, and animosity were all prevented by the dynamism of universal love, his listeners responded that this might be very well, except that the practice of universal love is too difficult to be attained. The presumed difficulty, Mo-Tze responded, lies simply in misunderstanding. Everyone agrees that the personal sacrifice demanded by warfare, often to the extent of the sacrifice of one's life, is difficult. Yet when a ruler asks for this sacrifice in war, his people readily grant it. To ask people all to love one another, he went on, is to ask much less of them. "Those who love others will be loved by others. Those who benefit others will be benefited by others. Those who hate others will be hated by others. And those who harm others will be harmed by others. Then what difficulty is there in this universal love?" The only real difficulty, he concluded, is that rulers do not make it their governmental policy and officials do not set this example for their people.

Confucius and Mencius condemned the tendency of the unphilosophical to seek profit or benefits, rather than to pursue righteousness. Mo-Tze frankly and fully accepted what he regarded as a fundamental of human nature, that individuals will pursue what they conceive to be their own self-interest. What he sought to teach was that benefit for oneself may be found only through dedication to righteousness, expressed in universal love.

This was the foundation of his rhetoric: a view that persuasion operates best not by trying to attain dominance over others but by manifesting a unifying and harmonizing love for them. It was an ethical view that confounded sophistry by equating effectiveness with philanthropy. To six generations of Chinese this rhetoric was wondrously appealing. In the twentieth century, when it is remembered again, the difficulties of manifesting universal love seem especially apparent. But so, too, does the urgency of the need for it. Today, after two thousand years of neglect, Mo-Tze has an audience again.

THE RATIONALISTIC RHETORICIANS

Chinese logic, from its beginnings, has been more concerned with how matters *appear* to be than with how they actually *are*. According to Hu Shih, the logic which has dominated Chinese history from about the sixth century B.C. "is an inductive method without the requisite details of procedure."[22] In effect, the Chinese said to one another, *study a subject thoroughly and you will know what is true about it.* In *The Great Learning,* a classic of Confucian scholarship which has dominated Chinese education, the principle is stated as follows: "When knowledge is extended to the utmost, our ideas will be made true."[23] In another translation, the same sentence reads: "Their knowledge being complete, their thoughts were sincere."[24]

Since Chinese civilization has been dominated by the ideal of social harmony, it is not strange that *what is factual* mattered less than *what is accepted as being factual;* that being *right* was secondary to being *sincere. Dependability* to them always meant *interdependability.* A statement is true when it is held to be true by the people considering it—when it serves their needs—when under all anticipated circumstances it may serve as a guide to their conduct. In Western terms, this kind of thinking is not rational but rationalistic; not logical but rhetorical. Not strangely, then, the so-called Chinese logicians have been sophistical rhetoricians.

One of the earliest of whom record remains was Hiao-Cheng Mao, who is said to have been executed by Confucius during the philosopher's brief tenure as Minister of Justice, because Mao "was capable of gathering about him large crowds of men; . . . his arguments could easily appeal to the mob and make perversity appear respectable; and . . . his sophistry was sufficiently recalcitrant to take a stand against the accepted judgments of right."[25] The nub of the charge against him was not that he was wrong as to fact but that it was wrong to arouse the people against "accepted judgments."

Another of the rationalistic rhetoricians, also executed for unsettling the minds and loyalties of the populace, was Teng Shih, who was so eloquent that "He could argue a right to be wrong, and a wrong to be right. With him right and wrong had no fixed standard, and 'yea' and 'nay' changed every day. What he wished to win was always won; and whom he desired to punish was always punished."[26] Like the Sophists of Athens, he taught the people how to plead their own cause in the law courts; and like them he took pay for his instruction. His career is recounted in a third-century B.C. compilation known as the *Lu shih ch'un-ch'iu,* or *The Spring and Autumn Annals of Mr. Lu,* which goes on to warn that "words often seem to be wrong when they are actually right, and often seem to be right when they are actually wrong." As an instance, the compiler explained: "One must be critical when dealing with words. When a story has been passed along from one person to another a number of times, white often turns into black and black becomes white. A dog resembles a baboon, a baboon resembles an ape, and an ape resembles a man; but a man is a long way from being a dog. This is just how fools are led into serious error. If people stop to consider what they hear, they will win good fortune; but if they fail to do so, it would be better that they didn't hear anything at all." Then the narrator added: "And how does one go about being careful? Only if one examines what he hears in the light of the logic of things and the common sense of human affairs will he get at the truth."[27] Once again, the court of final appeal is "the common sense of human affairs." In a political society, in which harmony is the greatest good, what everyone believes is what everyone must believe.

In the writings of Hsüntze, to be considered in the concluding section of this chapter, Teng Shih is linked with a greater logician, Hui Shih—both of whom Hsüntze ridiculed because they were more interested in abstract logic than in the practical usefulness of ideas. "They are very critical," he says, "but do not care about the usefulness of their ideas; they debate but impractically. They make much fuss but accomplish little; their doctrines cannot be the unifying bond of good government. Yet what they support seems reasonable; their teachings are plausible, sufficiently so to deceive and mislead the ignorant multitude."[28]

Hui Shih attracted so much attention with his contradictory aphorisms and paradoxes that Chuang-Tzu paid him the compliment of concluding his book with an attack upon him. In his view, "Hui Shih became the cynosure of the world's eyes, for he did know how to debate." His faults were that "he expounded upon all things . . . without stopping, just as when there is not much to say, one adds striking remarks to one's tale." His aim, so Chuang-Tzu believed, was "to gain a reputation for arguing others down," but he failed finally to win the hearts and minds of the people.[29]

Another Chinese historian, Wing-tsit Chan, agrees that "logicians" is a term scarcely applicable to these rationalistic rhetoricians. "Actually," he writes, "they neither evolved any syllogism nor discovered any law of thought. They expressed themselves in dialogues, aphorisms, and paradoxes instead of systematic and cogent argumentation."[30] Despite the label commonly applied to them, they were not logicians but rhetoricians. The question they asked themselves was: *how does the mind of a speaker work when he confronts a proposition which he wishes to have accepted by specific listeners?* Their theme was persuasion, not logic. The particular persuasive approach they favored was to confound opposition by presenting a statement which startled the mind of the listener out of its customary patterned responses and invited acceptance of the notion the speaker wished to implant.

Despite what we are told by his contemporaries about the debating skill of Hui Shih, all that is attributed to him that is still extant is a series of individual paradoxical statements, none elaborated. Some of these are suggestive of their extended meanings. For example, "One goes to the state of Yueh today and arrives there yesterday" probably means to remind us that the mind, in anticipation, flies far ahead of the body. "The egg has hair" is an indirect assertion that a thing is what it is capable of becoming. "A dog can be a sheep" must be a reminder that larger categories ("animal") can incorporate entities which appear to be entirely separate. "The eye does not see" leads to the conclusion that perception is at best partial and misleading.

"When the sun is at noon it is setting; when there is life, there is death" is, upon reflection, a truism—yet it would be useful as an aphorism to remind enthusiasts (or pessimists) that what they most admire (or dread) is inevitably of short duration. "Fire is not hot" may serve to suggest that the effect a thing has may be different from the nature of the thing itself. "The shadow of a flying bird does not move" is a reminder that how a thing appears depends upon the point of view from which it is observed; for, to the bird, looking down, its shadow must appear always to be immovably fixed beneath it.

Such a rationalist was Hui Shih—a man who delighted in breaking through the established mental patterns of his associates and forcing them to look anew at their own understandings of things. It is probable that he applied this abstract reasoning to current problems, for Chuang-Tzu says of him: "Hui Shih, out of his great knowledge, carried on debates every day with others. He was a perfect marvel when compared with the other dialecticians and sophists of the world." His greatest fault, at least to Chuang-Tzu, was that his interests were too diverse, his imagination too far ranging. "He scattered himself insatiably over the whole of nature and ended with a reputation for cleverness in dialectic. How sad it is! Despite his inspiration, Hui Shih was too diffuse, so he did not succeed."[31] Regrettably, no more is known of him than this—not even the end to which he came.

In the opinion of his contemporaries, the greatest of the so-called logicians was Kung-Sun Lung, who in our own time would probably be considered a semanticist. According to his disciples, "He was grieved by the confusion and divergence in names and realities."[32] His forte was classification, which in turn was dependent upon definition. As he well understood, men are led into numerous errors because they mistakenly confuse their own understanding by forming false classifications based upon misleading or incomplete or inadequately considered definitions. In his own time (from about 320 to about 250 B.C.) he won such high favor that he was successively pampered and honored by the Princes of Chao and of Wei. But among the scholars he was unpopular—perhaps because, like Socrates, his method was to lead them through questions and challenges to confute themselves and to deny their own prior assumptions. As a motivational theorist, he understood how to dominate men's minds but not how to satisfy their egoistic needs.

One of his favorite themes was that "a white horse is not a horse"—meaning that a subdivision of a species is not the same as the species itself. "Color is not shape," he explained, "and shape is not color. When color is spoken of, shape should not be included, and when shape is spoken of, color should not be brought up. Now, to make one object out of a combination of both is not correct." Then he went on to explain that if a man looking for a white horse went into a barn which held many black and brown horses, he would not find what he was looking for, even though the barn contained many horses. Accordingly, "a white horse is, indeed, not a horse."[33]

In another discourse he maintained that "two does not contain one," for he insisted that "two" is an entity comprised of one-and-one, not one and one. Hence *two* is a separable classification, just as *one* is. In the text that has been transmitted, which contains only a few fragments of the lifelong discourses of Kung-Sun, he does not offer any practical illustration of this abstract conclusion. It is obvious, however, that there is a qualitative (not merely quantitative) difference between having one wife and having two wives. It is precisely the distinctions of quality which Kung-Sun insisted must be kept in mind.

The method of teaching employed by Kung-Sun, which undoubtedly contributed to his unpopularity, may be illustrated in the discussion between Yin Wen and the King of Ch'i, which he presented in Chapter 3 of his book:

> The King of Ch'i said to Yin Wen, "I am very fond of accomplished men. Why is it that in Ch'i there are none?"
>
> Yin Wen replied, "I should like to know what Your Majesty considers to be an accomplished man?"
>
> The King of Ch'i could not say. Yin Wen went on. "Let us suppose that here we have a man who serves his sovereign loyally and his parents filially, who is faithful to his friends, and at peace with the members of his community. Embodying these four qualities, can he be considered an accomplished man?"
>
> The King of Ch'i rejoined, "Good, that is exactly what I consider an accomplished man."
>
> Yin Wen said, "If you had such a man, would you appoint him to be a minister?"
>
> The King replied, "I would be only too glad, but I cannot find such a man."
>
> At that time the King of Ch'i set high store upon courage. Therefore, Yin Wen asked him, saying, "Suppose such a man were insulted in open court before a crowd of people, but did not dare to fight, would you appoint him to office?"

The King said, "Why, for a gentleman not to avenge his insult with his sword is a dishonor. A dishonored man I would not like to have in my employ."

Yin Wen remarked, "Although the man does not draw his sword upon being insulted, he does not lose thereby the four above-mentioned qualities. Not having lost these, he is still a gentleman. But Your Majesty would in the first case take him into your service, and in the second case would not. Is then what we considered a gentleman before no gentleman?"

The King could not answer.

Yin Wen, however, was inexorable. Through a continuing series of questions he led the King to assert that laws should forbid violence and that there should be rewards for those who contribute to public order, with punishment for those who violate it. Yin Wen then showed him that the gentleman who refused to fight when insulted was contributing to public order, yet the reward of office would be refused him and instead he would be punished by the disgrace of dismissal. "Thus, rewards and punishments, approval and condemnation, are confounded with one another. Under these circumstances, even a man ten times as able as the Yellow Emperor could not keep order." The king, of course, was forced to agree that his own conduct and understanding were in error; but in all probability, nevertheless, he must still have felt that a man unwilling to defend his own honor might not make a good minister—and he may have concluded that what was truly at fault was an incompleteness in the original definition of "an accomplished man." This, however, is a conclusion that Kung-Sun Lung did not draw.

The rationalistic, sophistical rhetoricians had only a brief flurry of fame in the fourth century B.C. They were soon forgotten. The example they set proved not to be appealing, and logic never developed as a science in China. What they did do, however, was to show that the human mind is susceptible to skilled manipulation, even against its own habitual modes of operation. Hu Shih, in *Development of the Logical Method* (p. 130), says that because of them " 'logical' was identified with the paradoxical, the sophistical, and the unintelligible." Men, they revealed, can be led to conclusions that are contrary to their desires and to their own views of what is reasonable. This was a rhetorical contribution of limited validity but of a distinctive nature. They are to be remembered in a history of rhetoric for what they perceived and taught about the gullibility of the human mind and how it may be manipulated.

Hsüntze: Guide to Superior Speech

Hsüntze brought the consideration of human motivation to the highest form it achieved among the ancient Chinese; indeed, his speculations rank respectably with the findings of modern psychologists. He has been called the "Moulder of Confucianism" because, like Aristotle—who was his elder by perhaps sixty-five years—his genius lay particularly in the systematizing of knowledge and ideas. But, also like Aristotle, he was keenly analytical and exceedingly perceptive concerning the nature of man and the means by which he might be educated, or influenced, or led into good or evil by his own desires or by the persuasion of others. It would also be correct to designate him as the father of psychology, since he was a pioneer in attempting the full-blown analysis of the nature of human nature.

Hsüntze was born in the state of Chao, about 320 B.C. When he was around fifty years of age he went to Ts'i-hsia, a famous college established through the influence of Mencius, where he joined the scholarly faculty, with the title of Ranking Great Prefect. He became known as the principal defender of orthodox Confucianism and was honored by being three times invited to offer wine in the annual Great Sacrifice. Then, probably through loss of the King's favor because of the severity of his Confucian principles, he left Ts'i-hsia to wander from court to court offering counsel to whatever ruler would listen. Book IV of his *Works* contains a moving account of a debate in which he engaged, at about the age of sixty, with a military general, concerning the means of waging a war. Afterwards, in Ts'u, he accepted the relatively humble office as magistrate of the city of Lan-ling, where the duties were not strenuous and he used his leisure for writing out his *Works*.

With a crusty personality and little skill in conciliatory appeal, he had few disciples; in consequence, he wrote out his own teachings, instead of leaving them for composition by his students. Sometime around 235 B.C. he died, while living at Lan-ling in retirement, at about the age of eighty-five. He appears to have been well loved by the people he sought to serve; and he left two disciples who were to become notorious in Chinese history and who also made significant places for themselves in the history of rhetoric: Han Fei-tzu and Li-Ssu, of whom more will be heard later.[34]

The text of Hsüntze's writings appears to be well authenticated. Liu

Hsiang established the official text in a carefully edited edition which he published during the Han dynasty, some two hundred years after Hsüntze's death. In A.D. 818 a scholar named Yang Liang published a commentary so searching that it has remained the foundation for interpretation of all doubtful passages. The Imperial edition, published in 1891, provides the most authentic text, plus all the extant commentaries. Prior to the English translation by Dubs, only three or four chapters of Hsüntze's book had been translated into any European or other language. Despite his importance, then, he has remained relatively unknown outside of China.

The teachings of Hsüntze which aroused the greatest interest (and opposition) in his day was his view—directly contradicting Mencius—that human nature is naturally corrupt. "The nature of man is evil," he declared flatly; "his goodness is only acquired through training. The original nature of man today is to seek for gain. . . . Man originally is envious and naturally hates others. . . . Man originally . . . likes praise and is lustful."[35] Left at this point, Hsüntze's view of mankind seems deeply pessimistic. However, this was his starting, not his stopping, point. In his view, the natural corruption of man's original character is countered by his possession of a free and independent will, through which he can choose to improve. "If a person's will is cultivated, then he can be prouder than the rich and the honourable."[36] Self-control, laws, etiquette, and education can be used for infinite improvement of man's innate nature, he believed.

A society, in his view, does well to establish laws, to maintain etiquette, and to support teachers, for all these are means by which the improvement of men may be aided. Fundamentally, however, each man becomes what he wills to be. Freedom of the will, and with it responsibility for one's own character, was the cornerstone of his philosophy. Very definitely, he disagreed with the view of Mencius, which has been noted earlier, that the emotions are the primary expression of man's true nature and that it is emotion which finally determines one's conduct. "The mind is the ruler of the body and the master of the spirit," he taught. "It gives commands and all parts of the body obey. It itself makes prohibitions; it itself gives commands; it itself makes decisions; it itself makes choices; it itself causes action; it itself stops action."[37] When one argues that man's naturally selfish emotions must dominate his choices, Hsüntze retorts: "The mind selects from among the emotions by which it is moved—this is called reflection."[38] More elaborately, he explained: "The mind from birth has the capacity for knowledge; this knowledge contains distinctions; these distinctions consist of at the same time perceiving more than one thing. To perceive more than one thing at the same time is plurality. Yet the mind has that which may be called a unity. That which does not allow one impression to distort another impression is called the mind's unity."[39]

In summary, then, it was Hsüntze's contention that man's original nature is corrupt; that infinite improvement is possible by action of the will; and that free and responsible judgment develops as individuals use their free will wisely. He did not, however, believe that all men are equally willing to make wise use of this capacity for choice. If they willed to do so, he believed, all could succeed. "The mouth can exert itself forcibly," he insisted, "and convert silence to speech; the body can exert itself forcibly and make the bent straight." The capacity exists, if it but be used. "Hence I say: the mind must bear what it chooses."[40]

Since Hsüntze observed that in his society there clearly were superiors and inferiors, and since he noted that the superiors actually appeared to possess greater knowledge, more refined taste, and higher standards of behavior, he accepted the fact of acquired differences—insisting only that they were indeed acquired, not innate. From this position, he devoted considerable attention to analysis of what were the significant differences between those whom society designates as superior and those who are marked as inferior.

Always in his analysis the content and manner of an individual's speech are considered keys to his proper status. Because the sincere speech of an honest man offers the best insight his associates may have into his real character, it is through "speech in accordance with the right" that "the superior man will show his superiority."[41]

"The superior man is not called a dialectician," he warned, "because he can dispute concerning all that dialecticians dispute about."[42] Far from being merely skilled in argument, so that he could speak with equal facility on any side of any question, he must be searchingly sure that his words convey only the meaning he intends—and that this be a meaning which will aid in maintaining the harmony of the state:

> The speech of the superior man is deep but yet refined, reaching down to people's understanding but yet systematic, making distinctions but yet having unity. He corrects his words and makes his speech appropriate, in order to make clear his meaning. The terms he uses and his speech are his messengers of his meaning. When they are sufficient to be understood, he stops. To use them wrongly is wickedness. Therefore, when his words are sufficient to point out the reality, and his speech is sufficient to make his end manifest, he stops. In anything more than that, he is called slow of

speech. This is what the superior man rejects and the stupid man picks up and considers as his treasure. For the speech of the stupid man is hasty and coarse, or else mysterious and unsystematic, babbling and bubbling. He sophisticates his words and makes his speech mysterious, but has no depth to his meaning. Hence he travels far but does not come to any goal; he works hard without result; he desires but does not obtain renown. Reflect on the speech of the wise man and it is easily understood; carry it out and you will easily be at peace; hold to it and you will easily be established; bring it to accomplishment and you will certainly obtain your desire, and not meet with what you hate; but the stupid man is just the opposite of this.[43]

In this single concise paragraph is comprised a cohesive body of rhetorical doctrine. The goals of desirable discourse are: to help listeners to attain peace of mind; to help listeners to attain to their proper social station; and to help listeners to fulfill their natural capacities.

A superior man is one whose speaking, aiming to accomplish those socially useful goals, has the following characteristics: it penetrates into the depths of truth in a style so simple, clear, and direct that it is readily understood by attentive listeners; the style and diction are adjusted to the capacity of the audience; the speech does not contain embellishments designed to impress listeners with the skill of the speaker; rather, "the terms he uses are messengers of his meaning."

The inferior (stupid) man aims in his speaking to attain personal renown, which, however, he fails to win because: his style is coarse, or abstract (mysterious), and his organization is unsystematic, because he speaks up hastily, without sufficient consideration of what he is going to say; he tries to substitute impressive or sophisticated diction for depth of meaning; when he has concluded, the listeners are not clear as to what he has said and they have gained no advantages from it; hence, he "comes to no goal," "he works hard without result," and he fails to win the renown which he seeks.

To Hsüntze rhetoric and philosophy are inextricable. Good speaking depends upon wise understanding and upon a solid sense of social responsibility. Under his rhetorical doctrines, demagoguery could not be considered eloquent, although he well realized that it might be sufficiently effective to result in disruption of the society—the very opposite of the true goal toward which superior speech should aim. In his analysis of human motivation, he pondered the question of how good conduct is to be attained by men who by nature are corrupt and therefore pursue selfish ends. It was the prime question that must be answered if a harmonious society were to be a practical reality.

The problem, as he conceived it, is deep-seated. "Man by birth has desire. When desire is not satisfied, then he cannot be without a seeking for satisfaction. When this seeking for satisfaction is without measure or limits, then there cannot but be contention. When there is contention there will be disorder; when there is disorder, there will be poverty."[44] The ordinary man, confronting this innate difficulty, "desires to foster his enjoyment, but he attacks his mind; he desires to foster his fame, but he disorders his actions." If left to himself, to try to solve his own problems of wrong desires as best he might, his behavior would be so inefficient or harmful to his community that even if his station were that of a marquis or a prince, he "would be no whit different from . . . a robber . . . or a footless cripple."[45]

Like all the other Chinese political thinkers who thus far have been considered, Hsüntze believed as a basic article of faith that no people can be governed by force. To him as to his intellectual forebears it was axiomatic that government must be by consent of the governed. Yet somehow the people must be induced to behave differently and better than their own natures incline them to do. The means by which this amelioration and improvement of social conduct may be obtained are twofold: first, rules of propriety had been established in ancient times by sage kings who understood rightly that people will live together in harmony only when they follow prescribed and expected modes of conduct which are designed to protect their fundamental rights and their personal dignity; and, second, people will adhere to these social rules only if they are continuously persuaded to do so by the effective speaking of superior men.

With this fundamental view of social processes, it was inevitable that Hsüntze should center much of his thinking around the particular requirements of the speech of those who must set standards and uphold them. It is a theme from which he never far departed:

> The speech of the superior man has limits; his actions have standards; in his way of conduct there is one thing which he emphasizes. In speaking of what should be sought for in government, he does not descend below the plane of the peace and care of the people; in speaking of what purposes should be set up, he does not descend below those of an officer; in speaking of what should be sought for in the way of life and virtue, he does not differ from those of the later kings. A way which antedates that of the three

dynasties (Hsia, Shang, Chou) is vague; a method which is different from that of the later kings is incorrect. If his speech is elevated or depressed, made small or great, it does not go outside the foregoing.[46]

Refining his concepts still further, Hsüntze particularized three levels of discourse. The highest level, represented by the discourses of the outstanding sages in Chinese history, consisted of a gentle but continuous flow of talk, penetrating into every detail of a subject, yet "through a thousand turns and changes" making clear the essential unity of the theme. On a second level, "To speak little, but to the point and sparingly, coherently, and according to rule, as if a thread ordered the speech —this is the wisdom of the scholar or superior man." On the lowest level the speech of the little-minded or menial man is "flattering," "wrong," marked by "sharp retorts and triflingly clever," "without great usefulness, quickly making many distinctions but not going to the point, not caring for right or wrong, not considering error or truth, and having for an object the overcoming of an opponent."[47]

So seductive are the apparent advantages of menial speech that self-seeking individuals (which means people in general) will not rise above the lowest level of discourse unless they are well taught and surrounded by associates of high ideals. Accordingly, Hsüntze concluded his book with the following injunction: "Thus although a man has fine natural qualities [potential] and knows how to discuss, he needs to seek a virtuous teacher and serve him as a disciple; he needs to pick out good friends and attach himself to them."[48] In sum, good speech is the highest attribute of social superiority, and it is attained through careful study and assiduous practice under critical observation. This was the message Hsüntze left.

HsÜNTZE AS SPEAKER

Unlike many other rhetoricians, Hsüntze boldly subjected himself to the observation of his practice in persuasive speech. Perhaps he felt induced to do this because he realized his prickly personality and the severity of his demands for superiority resulted in his having no large body of devoted disciples. It may be that in response to the general view that he was not himself persuasive (and therefore might not be qualified to provide injunctions for the persuasiveness of others) he felt compelled to offer an example that would at least show how he selected and patterned his arguments to render them effective. In any event, Chapter 15 of his book consists of a report of a debate between Hsüntze and General Lin-wu-chuin, before King Hsaio-ch'en, in the state of Chao.

As a debater, Hsüntze presented forthrightly the Confucian viewpoint that a people cannot be conquered by force—or, even if they should be overcome, they would still harbor such resentment that to govern them would be more troublesome than beneficial to the ruler. Rather, they can only be overcome by demonstrating justice and righteousness of so high an order that they will wish to come under the new reign. Implicit in this argument is the political philosophy that a people does not owe loyalty explicitly to their own ruler but only to the ideal of a ruler who manifests benevolence in his governing. Both the argument and the mode of presentation are so strictly orthodox that they constitute a model of the Confucian debate.

General Lin opened the debate by summarizing the important points for managing an army: "On the one hand observe the seasons [for soldiers could not be conscripted when crops were to be cultivated or harvested], on the other take an advantageous position; observe the movements of the enemy; when following the enemy attack them; when preceding them, reach the goal first." Hsüntze replied, "No, . . . everything depends on uniting the people. . . . The man who can get the accord of the people is the best man at managing an army."

General Lin quickly brushed this amateurish suggestion aside. "No. What is valuable in military affairs is strength and advantage; what is done is sudden alteration of troop movements and deceitful stratagems. He who knows best how to manage an army is sudden in his movements; his plans are very deeply laid; and no one knows whence he may attack." To this Hsüntze retorted: "What you value is planning on the instant, strength, and advantage; what you do is attacking, capturing, sudden alteration of troop movements, and deceit."

Then, having shown that he understood and took honest account of the militaristic knowledge of his opponent, Hsüntze shifted the ground to his chosen line of reasoning. With a profusion of specific incidents drawn from Chinese history, he showed that when commanders depend upon sheer force and strategy, they unite the enemy in opposition and disrupt the loyalty of their own troops and the people of their own kingdom. Warfare of the sort advocated by General Lin, Hsüntze pointed out, can only arouse the resentment of those who are attacked and also of those who are forced to do the attacking—for both suffer. But when a commander observes true benevolence toward his own people, they respond with devotion: "The subject serves his prince, and the inferior

serves his superior as the son serves his father or the younger brother
serves his elder brother, or as the hand and arm defend the head and
eyes and cover the breast and abdomen. . . . His wisdom and his admonitions will certainly strike the people harmoniously and unite them."

Then, in addition to having his own people united behind him, the
benevolent ruler will also undermine the morale of the attacking force,
for it will be apparent to them that their own welfare would be advanced
if they should abandon their prince and attach themselves to the ruler
marked by benevolence. If I, with my philosophy, Hsüntze asserted, were
to fight an enemy who used the militaristic approach advocated by General Lin, "his people would be attached to me; and they would rejoice
in me as their father and mother. . . . On the other hand, they would
regard their superior as a branding iron or a tattooing needle, as an
enemy."

King Hsiao-ch'en, who had to formulate his governmental policies
in terms of which point of view he considered the better, was impressed
by Hsüntze but not yet ready to abandon the traditional modes of military attack and defense. "What methods do a king's armies use?" he
asked Hsüntze. "What movements are permitted them?"

Hsüntze replied that "Among all the things in the minds of the great
kings, the normal methods followed by generals and leaders were the
least important matters." Then he went on: "If the prince is a worthy
person, his country is well-governed and prosperous; if the prince is
without ability, his country is ill-governed and decadent. The country
which magnifies the rules of proper conduct and honors justice is well-
governed and prosperous; the country which treats negligently the rules
of proper conduct and which esteems justice lightly is ill-governed and
decadent. The one which is well-governed and prosperous is strong; the
one which is ill-governed and decadent is weak. These are the sources
of strength and of weakness. If the ruler can be relied upon, he is able
to use his subjects for his purposes; if the ruler cannot be relied upon,
he is unable to use his subjects. He who is able to use his subjects is
strong; he who is unable to use his subjects is weak—this is the abiding
principle of strength and weakness."

This argument was so convincing that both the king and the general
accepted it. But they could not go so far as to abandon wholly the traditional approach of entrusting the nation's defense to its military men.
What, they then asked, are the qualities that make a good general?

It was at this point in the debate, after Hsüntze had won a partial
victory but had still to accomplish the decisive reversal in the thinking
of the king and the general, that his great persuasive skill was most

surely manifested. Now that the two militarists had conceded their willingness to agree with much that he had argued, Hsüntze swiftly and even willingly paid high tribute to the militaristic qualities which they most admired. "In wisdom there is nothing better than getting rid of doubts," he said in reply to their question; "in action there is nothing better than being without mistakes. . . . Hence my orders and edicts should be severe and awe-inspiring; my rewards and punishments should seek to be certain and believed in; my camps and storehouses should seek to be safe and stable; they should seek to be quick and speedy. In spying upon the enemy and watching their movements I should seek to be hidden and deep. . . . In meeting the enemy and in a decisive battle, I should do what I am certain about, not what I am uncertain about. . . . Thought must precede action. . . . Be careful of the end as of the beginning, to have the end and the beginning alike. . . . Success in all things comes from being attentive; defeat in being careless."

By this time the king and the general were impressed that Hsüntze, even with his revolutionary ideas about warfare, both understood and appreciated the extremely difficult requirements of managing an army in the field. General Lin asked him, "What are the basic military regulations?" Hsüntze answered him in his own terms: "To obey orders is the most important thing; to gain glory is secondary." Then, apparently feeling that he had established an identity of understanding and a trust in his general insight and intentions, he shifted the line of reasoning back toward his own essential point. When your armies are successful in the field, he urged: "Do not kill the aged or the weak; do not march over the crops. Do not seize those who submit; do not let go those who are obstinate; do not arrest those who hasten to obey. Whomever you kill, do not kill his subjects; kill those who cause the people to rebel; but if among the people are those who defend these injurious individuals, they too are injurious. Hence those who yield to the sword shall live; those who resist the sword shall die."

Then, reverting even more closely to his fundamental theme, he cited an instance from Chinese history in which a victorious king treated his conquered enemies generously. "Hence those who were near sang and rejoiced; those who were distant fell prostrate and hastened to submit. There was no darkened or rustic state which did not hasten to send envoys and joyfully seek peace. Within the four seas [that is, throughout the continent] it was as if there was one family. No enlightened people failed to comply and submit. The foregoing is what is meant by being a leader of men."

At this point, in a swift recapitulation, he reiterated his theme:

"Hence the people of countries which were ill-ruled rejoiced to learn of the well-governed nation; and not being satisfied with their own rulers, they wished for the benevolent ruler to come to govern them." To this General Lin assented, apparently being well satisfied with the policy Hsüntze advocated, for his only comment was, "Good."

King Hsiao-ch'en, however, having the responsibility for determining the state's policies, needed to have a fuller and clearer interpretation of the proper course. How is it, he asked, that when you speak of military affairs you stress benevolence and justice as being at the roots of action? "The benevolent man loves others; the just man follows principle; then why do you speak of military actions? All the armies are good for is to contend and take things from others." Hsüntze recognized this question as driving to the heart of the problem under discussion, and he answered it strictly in the tradition of basic Chinese moral principles, which were not pacifistic, but accepted war only as a last resort to prevent injustice.

"It is not as you think," Hsüntze told the king. "This benevolent man loves others. He loves others, hence he hates what injures others. This just man follows principle. He follows principle, hence he hates those that lead others astray. These armies are for the purpose of stopping tyranny and getting rid of injury, not to contend and take things from others. Hence when the armies of the benevolent man remain in a place, it is peaceful and prosperous; when they enter into a place, civilization develops. Their coming is like the falling of a timely rain."

At this point, a disciple of Hsüntze's who was listening to the debate—Li-Ssu, who was to be notorious for his philosophy of brutal suppression—spoke up in sharp dissent: "Ch'in's armies for four generations have been victorious; it is the strongest state in the country; it has overawed the feudal princes; this has not been done by benevolence and justice but merely by taking advantage of the course of events."

Li-Ssu's point was historically accurate, as all who heard it knew. What they could not know was that the armies of Ch'in were shortly to conquer all China; that Li-Ssu should become the prime minister of the empire; that there would be a brief decade of tyranny unexampled in all the remainder of Chinese history; and that then the militaristic empire would quickly fall apart. Hsüntze knew no more of this forthcoming course of events than did his audience; but he had full faith in the principle he espoused.

"It is not as you think," he replied calmly. "What you call advantage is an unadvantageous advantage. What I call benevolence and justice is the most advantageous advantage. This benevolence and justice is that wherewith I reform my government. When the government is reformed, the people are attached to their ruler; they rejoice in their prince, and easily die for him; for this reason I have said, 'Of all that pertains to military affairs, generals and leaders are the least important.' Ch'in for four generations has been victorious, but it has been fearful, continually fearing that the whole country would unite and crush it." Then he concluded the debate with a pointed piece of advice which, unhappily, the protagonists of Ch'in did not follow: "Do not look for the principle of right action in the beginning of the action, but search for it at the end. It is through failure to follow this precept that the present generation is misled."

Thus ended the great debate on militarism. Hsüntze won over the king and the general, and established a point of view that was to dominate Chinese scholarship (though not its political leaders) for many hundred years. As happens for all great teachers, his disciples remained after he was gone. And in his train Hsüntze left a great divergency: on the one hand, his teachings became so widely influential that he became known as the "moulder of Confucianism"; and, on the other hand, the only two among his disciples who remained known to history both renounced and flouted his teachings—with great damage to themselves and with catastrophic results for China. Hsüntze's persuasion was greatly successful, and it also greatly failed. With both outcomes, his influence was so notable that he deserves better than public neglect.

In reviewing the lasting worth of all the rhetoricians considered in this chapter, what matters most is not the specific conclusions they reached but the method they espoused. Their effort was to see men steadily and to see them whole. They were, above all, students of human motivation. Like modern personality theorists, they sought to interpret how men would behave in terms of their entire panoply of needs, hopes, fears, abilities, and limitations, all affected by the circumstances surrounding them. In the long run this was their greatest achievement. For the short term, however, as has been indicated concerning Hsüntze, their method was rejected. Under the influence of Hsüntze's greatest disciples —and, even more, under the circumstance of China's domination for the first time by an all-conquering militarism—for a short generation rhetoricians turned their attention from internal motivation to external force. The next chapter belongs to theorists who renounced what these psychological rhetoricians most deeply believed. And from their own chosen perspective they, too, adduced a kind of truth that human nature and human history have often reaffirmed in the centuries since.

CHAPTER 12

The Legalistic Rhetoricians

TUTORS OF TOTALITARIANISM

BASICALLY, legalism and rhetoric are contraries. The one attempts to impose conformity in the name of equality through use of either actual or presumptive force. The other sets out to secure acquiescence based on free choice through the use of persuasion. What the policeman says must be done is in a different category from what the speaker says ought to be done. This, at least, is the theoretical difference between them. In practice the distinction often blurs and may indeed disappear.[1]

Ancient China notably preferred rhetoric over legalism. The society sought to control its members by tradition, custom, ritual, ceremony, etiquette, and example. Court counsellors tried to shape the conduct of the court into patterns that would win the willing loyalty of the populace. Humanistic by inclination, the Chinese did not accept the idea of an all-powerful deity by which the world was ultimately controlled. The standard by which they judged what behavior to approve was that of a contented individual living in a tranquil community. Their study of psychology, sociology, and political science was in a sense also a study of rhetoric; for their central concern was how to induce individuals to make the choices that conduce to righteousness, propriety, and justice, thereby enhancing personal welfare and social harmony.

Their approach to the problem of maintaining social order is well illustrated in a speech delivered in 542 B.C., quoted in the *Tso Chuen,* a commentary on Confucius' *Spring and Autumn Annals.* Wan-Tze, a counsellor, explained to the Marquis of Wei that every man must behave in a manner appropriate to his station, in order that the people not be confused: "Having majesty that inspires awe is what we call dignity. Presenting a pattern which induces imitation is what we call manner. When a ruler has the dignified manner of a ruler, his ministers fear and love him, imitate and resemble him, so that he holds firm possession of his state, and his fame continues through long ages. When a minister has the dignified manner of a minister, his inferiors fear and love him, so that he can keep sure his office, preserve his clan, and rightly order

210

his family. So it is with all classes downwards, and it is by this that high and low are made firm in their relations with one another."[2]

The theory underlying this injunction was purely Confucian: that social influence is to be exerted through example based on tradition. But in the fourth century B.C. a new political order began to emerge that gave rise to new problems and encouraged new theories for dealing with them. China came to be unified as a broadly inclusive empire; and the enlargement of relationships resulted in added complexities and an impersonalization of society which called for new means of achieving social control and order.

Under these circumstances, a new set of rhetoricians, known as legalists, came into prominence. Confronted by unprecedented problems requiring solutions not defined by tradition, they naturally differed widely among themselves. But they resembled one another in the cardinal respect that they sought to enshrine law as the chief moulder of human behavior. And they resembled the psychological rhetoricians discussed in Chapter 11 in the depth of their interest and insight in the problems of human motivation.

When their society undertook to impose law as a substitute for custom, striking changes occurred in human relationships. Old freedoms and old choices vanished. Certain injustices disappeared; others took their place. Benevolence, righteousness, gentlemanliness, and propriety came to be considered too imprecise to serve as reliable guides to conduct. Law seeks to impose equality of treatment upon individuals and circumstances that never are and cannot be equal.[3] Force comes to replace persuasion as the principal means by which order and harmony are to be maintained. So it was, almost, in the new China of the empire of the Ch'ins; almost, but not quite. For two thousand years of history had left a legacy of stress on gentility and propriety that could not be erased.

The Period of the Warring States, before the Ch'ins conquered China, was marked by a diversity of opinions that reflected the social disorder. Mencius, defending the old order, complained that "Unemployed scholars indulge in unreasonable discussions."[4] The historian Ssu-ma Ch'ien related that "King Hsuan of Ch'i delighted in traveling scholars who could talk on literary matters. Thus he conferred honors on a total of seventy-six men . . . who could carry on their discussions without having any administrative duties. This is how the scholars at Chi-hsia became numerous, until they amounted to several hundreds and thousands of men."[5] Among the many ideas that were fomented in these discussions was the concept of legalism.

The man chiefly credited as the precursor of legalism was Prime Minister Kuan Chung, who had lived much earlier, in the seventh century B.C. Known as the father of bureaucracy, it was his faith that through extensive governmental control of all aspects of communal living by a professional class of trained administrators, prosperity could be insured for the people. Kuan Chung was both successful and disingenuous in admitting how his methods worked: "I and my partner Pao-shu once did business together. In dividing the profits, I always took more than my share. Pao-shu never thought that I was greedy. He knew I was poor. Once I tried to get an official position for him and failed. Pao-shu did not think I was a fool. He knew that the chances of success were against me. When subsequently I went into government work for myself, I was dismissed by my king three times in succession. Pao-shu did not think that I had no ability. He knew my time had not come. I was also in war three times. Each time I ran away. He did not consider me a coward. He knew I was worried about my aged mother."[6] Kuan Chung became famous as a rationalistic persuader, and the methods illustrated in this quotation won renewed popularity for him in the fourth and third centuries B.C.

Among Kuan Chung's successors was one T'ien P'ien, of whom little is known except that his eloquence in speaking won him the cognomen "Heavenly Mouth." One of his comments which has been preserved was that the harmony of society derives not from the greatness of a wise ruler but from effective administration of laws.[7] This idea took especially strong root in the state of Ch'in, where the ambitious ruling clan was commencing to dream of creating a vast empire by conquering all of China. To accomplish this they needed a philosophical base quite different from the Confucian idea of uniting people by manifestations of benevolence. The philosophy they required was furnished to them first by Lord Shang, then by Li-Ssu, and finally, more completely, by Han Fei-Tzu.

Lord Shang, or Shang Yang, was a scholar statesman who died in 338 B.C., but not before he had given currency to a set of ideas that justified absolutism, autocratic rule and tyranny, while picturing "mercy and benevolence as the sources of error." The point of view was clear and it was stated plainly. Shang's ideas were presented in a book of twenty-four short sections, partly essays and partly dialogues between him and Duke Hsiao, which was put together by his disciples. The first English translation of The Book of Lord Shang, made by J. J. L. Duyvendak, was published in London in 1928. There is little in modern totalitarianism which was not adequately foreseen by Shang.

In primitivistic society, he speculated, the way of life of the people was "to love their relatives and to be fond of what was their own. From loving their relatives came discrimination [in their views of people], and from fondness of what was their own, insecurity." As disputes arose because of this discrimination and insecurity, men of talent conceived the ideas of equity, justice, and unselfishness, and taught the people to delight in moral virtue. However, as population and wealth increased, it proved necessary to enforce justice with decrees that were administered by officials under orders from their ruler. "Once a hierarchy had been set up, the idea of honoring talent disappeared and that of prizing noble rank arose." Then, to justify his conclusion that Confucian ethics must be replaced by a system of laws, he concluded: "When the guiding principles of the people became unsuited to the circumstances, their standards of value must change. As conditions in the world change, different principles are practiced."[8]

Basic to the "different principles" advised by Lord Shang was the decree that "the people be organized into groups of families, which should be mutually responsible for each other's good behavior and share each other's punishments." The laws were to be supported by generous rewards on the one hand and cruel punishments on the other. "Anyone who did not denounce a culprit would be cut in two at the waist; anyone who denounced a culprit would receive the same reward as if he had cut off the head of an enemy soldier."[9] Finally, to make emphatic his view of the sanctity of the laws, Shang punished not only those people who violated the laws but also those who praised them—his point being that the decrees of the court must be accepted as inviolate and inevitable, not at all subject either to the blame or the approval of the multitude.

An alert student of Lord Shang's doctrines was Li-Ssu, who had studied under Hsüntze. He accepted fully Hsüntze's theory that human nature is basically evil, and accordingly found no difficulty with Shang's belief that men must be rigorously controlled by precise laws backed by severe punishment. Li-Ssu was a man of persuasive eloquence who appeared at the right time and place in history to give his words of counsel their maximum effect. He became a key participant in the remoulding of China by the Ch'in dynasty, the most basic revolution that has occurred in the long history of China.

Shih Huang Ti was king of Ch'in while the various states of China were still rent by continuous conflict and weakened by division. In 221 B.C. Emperor Shih Huang, as he styled himself, accomplished the complete conquest and unification of all of China—with Li-Ssu as his prime minister and counsellor. Immediately, sweeping changes were installed.

A standardized system of weights and measures replaced the diversity of systems which had stalled commerce in the past. The numerous systems of writing were unified into the ideographs which were to survive down to the present day. The Great Wall was built along the northern border, to ward off invasions by Mongol tribes, extending for a distance of fourteen hundred miles and costing the lives of perhaps a million impressed prisoners and slaves. A palace was built that was probably the largest ever to be erected by human hands. A network of roads was constructed, uniting the capital with every remote quarter of the kingdom. The length of the axles of carts was standardized, so that all carts could use roads into which deep ruts were dug by the wheels in wet weather. The feudal system was destroyed and monarchal control was extended to every part of China and into every aspect of individual and communal life. So dynamic and dramatic were the accomplishments of this regime that it is by its name, China, that the nation has since been known. The Empire of Ch'in lasted only fifteen years, out of the five thousand of Chinese history, but its impress could not be shaken off.

The gigantic task which Li-Ssu and his master, Shih Huang Ti, undertook was the complete remaking of the mind of the Chinese people. The slate of history was to be wiped clean, and a new beginning was to be made. The magnitude of their daring staggers the imagination. China already had a civilization several thousand years old. Its governing ethics and customs were not only deeply enshrined in practice but were strongly buttressed by the tremendous prestige of the teachings of Confucius, Mencius, and many other honored scholars. Moreover, the state of Ch'in, which harbored Shih Huang and Li-Ssu, was a semi-barbarous outland which scarcely was considered a part of the great Middle Kingdom. The effrontery of attempting to remake China completely from such a base seemed incredible.

Li-Ssu understood well that the enormity of the undertaking required the most drastic of measures. In a series of debates with other ministers at court, he convinced Shih Huang that he should depart from the ancient system of installing his own sons on conquered thrones, and instead should establish a centralized rule.[10] Then, boldly taking his life in his hands—for in the excited autocracy of the court of Ch'in, intoxicated by military successes which had undermined all the opposing states, to offer advice which proved unacceptable could very easily result in the execution of the adviser—Li-Ssu argued:

> . . . in the past the empire was troubled and divided. No one could succeed in uniting it. Thus the princes ruled simultaneously. In their discussions the scholars speak of ancient times in order to

decry the present. They use false examples to stir up confusion in the actual state of affairs; they proclaim the excellence of the doctrines they have studied to abuse what Your Majesty has established. Now that the Emperor possesses the whole land and has imposed unity, they honour the past and hold private consultations. These men who oppose the new laws and commands, as soon as they hear of a new edict, discuss it in accordance with their doctrines. When they are at Court they conceal their resentment, but when they are elsewhere they debate these matters in the public streets and encourage the common people to believe calumnies.[11]

To remedy this tendency of critics to derogate the present by comparing it with the past, Li-Ssu proposed the bold expedient of calling in all copies of all the ancient books (except those kept in a few carefully restricted libraries) and of having them burnt. Then he added a further cruel proviso: "Those who praise ancient institutions to decry the present regime shall be exterminated with all the members of their families." The Emperor approved this advice; and it was done.

The Burning of the Books occurred in 213 B.C. Subsequently, four hundred and sixty of the greatest scholars, who were suspected of knowing the books so thoroughly that they could teach their doctrines from memory, were all buried alive. The power of the Confucian scholars was broken—for the time being. The texts of many old classics were lost forever; others survived only in part. The remaking of China was as thorough as possible. Yet another eight years after the books were burned and the scholars killed, a new dynasty came to the throne—the Hans—and shortly Confucianism was not only revived but established by law as the accepted intellectual orthodoxy, a decision that in a gentler way proved almost as stultifying to China as did Li-Ssu's destruction of the books. Li-Ssu himself was put to death by torture by Shih Huang's son and successor.

Ssu-ma Ch'ien, the Han historian, detailed the fall of Ch'in with gloomy relish. The King of Ch'in, he related, "multiplied the tortures and made the punishments more terrible. His officers governed with the greatest severity. The rewards and penalties were unjust. The taxes and levies were unbearable. The empire was crushed under forced labor, the officials could not maintain order. . . . Then crime broke out in every place and the Emperor and his subjects deceived each other mutually. The condemned were an innumerable multitude; those who had been tortured and mutilated formed a long procession on the road. . . .

From the princes and ministers down to the humblest people every one was terrified and in fear for their lives."

Such was the terrible price China had to pay when its rulers departed from the customary use of rhetoric to pursue the newly enticing method of brute force. Persuasion, they felt, was too slow and too uncertain, but they soon saw how speedily uncertain was the use of force. Without delay or qualification, the Empire of Ch'in collapsed. Totalitarianism had its day but briefly. It left, however, the works of a major rhetorician, Han Fei-Tzu, the Machiavelli of ancient China.

HAN FEI-TZU: THE RHETORIC OF POWER

However much a legalistic, or totalitarian, state may depend upon force, it cannot avoid situations which require persuasion. The history of Ch'in offers no exception to this rule. Especially in the circles of the court there was much conniving among the politicians who strove for favorable positions. In such a contest for power, even good friends fell out. Not strangely, a savage enmity developed between Li-Ssu and Han Fei-Tzu, both of whom had been students and disciples of Hsüntze, and both of whom were induced by consciousness of personal talent to develop inordinate ambitions.

Han Fei-Tzu was a prince of the royal family of the state of Han, and this foreign connection was used against him by Li-Ssu, who (when his own position at the court of Ch'in was unassailable) told King Shih Huang Ti: "Fei came here most probably with the intention to elevate his own position in the Han Government by demonstrating his ability to save the Han State. By means of eloquent speeches and beautiful phrases he embellishes lies and falsifies plots in order thereby to fish for advantages in Ch'in and watch Your Majesty's mind on behalf of Han."[12]

Li-Ssu well understood such duplicity, for he proceeded at the same time to propose that Shih Huang send him to Han as an ambassador to invite the King of Han to Shih's court. Then he added: "When he comes, Your Majesty retains him and never sends him away, but, instead, summons a few important ministers from the Han Government to make bargains with them."

Duplicity flourished under the legalistic theory of the "rule of law." The end of this particular rivalry was that Li succeeded in having Han Fei-Tzu arrested and then sent poison to him for a suicide death in prison—a death that saved Han from torture and Li from embarrassing disclosures at a trial. Brutality was the order of the day, with expediency as its justification. Han Fei-Tzu (and later, as has been noted, Li-Ssu as well) was caught in the net of his own devising. Both conceived of a rhetoric of power, and both were powerless to escape the effects of the crass duplicity of which they approved.

About all that is known of the life of Han Fei-Tzu is that he was a prince of Han; that he came to the court of Ch'in to seek his fortune where the stakes were highest and the dangers greatest; that his essays on political management brought him to the attention of King Shih Huang Ti, who exclaimed, "Had I only such a man as this by my side, I could face even death without regret!"[13] It is also known that his preferment at court aroused the jealousy of the powerful Li-Ssu, and that as a result he died in 233 B.C.—some twelve years after the Ch'in conquest of all of China had been completed. In the conniving circles of the court, Han competed with a severe handicap, stuttering so badly that he could not converse effectively, despite Li-Ssu's reference to his "beautiful speeches," and therefore had to present all his advice to the king in written form. Fifty-five of his essays are extant and were issued in a definitive text in 1896 by Wang Hsien-shen under the title *The Complete Works of Han Fei-Tzu with Collected Commentaries.* Partial translations were made in Russian, French, German, and English early in the twentieth century, but the first and thus far the only Western-language translation of Han's entire work is the 1939 English edition translated by W. K. Liao.

More than any of the other ancient Chinese philosophers, Han Fei-Tzu had a rounded and developed theory of rhetoric. He was also a keen student of human motivation, seeing as clearly as do modern social psychologists the interrelationships of motives and circumstances. His character was thoroughly Machiavellian, so he easily accustomed himself to toady to the Emperor and to advise whatever deception would serve the need of the moment. Even so, his rhetoric was far too consistent to be merely opportunistic. His view of human nature and of the social scene was carefully reasoned, and he had no doubt of the authenticity of his analyses. Consequently, just as Confucius and Mencius could argue confidently from their perception of traditional morality, without regard to the specifics of immediate problems, so could Han Fei-Tzu argue with equal confidence from his view of human motives, unhampered either by objective facts or by ethical restrictions. Unabashedly he set forth the principles of a rhetoric of power.

This rhetoric dealt not with what must be done under the law but with what could be done through persuasive exhortation, rationalization, and innuendo. His rhetoric in its own way was constructive, too. What he taught, knowingly and nakedly, was how power over people may be won and held through discourse that exploits every known weakness and appeals to every known cupidity. Unlike the sophists of Athens, who were charged with making the worse appear to be the better reason, Han Fei-Tzu was quite willing to advocate openly the worse reason as being the one which was the more likely to be effectual.

Han Fei-Tzu clearly sensed the importance of the interacting relationships of human nature and human society. In the opening paragraph of the essay "Eight Canons," which advises the ruler how to control his people, Han noted that social order "must accord with human feelings."[14] Since these feelings consist of likes and dislikes, the instruments of government must be rewards and punishments. The ruler will succeed in maintaining orderly control when he rewards the behavior he desires and punishes that which obstructs his aims. It is unrealistic to expect, as Confucius did, that rulers would be superior men who could rule through setting examples of high virtue. "As a matter of fact, most rulers in the world form a continuous line of average men."[15] It is equally unrealistic to expect that rulers, having mediocre ability, will be well served by counsellors who combine superior intelligence with superior virtue. On the contrary, a ruler must be forever suspicious of an adviser whose personal qualities are superior to his own, for the people will note the difference and will tend to shift their loyalties to the man of transcendent merit.[16] What is required as the basis for stable government is not high ability, benevolence, or righteousness, or even justice, but the strict enforcement of laws which provide high rewards for desired conduct and severe punishment for prohibited actions.[17]

Force alone, however, never will suffice for the government of men, in Han's view. Again and again he reiterated the need for effective persuasion. To dramatize this point, he related the story of Pien Ho, a man of Ch'u, who found a massive uncut jade in the hills and sought to curry favor at court by offering it to King Wu. However, the stone being uncut and unpolished did not reveal its precious quality and the king, considering Pien to be lying about its worth, had his left foot cut off in punishment. After the death of King Wu, Wen ascended the throne, and Pien offered the same uncut stone to him—with the result that his right foot was amputated. King Ch'eng, who succeeded Wen, observed Pien weeping bitterly by the roadside and inquired the reason. When Pien told him of the rejection of his jade, Ch'eng had a jeweler polish it, whereupon its great value became apparent.[18] The moral Han Fei-Tzu would have us draw from the story is clear: do not offer crude counsel to a listener, for it will be rejected and the speaker will be scorned or punished; refine the counsel and render it attractive if you would have it accepted.

So strongly did Han believe in the efficacy of skilled persuasion that he went to extremes in emphasizing it: "Who utters a word creates himself a name";[19] and "Wise men would advance their careers by improving their eloquence."[20] In an essay warning rulers about how they may be misled by self-seeking counsellors, Han pointed out that a king is necessarily insulated from real knowledge of affairs and must—to his constant peril—depend upon what trusted advisers tell him. "Accordingly, ministers find eloquent speakers from among the subjects of other feudal lords and sponsor able persuaders in the country, then make them speak about their self-seeking designs with skillfully polished words and fluent and convincing phrases, show the sovereign the direction of advantages and powers, overawe him with the location of calamities and disadvantages, manipulate all kinds of false sayings, and thereby deprave him."[21] In the history of world rhetoric, Han is the only rhetorician who valued persuasion so highly that he envisioned the utilization of whole corps of persuasive speakers to influence the shape of governmental policies, some selected and educated from local communities and some recruited from abroad.

The value of skill in speech preoccupied him—perhaps because of his own stuttering, perhaps because he observed such skills and noted their success. His tributes to persuasion recur in his essays again and again. It was "eloquence and penetration in wording" which Han considered to be the highest qualification for the office of Supreme Judge.[22] Even false envoys from abroad, serving as agents of self-seeking ministers, will be accorded high status at court if their words are pleasing and their arguments convincing.[23] In an essay criticizing various ancient philosophers, Han quoted one as having said that "whose words said inside the private room prevail upon everybody in the room, and whose words said inside the public hall prevail upon everybody in the hall, he can be called ruler of all."[24] The basis of Han's criticism is that effective words spoken even in private will be so influential that they will extend their effects over the countryside, so that it is needless to differentiate between "private" and "public" persuasion. Ability in persuasive speaking, he felt, is equal to power over people.

Han devoted one of his major essays to warning against "mere eloquence," which conceals lack of sense with appealing words. "The stupid sovereign," he pointed out, "in listening to words, admires their eloquence. . . . In consequence, it becomes the way of the officials, gentry and commoners to utter roundabout and high-sounding words." Han urged rulers to "take function and utility" as their standards in judging what is said to them, and not to be deluded by "words that are too minute to be scrutinized and too ineffable to be carried out." With heavy sarcasm, he then asked: "Supposing one listened to the scholars making glorious and exaggerated quotations from the early kings, might not the whole be unsuitable to the present age?" Then he cited the practice of Mo-Tze, who deliberately avoided eloquence because "If he made his phrasing eloquent, people might, it was feared, harbour the literature but forget the utility." In contrast, false counsellors "all speak with the words of eloquent persuasiveness and literary phrasing." Han concluded the essay with an analogical reminder that we take even bitter medicine if it will cure our illness; similarly, we should listen to even harsh words if they are guides to effective action.[25] Such an essay was needed, in Han's view, precisely because persuasion tended to be effective even when it aimed toward bad ends.

The right end of persuasion in his view was to serve neither truth nor the good of society, nor even the advantage of the speaker, but the requirements of the ruler. The cardinal test of a good counsellor was that "though he has a mouth of his own, he never speaks for his own advantage."[26] This was a severe test in a time and at a court where falling out of favor might easily lead to being beheaded. Even so, a counsellor's duty was, when necessary, to "offend the ruler's ear with loyal words," for "stubborn-minded rulers have good luck only through ear-offending words."[27] Only those should be at court who accept the rule: "It is the ministers who do the toil; it is the ruler who gets the spoil."[28] However, the minister would be unduly stupid if he did not at least safeguard his own interests by doing his best to phrase what he had to say in acceptable terms. "Ear-offending" should occur only as a desperate last recourse. Generally, even unpalatable advice could be put in attractive form. Thus Han placed emphasis upon the requirement of adaptation to the target audience. "To please madame is not the way to serve the master; to please the master is not the way to serve madame."[29] The mode of speaking should suit the circumstances and the persons addressed.

HAN FEI-TZU'S THEORY OF PERSUASION

The heart of Han Fei-Tzu's rhetoric is in his essay on "Difficulties in the Way of Persuasion." The winning of acquiescence from a listener, he declared, is difficult not from the speaker's lack of knowledge of the subject matter (which is readily obtained) or from lack of skill in argumentation (which may be learned), or from stage fright, which he described as the lack of "courage to exert my abilities to the utmost." Then he added: "As a whole, the difficulties in the way of persuasion lie in my knowing the heart of the persuaded in order thereby to fit my wording into it."[30] On this basis he proceeded to explain what should be known about the psychological processes of the one to be persuaded, pointing out how easy it is to misinterpret the cardinal motives that will lead to a decision:

> If the persuaded strives after high fame while you persuade him of big profit, you will be considered low-bred, accorded mean treatment, and shunned from afar. If the persuaded strives after big profit while you persuade him of high fame, you will be considered mindless and ignorant of worldly affairs and will never be accepted. If the persuaded strives after big profit in secret but openly seeks for high fame, while you persuade him of high fame, you will be accepted in name but kept distant in fact; and, if you persuade him of big profit, your word will be adopted in secret but your person will be left out openly. These points should be carefully deliberated.

This analysis reveals a sophistication and depth of understanding which merit for Han Fei-Tzu high status among the world's psychological rhetoricians. He knew well not only that persuasion must be based upon the precise motives which actually govern the listener's judgment concerning the matter being considered, but also that there is a strong probability such motives will be concealed and misrepresented. He also well understood the extreme delicacy of relationship between an adviser, who has no power except whatever trust may be placed in his words, and his ruler, who has all power and is suspiciously aware that it may be betrayed or undermined.

In a passage which must reflect his keen awareness of the dangers of his own position at court, Han pointed out: "Though you never intend to expose the ruler's secrets, yet if you happen to speak of anything he wants to conceal, you are then in danger. . . . When the persuader has devised an extraordinary scheme which suits the ruler, if another wise man finds it out by inferring it from other sources and divulges the secret to the world, the ruler will think he has divulged the secret, wherefore he is in danger. If the persuader exhausts all his wisdom before his master's favour becomes firm, then though his persuasion prevails and has merits, his fruitful service will be forgotten with ease. If his persuasion takes no effect and has demerits, he will fall under suspicion. In such a case he is in danger."[31] These are all problems that in a sense

are extrinsic to rhetoric, since they arise from the conspiratorial nature
of the court circle; but Han was keenly aware that the persuasive counsellor must protect himself against such flank attacks while simultaneously directing his best efforts to persuade the ruler of the merit of his
ideas.

Han then reverted to his principal theme—the difficulty of knowing
the heart of the listener. "Supposing," he continued, "the ruler had an
aptitude for certain faults and the persuader spoke plainly on propriety
and righteousness and thereby challenged his vices, he would be in danger. . . . Whoever urgently persuades the ruler to do what he cannot
do and not to do what he cannot stop doing is in danger." Audience
analysis, obviously, was for Han the *sine qua non* of persuasive discourse.

He also, however, was a psychologist who believed implicitly in the
commonality of basic characteristics. Since it is impossible to know fully
and confidently the precise motivational pattern of a listener (and since
the persuader may need to deal with many listeners at once), it is necessary to have a clearly delineated concept of general human nature. Han
did not doubt the fundamental nature of man: it is selfish, suspicious,
envious, fault-finding, without gratitude, and cruelly demanding. It was
his conviction that to think the worst of an individual is to come close
to understanding what he most certainly is. Accordingly, the persuader
must be aware that whatever he may say is liable to culpable misinter-
pretation:

> . . . if you talk about great men to him, he thinks you are intimat-
> ing his defects. If you talk about small men to him, he thinks you
> are showing off your superiority. If you discuss an object of his
> love, he thinks you are expecting a special favour from it. If you
> discuss an object of his hate, he thinks you are testing his temper.
> If you simplify your discussion, he thinks you are unwise and will
> spurn you. If your discussion is lucidly wayward [inclusive] and
> extensively refined, he thinks you are superficial and flippant. If
> you omit details and present generalizations only, he thinks you
> are cowardly and incomplete. If you trace general principles and
> use broad illustrations, he thinks you are rustic and arrogant.

Then Han added a warning: "These are difficulties in the way of persuasion which every persuader should know."[32]

From warning of the dangers to be avoided, Han went on to advise
about persuasive methods that should succeed. In general, he advised
rationalization—to show the listener how he might accomplish whatever

he wishes to do under some guise that will appear eminently respectable, regardless of what action is being contemplated. Well realizing, as he pointed out elsewhere, that "to choose safety and profit and avoid danger and trouble, this is human nature,"[33] he declared that "in general, the business of the persuader is to embellish the pride and obliterate the shame of the persuaded." Then in a long passage he explained the modes of rationalization which every persuader should attain skill in utilizing:

> If he has any private urgent need, you ought to encourage him with the cause of public justice. If the persuaded has a mean intention but cannot help it, you ought to praise its excellent points and minimize its harmfulness to the public. If he has a high ambition in mind but his real ability falls short of the mark, you ought to enumerate its mistakes, disclose its disadvantages, and esteem his suspension from realizing it. If he aspires to the pride of wisdom and talent, you ought to enumerate different species of the same genus with reference to every subject of knowledge and thereby supply him with abundant information and let him derive ideas from you but pretend to ignorance of his derivation so as to elevate his wisdom.[34]

Han then laid down two generalizations governing the persuasive presentation a counsellor might make in behalf of governmental policies he himself wants to have adopted. "If you want the persuaded to adopt your suggestion to cultivate inter-state friendship, you ought to explain it in the light of a glorious cause and intimate its accord with his private interest. If you want to warn against things dangerous and injurious to the state's welfare, you ought to enumerate the reproaches and slanders against them first and then intimate their discord with his private interest." Then he returned to the depiction of rationalizations useful in all kinds of persuasive situations: "Praise those men doing the same things he does. Esteem the tasks under the same scheme as his tasks are. In regard to men having met the same failures as he has met, be sure to bring out their incurring no loss. If he makes much of his own strength, do not bring in any difficult task that impedes him. If he thinks his own decisions brave, do not point out their unlawfulness; that angers him. If he thinks his own scheme wise, do not recall his past failures which embarrass him."

Han then pointed to the advantages that are to be gained by acceptance of his persuasive theories. "When your meaning is not offensive and your wording is not flippant," he declared, "you are then under way to use all your wisdom and eloquence to persuade anybody. In this way you can become near and dear to your ruler, avoid all suspicion, and exert your speech to the utmost."

In concluding this section of his essay on persuasion, Han indulged in a bit of defensive rationalization, in which he claimed that all the devious devices he had advocated were only for the sake of entrenching the persuader in the favor of his ruler, so that he might finally engage in sound counsel leading toward advantages for the state and the people. "Indeed," he meditated, "as days multiply in the long course of time and favour with the ruler grows well-grounded, when you are no longer suspected of devising schemes profoundly and not convicted in joining issue with the ruler on any point, then you may frankly weigh the relative advantages and disadvantages of the trend of the times . . . and straightly point out what is right and wrong in the course of government and thereby assert yourself." Finally, he added: "If ruler and minister stand together in such relationship, it is due to the success of persuasion."[35]

In the succeeding section of his essay, Han presented a series of specific incidents supporting the general theories he had advocated. One relates how the Duke of Wu, intending to invade Hu, encouraged a trusted counsellor to advise him publicly to do so. Then he put the counsellor to death as a dramatic way of reassuring the ruler of Hu concerning his pacifistic intentions. Afterwards, with Hu disarmed, Duke Wu launched a surprise attack and seized the country. Han intimated not the slightest criticism of the deception or of the deliberate murder of the faithful minister. By implication, at least, the king acted wisely and well. Any scheme is admirable if it works.

Two succeeding anecdotes stress Han's belief in the highly persuasive effects of ethos. He tells of a rich man in Sung whose protective mud fence collapsed in a heavy rain. Both his son and a neighbor warned that unless the fence were immediately repaired, burglars might break in. That very night the house was indeed burglarized. The rich man thereupon praised his son's foresight but was suspicious that the neighbor might have been the thief. Next Han related a more complicated narrative, illustrating how the same man will be believed when in favor and disbelieved if he becomes disliked. A counsellor of the Duke of Wei, one Mi Tzu-hsia, once in the dead of night, learning that his mother was ill, took the duke's own carriage in order to hasten to her bedside. The next day the duke praised him for his dutiful attentiveness to his mother, which led him to ignore the danger of incurring the wrath of his ruler. Another time, while the duke and Counsellor Mi were stroll-

THE LEGALISTIC RHETORICIANS

ing in the orchard, Mi munched upon an unusually sweet peach, and because it was so good he forebore to finish it but gave the remainder to the duke to eat. The duke praised him for his generosity and self-forgetfulness. But in due course Mi Tzu-hsia fell from favor. Then, when something he did offended the duke, the ruler said: "This fellow once rode in my coach under pretence of my order and another time gave me a half-eaten peach." Han pointedly made the moral clear: "The deeds of Mi Tzu had themselves never changed. Yet he was at first regarded as worthy and later found guilty because his master's love turned to hate." Then he added: "For this reason, whoever attempts remonstration, persuasion, explanation, and discussion before the Throne must carefully observe the sovereign's feelings of love and hate before he starts persuading him."[36]

Considering ethos in the general sense, however, Han Fei-Tzu regarded it as a handicap rather than an advantage. Mencius, it will be recalled, had praised especially the courage of flouting the will of the ruler publicly, in order that the judgment of the counsellor would be known as utterly independent. To Han this was incredible. He related the story of a man named Ch'ang, during the Chou period, who was highly popular with the nobles and the people because of his benevolence and justice. For this very reason, the king was advised to put him to death—for the popularity of a worthy man was always a danger to the ruler, leading to insidious comparisons with his own person and actions. The only kind of ethos Han believed to be persuasively efficacious was the specific approval of the speaker by the one whom he seeks to persuade.

In another respect, Han's persuasive theory was more nearly akin to that of Confucius—though on a cynical basis. Like the great sage, Han believed that the monarch must woo the favor of the people and without it would be greatly handicapped if not actually dethroned. "For instance," he observed, "though you have the wisdom of Yao but have no support of the masses of the people, you cannot accomplish any great achievement."[37] Han well realized that "On the whole, such is the general nature of mankind that people regard each other as right if their matters of acceptance and rejection are in common, and as wrong if their matters of acceptance and rejection are diverse."[38] Such reasoning, he made clear, is foolish; for, as a matter of fact, right is right and wrong is wrong regardless of how many may believe one way or another. In a dialogue between a minister named P'ang Kung and the King of Wei, Han revealed both the falsity of this line of thinking and at the same time its persuasive effectiveness:

Said P'ang Kung: "Now if someone says there in the market place is a tiger, will your Majesty believe it?" "No, I will not believe it," replied the King. "Then if two men say there in the market place is a tiger, will your Majesty believe it?" "No, I will not believe it," was another reply. "If three men say there in the market place is a tiger, will your Majesty believe it?" "I will believe it," affirmed the King finally. Thereupon P'ang Kung said: "That there is no tiger in the market place is clear enough, indeed. Nevertheless, because three men allege the presence of a tiger, the tiger comes into existence."[39]

Majority opinion, or the weight of multiple testimony, was well understood by Han to have both great and unmerited persuasive power.

Simply because his persuasive theory was both sophisticated and cynical, Han was also keenly aware of the need for critical and evaluative listening. In part his emphasis was upon the mutual responsibility between speaker and listener to make communication effective; in part he wished to remind his readers that the rule of *caveat emptor* means the speaker is entitled to fool any listener who is not sufficiently attentive to protect himself against deception. "Though you have faith in the counsellor's words," he advised rulers, "you must not listen to them blindly."[40]

The need for protective listening is illustrated in a story Han related of a man who divorced his wife because, when he asked her to weave for him a silk band like one he showed her, she instead wove one that was better than the model.[41] On other occasions, Han blamed poor listening for the prevalence of false conclusions. When critics of sophistry charged that "speeches which are eloquent and delightful to the ear are in discord with the cause of righteousness," Han declared this to be an absurd judgment; for the listeners would be either gentlemen, who would be alert to the moral significance of the utterances despite the beguilement of their style, or they would be rascals, who would be prone to ignore the moral quality of the speech whether or not the style were entrancing. In either case the effect of the communication depended primarily upon the preconception of the listener.[42] Again, he asserted that if "those who are generous, sincere, genuine, and faithful, and are active in mind but timid in speech, are called spiritless," whereas "those who speak on big subjects and talk about fundamental but impracticable principles, and act contrary to the beaten track of the world, are called great men," the fault lies squarely upon indiscriminatory listening.[43]

In an essay which he wrote "On the Difficulty of Speaking," Han did not excuse himself by the fact that he was a stutterer, but drew the broader conclusion that to speak is dangerous because of the probability of being misunderstood. By nature, he insisted, he was not diffident in speaking. Nevertheless, he hesitated to present his views orally because

> if his speeches are compliant and harmonious, magnificent and orderly, he is then regarded as ostentatious and insincere; if his speeches are sincere and courteous, straightforward and careful, he is then regarded as awkward and unsystematic; if his speeches are widely documented and subtly composed, frequently illustrated and continuously analogized, he is then regarded as empty and unpractical; if his speeches summarize minute points and present general ideas, being thus plain and concise, he is then regarded as simple and not discerning; if his speeches are very personally observing and well-versed in the inner nature of mankind, he is then regarded as self-assuming and self-conceited; if his speeches are erudite and profound, he is then regarded as boastful but useless; if his speeches touch the details of housekeeping and estimate each item in terms of numerals, he is then regarded as vulgar; if his speeches are too much concerned with worldly affairs and not offensive in wording, he is then regarded as a coward and a flatterer; if his speeches are far from commonplace and are contrary to human experience, he is then regarded as fantastic; if his speeches are witty and eloquent and full of rhetorical excellences, he is then regarded as flippant; if he discards all literary forms of expression and speaks solely of the naked facts, he is then regarded as rustic; and should he quote from the *Books of Poetry and History* from time to time and act on the teachings of the former sages, he is then regarded as a book chantor.

"These considerations," he concluded, "explain why thy servant Fei is diffident in speaking and worried about speaking."[44]

Precisely as in his essay on "Difficulties in the Way of Persuasion," Han Fei here placed the primary blame for ineffectiveness in communication squarely upon the listener, or upon listener responses which do not properly reflect the speaker's intentions. The essay continues on the theme that not even the wisest of men can convince fools; and even when the wise man speaks to the sanest of men, the difficulties of communication are so great that his message may not at first be properly interpreted. The sages and worthies of ancient times, he concluded, often were punished for their counsel simply "because of the difficulty of persuading fools." Then he added in what is certainly the bravest comment preserved from his life work: "Even the best speech displeases the ear and upsets the heart, and can be appreciated only by worthy and sage rulers. May your Majesty therefore ponder over this memorial of thy servant!"[45]

Not always, however, did Han place the blame for ineffective persuasion upon the listener. Speakers must understand human psychology and must select motivational appeals realistically. He devoted one essay to the theme that to be well-versed in the strategy of persuasion requires one to be "always far-seeing and clearly observing." Otherwise, the speaker may not discern how to develop his persuasive appeal in accord with (rather than contrary to) the selfishness inherent in the listener. Han then proceeded to set forth a veritable catalog of effective and ineffective appeals: "Indeed, the strange and distant, when contesting with the near and dear, have no reason to win; newcomers and travellers, when contesting with long acquaintances and old intimates, have no reason to win; opponents of the sovereign's opinion, when contesting with his supporters of the same taste, have no reason to win; the humble and powerless, when contesting with the noble and powerful, have no reason to win; and a single mouth, when contesting with the whole country, has no reason to win."[46]

Han went on to point out that the trusted confidants of the ruler might well be either fools or ruffians, or both. If wise counsellors should be forced to subject their advice to the criticism of these fools and ruffians, they would naturally guard most cautiously whatever they might say. It is at this point that Han declared, as previously noted, that "wise men would advance their careers by improving their eloquence." But the ability of listeners to understand clearly should be matched by the skill of speakers in setting forth these good ideas with persuasive effectiveness. Then good ideas would not have to be mangled in transmission through inferior channels.

In his "Eight Canons," which is a compendium of significant points on how men are to be ruled, Han Fei-Tzu conjoined listening and speaking, declaring: "Speak explicitly and thereby persuade people to avoid faults. Humbly follow others' speeches and thereby discriminate between earnest men and flatterers."[47] Then he set forth a series of precautions by which a ruler might judge of the soundness of the various policies which are presented for his decision:

> If speeches heard from ministers are not compared, the ruler will find no reason to call the ministers to account. If speakers are not held responsible for the practicality of their advice, heretical theories will bewilder the ruler. A word is such that people believe it because its upholders are numerous. An unreal thing, even if its

experience is asserted by ten men, is still subject to doubt; if its existence is asserted by a hundred men, its reality becomes probable; if its existence is asserted by a thousand men, it becomes undoubtable. Again, if spoken about by stammerers, it is susceptible to doubt; if spoken about by eloquent persons, it becomes believable. Wicked men, when deceiving their superior, rely on the support of the many for their evidence and display their eloquence by quoting forced analogies in order to misrepresent their selfish acts.[48]

Speakers, Han Fei-Tzu insisted, must be held strictly accountable for the utility, *not* for the truthfulness, of what they say. A ruler to whom policies are being recommended through the persuasive arguments of his various ministers must test what is said to him by the outcome of following the advice. "Whoever displays useless eloquence should never be kept at court; . . . and whoever talks big and exaggerates everything should be driven to his wit's end by the disappointing outcome." Han's standards for the judgment of speech were not ethical, but they were strict. If any word of counsel does not accurately forecast the results of the policies the speaker represents, it is a fraud, he asserts. He left little leeway for honest mistakes of judgment. His requirement was stringent: he who does not understand should not speak.

Absolute responsibility for the consequences of what one says was, to Han, of paramount importance. "Ministers usually present as many counsels as possible to display their wisdom," he warned, "and let the ruler choose one of them, so that they can avoid responsibilities." Han pointed out that this kind of ministerial irresponsibility led to chaos. A king needs to be surrounded by counsellors, each of whom will present his own best recommendation for a course of action and then stand by it. The ruler will, of course, have to decide among the various policies that are presented to him by his officials. But no minister should be in a position to assert that a course of action which he proposed did not, after all, represent his own best judgment. As Han said, "The way of the intelligent sovereign never tolerates two different counsels by one minister, but restricts one person to one counsel at one time, allows nobody to act at random, and always synthesizes the results by comparison."[49]

THE ELEMENTS OF HAN FEI-TZU'S RHETORIC

The rhetorical views of Han Fei-Tzu were strictly legalistic. Persuasive speech, in his view, was a primary means of exerting power over people.

The purpose of speech, as he viewed it, is not to reveal established truth; it is to accomplish practical results. Such an accomplishment must be one of two kinds: to merit the approval of the sovereign through speech aimed to enhance his welfare, or to pursue the selfish advantage of the speaker while pretending to serve the well-being of the kingdom and the sovereign. Every speech should be evaluated strictly in terms of its usefulness in serving the purposes of the speaker—or, perhaps, the interests of the listeners.

In view of the inherent selfishness of people, he believed that speech always tends to be rationalistic rather than rational. Eloquence takes the form of embellishment, analogizing, quotation from ancient sources, and exaggeration, all designed to conceal the lack of sense in the substance and to win praise for the ability of the speaker. In order truly to persuade listeners, in his view, it was necessary to either "embellish the pride" or "obliterate the shame" of the one who was to be persuaded. Whatever the ruler might want to do, the speaker must praise; whatever faults he has must be interpreted as being virtues; however unrealistic his aims might be, the speaker should approve them even while seeking to divert the sovereign from pursuing them. Such were the methods of rationalization Han recommended.

There are, he believed, genuine motives so deeply seated in human nature that appeals to them would unfailingly be persuasive. These he considered to be self-interest, which always is the controlling factor in voluntary behavior; the tendency to associate one's own beliefs and conduct with whatever is approved by large numbers of people, which gives weight to multiple testimony; adherence to power, so that listeners may be assured of their personal safety through adhering to what is sanctioned by the state; and a true affection for one's own family, friends, and country. These are the motives that should provide the convincing supports for a speech since they are the sources of the belief and action of the audience.

One special aspect of Han Fei-Tzu's rhetoric was his strong insistence that both speaker and listener should be held strictly accountable for their respective communicative responsibilities. A speaker's words should always be strictly tested by the practicality of the advice he gives: will it work? Speakers must evaluate intelligently what they hear because self-seeking speakers are always likely to be trying to deceive them, and because matters of fact are usually so complex that their true meaning can only be apparent when the minds of the listeners assist the mind of the speaker as he tries to explain them.

Fundamental in the views of Han was the judgment that speech may not only be a principal avenue of advancement at court, but that indiscreet or unskillful speech can be exceedingly dangerous for the speaker.

From the standpoint of the state, persuasive speech is of such high importance that corps of persuasive speakers should be developed and maintained to insure that all the varied courses of action and of policy will be adequately examined, depicted, and defended. These speakers should be strictly controlled and held accountable by the sovereign, to insure that their speaking will be directed to serve the general interests of the state rather than the selfish individual purposes of the speakers or of special groups.

His view of *ethos* was both sophisticated and cynical. Like all rhetoricians, East and West, he held that the confidence of the listeners in the character and goodwill of the speaker is the principal source of persuasion. But he also pointed out that a speaker of outstanding merit is a source of danger to the sovereign, since he may win to himself the loyalties and affection of the people.

Persuasion often fails to achieve its purpose, and the reason primarily is that the speaking is directed to false rather than true motives. The motives by which men seek to live are hidden behind a façade of pretenses that are designed to win social approval, so that it is always difficult to discern the motives that will be practically operative. Moreover, listeners are prone to take pains to conceal or to misrepresent the motives by which they are truly influenced, thus making the task of the speaker harder. The communicative transaction, in Han's view, was unlikely to be cooperative. Speaker and listener were in a sense opponents, striving to get the better of one another.

In conclusion, Han Fei-Tzu regarded persuasive speaking as a high art concerned with such a complexity of motivational factors that it required great care in order to master it. The difficulty speakers encountered was not in knowing the subject matter to be discussed, or in mastering the rules and methods of argumentation, or in gaining ease and confidence in speaking. The difficulty simply and unmistakably lay in penetrating through the maze of fabricated pretense to discover the true motives of the listeners. This could be accomplished only through careful study and preparation. To Han, speakers were not born; they were made. Speech was an art requiring the utmost of careful study and constant consideration.

There were, he felt, many who claimed or were accorded praise as eloquent speakers who were far from deserving of such an accolade. He likened those speakers who embellished their speeches with scholarly references to antiquity or with niceties of style to children who play at housekeeping, so that "when they play together, they take soft earth as cooked rice, muddy water as soup, and wood shavings as slices of meat. However, at dusk they would go home for supper because dust, rice, and mud soup can be played with but not eaten. Similarly, tributes to the legacy of remote antiquity are appreciative and eloquent but superficial; and admiration of the early kings for their benevolence and righteousness cannot rectify the course of the state."[50]

In an essay, "On Pretensions and Heresies," he wrote: "In general, wisdom, ability, cleverness, and erudition, if properly employed, take effect; otherwise, all comes to nought." Consequently, it would be risky and unwise for any court counsellor to attempt to rely upon the natural shrewdness of his native wit. Instead, he required the most sophisticated education in the processes of persuasion, to thread his way through the dangers that lay on every side. "To discard the compasses and trust to skillfulness, and to discard the law and trust to [one's own] wisdom, leads to bewilderment and confusion," he concluded.[51] In sum, persuasive speaking is of far too great importance to be neglected, and its difficulties are far too great for any man, however intelligent, to undertake to be a speaker without exceedingly careful education and preparation.

It is obvious that Han Fei-Tzu's rhetorical theories were in part a deliberate renunciation of Confucianism. He ridiculed the Confucian appeal to the traditions of antiquity; and he had no faith in influence exerted through example. In two lengthy essays on Taoism—the mystic set of beliefs that became the principal rival of Confucianism—he indicated also a distaste for the Confucian emphasis upon propriety and a preference for Lao-Tzu's faith in intuitive insight. "The ears and the eyes are exhausted by sounds and colors," he pointed out, rejecting empiricism as a basis for dependable understanding. "Mental energy is exhausted by outer attractions," he went on, showing no more confidence in rational thinking. "As a result, there is no master in the body. If there is no master inside the body, then though all kinds of good and bad luck pile up like hills and mountains, there is no way to know them."[52] He did not directly say what this "master inside the body" is; but in another essay on Lao-Tzu he rejected conventional propriety as being an external copy of traditionally proper behavior. Instead, he said, individuals should behave in accordance with their natural or untaught perception of what is right and wrong.[53] Intuition would seem to be Han's way to understanding.

When, however, he thought of precautions which the listener should take to test the value of what he hears, he abandoned intuition in favor of practicality. The ruler "ought to know the motive and purpose of every speaker," Han warned, "in order to hold his words responsible for the equivalent fact."[54] In the same essay he pointed out that while some ministers may err in that they "utter words which have neither beginning nor ending or an argument that has no proof," others will "attempt to evade responsibilities by not giving any opinion so as to maintain their high posts." Han concluded that "both speaking and silence equally involve accountabilities." Elsewhere, on this same theme, he gave some rather peculiar but perhaps efficacious advice: "The right way to hear different utterances [to listen to speakers representing diverse viewpoints] is to look drunken. Never start moving your own lips and teeth before the subordinates do." Then he added: "The longer I keep quiet, the sooner others move their lips and teeth. As they themselves move their lips and teeth, I can thereby understand their real intentions. Right and wrong words coming to the fore in such fashion, the ruler does not have to join issue with them."[55]

It is notable that in the theorizing of Han Fei-Tzu, as in that of all the other Chinese philosopher-rhetoricians noted here, there is an absolute faith that the words men speak and the manner in which they speak them are far more dependably accurate indexes to their actual intentions and real character than are even the deeds which they may perform. *Speech most shows the man* is a central theme that recurs constantly, even in such a cynic as the legalist Han. Along with this belief, inevitably, there went a sharp emphasis upon the necessity for penetrating and discriminatory listening. The difference between what a man meant and what he said could always be detected, in the view of Han and the others, provided the listener were sufficiently acute. And if the listener was not wary, in Han's view, there was no safeguard (and actually no reason) to prevent the speaker from deceiving him.

But even with this un-Confucian amorality of Han's in mind, it is noteworthy that he, like the other Chinese rhetoricians, found his rhetorical goal in the harmony or at least in the stability of the state. *Whatever is* is not to be disturbed. *Whatever is* is to be supported. This was, throughout all ancient Chinese rhetoric, the predominant theme. Not to innovate but to preserve was the intellectual and moral aim.

CHAPTER 13

Rhetorical Implications of Taoism

LAO-TZU: THE MYTH OF THE OLD ONE

TAOISM is the only system, prior to the advent of Buddhism in China in the third and fourth centuries A.D., that offered a continuing challenge to Confucianism. Students of Asian philosophy conclude that "no other doctrine of the ancient period except Confucianism has for so long maintained its vigor and attractiveness to the Chinese mind."[1] Like Confucianism, Taoism was an effort by a small number of thinkers to systematize and establish the study of a set of tendencies which they found to be exercising a central influence in the gradual growth of Chinese society. In the view of Burton Watson, an astute expert on the period, "Essentially, all the philosophers of ancient China addressed themselves to the same problem: how is man to live in a world dominated by chaos, suffering, and absurdity?"[2] Under such conditions, how may harmony be maintained while individuals seek for themselves the qualities of the good life? The answers given by Confucius, Mo-tze, Mencius, Han Fei-Tzu, and the others were all different, yet each sought practical solutions based on his observation of life as he found it. The Taoists chose a different approach. They looked through and beyond the conditions of life to an ideal which they posited. Rather than being rationalists or pragmatists, they sought to be mystics.

Taoism encouraged insight and discouraged bookishness. It sought harmony through allegiance to nature rather than conformity to social traditions. The Taoists stressed an individualized search for ultimate meanings that turn out to be so elusive that it was difficult to tell when or whether the sought-for truth had actually been unveiled. Confucius and Mencius insisted there was a Great Way (the Tao), clearly evident when looked for, that would guide the conduct of all who followed it. To the Taoists man seemed to have lost his way by having separated himself from nature. It is because they devoted themselves assiduously to trying to find the way that was lost that they came to be known as Way-followers, or Taoists.

In view of the dominance of Chinese life by Confucianism, it is suggestive to encounter the judgment of Lin Yutang that Lao-Tzu's *Tao-Teh-Ching* is the "one book in the whole of Oriental literature which one should read above all others."[3] Going further, he called it the one book "that is necessary to the understanding of characteristic Chinese behavior." Then he explained what it is that he found to be basic in its teachings. It "contains the first enunciated philosophy of camouflage in the world; it teaches the wisdom of appearing foolish, the success of appearing to fail, the strength of weakness and the advantage of lying low, the benefit of yielding to your adversary and the futility of contention for power." As a result of these factors, Lin concluded, Lao-Tzu's influence "accounts in fact for any mellowness that may be seen in Chinese social and individual behavior." It is an impressive claim, quite sufficient to induce the careful reading of the *Tao-Teh-Ching*.

All these characteristics identified by Lin Yutang indicate that the *Tao-Teh-Ching* is, among other things, a work on rhetoric. The factors he cataloged constitute a methodology of persuasion, one that seems to be deliberately deceptive. Lin's statement suggests that he considers his countrymen to be skilled in pretending to yield, in order to . . .

In order to . . . Here is the puzzling hiatus in Lin's argument. In order to what?

Is it so that the adversary will feel sorry for the ostensibly incapable pleader? Or is it that the opponent will be disarmed by the seeming incompetence of the speaker and thus may be caught off guard? Is it indeed the characteristic behavior of the Chinese people, or was it recommended by Lao-Tzu, to camouflage their intentions so that they appear to be yielding in order to be granted or to seize some advantage they could not attain directly? This seems to be what Lin Yutang has said. This apparently is his interpretation of the *Tao-Teh-Ching*.

The record, however, appears to read otherwise. Far from constituting an unethical rhetoric of deliberate camouflage, the *Tao-Teh-Ching* presents a substantial case for two propositions that five centuries later were to be enunciated by Jesus of Nazareth—namely, "the meek shall inherit the earth," and "he who would find his life must lose it."

The rhetorical contribution in the writings derived from Lao-Tzu is their insight concerning the futility of argument and contention, their recognition that nobody wins an argument, that he who appears to win actually loses more than he gains. In place of contention, Lao-Tzu presented an alternative. His philosophy of persuasion came full circle. He not only renounced the methodology of crushing opposition through strength—whether it be of fact, or of argument, or of personality—but he also showed how to surmount opposition by encompassing it within one's own goals. He recommended identification of the contesting viewpoints with a higher good so inclusive of complementary ideas that their true unity becomes evident.

This theory of persuasion quickly won high favor among the elite of China. Even while Confucianism was being established as the basis of formal education and consequently as the means by which individuals could rise to power, the *Tao-Teh-Ching* was required reading at court.[4] Among the nobility it was realized that Lao-Tzu's persuasive methods offered greater security than military or political power.

"The greater one's understanding of the Way," they told one another, "the more security he enjoys; but the greater one's power, the more danger threatens him."[5] And the Grand Historian of the Han dynasty, examining the historical record, agreed that this was true. The results of adhering to Taoism, according to Ssu-Ma Ch'ien, were impressive. Of one royal student of these doctrines, the historian noted: "In executing his duties and governing the people, he valued honesty and serenity, selecting worthy assistants and secretaries and leaving them to do as they saw fit."[6] For the populace at large, the persuasive method of self-abnegation was too difficult. Among the people, the historian wrote, "bodies have delighted in ease and comfort, and hearts have swelled with pride at the glories of power and ability. So long have these habits been allowed to permeate the lives of the people that, though one were to go from door to door preaching the subtle arguments of the Taoists, he could never succeed in changing them."[7]

The origin of the Taoist teachings is obscure. Like Confucianism, they antedated, at least in part, their presumed author, and they were greatly expanded and elaborated by succeeding interpreters. The very existence of the principal expositor of Taoism has been questioned. Like Homer, whose *Iliad* and *Odyssey* were the fruition of many legends from many sources, Lao-Tzu must have put together the *Tao-Teh-Ching* from many existing materials. Both Ssu-Ma Ch'ien and Chuang-Tzu represented him as the author of Taoism and report debates between him and Confucius. H. G. Creel insists that these debates are merely literary devices; and he cites evidence that if Lao-Tzu existed at all he must have belonged to a later period, when the Confucian ideas had already been extended and applied in education and in court practices. It would be ridiculous, however, to assume that the *Tao-Teh-Ching* somehow just emerged as a catch-all collection of aphoristic terms. It presents such a consistent philosophy, and one so original, that internal evidence suggests an author of singular personality and understanding.

Many able scholars still maintain the traditional view that Lao-Tzu was born in 570 B.C.[8] or perhaps even as early as 604 B.C.[9] Others date the Tao-Teh-Ching as "probably no older than the third or fourth centuries B.C."[10] Fanciful legends about him multiplied, including one that he was immaculately conceived by a shooting star, was carried in his mother's womb for sixty-two years, and was born a white-haired old man.[11] Ssu-Ma Ch'ien, his earliest biographer, wrote unequivocably of him that

> he came from the Good Will Corners section of Grindstone Village in the Hardpan District of Ch'u. He belonged to the Plum family clan. His given name was Ear and, familiarly, he was called Uncle Sun. Posthumously he was called Tan. He was an historian in the secret archives of Chou. . . .
>
> Lao-Tzu practiced the Way and its Virtue. He learned to do his work in self-effacement and anonymity. For a long time he lived in Chou, and when he saw that it was breaking up, he left. At the frontier, the official Yin Hsi said: "Since, Sir, you are retiring, I urge you to write me a book."
>
> So Lao-Tzu wrote a book in two parts, explaining the Way and its Virtue in something over 5,000 words. Then he went away. No one knows where he died.[12]

However dubious may be the authorship, the authenticity of the text of the Tao-Teh-Ching is well established. Four separate editions of it were listed in the catalog of the imperial library of the Han dynasty, compiled prior to the opening of the Christian era. Many more editions are listed in the catalog of the imperial library of the Sui dynasty (A.D. 589–618). The first Western-language translation was a Latin version, made by Jesuit priests and presented at the Royal Society in London in 1788. A French translation was made in 1842. From that time, translations multiplied. As early as 1867, a historian of Chinese literature wrote that "the various editions of it are innumerable; it has appeared from time to time in almost every conceivable size, shape, and style of execution."[13] Lin Yutang declares it to be "the most translated of all the Chinese books."[14] Burton Watson notes that every translation is an interpretation, since the translator "must choose one of a number of possible meanings before he can produce any kind of coherent version."[15]

Comparative reading of the many translations indicates a very wide range of interpretations of specific passages. But Watson is surely right when he insists that, though particular passages may be obscure, the general meaning of the whole is inescapable. The style is varied, being sometimes sharply clear and at other times suggestively ambiguous or even vague; but its central meaning is repeated many times in many ways.

Preparatory to establishing this central meaning, Lao-Tzu had to clear away clusters of misunderstandings. What the world calls knowledge, skills, and cleverness he declared are only shams concealing the lack of genuine capacity. Similarly, righteousness, justice, and love are also shams—modes of behavior adopted deliberately and maintained by rule as a substitute for the lost or abandoned feeling of identity. Philosophically, Lao-Tzu was a monist. In his view, all substance, all being, is essentially one. Seeming differences are illusions. The great art of living is to learn how to re-identify with the natural unison of the universe. And the means of doing so are irrational. We do not *think* ourselves into harmony with all being, including other people; we *feel* our way to such unity. The making of explicit distinctions, through analysis, definition, and classification, does not clarify meaning; neither does it penetrate into the inner truth of a subject. On the contrary, such particularization and dismemberment destroy the reality that is being sought. Actuality is sensed; it is not understood. The brain is no more truly an organism of man than is stomach or skin; why, then, emphasize its importance? Distinctions divide, and therefore they do violence to nature; confrontation with distinctions causes confusion and conflict. Whatever seems to be different is imperfectly comprehended. We should, therefore, relax into a quietistic receptivity that invites awareness of undifferentiated reality.

Such a philosophy is in usual terms anti-rhetorical. Indeed, many isolated passages from the *Tao-Teh-Ching* seemingly renounce rhetoric—and even communication itself. "In much talk there is great weariness. It is best to keep silent." This is the theme of the fifth of the eighty-one poems that comprise the *Tao-Teh-Ching*.* "Root out your preachers, discard your teachers, and the people will benefit a hundredfold," reads part of the suggestive nineteenth verse. "Wise is the man who teaches by deeds, not by words," we are advised in verse two; and in verse forty-three we again are told that "The best instruction is not in words."

* Many translations are collated for the quotations from Lao-Tzu, especially those by Waley, John C. H. Wu, Lin Yutang, Legge, Blakney, Duyvendak, Giles, Bynner, and Chu'u Takao. As Watson recommends, my practice is to try to interpret particular passages in terms of the general meaning of the whole work.

The primary business of life, Lao-Tzu believed, is to live, not to influence others. Therefore, as verse seventy-two points out, "The wise man knows himself but does not reveal his inmost thoughts." "A good man," verse eighty-one advises, "does not argue." The reasons are various, but among them is the simple fact of which verse eighty-one also reminds us, that "true words may not sound fine and fine words may not be true." A better reason is adduced in verse seventy-three, one with which translators have had the most trouble; yet the basic meaning clearly is that the ways of nature are inscrutable. In paraphrase, the content of this verse is as follows: Bravery may assert itself in killing, or in avoiding killing. We know that either of these kinds of courage is both praiseworthy and blameworthy. Even sages consider it difficult to tell what is ultimately advantageous. The natural processes of nature are not designed to assure advantage, yet somehow they do work out harmoniously. Nature does not carry on a dialogue with men, yet it responds properly to their questions and their answers. Natural processes affect us all even though we do not seek them out; there is no evidence that nature has any anxiety about its own functioning, yet it dependably follows a natural sequence. The conclusion must be that nature is adequate to all needs if its functioning is quietly accepted. This philosophy of quiet acquiescence is paramount in the *Tao-Teh-Ching;* and in this emphasis it is indeed anti-rhetorical.

The general tenor of the work, however, is precisely rhetorical, for it teaches a way of dealing with other people which is designed to attain the ultimate goal of both the individual and his society. Paradoxically, the very method is what appears on first encounter to be the renunciation of method. In verse forty-five we are warned that "the greatest eloquence is like stuttering," in a context which makes clear the meaning that amidst great difficulties the difference between high and low skill becomes extinguished. The sentiment might be rephrased: *when problems abound, glib cleverness is as futile as inarticulate awkwardness.*

The Taoist rhetorical method begins to emerge more clearly in verse forty-three, where it is averred: "If you do not quarrel, no one on earth will be able to quarrel with you." It is even more explicit in verse eighty-one, which observes: "The female always overcomes the male by her stillness." This same eighty-first verse continues: "Those who are skilled do not dispute; the disputations are not skilled. . . . The sage constantly keeps the people without knowledge and without desire; and where there are those who have knowledge, he prevents them from presuming to act. . . . He who tries to govern a state by his wisdom is a scourge to it, while he who does not do so is a blessing." *Leave well enough alone* is a proverb long familiar in the West. Lao-Tzu would add to it, *also leave ill enough alone.*

The principal teaching of the *Tao-Teh-Ching,* according to the Sinologist H. G. Creel, is that we "should be in harmony with, not in rebellion against, the fundamental laws of the universe."[16] This is a way of saying that behavior should be natural, untrained, unsophisticated. Its goal is not so much serenity, which might be interpreted as the philosophical acceptance of whatever must be, whether it be good or ill; it is, rather, passivity, a flowing into and becoming one with nature. Using water as his analogy, Lao-Tzu, in verse forty-three, pointed out that the "softest thing in the world overcomes the hardest things," and that water flows into and occupies spaces that had not even appeared to exist. He concluded the verse with the regretful observation that "few in the world can understand teaching without words and the advantage of taking no action."

The cardinal concepts of Lao-Tzu would seem to be *wu-wei, wu-hsin,* and *te,* which might be translated as: "passive nonaction," "mindlessness," and "spontaneous righteousness." All three of them have rhetorical implications. His theory of persuasion was that fundamentally people tend to think, feel, and act in accordance with their own basic nature, which is akin to and even indistinguishable from nature in general. Since natural forces are genuinely inscrutable and nonreasonable, it is futile to try to "understand" them or to foster understanding by others. Far better is it to avoid purposive action, to abandon the mind to its own vacuous wanderings, and to be naturally good in the sense of living effortlessly in harmony with natural characteristics.

If there can be a rhetoric of mysticism, Taoism should qualify. In verse twenty-five, Lao-Tzu averred: "The principle of the Tao is spontaneity." In verse seventy-eight, he advised us to note that: "Nothing in the world is softer or weaker than water; but for attacking the hard and strong, there is nothing like it! That weakness overcomes strength and gentleness overcomes rigidity, is known to all, though no one can put it into practice." Then, in verse nineteen, he said abruptly: "Cut out sagacity; discard knowingness." The meaning which most matters, the true essence of a matter, he explained in verse twenty-one, is to be sensed intuitively rather than discovered through analysis:

> The Tao is something blurred and indistinct,
>   How blurred! How indistinct!
> Yet within it are images.
>   How blurred! How indistinct!

> Yet within it are things.
> How dim! How confused!
> Yet within it is mental power,
> Because this power is most true,
> Within it there is confidence.

The insight needed to understand truth and to communicate with one another consists of spontaneous identification—much like the modern concept of empathy. According to Holmes Welch, one of Taoism's best interpreters: *"Te* (spontaneity) cannot be achieved, however, until you have erased the aggressive patterns etched by society into your nature. . . . When you discard some of your wishes, you will have them all."[17]

With apologies to Lin Yutang, another very great interpreter of the Chinese spirit, this Taoistic rhetoric is quite the contrary of camouflage. The message of Lao-Tzu, rather, is this: Be what you are; do not pretend; do not attempt the impossible task of trying to conform to the vast network of often conflicting and never adequate social beliefs and customs. Moreover, do not try to understand nature, either; for such an effort at understanding would require analysis, and this would fix upon the object your own mode of interpreting it. The recipe that Lao-Tzu recommended is simple to state, though perhaps impossible fully to attain: avoid action, empty your mind, and be passively receptive to spontaneous insight.

Taoism is generally considered the leading Chinese alternative to the formalistic conventionality of Confucianism. However, when Lao-Tzu advised against conventionality, he did not advocate deliberate flouting of the social norms. In old China, just as truly as in the world of the twentieth century, the avowed rejection of social values would have invited stern punishment, perhaps to the extent of imprisonment, amputation of a limb, exile, or death. Flagrant individualism has never been a Chinese ideal; it was surely not the Way Lao-Tzu envisioned as leading toward insight and peace. Arthur Waley, for example, one of the best exponents of Chinese thought, quotes the *Kuan Tzu,* a work presumably dating from the seventh century B.C., as saying: "A ruler should not listen to those who believe in people having opinions of their own and in the importance of the individual. Such teachings cause men to withdraw to quiet places and hide away in caves or on mountains, there to rail at the prevailing government, sneer at those in authority, belittle the importance of rank and emoluments, and despise all who hold official posts."[18] Becoming "unconventional," in terms represented in the *Tao-*

Teh-Ching, meant attaining a degree of sophisticated understanding that reveals social conventions to be arbitrary and artificial constructs which serve expedient ends but do not represent illimitable truths.

Lao-Tzu's plea was that culture and custom should not be accorded the kind of acceptance which must be given to natural laws. The social agreements by which human relationships are governed have gained currency, he felt, because of their transient or current usefulness. His view appears to have been very much like that of the post-Kantian German philosopher, Hans Vaihinger, who wrote: "It must be remembered that the object of the world of ideas as a whole is not the portrayal of reality—this would be an utterly impossible task—but rather to provide us with an *instrument for finding our way about more easily in this world.*"[19]

Lao-Tzu's perception was like that of Walter Lippmann, when he wrote: "In the great blooming, buzzing confusion of the outer world we pick out what our culture has already defined for us, and we tend to perceive that which we have picked out in the form stereotyped for us by our culture."[20] The central theme of Taoism is that man should strive to penetrate through appearances to the reality which is veiled from ordinary perception by strongly entrenched traditional modes of interpretation. The *Tao-Teh-Ching* carries this message basically throughout, but nowhere more clearly than in its nineteenth verse:

> Banish wisdom, discard knowingness,
>   And the people will be a hundredfold benefited.
> Banish love, discard justice,
>   And the people will resume their natural affections.
> Banish shrewdness, discard self-seeking,
>   And there will be no more thieves or brigands.
> Since these three are external and inadequate,
> The people have need of what they can depend upon:
>   Seek the real self;
>   Embrace primal nature;
>   Check selfishness;
>   Curtail desires.

The basic difference between Confucianism and Taoism emerges clearly in contrasting this Taoist declaration with the statement by the Confucianist T'ang, in his commentary on *The Great Learning,* when he said: "Riches adorn a house, and virtue adorns the person."[21] Lao-Tzu would surely have agreed heartily with this sentiment; but Confucianism recommends such adornment, whereas Taoism condemns it. To Confucius, the development of human nature by the acquisition of social graces and humane sentiments is the proven pathway to individual and social moral improvement. To Lao-Tzu the disfigurement of human nature by diversion from natural tendencies through acceptance of culturally established forms of thinking and behaving is the pathway to pretense, frustration, and futility.

Lao-Tzu argued that it is because of our socially induced refusal to live in immediate relations with reality that we have had to invent such prescriptive concepts as *love, honor, charity,* and the whole panoply of directives which we call *education.* Instead of looking around to observe the ideals and the prohibitions contrived by men in relationships, the Taoist urged that we try to resume the innate ability to relate our own perceptions and feelings to what F. S. C. Northrop, an acute Western critic, has termed "the immediately apprehended esthetic continuum," within which "there is no distincttion between subjective and objective," for it is "a single all-embracing continuity."[22] Amorphous as the idea may seem, it is close to the advice Jesus is reported, in Luke 10:41, to have given to Martha: that she cease hurrying about to provide comforts for him and simply sit in silent attentiveness, so that insight might help her not to *do* but to *be* good.

Since social codes constitute a screen standing between original nature and actual behavior, hypocrisy has become the ruling social virtue. Motivational impulses themselves have been twisted so that they originate in pretense, and behavior is carefully calculated to meet the test of the prying eyes of neighbors. Such social norms may indeed be recognized as having utility, but they are inevitably not in harmony with nature. Taoism, interpreted in this view, actually aims to assist individuals to pierce through the camouflage maintained by society. Its aim is to help us to penetrate through the exterior masks to the inner reality. Taoism assumes a deep-seated conflict between self and society. Moreover, Lao-Tzu saw clearly that anxieties are not to be avoided and peace attained by the flouting of social conventions. Neither does the proper method consist of hypocritical subservience to their dictates. Rather, in Lao-Tzu's observation, there is a better way which consists of sufficient outward conformity to avoid social rejection, while simultaneously remaining true to one's own inner vision of truth. Only in this sense was Lin Yutang right to call Taoism a rhetoric of camouflage. It might better, perhaps, be termed a rhetoric of sophistication, even though sophisticated insight leads directly to primal simplicity.

The rhetorical ideas in the *Tao-Teh-Ching* accord with Lao-Tzu's general philosophy. To him, the purpose of communication is communion. The aim is to establish an identity with what is being talked about and with those who are listening. As verse eighty-one avers, "It is not good to settle a grievance if the settlement leads to other grievances. Care should be taken that communication not become divisive."

The only acceptable message to be communicated, in his view, is the truth. And he believed that truth could indeed be determined by a process of (1) freeing the mind from socially established and hence artificial conventions; (2) attaining the ability to subordinate one's egoistic feelings and self-centered thoughts so that the message is presented objectively, rather than in accordance with the feelings of the speaker; and (3) resuming the inherent ability to identify oneself with the unitary essence of nature.

In view of the purpose and the message that have been recommended, it is understandable that Lao-Tzu believed that style, organization, and delivery must be nonassertive and nonargumentative. The message that is unqualifiedly true and that is identified with the listener's own feelings will be accepted by him most readily as he hears it set forth with utter and categorical simplicity—with no qualifications and no argumentative supports.

The demands of speech which aims to make truth so self-evident that it will be accepted without explanation or support are difficult. As verse twenty-seven warns, "Just as a good runner leaves no tracks, so does a good speaker make no blunders." The skills required for effective speaking, however, are not "learned" but are "recovered"—by relaxing into one's own essential nature. This point is emphasized again and again. For example, verse twenty-four reminds us that "He who raises himself on tiptoe cannot long remain steady." Verse forty declares that "There is no greater misfortune than not to know when one has had enough." And in verse nine Lao-Tzu piled up examples:

> If you would not spill the wine,
>> Do not fill the glass too full.
> If you wish your blade to hold its edge,
>> Do not make it over-keen. . . .
> When you have done your work and established your fame,
>> Withdraw!
>> Such is the Way.

Always for Lao-Tzu the basic requirement is to know what is true. This cannot be accomplished by reason or by analysis but requires a nonmental, nonseeking, spontaneous insight. "He also sees," John Milton might have said, "who only stands and waits." Alan Watts interprets the Taoist method as using "the peripheral vision of the mind."[23] In ordinary living, Watts observes, we do best that to which we give the least thought. Speech is an excellent example: we could not utter a sentence if we tried consciously to direct the complex of muscles and nerves that are involved. Breathing and walking, also, are done best when there is no thought of what is being done. Riding a bicycle becomes skilled when the rider no longer thinks about how to maintain balance. Watts dramatizes the method as follows: "For it is really impossible to appreciate what is meant by the Tao without becoming, in a rather special sense, stupid. So long as the conscious intellect is frantically trying to clutch the world in its net of abstractions, and to insist that life be bound and fitted to its rigid categories, the mood of Taoism will remain incomprehensible; and the intellect will wear itself out."[24] Greater efficiency— even greater mental efficiency—requires the withdrawal of the mind from active supervision.

True insight is likely to come from ceasing to strive, to criticize, or to think. Intelligence, then, is not to be identified with the analytical and associative centers of the cortex. Genuine understanding depends upon a feeling tone which emanates from a multiplicity of factors within the observer and within or about the object being observed. The *Tao* is "blurred and indistinct . . . yet within it are images." These images are to be discerned not by intellectual probing but by a merging of the Self with nature. The mind should behave like a mirror: neither seeking nor rejecting, just reflecting. Above all, thinking should not be purposive. For to think purposively requires a sharpening of focus, a delimiting of the field of observation, a shutting out or diminishing of all that does not contribute toward illumination of the preconceived item. To think purposively, Lao-Tzu would warn, is to court the danger of imposing one's own conclusions upon the matter under consideration.

Lao-Tzu's rhetoric suffers difficulties arising from its vagueness, since he denied the validity of definition and classification. It must, therefore, be implicative rather than definitive. For of one thing Lao-Tzu was certain: to break truth into separable fragments is to destroy it. Nothing has meaning except in context—and context is all-inclusive. This view produces a rhetoric that is difficult both for speakers and for critics of communication. It might require, as is declared in a book derived from Lao-Tzu's teachings, the *Lieh-Tzu,* a span of nine years of concentration before a disciple may attain a state of disassociation in which his "mind gave free rein to its reflections, his mouth free passage to its speech." There is much to unlearn before one may even commence to use the "peripheral vision of the mind." A rhetoric based on such mental discipline is extremely demanding. But, in its emphasis upon the unitary nature of reality, it subjects all rhetorics based upon manipulatory strategies to new scrutiny.

CHUANG-TZU: THE DREAMER AND THE DREAM

Since appearances belie reality, what we perceive, what we say, and what we seek to accomplish may as often be wrong as right. This was a cardinal principle in Lao-Tzu's teaching, and it was emphasized also by his chief disciple, Chuang-Tzu. Chuang, as was his way, made the point with an illustrative story: "Once," he wrote, "when Hsi Shih, the most beautiful of women, was frowning and beating her breast, an ugly woman saw her and thought, 'Now I have found out how to become beautiful!' So she went home to her village and did nothing but frown and beat her breast. When the rich men of the village saw her, they bolted themselves into their houses and dared not come out; when the poor people of the village saw her they took wife and child by the hand and ran at full speed. This woman had seen that someone frowning was beautiful and thought that she had only to frown in order to become beautiful."[25]

Such confusions of reality and illusion were the root cause, he felt, of most personal unhappiness and social turmoil. Further to dramatize the point, he related a dream he had had: "I, Chuang Chou, once dreamed that I was a butterfly flitting about. I did whatever I wished! I knew nothing about any Chuang Chou. Then I suddenly awakened a Chuang Chou with all his normal trappings. Now I don't know whether Chuang Chou dreamed he was a butterfly, or a butterfly is dreaming he is Chuang Chou. There must be a difference between Chuang Chou and the butterfly, and that is what is meant when we say that things undergo transformation."[26] Yes, there are transformations. What is true comes to appear as something false; and the false sometimes seems unquestionably true. Which, finally, is which? This was the question Chuang-Tzu could not follow to a certain conclusion.

"How do I know that loving life is not a delusion?" he asked. "How do I know that in hating death I am not like a man who, having left home in his youth, has forgotten the way back?" Then, to enforce the point, he related a story of Lady Li, who was heartbroken when she was captured and taken far away from her home to be made a concubine of a king. But when she found her status at court was one of elevated luxury, she wondered why she had dreaded it. "How do I know," Chuang concluded, "that the dead do not in the same way wonder why they ever longed for life?"[27]

The author of these lively anecdotes is renowned in Chinese history for the strength of his imagination. He should as well be known as a rhetorician of singular penetration. He rendered the implicit teachings of Lao-Tzu explicit, and to them he added rich insights of his own.

Chuang-Tzu's dates are tentatively accepted as 369 to 286 B.C., which would make him Mencius' junior by ten years. For a time he held a minor clerkship in his local district of Meng, in the state of Sung; but he seldom mentioned his own career, and almost nothing is known of it. After he had achieved fame as a teacher, according to his own account, he was approached by a messenger from the King of Ch'u, who wished to offer him the post of Prime Minister. "I have heard," Chuang replied to him, "in your king's possession is a sacred tortoise, dead these three thousand years, and that your king keeps it wrapped in a cloth in his ancestral temple. Now, were the tortoise to have a choice, would he die so as to leave his bones as relics to be treasured by men, or would he rather live and wag his tail in a mud pool?" When the messenger replied that the tortoise would rather live, Chuang turned away, saying: "Please be gone. I want to wag my tail in the mud pool."[28] It was a most un-Confucian reply—renouncing public responsibility for personal pleasure; but then Chuang-Tzu was a most un-Confucian man.

What he taught, according to the Grand Historian Ssu-ma Chien, poured out across China "like an overwhelming flood, which spreads at its own sweet will." Then the historian added that since the teachings were sweepingly comprehensive, they could not be put to any definite use. It would be impossible to abstract from Chuang-Tzu a maxim or set of maxims with which to deal with specific problems. His philosophy was all of a piece—an unbreakable unity. What he asked of his followers was complete acceptance of the Way as he depicted it: this or nothing. He offered them no halfway point at which to come to rest.

The corpus of his work once totaled fifty-three chapters, of which thirty-three are preserved; and of these, Chapters 19–32 are suspected to have been later additions written by his disciples. Chapters 1, 2, 4, 5, 22, 24, 27, 29, and 33 are the primary sources of his explicit rhetorical ideas, though all the rest are also relevant. The earliest known edition, in ten volumes, was edited by Kua Hsiang, at the close of the third century B.C.—perhaps a hundred years after Chuang's death. This, however, shows evidence of having been based on an even earlier edition. A definitive edition was issued in the seventeenth century by Lin Hsi-Chung; it is this which serves as the foundation of present-day studies of Chuang-Tzu. The first English-language translation was issued in Shanghai and London in 1881, by Frederic Henry Balfour, under the title *The Divine Classic of Nan-hua*—because Chuang is supposed to have composed his book in his later years while living in retirement on Nan-hua Mountain. Later and better translations are by James Legge, for the *Sacred Books of the East* series, in 1891; by H. A. Giles, in 1889 and 1923; and by James R. Ware in 1963. (Arthur Waley, from whom selections have been cited, translated only fragments of this work.) After Confucius, in the opinion of Ch'en Shou-Yi, a Chinese literary historian, "none was to wield greater influence on posterity in art and letters than Chuang Chou."[29] Yet he never has been widely known, and his prolific and suggestive ideas on rhetoric have passed without special notice.

James Ware, the most recent translator of Chuang-Tzu, finds his monistic philosophy "titanic in scope and incandescent with potential," bringing "all of past, present and future into one focus."[30] Chuang never stooped to write below the grand scale. As he says in the opening of his book, "Petty knowledge is not comparable with knowledge on the large scale any more than youth is comparable with age." The conclusion of his opening chapter is a conversation with the rationalistic rhetorician Hui Shih, who finds him "awkward in the use of magnitude," and thinks him "weedy-minded," apparently because his ideas spring up so pro-lifically and have no obvious usefulness. Then Hui said to him: "There is a tree on my place with a large trunk so gnarled that the plumb line cannot be used on it. Its branches are so twisted that the compass and square cannot be used on them. Although it stands by the road, carpen-ters do not give it a thought. Similarly, your talk is on such a grand scale that it is useless and the people unanimously reject you."[31] Chuang no doubt included this comment in his book because he was glad to preserve it. It was never his intent to speak plainly of simple things; and neither a day-by-day utility nor popularity were among his goals. In his opening chapter he was pleased to signal to his readers that if they would find what he meant to convey, they must be prepared to read between the lines.

Chapter 2 is rich in rhetorical judgments. Chuang-Tzu manifested at once that in his view the way a man speaks is the surest indication of his character and ability, for which reason speech is worthy of the closest attention. And just as human capacity in general varies from high to low, so does speech. As he said: "Just as knowledge in its great form is all-encompassing and petty knowledge is hairsplitting, so speech in its great form is brilliant and petty speech is verbose." Then he par-ticularized the differences to be noted between "brilliant" and "petty" speech. "When a remark comes like an arrow from a crossbow," he said, "rights and wrongs are in question. When the speaking is deliberate, as in prayers and oaths, we are dealing with a defensive effort to achieve victory. When the talk diminishes like daylight in fall and winter, it means that the mind, like day, is drawing toward its close. To a torrent of speech, no reply can be made. When the remarks are only mumbled, it is an indication of great age."

In the remainder of the chapter, after noting that joy, anger, grief, and anxiety intermingle and shade into one another, he asked: "Is man's life actually as confused as it seems to be? Or am I the only one confused?" Again he turned from this query directly to the patterns of speech, since these indicated to him the typical revelations of a man's character. "Speech," he declared, "is not merely blowings of the breath. A speaker says something, but before he himself knows what he means, is there speech or not? The speaker assumes that his speech differs from the peepings of fledglings, but perhaps that can be argued." Then he revealed the reason for his perplexity. "Where is the Truth hidden, so that what appears to be true or false can be apparent? Where is speech so twisted that its distinctions between right and wrong are obscured?" And at the end of this passage he presented his own conclusion: "The Truth is concealed from understanding by an insufficiency of insight; speech misleads as to distinctions between right and wrong by social influences that cause the speakers to try to be impressive."

Chuang then approached the same problem more fundamentally. Everything is either objective or subjective, he declared. But actually this distinction loses its validity; for the objective item must be perceived and understood, which renders it subjective; and subjective impulses or feelings are related to externals, which makes them also objective.[32] So far as human relations are concerned, "a thing is whatever we call it only so long as people accept that name for it. . . . But particularization is a denial of the actual unity of being. Words bring compartmentalization, by which I mean left, right, rules, propriety, analysis, argument, strife, and quarrels, which," he added sarcastically, "are called the Eight Perfections."

In the remainder of this chapter Chuang-Tzu made his primary contribution to rhetoric, namely: that knowledge is far too uncertain to justify its persuasive presentation, and that even when a speaker feels sure of what he knows, his perception is too inclusive and undifferentiated to be stated in discursive language. The true sage, he felt, is "eloquent in silence, or in speaking unspecifically." Or, putting the same idea another way, the wise man "speaks without speaking; he does not speak when he speaks."

The disciple to whom Chuang addressed these observations found them exceedingly perplexing. Confessing his inability to understand them, he said that in his view, "Such language only means that the sage man keeps his mouth shut, and turns aside questions that are uncertain and dark." Such an explanation, he suggested, must be unsatisfactory, for it makes the sage seem stupid and ignorant.

Chuang tried again: "Let me put it this way: how do we know that what I call knowledge is not ignorance? Or that what I call ignorance is not knowledge?" He then gave numerous examples of divergent judgments, typical of which was a reminder that a woman whom men consider to be beautiful would seem dangerous and frightening to fish, birds, and animals. "From my point of view," he concluded, "the teaching of morality and etiquette, as well as the dubbing of things as right or wrong, produce only utter confusion. How can I effectively discuss them?" In the view of Burton Watson, "He saw the man-made ills of war, poverty, and injustice. He saw the natural ills of disease and death. But he believed that they were ills only because man recognized them as such. If man would once forsake his habit of labeling things good or bad, desirable or undesirable, then the man-made ills, which are the product of man's purposeful and value-ridden actions, would disappear and the natural ills that remain would no longer be seen as ills."[33]

When the disciple again demurred, unconvinced by these instances, Chuang-Tzu again tried to put into words the concept which he felt was actually wordless. "I will try to explain the thing to you in a rough way," he said; "do you in the same way listen to me." Then he continued:

> Suppose that you and I debated and you bested me, would it mean that you were naturally right and I was naturally wrong? Or even vice versa? Or would one be partially right and one partially wrong? Or would both be both right and wrong? If you and I cannot come to a mutual understanding, others assuredly will experience the same difficulty.
>
> Whom, then, could we get to adjudicate the controversy? Anybody agreeing with me will only repeat my arguments, and we shall still be in the dark. Somebody differing with both of us merely offers a third point of view, and somebody agreeing with both of us simply brings us back to the starting point. You and I and all those others would not be able to come to a mutual understanding.

Of what, then, Chuang continued, does argument really consist? "There is affirmation and denial; and there is the assertion of an opinion and the rejection of it. If the affirmation be according to the reality of the fact, it is certainly different from the denial of it—there can be no dispute about that. If the assertion of an opinion be correct, it is certainly different from its rejection—neither can there be any dispute about that. Whether voices that are ever changing come to agreement or not, the ultimate answer must remain unknown in the infinity of the whole universe. Let us forget the lapse of time; let us forget the conflict of opinions. Let us make our appeal to the Infinite and take up our position there."

The ontological problem was endlessly fascinating for Chuang-Tzu. Chapter 3 opens with the query: "The life in us being limited, but knowledge unlimited, it is dangerous to pursue the unlimited with the limited." Chapter 5 returns again to the rhetorical problem of how unknowables may be communicated. "Is there really such a thing as wordless instruction?" he asked; and he answered it by relating anecdotes of three crippled beggars who lived in serenity because they contemplated the wholeness of life, which, in perspective, reduced the loss of their amputated toes to insignificance. People learn much about true meanings simply by observing them, without oral instruction. Indeed, "nobody uses flowing water as a mirror, only still water"; wherefore, silent instruction may be the best. Moreover, "a mirror is bright when there is no dust or dirt on it"; hence, we learn most from observing the lives of superior men.

Still teaching through examples, Chuang continued in Chapter 5 with the story of a deformed man so ugly that he was called T'o the Horrible; yet so attractive was he that women longed for his love, all men were friendly with him, and he was offered the post of prime minister. The reason? "Because he never took the initiative in anything; he was simply always agreeable." Rather than taking the lead in discussions, he seemed always to share the opinions of his associates. He never exhorted people but manifested his sympathy with them. Then, instead of stating directly what conclusion should be drawn from this instance, Chuang, as was his wont, indicated his meaning obliquely, with another anecdote. "A litter of young pigs was suckling their dead mother; but after a while they looked at her, and went away. After all, it was not their mother they loved but her function."

The function a wise man should pursue is to be, not to do. Chuang became more explicit: "But mankind forgets not that which is to be forgotten, forgetting that which is not to be forgotten. This is forgetfulness indeed! And thus, with the truly wise, wisdom is a curse, sincerity is like glue, virtue is but a means by which to acquire, and skill nothing more than a commercial capacity. For the truly wise make no plans, and therefore require no wisdom. They do not analyze and differentiate, therefore they need no glue. They want nothing and therefore need no virtue. They sell nothing and therefore are not in want of commercial capacity." Hui Shih, the debater, then asked: "Are human beings without any functions?" To this Chuang replied: "When I say they have no function, I mean that they have no business to wound themselves inwardly with preferential judgments. They should constantly accept the universe spontaneously." This ended the discussion, but Chapter 6, as though continuing the theme, opens with the pointed comment that "when men are defeated in an argument, their words are retched out as though they were vomiting."

Chuang-Tzu's book seldom departs from the principle that to follow the Way means to live in unquestioning harmony with nature. In Chapter 13 he again made explicit the rhetorical significance of his philosophy, declaring that the quietude of the sage teaches mankind just as (to repeat his earlier image) still water gives a more dependable reflection than water in motion. Then he explained: "Worldly men value words, believing they are necessary to explain the Way. But words are valuable only for the thought they contain; and thought has qualities that may not be contained in words. Therefore, although the world values words, they are not of value." Neither, he insists, is understanding furthered by what is generally considered to be skill in the presentation of arguments. How does the persuasive speaker appear to a perceptive listener? "Your countenance is stern, your eyes piercing, your forehead high and prominent, your mouth roaring, and your attitude threatening. You stand like a tethered horse. . . . You examine things and are discerning; in your cleverness you have an eye to the grand manner." And the result: "All these things invite distrust." In Chapter 14, still on the same theme, he commented that words, however fine, are like footprints. They indicate passage but are far from being the identity to which they merely attest.

In Chapter 15 he urged his disciples: "In all your brilliance, do not shine." Then, in Chapter 19 he identified the proper posture for them: "Don't deliberately conceal yourself; don't deliberately vaunt yourself; stand with poise in the middle." Whatever we do, he observed, should be done without effort, without anxiety. "When the shoes fit, the feet feel easy." To strain to correct someone's erroneous assertion is needless, for: "If he was right and you were wrong, wrong will never drive right into doubt. If, on the other hand, he was wrong and you were right, he brought his error with him and you were not responsible." This sentiment is again the un-Confucian view that no man is his brother's keeper. Chuang reverted in Chapter 21 to his more basic theme that the only thing worth speaking about is ultimate meaning, and that this is both too difficult to be understood and too amorphous to be put into words. The whole of Chapter 22 reiterates and elaborates this point, that when men seek to discuss the unknowable and the inexpressible they are but chattering aimlessly. Nature itself reveals truth but does not expound it. Discussion of even the most profound topics is worthless when the real meanings are beyond comprehension.

The view that discussion should be avoided was not, however, Chuang-Tzu's ultimate position. Chapter 24 warns that "strife is illness," and urges: "Don't subdue others with tricks and plots." It recognizes that "Dialecticians are unhappy when no logical discussions are in progress," but points out that when we "flail one another with our statements and fortify ourselves with our shoutings, no one is led to adjudge himself in error." An expositor does not win adherents if "he never forgets a mistake a person has made." But this disparagement of useless talk was but prelude, before he came to the point of his own persuasive methodology: "When superiority lords it over others, it never succeeds in winning hearts; when it humbles itself, it always wins hearts."

In his customary manner, he enforced his point with an illustration: a monkey, to exhibit its skill, grabbed an arrow that was shot at it and threw it back; whereupon, the group of hunters shot a shower of arrows at it and killed it. "Let this, alas, be a warning," Chuang said. "Do not exhibit your pride before others." Then he added: "no man is thought superior because he speaks well."

The conclusion of Chapter 24 points out, almost as a matter of indifference to its author, that persuasion is easy for those who choose to practice it. The technique is clear and simple: "There is no difficulty in winning the people. Love them and they will draw near. Profit them and they will come. Praise them and they will vie with one another. But introduce something they dislike and they will be gone." In the following chapter he noted the characteristics of a man who is not persuasive: "His mouth may speak, but his heart and mind have never spoken."

Chapter 27 reverts again to his habitual distrust of glib talk. Ninety percent of discourse, he says, consists of metaphors, which skirt the subject without illuminating it; and seventy percent consists of the parroting of other men's opinions. Moreover, "men assent to views that accord with their own, and oppose those which differ." Language flows about us like water, but, "constantly spoken, it is as though not spoken." True discourse is wordless. "One may talk a lifetime and never say anything; conversely, one may say nothing in a lifetime and still be eloquent."

In Chapter 29 Chuang let his fancy roam free and depicted an imaginary debate between Confucius and a brigand named Chih, who was "eloquent enough to make evil look fair." Confucius attempted to appeal to him to live righteously because this would promote social harmony, but got only the sneering response: "Agitating your lips and flapping your tongue, you presume to say what is right and what is wrong to the point of confusing the leaders of the world and keeping students from their basic occupation." Confucius tried to turn aside his hostility with praise, pointing out that he had such high abilities that if he gave up highway robbery he might become a natural ruler and sage. Chih, however, brushed this aside rudely, saying: "I have been taught that anybody good at praising a man to his face is also good at maligning him behind his back." The brigand continued his denunciation, citing Confucius for his "finicky dress, contrived speech, pretentious behavior, and honeyed talk," after which Confucius, badly shaken, bowed twice and hurriedly departed.

The scene is fully in accord with Chuang's views. The man of wisdom who presumes to give advice opens himself to just ridicule. What Chih represented was indeed evil, however fair he could make it seem; but for Confucius to believe that exhortation can reform a determined evil-doer was the height of foolishness. As Chuang rather cattily observed in Chapter 31: "Undertaking what is not one's own business is arrogance." Then he added: "By understanding and yet not putting into words, one attains harmony with nature. By understanding and putting into words, one attains artificiality." The sentiment is similar to the famous injunction which Ralph Waldo Emerson, two thousand years later, wrote in his lecture on "Social Aims": "Don't say things. What you are stands over you the while and thunders so that I cannot hear what you say to the contrary."

Chuang-Tzu's rhetorical concepts may be summarized clearly, for despite his tendencies toward ambiguity and obscurity, his rhetoric emerges unmistakably. In some respects his rhetoric resembles that of Lao-Tzu, but Chuang's views on communication were more detailed, more discriminating, and more inclusive than those of his master. Both agreed that the sole worthy purpose of discourse is the exposition of truth and that the primary requirement for good speaking is to know the truth. Chuang, perhaps more than Lao-Tzu, realized the extreme difficulty of ascertaining what truth is. One difficulty that he noted is that superficial appearances, since they are external and therefore readily observable, tend to be mistakenly accepted as reality. When individual seekers after truth try earnestly to depend upon the reality of their own experiences, they are hampered by the fact that on every side they are surrounded by the artificial conventions created by society. Since these conventions are fabricated rather than natural, they are untrue; but since they have great durability, wide acceptance, and obvious social utility, they seem to be real and actual. Thus to penetrate through the maze of conventional unrealities into the hidden, uncorrupted nature of truth itself is no easy task.

Because truth is difficult to discern, Chuang felt that much speaking is the representation of mistaken views and therefore is harmful. The speaker may unknowingly recommend to his listeners views that are false simply because he himself is confused about reality. Beyond this, it is difficult to put into finite discourse anything that is not particular, local, and immediate—which means that what is uttered is generally contradictory to illimitable and universal truth. Words, he sensed, are never adequate to represent the thoughts which they seek to depict, so that the speaker simply cannot make clear what he does understand and wants to communicate. Worse, speakers are often deliberately untruthful because they are less determined to present truth than they are to sound impressive or to appear "sensible" in terms of established social usages. But speakers must beware of these temptations and try to surmount the difficulties, he warned, for (as he explains in Chapter 4), "Those who speak evil of others are liable to have evil spoken about themselves." It should be noted that what he is warning about is something much more basic and much worse than mere gossip or personal vilification. What is at stake is the adjustment of individuals and of society itself to the elemental truth. If speakers do the basic evil of misrepresenting reality, they induce their listeners to live unreal and unnatural lives. And as they do to others, so also is it done in turn to them. This is the price mankind pays for misleading discourse.

When a speaker does think he understands truth and desires to convert his listeners to his own vision of reality, it is useless for him to try to argue with them. In the first place, it is impossible to be truly and intelligently confident that one is right, for this is a subjective judgment that stands outside of the reality of the truth being examined and thereby casts its own partial and misleading light upon it. Moreover, it is unlikely that any argument would establish the right view, since in an argument it is not truth but skill that prevails. More basically, it is unproductive to argue, since the very fact of taking divergent positions concerning a proposition presupposes differentiation between what is right and what is wrong; whereas whatever exists has to be a portion of the all-inclusive unity of all being. Hence, the very existence of differentiation is itself a denial of essential reality and therefore a negation of truth. Finally, mere observation shows that argument tends to arise easily when feelings are excited and that it plays, however fiercely, upon the surface of topics, rather than even seeking to penetrate into their essence. As Chuang explains, again in Chapter 4, "Speech is like wind to wave. . . . By wind, waves are easily excited. . . . Thus angry feelings rise up without a cause. Specious words and dishonest arguments follow, like the wild random cries of an animal at the point of death. Both sides give way to passion. For where one party drives the other too much into a corner, resistance will always be provoked without apparent cause." Argument, therefore, is not only ineffective; it is actually harmful in that it produces increased misunderstanding, exaggerated differences, and ill feelings.

Despite all the problems surrounding discourse, speech is of the utmost importance for two very fundamental reasons. It is the most accurate gauge of an individual's inner character; speech much more than action shows the man as he truly is. We can and do control how we act; but it is far more difficult to avoid revealing our nature through what we say and the nuances of style and manner by which we say it. Secondly, discourse is of basic importance because it provides the best available meeting place for human minds. The difficulties and falsities of discourse were very apparent to Chuang. Nevertheless, he plaintively noted in Chapter 2, "When the talk diminishes like the daylight of Fall and Winter, it means that day is drawing to a close." Amidst the twilight darkness in which individual man must grope his way, as he explained in Chapter 4, "With others, one must invite loyalty by one's words."

It is true, as he often declared, that the best communication is wordless example and that verbal persuasion is suspect because it may be "eloquent enough to make evil look fair." These were caveats stated much as they had been by Lao-Tzu and for similar reasons.

Even so, Chuang was much concerned with the sources of effectiveness and of ineffectiveness in persuasive discourse. To be truly persuasive, he insisted, demands of the speaker that he maintain a middle ground between abjectness and arrogance. He must manifest a humble eagerness to serve the wellbeing of his listeners. He must take the utmost care to put into his words and voice the same message that he nurtures in his own mind and heart. And he must always recommend his views in terms of love, profit, and praise for those whom he seeks to persuade.

For, as he concludes in Chapter 23, "If people cannot be won over to your side through what they like, they cannot be won at all." Ineffectiveness, on the other hand, derives from insistence upon conducting logical arguments, assertive statements delivered in a loud voice, a positive and dogmatic manner of speaking, and talking about what the speaker does not himself understand.

In the concluding chapter of his book Chuang described the good speaker and the good citizen—for in his view the two were one—as one who follows a prescribed code of public service: "To adopt the public interest and not form cliques; to be fair and unselfish; to decide without prejudice; to go straight to the goal without hesitation; not to be indecisive; not to be devious; to show no biased preference among people but to take them as they come."

And then, before ending his book, he inserted among a series of brief critical commentaries on his leading rivals and contemporaries a portraiture of himself as a thinker and teacher which seems reasonably objective and sound: "Employing paradoxical explanations, terms for vastness, expressions for infinity, he was not treating his subject lightly, even though he constantly indulged in hyperbole. He does not reveal his topic under one rubric. . . . Making no judgments about right and wrong, he lives along with his age. . . . Though his language is both factual and fanciful, his wit is worthy to be observed. . . . No matter how much he may confuse us or leave us in the dark, he proves inexhaustible."

As rhetoricians the advice of both Chuang-Tzu and Lao-Tzu was: Strive always to know truth and to live it; then speak in such a manner that your truth will be accepted as a truth common to all. Above all, never forget that differences which lead to strife are evidence of error, for perceptive insight would reveal that a pervasive unity encompasses into one whole all the superficially conflicting views. If this vision of ultimate reality is not apparent, we should remember that life itself is only a tiny segment of universality and that what seems most urgently real to us may be a dream and we but dreamers. And when we strive most earnestly to do what we believe to be true and right, perhaps we are but as one who is frowning and beating our heads in a futile effort to be beautiful. Much of their advice was negative, but it had a central core: speech is the prism through which one's identity with nature should be revealed. Anything less than this or anything that seeks to go beyond this aim can only be artificial or contrived.

CHAPTER 14

Characteristics of Asian Rhetoric

RHETORIC AND PHILOSOPHY

THE GERMANE RELATIONSHIP between rhetoric and philosophy has always been close, but it has not always been adequately recognized. Whenever rhetoric has been considered practically rather than theoretically—that is, when rhetoric has been interpreted as a set of practical guidelines to effective speaking or to critical evaluation, rather than as an interpretation of the communicative function—its philosophical foundation has been blurred. This has happened more often in Europe and America than in ancient Asia.

Aristotle and Plato were concerned with the relative roles of dialectic (which is devoted to the discovery of knowledge) and rhetoric (or persuasion). Cicero and Quintilian popularized a rhetoric of method, which emphasized the devices as well as the functions of rhetoric. This approach tempted the persuasive theorists who followed them; yet, as Otis Walter has pointed out in a perceptive essay, the quality of any rhetoric is necessarily predetermined by the philosophical premises from which it is derived.[1] A general value system inevitably encompasses and determines specific standards of judgment.

Even more broadly, Maurice Natanson has argued that whenever rhetoric is united with dialectic—that is, when rhetoric is as much concerned with determining the nature of truth as it is with the problem of seeking to influence individuals to accept the speaker's version of what is true—then rhetoric no longer may be defined as "the faculty of discovering in the particular case what are the available means of persuasion";[2] instead it becomes "the conceptual ordering of propositions into coherent structures of an *a priori* nature."[3] Rhetoric as a branch of philosophy, in this view, is the art of phrasing propositions in such a manner that their truth is self-evident.

As the foregoing chapters should make clear, this in general terms is what rhetoric meant in the classical periods of India and China. As such, its preferred methodology was not argument but exposition; its aim was not to overwhelm an opponent but to enlighten an inquirer. Its characteristic style was not the fervor of conviction but the earnestness of investigation.

Even more importantly, ancient Asian rhetoric was not—like that of the West—subordinate on the one hand to logic and on the other to politics. However ambiguous may be the relationship between Aristotle's enthymeme, which he designated as the instrument of persuasion, and the syllogism, which he denoted the principal element in logic, there is no doubt whatever that in his view the ultimate court of appeal in any persuasive situation is logic. As he said, "The man who is to judge would not have his judgment warped by speakers arousing him to anger, jealousy, or compassion. One might as well make a carpenter's tool crooked before using it as a measure."[4] However beset by emotionalism men may be in a given instance, they are fundamentally rational beings and may be required, provided the speaker has sufficient skill, to accept conclusions that are logical. In Asia, on the other hand, as we have seen, no real logic was ever developed, precisely because intuitive insight was considered to be the superior means of perceiving truth. Asian rhetoric, therefore, did not presume logical argument but the explication of self-evident propositions. And while the renunciation of logic provided one basis for the preference for informational over argumentative discourse, the Asian view of politics provided still another.

Aristotle, it may be recalled, considered rhetoric to be an offshoot not only of dialectic (which rendered it basically logical) but also of politics,[5] which rendered it audience-centered. In Athenian society, speeches were directed to free men who rendered decisions by majority vote. The purpose of the speaker was to win as many votes as he could. The measure of desirability of a proposal was whether it rendered the greatest good for the greatest number. Hence, in its very interior nature, rhetoric was directed not only toward the explication of truth but, concurrently and also contrarily, toward the satisfaction of the prejudiced and personalized views of the listeners. It was precisely because of this inner conflict in the Aristotelian concept of rhetoric that, as Natanson has showed, Western rhetoric was turned away from philosophy and became not a mode of inquiry but a study of methods by which agreement might be manipulated.[6]

This is a dichotomy which did not occur in Asia, for the reason that politics did not mean in the East what it meant in the West. Whereas Western political theorists have been concerned with how societies may be brought to reflect the will of the general population, in Asia the concern has been with the maintenance of harmony. Asian speaking was indeed generally political, but it aimed toward rationalization of the status quo rather than toward reformist efforts to produce improvements. In the East, as in the West, the listeners indeed had to be pleased; but an insistence upon an independent right to decide in accordance with one's own preference was not stressed. In India and in China, though for quite different reasons, the norm was acceptance rather than resistance.

The reality of these differences between East and West becomes most strikingly apparent in the difference in the ways in which rhetoric has been considered in these two parts of the world. The West has been both intensively and extensively interested in rhetoric as a separate subject area. From Aristotle, Cicero, and Quintilian to Blair, Whately, and Campbell—with many more before, after, and between these notable rhetoricians—the amount of writing about rhetoric has been impressively large. A bibliography of Western rhetorical writings would be exceedingly lengthy and would be steadily increasing. The exact opposite has been true of the East. In fact, in all the vast accumulation of Asian writings, there is virtually no work whatever that is explicitly devoted to rhetoric. A bibliographic survey of Asian literature would seem to indicate that rhetoric simply did not exist in that part of the world.

The reason for this difference is greatly significant. In the West, rhetoric has been of such high importance that it has received very considerable attention as a separate field of inquiry. In the East, rhetoric has been of such even higher consequence that it never has been separated from philosophy but has received continuous attention as an essential and integral part of generalized philosophical speculation.

The consequences of this divergence of ways of looking at rhetoric has been that, in the West, effort must be continuously expended to reconcile rhetoric with philosophy and to repair the damage from its separation, whereas in the East the effort needs to be made to discern the specific rhetorical particulars amid the general philosophy and to identify its special nature and effects. Philosophy in the West may be only accidentally and occasionally concerned with rhetoric; but in the East philosophy almost always has had a direct rhetorical concern. The reason may be that in the West philosophers have tended to be interested in abstract truth, in the East, in the assessment of the results of immediate observation and experience.[7] As we have seen in our examination of the foundation philosophies of Gautama Buddha and of Confucius, both of these men insisted upon commencing their speculations with interpretations of mankind as they observed it, in the midst of existent circumstances; nor would they permit themselves to be pushed into extension of their thinking beyond the realm of experiential observation. The focus of their concern was: being what we are, and seeking what we seek, what should we do and how should we do it? Such a focus was not, of course, exclusively rhetorical. But since both in China and in India social harmony was considered a fundamental value, the question of what to do and how to do it inevitably revolved to a large degree about the ways in which people should deal with ideas and with one another. Rhetoric was never far from the thoughts of the philosophers in Asia. What is essential in studying Asian rhetoric is to disentangle it from the philosophy and to attempt while doing so to avoid distorting it.

The most likely distortion is to seek to depict the rhetoric thus extracted in Western terms. It is tempting to look in the philosophy for what appear to us to be rhetorical universals, such as invention, disposition, style, delivery, and memory, and the three Aristotelian modes of proof—ethos, pathos, and logos. In effect unless we find a Western rhetoric, it is a temptation to conclude there is no rhetoric there at all. And, equally lamentably, whatever rhetoric is found is very likely to be labeled and described in Western rhetorical terms—since, otherwise, we would scarcely be aware that rhetoric is what we are in fact dealing with. This is almost tantamount to declaring that rhetoric is a Western artifact whether or not it exists in the East. And this brings us back, full circle, to the discussion included in Chapter 1. Perhaps it is sufficient to repeat that no civilization could exist without rhetoric, and assuredly the cultures of the Orient were not devoid of it.

FOCAL POINTS IN ASIAN RHETORIC

Instead of attempting to discover in Asia judgments which may be compared or contrasted with Western pronouncements concerning the major classical canons of rhetoric, it is more fruitful to attempt to assess the rhetorical theories of Asia in their own terms—to go with them wherever they may take us, regardless of whether this may be close to or far from the kinds of rhetoric with which Westerners are familiar. When this method is followed, the following focal points of Asian rhetoric may be discerned.

First, the primary function of discourse is not to enhance the welfare of the individual speaker or listener but to promote harmony. In China the goal generally was a harmonious society, in India a harmonious relationship of the individuals with the course of nature—which, as we have seen, was also the goal of the Chinese Taoists. One effect of this view of the function of discourse was to depersonalize it. Emphasis was removed from the specific individual purposes of speakers and listeners and was placed, instead, upon their participation in the common lot of mankind. Another effect was to magnify both the importance and the seriousness of discourse. Its generalized function was of far too great significance to permit it to be undertaken lightly or conducted carelessly.

Second, rather than encouraging individuality of style or of method, the traditions in both India and China stressed the value of adhering strictly to patterns of expectation. Originality was discounted. Effectiveness was achieved primarily by identification of the speaker with accepted tradition. This principle affected both what was said and the manner of saying it. Speakers who wished to have a favorable effect took care to stress that what they presented was not their own idea but was derived directly from ancient authority. And they took equal care to make it clear that they were phrasing and presenting their message in a mode that was precisely prescribed. Listeners were no less constrained than were speakers to behave in a manner that was predetermined by custom. The dynamic vitality of change and progress was thereby exchanged for social stability and dependability. Individuals were taught to look not for ways by which they could manipulate circumstances for their own best interests but how they could accommodate themselves to situations with the least possible disturbance of them.

Third, discourse which aimed toward social harmony rather than at the specific wellbeing of the participants, and which somewhat ritualistically adhered to approved patterns, naturally tended to avoid argumentation and persuasive fervor. The characteristic mode was exposition. What the West has generally designated as a search for common ground between speaker and listener was in ancient Asia the natural and virtually the universal method of conducting a discussion.

Fourth, as was indicated in Chapters 2 and 6, both in India and in China the very insistence of the societies upon restrained and ceremonial discourse resulted upon occasion in wild bursts of quarrelsomeness. In India particularly these outbursts often resembled the temper tantrums of children. But their purpose was expressive rather than communicative. The free vent of the emotions simply emphasized the fact that generally they were decorously controlled. And in China, more particularly than in India, the quarreling was subject to well-understood and observed rules that gave even to the quarrels the appearance of a well-rehearsed drama.

Fifth, more specifically than in the West, the Asians (and especially the ancient Chinese) emphasized the dual and reciprocal responsibility of speakers and listeners. This emphasis was a natural result of their point of view that discourse should properly aim not toward accomplishment of personal desires of the particular participants in a discussion but toward the general advantages of society as a whole. Listeners were advised not only to be attentive but to bring to the problem of interpretation of the speaker's meaning all their resources of knowledge and of critical judgment. Since individuals are liable to err, speakers might through ignorance, lack of skill, or selfishness fail to further the welfare of the community, just as listeners, through careless inattention, prejudice, or selfwill, might fail to interpret what was said in terms of the general needs of society. Each must be alert to compensate for the possible incapacity of the other.

Sixth, the principal sources of proof on which judgment should be based were authority and analogy. Speakers took care to represent ideas as being not their own but an authoritative derivation from ancient precepts or practice. Further support was sought through the use of analogies, which had the twin functions of clarifying the speaker's viewpoint while, at the same time, appealing through comparison to the everyday experience and observation of the listener. Authority and analogy were used almost to the exclusion of both formal logic and citation of specific evidence or supporting facts. The Indians did develop a complicated system of pseudo-logic, which rested basically upon intuitive insight and the Chinese did employ a "chain of reasoning" which was in effect an appeal to commonsense observation. But in both cultures what was finally persuasive was appeal to established authority, buttressed by analogical reasoning which sought to clarify the unfamiliar through comparison with the familiar.

Seventh, in contrast to the West, Asians were inclined to believe that an individual could more truly be judged in terms of what he said than what he did. Actions, they felt, could be manipulated for hypocritical effect; but speech is sensitively revelatory of character, for two reasons: first, because the words, the accents, and the gestures form a complicated pattern so responsive to the inner impulses of the speaker that they cannot successfully camouflage his actual sentiments; and second, because the speech establishes a record to which the individual subsequently may be held. Hence, whereas in the West warning often is given to look behind and beyond the words to see how the speaker actually behaves, in ancient Asia the counsel was, rather, to look beyond the behavior to see what the individual was saying and to note how he said it. Speech, they felt, most shows the man. It was the criterion of character to which they were most continually alert.

Eighth, another focal point of Asian rhetoric is the value which it attached to silence. In Western society, silence is awkward and embarrassing. When a conversation is broken by a lengthy pause, the suspicion is that the participants have nothing to say (which is an admission of ignorance or of lack of interest) or perhaps that they have something in mind which they do not wish to communicate or do not know how to state, or even that the subject of discourse has skirted upon a subject area that is embarrassing or disagreeable. When a pause develops, it is felt to be a social responsibility to say something—almost anything— to get the discourse reanimated. In the ancient Orient, on the contrary, silence was valued rather than feared. If a group of people fell silent, the reason might be any one of four: (1) perhaps no one had anything he wished to say—meaning there was no sense of urgency to be discussing the particular subject; or (2) perhaps the subject was felt to be wordlessly ambiguous, so that whatever meaning it had could be sensed but could not be phrased; or (3) perhaps it was generally felt that all were in substantial agreement, so that no affirmation was needed; or, finally, (4) if the subject matter were sensitive, it might be that to speak would be an unwise commitment of one's judgment—a risk that ought not to be taken. For a variety of reasons, silence in Asia has commonly been entirely acceptable, whereas in the West silence has generally been considered socially disagreeable.

And ninth, the insistence in the West upon everyone's equal right to have and to express his own opinion has been countered in the East by the tradition that opinion-formation was primarily the responsibility of those who were elderly, or in a position of authority, or were scholars and teachers. This difference resulted in a more clear-cut understanding in Asia than in the West as to who should do the speaking, and under what circumstances. In Asian rhetoric the principle was accepted that individuals do not have the right to speak until or unless they have earned it. Concurrently, Asians have felt that speaking carries with it a direct responsibility to abide by the consequences, for which reason the speaking about particular subjects should be done primarily by those who have the power and authority to take actions which correspond with their words. This point of view has been especially prevalent in China. In India the theory and the practice have been more nearly in accord with the Western emphasis upon both the freedom of speech and the values of hearing all sides of every question from all who are involved in it. Even in India, however, the establishment of the Brahmin caste to include those who teach, judge, and legislate has had the effect of restricting the most meaningful discourse to select members of the society.

Such are significant focal points of Asian rhetoric, which indicate substantial ways in which it differs from the traditional rhetoric of the West. They reflect a society, a philosophy, and a view of individuality that are constituents of the culture of that part of the world. Their theories of communication are an integral part of their ways of thinking and of living. Even the effort to compare them with Western beliefs and practices results in some degree of distortion. But the fact that such a comparison is to some extent possible indicates the usefulness which this rhetoric may have for the West.

COMPARISONS WITHIN RHETORICAL CATEGORIES

When major rhetorical categories are considered, significant differences emerge between Western and Eastern rhetorics. These categories may be determined to include the following concepts: the speaker, the message, the audience, the channel of communication, the purpose governing the discourse, the effect or result which the speaker aims to achieve, the tone of the discourse, the motivation through which the speaker attempts to support his conclusion, the basis for the ethos or personal authority of the speaker, the style of the discourse, and the manner of the delivery or presentation of it. Each of these categories is subject to widespread variations both West and East; yet, concerning each of them, meaningful generalizations may be rendered that arise from the cultures within which the rhetorics are formulated.

The speaker

In Western rhetoric the speaker is conceived as an individual who has a purpose to accomplish, either on his own behalf or as an agent or spokesman for a group or an organization. In either instance, he is selected as a speaker because his special knowledge of the subject, or his position of prestige, or his skill in speaking makes him a potential instrument for changing the views of the listeners. In simplest terms, the speaker serves as an advocate, a champion of a cause, who stands to do battle with verbal weapons against any and all challengers who may doubt what he says. This same conception is not unknown in Asian rhetoric; but more commonly, in the ancient East the speaker was represented as an authority figure who "announced" the truth rather than as a combatant who sought to establish a particular point of view against all opposition. One was not supposed to speak until he knew; even then, he was not to speak until his right to determine what should be believed and done was generally recognized. In a situation which called for zealous persuasion—as in the evangelistic campaign which Gautama urged his monks to undertake—the speakers were to proceed confidently and to speak with authority, expecting concurrence as a matter of course.

The message

In the West the speaker's message is in some sense a mediation between the speaker and his listeners. It is their message, as well as his own. Its form and therefore in part its content is affected by their reactions, or feedback. The speaker is counselled to formulate his message in terms of the "common ground" which he can discover between himself and his audience. The unfamiliar or new portion of what he has to say is to be related as closely as possible to the familiar and accepted beliefs of his listeners. The process of preparing the message consists very largely of trying to see and depict it from the listener's point of view. For as Alexander Pope advised, "men must be taught as though you taught them not; and things unknown proposed as things forgot." Speech skill consists in part in the ability to present a message to an audience in such a fashion that it seems to the auditors as though it already had been their own.

Superficially, the same condition was advocated in Asian rhetoric; for the message was conceived as belonging not to the "invention" of the speaker but to the community as a whole. What was to be spoken was traditional wisdom—the fundamental understanding that derived from communal experience. Above all, the message was to be social rather than individual; to the extent that it represented an idiosyncratic particularity of the specific speaker, it was to be rejected. The principal claim to authenticity was that it was no less (it could scarcely be more) than a distillation of sound tradition. In comparison with Western preference and experience, in the East the message belonged not so much to either the speaker or the listeners. The message was generally conceived as being the sense of the community. What the speaker was to say was what was true—not what either he or his audience wished or believed or hoped might be true. The message was not to be distinguished by originality, which would be considered not a virtue but a defect. Its value lay precisely in the fact that it was not original or individual, but traditional and communal. The speaker did not create it; neither did his listeners. Both simply recognized that it was there.

The audience

In Western terms, the listeners are cooperative and active participants in the communicative situation. Realistically, their preferences help to determine the subject matter of the discourse; their characteristics are largely influential in shaping the style, the choice of illustrations, the kinds of proof, and the arrangement of the materials. Their reaction is the measure of the success of the discourse. In Asia all this was true to a much more limited extent. Rather, the listeners were considered to be subordinate (though never passive) recipients of the message. The speaker was to enlighten; they were to be enlightened. This was thought to be the principal justification for communication. And just as the speaker was selected on the basis of his superiority, the listeners were selected on the basis of their need for his guidance. He was the teacher; they were the students. He taught; they learned.

The channel

The actual delivery of the speech, in Western rhetoric, has been generally depicted as natural and unobtrusive. The speaker has been advised to talk in the idiom of his listeners. His posture, dress, and bearing are supposed to reflect sincerity and realism in the relationship between himself and those who hear him. The whole communication is to approximate the naturalness of social conversation. Neither the voice nor the diction, neither the style nor the delivery, is to detract from the listeners' concentration on what is said. The presentation is not to attract attention to itself but to be inconspicuous. This is the Western norm.

In Asian rhetoric, on the other hand, the mode of presentation has been rendered ceremonial and ritualistic. Care was taken not to diminish but to augment the differences between speaker and listener. Equal care was devoted to eliminate natural individual characteristics and to substitute for them a formalized method and manner which was deemed to be universally correct. There were right and correct ways for speakers and listeners to behave, and from these approved norms they were not to deviate. Naturalness gave way to formality.

The purpose

In the West the purpose has been considered the factor in the speaking situation which above all was to be dominated by the speaker. He might choose a subject matter on the basis of his listeners' interests; and he might organize and stylize his discourse to suit their capacities and preferences. But the purpose he was to hold sacred. The whole meaning of the communicative situation was derived from consideration of a speaker seeking to influence listeners in the direction of his own convictions. To abridge or amend his purpose in order to win audience approval was considered a serious breach of ethics. The goal toward which the speaker seeks to lead his auditors governs the entire strategy of the communication. It is precisely the reason for which communication takes place.

Asian rhetoricians have held that purpose *somewhat* dominates and *partly* shapes the process of communication; but the purpose which has this partial function is only to a limited degree derived from the individual will of the speaker. Again and again in the foregoing chapters it has appeared that in the purview of Asian rhetoric individuality is not a virtue but a defect. So it is in the realm of communicative purpose. Society has the dominant role. The needs of the community take definite precedence over those of any individual. Even the monarch was to be overthrown when he ceased to serve the people. This point of view, when applied to a specific communicative circumstance, meant that it was the responsibility of the speaker (and the listeners as well) to discern what in the situation would best serve social wellbeing. Since their own judgment could scarcely be adequate to so complicated a problem, the purpose was actually to be sought by an understanding search of the wisdom of the past. In short, a speaker was not to devise but to discover the proper purpose for a speech; and when found it would be not so much his own as that of the group. The focal point in preparation for discourse would not be *my purpose* but *our purpose*. This was a distinctive characteristic of Asian rhetoric which had far-reaching effects in the whole range of communicative principles and strategies.

The effect

In both Western and Asian rhetoric, the effect sought through communication is a movement of minds and feelings in the direction of unity. The speaker tries to influence his listeners (while they through their reactions are also influencing him) to understand a particular proposition more nearly as he does. Wherever discourse takes place, this is the impulse which underlies it. Even here, however, there is a difference—of degree if not of kind—between East and West. In Western rhetoric the assumption is that the speaker seeks to manipulate a change in the reactions of his listeners. His aim is (however gently) to coerce agreement from them. In the view of ancient Asian rhetoric, the speaker seeks from his audience not agreement but acceptance. The nuance of difference is small, but it is significant. The speaker does not expect from them an active grappling with his ideas and feelings to determine whether or not—and with whatever kinds of modifications—they should be approved; what he seeks is to win their concurrence. The difference is roughly analogous to that between an election and a plebiscite. The sovereignty was less divided between speaker and listener in Asia than in the West. When a communicative situation was normal and proper— that is, a superior addressing inferiors, for the purpose of enhancing communal wellbeing, and in an approved mode—the effect anticipated would not be the critical, dynamic, and active reaction indicated in approval but, rather, the passive acceptance represented by acquiescence.

The tone

By tone is meant the basic attitude which pervades and gives special character to the speech. In a very general sense, Western discourse tends to be animated, optimistic, dynamic, and favorable to experimentation and change. Europeans and Americans are likely to recommend new courses of action with the confidence that novelty in itself is appealing. There is also likely to be a curious intermingling of conciliation (because among equals agreement may not be demanded but must be wooed) and of sharp controversy (because the emphasis upon individualism and independence breeds disagreement). The tone of Western discourse is difficult to define, precisely because it is widely varied. Personal differences are magnified and each individual insists upon the right to be and to express himself, by which often is meant—to emphasize the ways in which he differs from his associates.

In Asia, as has been demonstrated again and again, the social pressures are in the direction of blurring individual differences in order to heighten the sense of harmony. When differences prove to be insurmountable, skill is exercised to "save face" by minimizing their nature or their effects. Conciliation takes the form of assuming that whatever present disagreement there may seem to be, in the long run and on fundamental matters there is and must be basic accord. Instead of a frenetic rushing toward new ideas and activities, there is a calm depiction of the satisfactions arising from accommodation to established and accepted norms. Individual differences are rounded off and ignored or explained as being mere incidentals. The general tone tends to be mellow, unexcited, gently authoritative, and matter-of-fact. There is seldom any real difficulty in identifying a particular specimen of discourse as being either Western or Eastern. Whatever the subject matter, the tone will be distinct.

The motivation

Motives are recognized as being exceedingly complex and variable. Nevertheless, in Western rhetoric it is clear that motivation is considered to be almost synonymous with self-interest. Self-preservation is said to be the first law of life. Individuals are represented as seeking what is pleasant and avoiding what is painful. No doubt this is sufficiently true of every living organism so that it is as much a universal as is likely to be found. East and West, it is difficult to conceive of a person as wanting to do that which he does not want to do. The satisfaction of one's own deepest and truest desires is certain to be the source of motivational appeals.

Even so, cultural influences differ with respect to motivation, just as they do in other aspects of rhetoric. Social customs and traditions in the West have tended to magnify the effects of self-interest by teaching the virtues of individualism, of ambition, of self-advancement, of seeking to be successful. A Western child is taught from babyhood that he should rise to a higher status than that of his parents. Our capitalistic free-enterprise system is founded on the hypothesis that if everyone seeks his own profit (under controlled conditions) society itself will benefit. In this respect the East differs from the West in its cultural emphasis, even though human nature on the Yangtze is the same as on the Hudson.

The traditional Asian child was taught from birth that he owed his primary duty to his family, his clan or caste or community, and his state. He was taught to accept whatever position he was born to in the social hierarchy. He was taught that to struggle against things as they are was sinful. The responsibility of caring for parents, for brothers and sisters, and for friends was deeply impressed upon him. In India there was the additional factor of an inescapable responsibility to his own destiny through the course of numberless incarnations. In all these ways, the immediate self-interest of the individual was curbed or amended by what Westerners might deem to be secondary (or even fanciful) considerations.

There is no basis for considering selfishness any less genuine in Asia than in the West; but there is nevertheless a realistic difference. Western rhetoric frankly advocates motivational appeals to natural human selfishness. Eastern rhetoric advises that the appeal be through or from selfishness to social duty. In the West the ultimate good is envisioned as individualistic; in the East it is clearly and firmly held to lie in social harmony: what is good for the community is in the long run also good for the individual.

Ethos

It is precisely because people differ that ethos, in Aristotelian terms, is a persuasive factor. Audiences are aware of a speaker's greater or lesser wisdom, of his courage or cowardice, of his good or bad character, of his pleasing or disagreeable personality, of his favorable or unfavorable reputation. In Asia as in Europe and America, rhetoricians have clearly understood that what and who a speaker is make a tremendous difference in his effectiveness. The difference between East and West lies in what it is that gives prestige and attractiveness to a speaker. In the West it is likely to be factors of individuality—experiences or qualities that render him unusual. In Asia the attractiveness and the prestige have been derived primarily from the unquestionable soundness with which the speaker represented the traditions of the society. The factors which constituted ethos for the speaker were those already noted—the feeling that he represented the whole group, that he spoke from and for established wisdom.

The style

If style is the man himself, there must be as many different styles as there are speakers or writers. And so it is, East as well as West. Confucius and Gautama Buddha, Han Fei-Tzu and Chuang-Tzu, Mencius and Mo-Tze—all of these differ from one another as genuinely as do the great speakers of Europe and America. If there are culturally generalized stylistic differences, they probably lie in a greater liveliness and variability in Western discourse, as against more ambiguity, ceremonial-

ism, and sententiousness in the Orient. Even this is doubtful. Style everywhere is highly individualistic.

THE MANY BEGINNINGS

Whatever now is must somewhere have had a beginning; but it is not
so clear that all things have an end. Much that is observed seems yet
to be growing and may not now have achieved its final or definitive form.

Western rhetoric had a beginning with Aristotle—and an earlier one
in ancient Syracuse—and a still earlier start in ancient Egypt. Asian
rhetoric had roots that penetrated deep down into the prehistoric social
patterns and preliterate philosophies of India and China. It had also
other beginnings that have not yet been explored: in Korea, in Japan,
in Tibet and Ceylon, in Muslim India and in the later Buddhist China.
For two thousand years the rhetorical theories depicted in these pages
intertwined and grew and changed, on down to the mid-nineteenth cen-
ury, when they began yet a new adjustment as they met and reacted to
the influences introduced from the West.

This initial exploration into the rhetorical domains of ancient Asia
is in itself a beginning—a conceptualizaton of theories and principles
that heretofore had not been considered separately. As is true of all
explorations, no doubt trails opened up that seem promising may prove
to be dead ends, and trails not taken will be found to lead into verdant
areas. The terrain that has been found and described will have to serve
as its own justification. Some will find it challenging and inviting and
their work will open new vistas to intrigue the interest of still others.

As has been true of the Orient in so many respects, its vagueness
and vastness make it seem more mysterious than it is. The people who
live and have lived there are a part of the brotherhood of us all. There
must be more beginnings, and then still more, until finally the roads they
trod come to seem familiar and their ideas come to be interrelated with
our own.

Notes to the Chapters

Notes to Chapter 1—CULTURE AND RHETORIC

1. For illustrations of the use of oratory as a political instrument in the democracies, see Timon (Viscount de Commenin), *Noted French Orators* (Chicago: Belford, Clarke, 1884); James H. McBath and Walter Fisher, *British Public Address* (Boston: Houghton Mifflin, 1970); and Robert T. Oliver, *History of Public Speaking in America* (Boston: Allyn and Bacon, 1965).

2. See Harry P. Harrison, as told to Karl Detzer, *Culture under Canvas* (New York: Hastings House, 1958).

3. In China there was a signficant exception, in 81 B.C., depicted in Huan K'uan, *Discourses on Salt and Iron: A Debate on State Control of Commerce and Industry*, trans. Esson Gale (Leiden: *Sinica Leidensia*, 1931), II, lvi and 165.

4. Hugh Dalziel Duncan, *Communication and Social Order* (New York: Bedminster Press, 1962), p. xxvii.

5. Margaret Mead, "Some Cultural Approaches to Communication Problems," in Lyman Bryson, ed., *The Communication of Ideas* (New York: Harper, 1948), p. 9.

6. Cf. the view that writing is a "mummified" derivative of oral speech, in Otto Jesperson, *The Philosophy of Grammar* (London: Horace Allen and Unwin, 1951), pp. 17–18; and Charlton Laird, *The Miracle of Language* (New York: World, 1953), p. 16.

7. Lyman Bryson, "Problems of Communication," in *Communication of Ideas*, pp. 2, 3.

8. Kenneth A. Oliver, *Our Living Language*, rev. ed. (Los Angeles: Occidental College, 1962), p. 3.

9. The influence of culture upon both personality and society is well depicted in two books that show the continuing effects of traditional value systems in Asia: Hajime Nakamura, *Ways of Thinking of Eastern Peoples*, ed. Philip P. Wiener (Honolulu: East-West Center Press, 1964); and Charles A. Moore, ed., *The Status of the Individual in East and West* (Honolulu: University of Hawaii Press, 1968).

10. Younghill Kang, *East Goes West* (New York: Scribners, 1937), p. 126.

11. William Franklin Sands, *Undiplomatic Memories: The Far East, 1896–1904* (New York: Whittlesey House, 1930), p. 15.

12. Quoted by Richard LaPiere and Paul R. Farnsworth, *Social Psychology* (New York: McGraw-Hill, 1936), p. 261.

13. Ina Corinne Brown, *Understanding Other Cultures* (Englewood Cliffs, N.J.: Prentice-Hall, Spectrum Book, 1963), p. 5.

14. Gregory Bateson, *Naven*, rev. ed. (Stanford: Stanford University Press, 1958), p. 175.

15. Donald C. Bryant, "Rhetoric: Its Function and Its Scope," *Quarterly Journal of Speech*, 39 (December, 1953), pp. 401–24.

16. See Chaim Perelman and L. Olbrechts-Tyteca, *The New Rhetoric: A Treatise on Argumentation*, trans. by John Wilkinson and Purcell Weaver (Notre Dame: University of Notre Dame Press, 1969); and Walter Fisher, "A Motive View of Communication," *Quarterly Journal of Speech*, 56 (April, 1970), pp. 131–39.

17. For a further elaboration of the argument that rhetoric is and must be culture-centered, see Robert T. Oliver, "Culture and Communication," *Vital Speeches of the Day*, 29 (September 15, 1963), pp. 721–24.

18. Edith Hamilton and Huntington Cairns, eds., *The Collected Dialogues of Plato* (New York: Pantheon Books, 1961), pp. 522–23.

19. Edwin Black, "Plato's View of Rhetoric," *Quarterly Journal of Speech*, 44 (December, 1958), 369.

20. Lane Cooper, trans. and ed., *The Rhetoric of Aristotle* (New York: Appleton-Century-Crofts, 1932), pp. 7, 8.

21. The subjectivity of knowledge is well depicted in Michael Polanyi, *Personal Knowledge* (Chicago: University of Chicago Press, 1958); Angus Sinclair, *The Conditions of Knowing* (New York: Harcourt, Brace, 1951); and Hans Vaihinger, *The Philosophy of 'As If,'* trans. C. K. Ogden (London: Routledge and Kegan Paul, 1924).

22. See Robert T. Oliver, "Sacred Cows, Asian and American: The Language of Social Behavior," *Vital Speeches of the Day*, 35 (August 15, 1969), 668–72.

*Notes to Chapter 2—*INDIA: THE RHETORICAL MILIEU

1. Surendranath Dasgupta, *History of Indian Philosophy* (Cambridge: Cambridge University Press, 1922), I, 10. The difficulties of any unitary interpretation, however, are stressed by a notable Indian anthropologist, G. S. Ghurye, who insists that "Hindu society was accustomed to free, desultory, and even contradictory and contending schemes of philosophical thought for about fifteen hundred years." "Indian Unity: A Retrospect and a Prospect," in Manilal B. Nanavati and C. N. Vakil, eds., *Group Prejudices in India* (Bombay: Vora and Co., 1951), p. 118. As is well known, it was precisely the existence of multiple contending sects that inspired Gautama Buddha to reassert the underlying unity of belief which underlay traditional Indian philosophies.

2. Sir Charles Eliot, *Hinduism and Buddhism: An Historical Sketch,* 3 vols. (London: Routledge and Kegan Paul, 1921), I, li.

3. Jawaharlal Nehru, *The Discovery of India* (London: Meridian Books, 1956), p. 10.

4. See Edward Conze, trans. and ed., *Buddhist Scriptures* (Baltimore: Penguin Books, 1966), particularly Chapter I, "The Buddha's Previous Lives."

5. To counter the inevitable simplification of the capsulized explanation of central Indian beliefs (comparable to the similar simplification of my encapsulation

of Judeo-Christian theology), readers are invited to consult a sourcebook that was designed to illustrate the divergencies of Indian thought: Wm. Theodore de Bary, *et al.*, eds., *Sources of Indian Tradition* (New York: Columbia University Press, 1958). Other works cited in other notes to this and succeeding chapters also invite consideration of the genuine differences of viewpoint that abound.

6. Pandharinath H. Prabhu, *Hindu Social Organization*, 4th ed. (Bombay: Popular Prakasham, 1963), p. 27. In many talks with Professor Prabhu while he was revising his book, I profited from his clarification of my understanding of Indian life—though he may not, of course, wholly concur in all my conclusions.

7. *Ibid.*, pp. 12, 83.

8. *Ibid.*, p. 78.

9. Eliot, *Hinduism and Buddhism*, I, xci and xcix.

10. Nehru, *Discovery of India*, p. 16.

11. Prabhu, *Hindu Social Organization*, pp. 212–14 and *passim*.

12. R. Fick, *The Social Organization in Northeast India in Buddha's Time*, trans. S. K. Maitra (Calcutta: University of Calcutta, 1920); and Romila Thapar, *A History of India* (Baltimore: Penguin Books, 1966), I, 50–53.

13. Eliot, *Hinduism and Buddhism*, II, 312.

14. M. Winternitz, *A History of Indian Literature* (Calcutta: University of Calcutta, 1959), p. 29.

15. D. M. Majumdar, *Caste and Communication in an Indian Village* (New York: Asia Publishing House, 1958), pp. 290–91.

16. Winternitz, *History of Indian Literature*, p. 34.

17. J. Allan, T. W. Haig, and H. H. Dodwell, *Cambridge Shorter History of India* (New York: Macmillan, 1934), pp. 9–14.

18. Thapar, *History of India*, p. 43.

19. T. W. Rhys Davids and C. A. F. Rhys Davids, trans. and eds., *Dialogues of the Buddha* (London: Luzac and Co., 1910, 1951), III, 79.

20. R. J. Majumdar and A. D. Pusalkar, eds., *The Vedic Age* (London: George Allen and Unwin, 1951), from Chapter XX by B. K. Ghosh, "Language and Literature in the Age of the Later Samhitas," pp. 410 and 412.

21. *Ibid.*, p. 420, cites passages showing that women were not allowed to attend council meetings.

22. *Ibid.*, pp. 225–27 and 341.

*Notes to Chapter 3—*CASTE AS RHETORIC IN BEING

1. Neither Indians nor Indologists find it easy to define Varna and Jati or to spell out their distinctions and relationships. One of the clearest efforts is that by Prabhu, in his *Hindu Social Organization*, Chap. VIII, "The Four Varnas."

2. Stephen Fuchs, *The Children of Hari* (Vienna: Verlag Herold, 1950), p. 18, points out that in rare instances persons expelled from their own caste might be admitted into a lower caste. An early (1815), somewhat naive but explicitly detailed description of caste regulations and practices is that of Abbe J. A. Dubois, *Hindu Manners, Customs and Ceremonies*, trans. by Henry K. Beauchamp, 3rd ed. (Oxford: Clarendon Press, 1906).

3. Nripendra Kumar Dutt, *Origin and Growth of Caste in India*, 2 vols. (London: Kegan Paul, Trench, Trubner and Co., 1931), I, 32.

4. John W. Wilson, *Indian Caste*, 2 vols., ed. by P. Peterson (Bombay: no publisher indicated, 1877), I, 13.

5. J. H. Hutton, *Caste in India: Its Nature, Function, and Origins*, rev. ed. (London: Oxford University Press, 1961), p. 48.

6. Adrian C. Mayer, *Caste and Kinship in Central India: A Village and Its Region* (Berkeley: University of California Press, 1960), p. 160.

7. Hutton, *Caste in India*, p. 72.

8. *Ibid.*, pp. 86–87.

9. According to G. Morris Carstairs, in *The Twice-Born* (Bloomington: Indiana University Press, 1958), p. 57: "the idea that one might have preferred to be born in a different caste was never expressed. One's own caste role was taken for granted, and so were those of one's social superiors, and those of the menial groups."

10. Hutton, *Caste in India*, p. 78.

11. Majumdar, *Caste and Communication*, p. 72.

12. *Ibid.*, pp. 211–18.

13. Carstairs, *The Twice-Born*, pp. 46, 47.

14. Fuchs, *Children of Hari*, pp. 22, 40.

15. Majumdar, *Caste and Communication*, pp. 213, 214, and *passim*. He devotes many pages (especially 32–33, 73–74, 77–78, 114–18) to describing the causes, conduct, and settlement of quarrels.

16. Fuchs, *Children of Hari*, pp. 40–43.

17. Ran Sharan Sharma, *Sudras in Ancient India* (Delhi: Motilal Banarsidass, 1958), p. 199. Also Dutt, *Origin and Growth of Caste in India*, p. 140.

18. Majumdar, *Caste and Communication*, p. 129.

19. Fuchs, *Children of Hari*, p. 35.

20. Eliot, *Hinduism and Buddhism*, I, xci.

21. Michael Banks, "Caste in Jaffna," in E. R. Leach, ed., *Aspects of Caste in South India, Ceylon and North-West Pakistan* (Cambridge: University Press, 1962), pp. 65–66.

22. Robert V. Russell and R. B. H. Lal, *The Tribes and Castes of the Central Provinces of India*, 4 vols. (London: Macmillan, 1916), III, 72.

23. Fuchs, *Children of Hari*, p. 137.

24. Hutton, *Caste in India*, p. 63.

25. E. B. Cowell, ed., *The Jātaka: Stories of the Buddha's Former Births*, 4 vols. (Cambridge: University Press, 1880 and 1925), IV, 245.

26. Fuchs, *Children of Hari*, p. 435.

27. *Ibid.*, pp. 167–76.

28. *Ibid.*, p. 81.

29. Will Durant, *Our Oriental Heritage* (New York: Simon and Schuster, 1942).

Notes to Chapter 4—HINDUISM AND OTHER PRE-BUDDHIST RHETORICAL THEORIES

1. Edmond Holmes, Introduction to S. Radhakrishnan's *Philosophy of the Upaniṣads* (London: George Allen and Unwin, 1924), p. 4.

2. Sures Chandra Chakravarti, *The Philosophy of the Upanishads* (Calcutta: University of Calcutta, 1935), p. 45. In Hymn 81 of Book X of the *Rig-Veda*,

the creator is given only one continuing function: he is to be worshipped as the god of speech. The reason was that speech most truly unveils mind and character and thus is the truest indicator of the nature of man.

3. *Ibid.*, pp. 91–92.

4. S. Radhakrishnan, *Indian Philosophy* (London: George Allen and Unwin, 1939), I, 89.

5. Max Müller, *Sacred Books of the East,* 50 vols. (London: Oxford University Press, 1894; reprinted, Delhi: Motilal Banaraidass, 1963, I, x.

6. R. D. Ranade, *A Constructive Survey of Upanishadic Philosophy* (Poona: Encyclopaedic History of Indian Philosophy, 1926), II, 3.

7. Radhakrishnan, *Philosophy of the Upaniṣads*, p. 18.

8. Cited as the key concept of the Upanishads by a lifelong student of their meaning, Juan Mascaro, in *The Upanishads* (Baltimore: Penguin Books, 1965), p. 11.

9. *Bhagavad Gita,* Chapter XVIII, verse 20. Franklin Edgerton, in his definitive English-language edition of the *Bhagavad Gita* (Cambridge: Harvard University Press, 1944), points out (on p. 139) that the Gita deals incidentally with the theme that in the Upanishads is absolutely basic: namely, that there is one monistic and indissoluble essence uniting and incorporating all that exists in this seemingly variable and diverse universe.

10. Radhakrishnan, *Philosophy of the Upaniṣads*, p. 14.

11. *Ibid.*, pp. 21–22.

12. For the summaries of the Upanishads which follow, the principal translations used are: Robert Ernest Hume, *The Thirteen Principal Upanishads,* 2nd ed. rev. (London: Oxford University Press, 1931); Juan Mascaro, *Upanishads;* Swami Gambhīrānanda, *Eight Upanishads,* 2 vols. (Calcutta: Advaita Ashrama, 1957); and Swami Nikhilananda, *The Upanishads,* 4 vols. (New York: Harper, 1949).

13. *Chhāndogya Upanishad,* Part VIII, sections 7–12.

14. For a development of this theme, see Lama Anagarika Govinda, *The Psychological Attitude of the Early Buddhist Philosophy* (London: Rider and Co., 1961). The Western view is well explained technically by George Herbert Mead in *Mind, Self, and Society,* ed. Charles Morris (Chicago: University of Chicago Press, 1939), and popularly by Walter Coutu, *Emergent Human Nature* (New York: Knopf, 1939). The difficulty of reconciling the Indian and Western views is apparent in the work of one who made a major effort to do so, Arthur Schopenhauer, *The World as Will and Idea* (Garden City, N.Y.: Doubleday, Dolphin Books, 1961).

15. K. N. Jayatilleke, *Early Buddhist Theory of Knowledge* (London: George Allen and Unwin, 1963), pp. 110–11.

16. *Ibid.*, pp. 46–48.

17. Jayatilleke cites these arguments, and others like them, as having been popular and as often occurring in pre-Buddhistic debates. *Ibid.*, pp. 103–104.

18. *Ibid.*, p. 106.

19. These attacks on debate are paraphrased from the *Dīgha Nikāya.* Among the half-dozen leading skeptics of the period, Jayarasi and Sanjaya were preeminent. The nature and the consequences of the skeptical schools are discussed by Jayatilleke, *Buddhist Theory of Knowledge,* especially in Chap. 3.

20. *Ibid.*, pp. 154–61. See also de Bary, *Sources of Indian Tradition,* pp. 42–43.

21. A. L. Basham, *History and Doctrines of the Ajīvikas* (London: Luzac and Co., 1951), pp. 13–14. See also Chap. 12, pp. 224–39.

22. *Ibid.*, p. 274.

23. Jayatilleke, *Buddhist Theory of Knowledge*, p. 160.

24. The metaphysical nature of Indian psychology is well explicated in Jadunath Sinha, *Indian Psychology*, 2 vols. (Calcutta: Sinha Publishing House, 1958).

25. This interpretation is based upon Nathmal Tatia, *Studies in Jaina Philosophy* (Banaras: Jain Cultural Research Society, 1951), especially Chapter 3; and Jagmanderlal Jaina, *Outlines of Jainism* (Cambridge: University Press, 1916). It should be considered in terms of the judgment of Sinha in his *Indian Philosophy* that "India psychology is based on metaphysics" (I, xvi).

26. Jayatilleke, *Buddhist Theory of Knowledge*, p. 165.

27. *Ibid.*, p. 163; also, Tatia, *Jaina Philosophy*, Chap. 4. Abraham Kaplan, in his excellent lecture on Indian philosophy, identifies this "combination of catholicity and individualization" as "*syadvada*, the 'maybe so' doctrine, or the doctrine of 'up to a point' or 'in a manner of speaking.' " Especially helpful are his lectures 6 and 7 in *New World Philosophy* (New York: Random House, 1963).

Notes to Chapter 5—THE RHETORICAL INFLUENCE OF GAUTAMA BUDDHA

1. E. Zürcher, *Buddhism* (New York: St. Martin's Press, 1962), p. 17. See also C. H. S. Ward, *Buddhism*, 2 vols. (London: Epworth Press, rev., 1947), who warns that it is "very difficult to decide what the original teachings were" (I, 21).

2. Edward Conze, ed., *Buddhist Scriptures* (Baltimore: Penguin Books, 1959), p. 11.

3. By Simon de la Loubere, in his *Descripion du Royaume de Siam* (Paris, 1691).

4. Edward J. Thomas, *The Life of Buddha as Legend and History* (London: Routledge and Kegan Paul, 1927), p. xiv. See pp. xiii–xciii for a depiction of scholarly European interest in Buddhism.

5. Hermann Oldenberg, trans. and ed., *Vinaya Pitika*, 5 vols. (London: Oxford University Press, 1929). The *Vinaya*, comprising the first Buddhist scriptures, consist not of doctrine but of regulations governing the conduct of monks. For an analysis of their importance, see Edward J. Thomas, *The History of Buddhist Thought* (New York: Knopf, 1933), especially Chap. 2, "The Ascetic Ideal"; and Sukumar Dutt, *Buddhist Monks and Monasteries of India* (London: George Allen, 1962).

6. Conze, *Buddhist Scriptures*, p. 14.

7. W. T. de Bary, *Sources of Indian Tradition*, p. 95.

8. Thomas, *Life of Buddha;* and Ananda Coomaraswamy, *Buddha and the Gospel of Buddhism* (Bombay: Asia Publishing House, 1956).

9. Zürcher, *Buddhism*, p. 17.

10. The best edition in English is edited by E. B. Cowell, *The Jātaka*, 6 vols. (Cambridge: University Press, 1895–1913), supplemented by T. W. Rhys Davids' *Buddhist Birth Stories* (Cambridge: University Press, 1880 and 1925).

11. *Majjhima Nikāya*, Sutta I, 240.

12. Edward Conze, *Buddhist Thought in India* (London: George Allen and Unwin, 1962), p. 217.

13. E. A. Burtt, ed., *The Teachings of the Compassionate Buddha* (New York: New American Library, Mentor Religious Classic, 1955), pp. 29–32.

14. In the *Majjhima Nikāya*, Sutta 63, Gautama brushed aside such questions as whether there is a soul, and if so whether it might have eternal life; nor, he declared, had he considered either the origin or the ultimate fate of the world. These matters were beyond knowledge, he said; but, nevertheless, "there still remain birth, old age, death, sorrow, lamentation, misery, grief, and despair, for the extinction of which in the present life I am prescribing." Thomas concluded that: "The Buddhist was convinced that he knew or could come to know quite enough about the universe in order to understand his relation to it, and what he must do in order to attain final happiness." *History of Buddhist Thought,* pp. 56–57.

15. Ward probably stated the matter rightly when he said: "there is a strong presumption that the *Pitakas* contain teachings actually given by the Buddha, and, possibly, some of them in the very form in which they were originally given, though not in the Buddha's own words, for we may be sure that he spoke to the people in their own vernaculars." *Buddhism*, I, 20–21. T. W. Rhys Davids believed the discourses were first written down some hundred seventy-five years after Gautama's death. *Buddhist Suttas* (Oxford: Clarendon Press, 1900), p. x. Another tradition has it that the collection and ordering of the sermons occurred at the Buddhist Council of Rājagaha, held soon after Buddha's death. See Thomas, *History of Buddhist Thought,* pp. 27–29; and N. A. Jayawickrama, *The Inception of Discipline and the Vinaya Nidāna* (London: Luzac, 1962). Edward Conze, in his *Buddhism: Its Essence and Development* (New York: Harper Torchbooks, 1959), p. 29, places the actual writing at "about four hundred years" after the discourses were spoken. It should be kept in mind that the Brahmins maintained a strictly verbatim body of oral literature.

16. Davids, *Dialogues of the Buddha,* II, xviii–xix.

17. *Ibid.,* p. xx.

18. This story, which appeared late in the Buddhist canon, was not related by Gautama but is within the style which he established. It appears in E. W. Burlingame's *Buddhist Parables* (New Haven: Yale University Press, 1922), pp. 92–94, taken from the *Anguttara Nikāya.*

19. Davids, *Dialogues of the Buddha,* II, 173–85.

20. Davids, *Buddhist Suttas,* p. 13.

21. *Ibid.,* pp. 175–76.

22. *Ibid.,* pp. 48–49.

23. *Ibid.,* pp. 37–38.

24. Davids, *Dialogues of the Buddha,* II, 4–5.

25. *Ibid.,* pp. 135, 157, and 319.

26. *Ibid.,* IV, 48–51.

27. *Ibid.,* III, 253.

28. Coomaraswamy, *Buddha and the Gospel of Buddhism,* p. 278.

29. *Ibid.,* pp. 268–69.

30. Quoted from the *Majjhima Nikāya* by Thomas, *Life of Buddha,* p. 82.

31. Davids, *Dialogues of the Buddha,* II, 3.

32. *Ibid.,* p. 38.

33. *Ibid.,* pp. 52–55.

34. A. Foucher, *The Life of Buddha,* trans. and abridged by Simone Brangier Boas (Middletown, Conn.: Wesleyan University Press, 1963), p. 245.

35. Conze, *Buddhist Thought in India,* Chapter 3.

36. See F. S. C. Northrop's discussion of the Buddhist dialectic of negativism in his *The Meeting of East and West* (New York: Macmillan, 1946), pp. 348–58.

37. *Ibid.*, p. 345.

38. Davids, *Dialogues of the Buddha*, II, 225.

39. *Ibid.*, IV, 111.

40. *Ibid.*, IV, 115.

41. Thomas, *Life of Buddha*, pp. 136–37.

42. From the *Dhammapada*, trans. and ed. by Max Müller (Oxford: Clarendon Press, 1881), I, 1.

43. *Dhammapada*, XII, 2.

44. Thomas, *Life of Buddha*, p. 179.

45. Richard A. Gard, *Buddhism* (New York: George Braziller, 1961), pp. 58–59.

46. *Ibid.*, p. 63.

47. *Ibid.*, pp. 64–65 and 68.

48. Davids, *Dialogues of the Buddha*, IV, 177.

49. *Ibid.*, II, 148.

50. *Dhammapada*, XXV.

51. Gautama's methods of conducting disputations are well depicted by Nalinaksha Dutt, in *Early History of the Spread of Buddhism and the Buddhist Schools* (London: Luzac, 1925), pp. 52–68.

52. From "The Great Chapter" of the *Sutta Nipata: Dialogues or Discourses of Gautama Buddha* (London: Oxford University Press, 1945), p. 65.

*Notes to Chapter 6—*CHINA: THE RHETORICAL MILIEU

1. See the section on the "Hundred Schools" of philosophy in C. P. Fitzgerald's *China: A Short Cultural History* (London: Cresset Press, rev., 1950), pp. 74–105.

2. Susanne K. Langer has said it well: "Every society meets a new idea with its own concepts, its own tacit, fundamental way of seeing things; that is to say, with its own questions, its peculiar curiosity," in her *Philosophy in a New Key* (Cambridge: Harvard University Press, 1942), p. 4.

3. Quoted from the *Annals and Memoirs of the Court of Peking* (London: Backhouse and Bland, 1914) by Fitzgerald, *China*, pp. 557–58. See also H. B. Morse and H. F. MacNair, *Far Eastern International Relations* (Boston: Houghton Mifflin, 1931).

4. The quotation is from the *Book of History*, to be examined in Chapter 7. Fitzgerald, in *China*, p. 17, noted the incident as evidence that in ancient China kings could not rule without the consent of their people; hence public criticism could not be ignored.

5. Yi-Pao Mei, *Motse: Rival of Confucius* (London: Arthur Probsthain, 1934), p. 64.

6. James R. Ware, trans., *The Sayings of Chuang-Chou* (New York: New American Library, Mentor Books, 1963), p. 23, cites Chuang's view that "among the ancients knowledge has attained the ultimate."

7. F. L. Hawks Pott, *A Sketch of Chinese History* (Shanghai, 1908), p. 51.

8. W. K. Liao, trans. and ed., *The Complete Works of Han Fei-Tzu*, 2 vols. (London: Arthur Probsthain, 1959), II, 3.

9. John Steele, trans., *I-Li or Book of Etiquette and Ceremonial* (London: Arthur Probsthain, 1917), I, 47.

10. *Ibid.*, pp. 233–34.

11. James Legge, trans., *The Doctrine of the Mean*, in *The Chinese Classics*, translated and edited by Legge, with extensive annotation, 5 vols. (London: Oxford University Press, 1893–95; reprinted, Hongkong: Hong Kong University Press, 1960), I, 406–407.

12. *Ibid.*, p. 418.

13. *Ibid.*, p. 407.

14. *Ibid.*, p. 395.

15. *Ibid.*, p. 396.

16. V. R. Burkhardt, *Chinese Creeds and Customs*, 3 vols. in one (Taipei: World Book Co., 1953), III, 68.

17. Burton Watson, *Early Chinese Literature* (New York: Columbia University Press, 1962), p. 226. The same ode is translated by James Legge, in *The She King or the Book of Poetry*, Vol. IV of *Chinese Classics*, p. 561. The difficulties of translating classical Chinese are revealed in Legge's rendition of the last lines, in which he says not that women and eunuchs are unteachable, as Watson does, but that they are unable to give instruction. Similar divergencies of meaning appear often among the translations cited in succeeding chapters. Since precise meanings are often uncertain, I have sought throughout to interpret particular passages in the context of each Chinese sage's general philosophy.

18. Charles K. Parker, *Dog Eats Moon* (Pittsfield, Mass.: Greylock Publishers, 1950), p. 66.

19. P. F. B. Du Halde, *Description of the Empire of China* (London: Edward Cave, Vol. I, 1738, Vol. II, 1741), II, 54. Although never in China, Du Halde writes of Chinese customs in great detail, basing his work on reports by Jesuit missionaries.

20. *Ibid.*, II, 109.

21. *Ibid.*

22. *Ibid.*, p. 111 (misprint for p. 110).

23. *Ibid.*, p. 124.

24. Yung Tai Pyun, trans., *The Analects of Confucius* (Seoul, Korea: Minjungsugwan, n.d. [1956]), p. 77.

25. Homer H. Dubs, trans., *Hsüntze: Moulder of Ancient Confucianism* (London: Arthur Probsthain, 1927), p. 249.

26. Pyun, *Analects of Confucius*, p. 79.

27. Arthur H. Smith, *Chinese Characteristics*, rev. ed. (New York: Fleming H. Revell, 1894), pp. 36–37.

28. Kenneth Scott Latourette, *The Chinese: Their History and Culture*, 2 vols. (New York: Macmillan, 1934), II, 209–13.

Notes to Chapter 7—THE BOOK OF HISTORY: AN ANTHOLOGY OF SPEECHES

1. Burton Watson, *Early Chinese Literature* (New York: Columbia University Press, 1962), pp. 40–66. Other notable commentaries, dating as did Tso's from the fifth century B.C., are discussed by Ch'ên Shou-Yi, in his *Chinese Literature: A Historical Introduction* (New York: Ronald Press, 1961), pp. 70–73.

2. Watson, *Early Chinese Literature*, p. 74; see also pp. 66–74 for Watson's analysis of the *Conversations*.

3. Wing-tsit Chan, trans. and ed., *A Source Book in Chinese Philosophy* (Princeton, N.J.: Princeton University Press, 1963), p. 11.

4. Ch'ên Shou-Yi, *Chinese Literature*, p. 62.

5. Legge, *Chinese Classics*, III, *The Shoo King, or the Book of Historical Documents*, "Prolegomena," p. 47.

6. *Ibid.*, pp. 41–49.

7. *Ibid.*, pp. 53–62.

8. *Ibid.*, pp. 64–65.

9. *Ibid.*, pp. 153–55.

10. *Ibid.*, pp. 168–69.

11. *Ibid.*, pp. 173–75.

12. *Ibid.*, p. 182.

13. Ssu-Ma Ch'ien, *Records of the Grand Historian of China, 209–100 B.C.*, trans. and ed. by Burton Watson (New York: Columbia University Press, 1961).

14. Legge, *Book of Historical Documents*, p. 177n.

15. Herbert A. Giles, *A Chinese Biographical Dictionary* (Cambridge: University Press, 1898, republished Taipei, n.d.), p. 206.

16. James Legge, *Chinese Classics*, II, *The Works of Mencius*, pp. 370–71.

17. Legge, *Book of Historical Documents*, p. 183.

18. *Ibid.*, pp. 79–83.

19. Giles, *Biographical Dictionary*, p. 352.

20. Legge, *Works of Mencius*, p. 370.

21. Legge, *Book of Historical Documents*, pp. 195–98.

22. *Ibid.*, pp. 209–19.

23. Cited by Watson, *Early Chinese Literature*, p. 218.

24. Quoted by Ch'ên Shou-Yi, *Chinese Literature*, p. 159.

25. Ssu-Ma Ch'ien, *Records of the Grand Historian*, II, p. 474.

26. Fitzgerald, *Short Cultural History*, pp. 20ff., and W. P. Yetts, "The Shang-Yin Dynasty and the An Yang Finds," *Journal of the Royal Asiatic Society*, July, 1933.

27. Legge, *Book of Historical Documents*. King Pwan-kang's first speech is on pp. 220–31, the second on pp. 233–41, and the third on pp. 243–47.

28. *Ibid.*, pp. 273–75.

29. *Ibid.*, pp. 326–27.

30. *Ibid.*, pp. 579–80.

31. Ssu-Ma Ch'ien, *Records of the Grand Historian*, II, p. 156.

32. Legge, *Book of Historical Documents*, p. 580.

33. *Ibid.*, pp. 580–87.

34. *Ibid.*, p. 628.

35. *Ibid.*, pp. 626–30.

Notes to Chapter 8—CONFUCIUS: THE AUTHORITY OF TRADITION

1. See Arthur E. Christy, *The Asian Legacy and American Life* (New York: John Day, 1942), pp. 16–37; Lewis A. Maverick, *China: A Model for Europe*

(San Antonio, Texas: Paul Anderson Co., 1946); H. G. Creel, *Confucius and the Chinese Way* (New York: Harper Torchbooks, 1960), pp. 254–78; and Arnold H. Rowbotham, "The Impact of Confucianism on Seventeenth Century Europe," *Far Eastern Quarterly*, 4 (1945), 224–42.

2. Eustace Budgell, *Letter to Cleomenes: King of Sparta* (London, 1731).

3. The limitations of the Confucian influence, however, are strikingly evidenced in the omission of any reference to Confucianism in Crane Brinton's *A History of Western Morals* (New York: Harcourt, Brace, 1959).

4. Arnold Toynbee, *A Study of History*, edited and abridged by D. C. Somervell (New York: Oxford University Press, 1947), p. 375.

5. Joseph R. Levenson, *Liang Ch'i-ch'ao and the Mind of Modern China* (Cambridge: Harvard University Press, 1965), p. 34.

6. *Analects*, XVIII, 6.

7. James I. Crump and John J. Dreher, "Peripatetic Rhetors of the Warring Kingdom," *Central States Speech Journal*, 2 (March, 1951), 16.

8. James Legge, trans. and ed., *The I Ching: The Book of Changes*, Vol. XVI of "The Sacred Books of the East," ed., Max Müller (London: Clarendon Press, 1898). Unexpected and sudden popularity was won by *The I Ching or Book of Changes*, trans. into German by Richard Wilhelm and thence into English by Cary F. Baynes (Princeton, N.J.: Princeton University Press, Bollingen Series, 1961).

9. *Analects*, VII, 16.

10. Creel, in *Confucius and the Chinese Way*, pp. 33–34, rejects the tradition that Confucius held one or several official positions.

11. Ssu-Ma Ch'ien, *Records of the Grand Historian*, II, 395.

12. See, for example, *Analects*, XIX, 25; XII, 7; XIII, 20; XIV, 18, 31; XV, 2; and XVII, 19.

13. Pyun, Yung Tai, *The Analects of Confucius*, p. 2.

14. Creel, *Confucius and the Chinese Way*, p. 27.

15. Pyun, Yung Tai, *The Analects of Confucius*, p. 4.

16. Legge, *Chinese Classics*, Vol. II, *Works of Mencius*, p. 192.

17. James R. Ware, *The Sayings of Chuang Chou* (New York: New American Library, a Mentor Classic, 1963), p. 200.

18. Legge, *Chinese Classics*, I, 357–59.

19. Arthur Waley, *The Analects of Confucius* (London: George Allen and Unwin, 1938), pp. 27–29; and Ch'u Chai and Winberg Chai, eds., *The Humanist Way in Ancient China* (New York: Bantam Books, 1965), p. 1.

20. Creel, *Confucius and the Chinese Way*, pp. 32, 80.

Notes to Chapter 9—THE RHETORIC OF BEHAVIOR: CEREMONY, ETIQUETTE, AND METHODOLOGY

1. R. G. H. Siu, *The Man of Many Qualities: A Legacy of the I Ching* (Cambridge, Mass.: MIT Press, 1968), p. vi. For a discussion of the whole body of major and minor ritualistic literature of Ancient China, see Watson, *Early Chinese Literature*, pp. 139–53.

2. Arthur H. Smith, *Chinese Characteristics* (New York: Fleming H. Revell, 1894), p. 37.

3. Du Halde, *Description of the Empire of China*, II, p. 38.

4. Liu Wu-chi, *An Introduction to Chinese Literature* (Bloomington, Ind.: Indiana University Press, 1966), p. 5.

5. The Confucian *Classic of Filial Piety* makes the interesting observation that "The Confucian gentleman . . . in teaching filial piety shows respect to all fathers in the world, and in teaching brotherly affection, he shows respect to all the brothers in the world." Quoted by Watson, *Early Chinese Literature*, p. 150.

6. *Li Chi*, Book XXII, para. 1.

7. Ralph Waldo Emerson, *Works*, ed. Edward Waldo Emerson (New York: Wise, 1929), VI, 172–73.

8. *Li Chi*, Book VIII, Sec. 2, para. 19.

9. This concept of the acculturation into personality of communicative acts and attitudes is presented by David Reisman and associates in *The Lonely Crowd* (New Haven: Yale University Press, 1950), and, more technically, by Gregory Bateson in "Information, Codification, and Metacommunication," in Jurgen Ruesch and G. Bateson, eds., *Communication: The Social Matrix of Psychiatry* (New York: Norton, 1951), pp. 168–86 and 212–14.

10. It was first published in London by Probsthain in 1917 and reissued by the Ch'eng-wen Publishing Co. in Taipei in 1966.

11. John Steele, trans. and ed., *The I-Li or Book of Etiquette and Ceremonial* (London: Probsthain, 1917), I, xiii.

12. *Ibid.*, p. 37.

13. *Ibid.*, pp. 42–43.

14. *Ibid.*, p. 47.

15. *Ibid.*, pp. 233–34.

16. Ch'ên Shou-Yi, *Chinese Literature*, p. 76.

17. *Ibid.*, p. 78.

18. James Legge, trans. and ed., *The Li-Ki*, 2 vols. (Oxford: Clarendon Press, 1885), I, 12. Source references for this book will be to the edition edited by Ch'u Chai and Winberg Chai, under the title *Li Chi: Book of Rites* (New Hyde Park, N.Y.: New York University Books, 1967). The paging is identical in the two editions.

19. Wilhelm and Baynes, *The I Ching*, p. xiii.

20. *New York Times Book Review Section*, May 18, 1969, p. 7.

21. Ch'ên Shou-Yi, *Chinese Literature*, p. 70.

22. Siu, *Man of Many Qualities*, p. 5.

23. James Legge, *The I Ching* (New York: Dover, 1963), p. 224.

24. *Ibid.*, p. 219.

25. For development of this theme, see Wilhelm and Baynes, *The I Ching*, p. xxiii, and Hu Shih, *Development of the Logical Method in Ancient China* (New York: Paragon reprint, 1963).

26. Legge, *I Ching*, p. 303.

27. *Ibid.*, p. 392.

28. *Ibid.*, p. 363.

29. *Ibid.*, p. 361.

30 *Ibid.*, p. 238.

Notes to Chapter 10—MENCIUS: THE BOLD PROPHET

1. Daisetz Teitaro Suzuki, *A Brief History of Early Chinese Philosophy* (London: Probsthain, 1914), p. 64.
2. Legge, *Chinese Classics*, II, *Works of Mencius*, p. 106.
3. Gung-Hsing Wang, *The Chinese Mind* (New York: John Day, 1946), p. 29.
4. Leonard A. Lyall, *Mencius* (London: Longmans, Green, 1932), p. xxv.
5. H. G. Creel, *Chinese Thought from Confucius to Mao Tze-tung* (New York: New American Library, Mentor Book, 1960), p. 64.
6. Legge, *Chinese Classics*, II, *Works of Mencius*, "Prolegomena," p. 6.
7. I. A. Richards, *Mencius on the Mind* (London: Kegan Paul, Trench, Trubner and Co., 1932), p. 28.
8. Brief selections from Mencius translated by Y. P. Mei are included in de Bary, *Sources of Chinese Tradition*, pp. 102–12.
9. The whole of Book I, Part 1 of the *Book of Mencius* is devoted to his colloquy with King Hui. Subsequent source references will be to Book, Part, Chapter, and paragraph (when pertinent) of this *Mencius*, facilitating reference by readers to whatever translation or edition may be available to them. Where publishers use different schemes of division, the Legge edition is followed.
10. *Mencius*, Bk. I, Pt. 2, Chap. 13.
11. *Ibid.*, Chap. 16.
12. *Ibid.*, Bk. II, Pt. 1, Chap. 2, para. 7.
13. *Ibid.*, Bk. III, Chap. 2, para. 4.
14. *Ibid.*, Bk. VII, Chap. 9.
15. *Ibid.*, Bk. III, Chap. 1, para. 5.
16. *Ibid.*, Bk. II, Chap. 2. See also Bk. III, Chap. 1 and Bk. V, Chap. 7.
17 *Ibid.*, Bk. VI, Chap. 2, para. 7.
18. *Ibid.*, Bk. VI, Pt. 1, Chap. 12.
19. Legge, *Chinese Classics*, II, *Works of Mencius*, p. 394n.
20. Richards, *Mencius on the Mind*, p. 22.
21. This is a continuation of the argument of Book VI. The same point is made equally cogently in Bk. VII, Pt. 2, Chap. 3, para. 1: "To believe the books without question is worse than having no books."
22. Translated from *Kung Tze Chia Yu* by Hu Shih, in his *Development of the Logical Method*, p. 12.
23. *Mencius*, Bk. VI, Chap. 15, para. 3.
24. *Ibid.*, Bk. V, Chap. 15, para. 1 and 2.
25. *Ibid.*, Bk. V, Chap. 15, para. 1 and 2.
26. *Ibid.*, Bk. VI, Chap. 16.
27. *Ibid.*, Bk. III, Pt. 2, Chap. 4, para. 6.
28. *Ibid.*, Bk. III, Pt. 2, Chap. 7, para. 4.
29. *Ibid.*, Bk. VII, Pt. 2, Chap. 31, para. 4.
30. *Ibid.*, Bk. II, Pt. 1, Chap. 2, para. 17.
31. *Ibid.*, Bk. IV, Pt. 1, Chap. 15, para. 1 and 2.
32. *Ibid.*, Bk. VII, Pt. 2, Chap. 32, para. 1.
33. *Ibid.*, Bk. IV, Pt. 1, Chap. 22.

34. *Ibid.*, Chap. 12, para. 3.
35. *Ibid.*, Bk. VII, Pt. 2, Chap. 33, para. 2.
36. *Ibid.*, Pt. 1, Chap. 4, para. 2
37. Richards, *Mencius on the Mind*, Chap. 4.

Notes to Chapter 11—THEORISTS OF HUMAN MOTIVATION

1. Cf. Calvin S. Hall and Gardner Lindzey, *Theories of Personality* (New York: Wiley, 1957), and A. H. Maslow, *Motivation and Personality* (New York: Harper, 1954).
2. Fitzgerald, *Short Cultural History*, p. 548.
3. For a more recent edition, see T'ang Ching-kao, ed., *Selected Texts of Mo-tze with Notes and Introduction* (Shanghai: Commercial Press, 1938, 4th ed., 1947). The name of the philosopher is variously spelled Mo-ti, Motse, Mo-Tze, Mo-tzu, Mehti, and Micius.
4. See Wilbur Henry Long, *Mo-tse: China's Ancient Philosopher of Universal Love* (Peiping, 1934) and H. Williamson, *Mo-ti: A Chinese Heretic* (Tsi-nan, 1927).
5. See Chiang Kai-shek, *All We Are and All We Have* (New York: John Day, 1943) and Madame Chiang, *This Is Our China* (New York: Harper, 1940).
6. See Hu Shih, *Development of the Logical Method*, p. 54, and Burton Watson, trans. and ed., *Basic Writings of Mo Tzu, Hsün Tzu, and Han Fei Tzu* (New York: Columbia University Press), pp. 1–17. Watson translated seven subsections which he thought best represent Mo-Tze's thought. Yi-Pao Mei, *Moral and Political Works of Motse* (London: Probsthain, 1929), omits the first five and the last eleven of the extant fifty-three chapers.
7. Yi-Pao Mei, *Motse: The Neglected Rival of Confucius* (London: Probsthain, 1934), p. 31.
8. Mei, *Works of Motse*, Chaps. 47 and 48.
9. James R. Ware, *The Sayings of Chuang-Chou* (New York: New American Library, Mentor Classic, 1963), pp. 224–26. The philosopher's name is more commonly transliterated as Chuang Tzu.
10. Ch'ên Shou-Yi, *Chinese Literature*, p. 91.
11. Mei, *Works of Motse*, Chap. 17.
12. Augustine Tseu, in his *Moral Philosophy of Mo-tze* (Taipei: China Printing, 1965), argues also that Mo-Tze was no pragmatist; he insists that Mo-Tze somehow drew his sanction from the will of God.
13. Mei, *Works of Motse*, p. 229.
14. *Ibid.*, p. 222.
15. *Ibid.*, p. 251.
16. *Ibid.*, p. 222.
17. *Ibid.*, p. 253.
18. *Ibid.*, p. 215.
19. *Ibid.*, p. 161.
20. *Ibid.*
21. *Ibid.*, Chap. 26.
22. Hu Shih, *Development of the Logical Method*, p. 4.

23. Legge, *Chinese Classics,* I, *The Great Learning,* "Introduction."
24. *Ibid.,* p. 358.
25. Hu Shih, *Development of the Logical Method,* p. 12.
26. *Ibid.,* p. 13.
27. Watson, *Early Chinese Literature,* pp. 188–89.
28. Homer H. Dubs, trans., *The Works of Hsüntze* (London: Probsthain, 1928), p. 79.
29. Ware, *Sayings of Chuang Chou,* pp. 230–31.
30. Chan, *Source Book in Chinese Philosophy,* p. 232.
31. Ware, *Sayings of Chuang Chou,* pp. 230–31.
32. *Kung-Sun Lung Tzu,* Chap. I, para. 1. The only available English translation is that by Y. P. Mei, "The Kung-Sun Lung Tzu: With a Translation into English," *Harvard Journal of Asiatic Studies,* 16 (December, 1953), 404–37.
33. Mei, "The Kung-Sun Lung Tzu," p. 415.
34. The only English-language biography of Hsüntze is that by Homer H. Dubs, *Hsüntze: The Moulder of Ancient Confucianism* (London: Probsthain, 1927).
35. *Ibid.,* p. 301.
36. *Ibid.,* p. 47.
37. *Ibid.,* p. 269.
38. *Ibid.,* p. 281.
39. *Ibid.,* pp. 267–68.
40. *Ibid.,* p. 269.
41. *Ibid.,* p. 97.
42. *Ibid.,* p. 96.
43. *Ibid.,* pp. 292–93.
44. *Ibid.,* p. 175.
45. *Ibid.,* pp. 298–99.
46. *Ibid.,* p. 118.
47. *Ibid.,* p. 315.
48. *Ibid.,* p. 317.

Notes to Chapter 12—THE LEGALISTIC RHETORICIANS

1. Both the distinction between enforced justice and persuasion and also their paradoxical relationships are well analyzed by Chaim Perelman in *The Idea of Justice and the Problem of Argument,* trans. by John Petrie (New York: Humanities Press, 1963), pp. 134–53 and *passim.*
2. Legge, *Chinese Classics,* V, *The Tso Chuen,* p. 566.
3. Perelman, *The Idea of Justice,* pp. 79–87.
4. Legge, *Chinese Classics,* II, *The Works of Mencius,* p. 282.
5. Bodde, in Fung Yu-lan, *History of Chinese Philosophy,* I, 133.
6. Quoted by Gung-Hsing Wang, *The Chinese Mind,* p. 87.
7. Liu Wu-Chi, *A Short History of Confucian Philosophy* (Baltimore: Penguin Books, 1955), p. 111.
8. J. J. L. Duyvendak, trans. and ed., *The Book of Lord Shang* (London: Probsthain, 1928), pp. 225–27.

9. *Ibid.*, pp. 14–16.

10. Fitzgerald, *Short Cultural History*, pp. 141–45.

11. *Ibid.*, pp. 144–45, from Chapter 87 of Ssu-ma Ch'ien's *Records of the Grand Historian*. For a rounded account of the career of Li-Ssu, see Derk Bodde, *China's First Unifier: A Study of the Ch'in Dynasty as Seen in the Life of Li-Ssu* (Leiden: E. J. Brill, 1938).

12. "Li-Ssu's Memorial to the King of Ch'in," in W. K. Liao, trans. and ed., *The Complete Works of Han Fei Tzu*, 2 vols. (London: Probsthain, 1939), I, 17.

13. Quoted by Giles, *A Chinese Biographical Dictionary*, p. 245.

14. Liao, *Works of Han Fei Tzu*, "Eight Canons," II, 258–59.

15. *Ibid.*, "A Critique of the Doctrine of Position," p. 204.

16. *Ibid.*, "Outer Congeries of Sayings, Lower Left Series," pp. 74–75. These six "Congeries of Sayings" are entitled by Bodde, "Inner and Outer Discussions." They could be thought of as "Random Observations." The notation, "Lower" and "Upper" Series refers to their placement in Han's book.

17. *Ibid.*, "Eight Canons," pp. 258–59.

18. *Ibid.*, "The Difficulty of Pien Ho," I, 113–16.

19. *Ibid.*, "The Tao of the Sovereign," p. 31.

20. *Ibid.*, "Solitary Indignation," p. 102.

21. *Ibid.*, "Eight Villainies," pp. 64–65.

22. *Ibid.*, "Outer Congeries of Sayings, Lower Left Series," II, 78.

23. *Ibid.*, "On Assumers," p. 224.

24. *Ibid.*, "Criticisms of the Ancients, Series Three," pp. 187–88.

25. *Ibid.*, "Outer Congeries of Sayings, Upper Left Series," pp. 26–27.

26. *Ibid.*, "Having Regulations," I, 40–41.

27. *Ibid.*, "Safety and Danger," pp. 262–63.

28. *Ibid.*, "The Tao of the Sovereign," p. 32.

29. *Ibid.*, "Ministers Apt to Betray, Molest or Murder the Ruler," pp. 125–26.

30. *Ibid.*, "Difficulties in the Way of Persuasion," p. 106.

31. *Ibid.*, p. 107.

32. *Ibid.*, p. 108.

33. *Ibid.*, "Ministers Apt to Betray," p. 118.

34. *Ibid.*, "Difficulties in the Way of Persuasion," pp. 108–109.

35. *Ibid.*, pp. 109–10.

36. *Ibid.*, pp. 110–12. The "mud fence" analogy is repeated in "Collected Persuasions, The Lower Series," p. 258.

37. *Ibid.*, p. 259.

38. *Ibid.*, "Ministers Apt to Betray," pp. 116–17.

39. *Ibid.*, "Inner Congeries of Sayings, Upper Series," p. 291.

40. *Ibid.*, "Wielding the Sceptre," p. 55.

41. *Ibid.*, "Outer Congeries of Sayings, Upper Right Series," II, 113.

42. *Ibid.*, "Criticisms of the Ancients, Series Two," p. 167.

43. *Ibid.*, "Absurd Encouragements," pp. 230–31.

44. *Ibid.*, "On the Difficulty of Speaking," I, 23–24.

45. *Ibid.*, pp. 27–28.

46. *Ibid.*, "Solitary Indignation," p. 99.

47. *Ibid.*, "Eight Canons," II, 267.

48. *Ibid.*, p. 269.

49. *Ibid.*, pp. 270–71.

50. *Ibid.*, "Outer Congeries of Sayings, Upper Left Series," p. 43.
51. *Ibid.*, "On Pretensions and Heresies," I, 164–65.
52. *Ibid.*, "Illustrations of Lao-Tzu's Teachings," p. 221.
53. *Ibid.*, "Commentaries on Lao-Tzu's Teachings," pp. 170–75.
54. *Ibid.*, "Facing the South," p. 153.
55. *Ibid.*, "Wielding the Sceptre," p. 56.

Notes to Chapter 13—RHETORICAL IMPLICATIONS OF TAOISM

1. de Bary, *Sources of Chinese Tradition*, p. 50.
2. Burton Watson, *Chuang Tzu: Basic Writings* (New York: Columbia University Press, 1964), p. 3.
3. Lin Yutang, "Laotse, the Book of Tao," in *Wisdom of India and China* (New York: Random House, Modern Library, 1942), p. 579.
4. Ssu-Ma Ch'ien, *Records of the Grand Historian*, I, 386.
5. *Ibid.*, II, 475.
6. *Ibid.*, p. 344.
7. *Ibid.*, pp. 476–77.
8. Mei, *Motse: The Rival of Confucius*, p. 23, and Ch'ên Shou-Yi, *Chinese Literature*, p. 36.
9. James Legge, *The Texts of Taoism* (New York: Julian Press, reprinted, 1959), p. 48, and Herbert A. Giles, *A History of Chinese Literature* (New York: Appleton, 1923), p. 56.
10. Creel, *Chinese Thought from Confucius to Mao Tze-tung*, pp. 84–85, and Watson, *Early Chinese Literature*, p. 157.
11. Witter Bynner, *The Way of Life According to Laotzu* (New York: John Day, 1944), p. 7.
12. R. B. Blakney, *Lao Tzu* (New York: New American Library, Mentor Book, 1955), pp. 27–28.
13. A. Wylie, *Notes on Chinese Literature* (Shanghai, 1867), p. 179.
14. Lin Yutang, *Wisdom of China and India*, p. 582.
15. Watson, *Early Chinese Literature*, p. 158.
16. Creel, *Chinese Thought from Confucius to Mao Tze-tung*, p. 88.
17. Holmes Welch, *The Parting of the Way* (London: Methuen, 1958), p. 83.
18. Arthur Waley, *The Way and Its Power: A Study of the Tao Teh Ching and Its Place in Chinese Thought* (New York: Grove Press, n.d.), p. 37.
19. Vaihinger, *The Philosophy of 'As If,'* p. 15.
20. Walter Lippmann, *Public Opinion* (New York: Macmillan, 1922), p. 61.
21. Legge, *Chinese Classics*, I, 367.
22. F. S. C. Northrop, *The Meeting of East and West* (New York: Macmillan, 1946), pp. 315–46.
23. Alan W. Watts, *The Way of Zen* (New York: New American Library, Mentor Book, 1959), Chap. 1.
24. *Ibid.*, p. 31.
25. *Chuang Tzu*, Chap. 14, section 40 (in Waley's translation).
26. Ware, *Sayings of Chuang Chou* (Waley's version).
27. *Ibid.*, p. 27 (Waley's version).

28. *Ibid.,* p. 116.

29. Ch'ên Shou-Yi, *Chinese Literature,* p. 93.

30. Ware, *Sayings of Chuang Chou,* p. 7.

31. *Ibid.,* pp. 15–16 and 18–19. The following quotations are, variously, from translations by Giles, Legge, Watson, or Ware.

32. A strikingly similar view, stated in terms of modern psychology, is that of Polanyi, *Personal Knowledge,* especially in Chaps. 1, 8, 9, and 10.

33. Watson, *Chuang-Tzu: Basic Writings,* p. 4.

Notes to Chapter 14—CHARACTERISTICS OF ASIAN RHETORIC

1. Otis M. Walter, "On Views of Rhetoric, Whether Conservative or Progressive," *Quarterly Journal of Speech,* 49 (December, 1963), 367–82.

2. Lane Cooper, trans. and ed., *The Rhetoric of Aristotle* (New York: Appleton-Century-Crofts, 1932), p. 6.

3. Maurice Natanson, "The Limits of Rhetoric," in Maurice Natanson and Henry W. Johnstone, Jr., eds., *Philosophy, Rhetoric and Argumentation* (University Park, Pa.: Pennsylvania State University Press, 1965), p. 98.

4. Cooper, *Rhetoric of Aristotle,* p. 2.

5. *Ibid.,* p. 9.

6. Natanson, *Philosophy, Rhetoric and Argumentation,* pp. 93–95.

7. This is the well-known distinction made by Northrop in his *Meeting of East and West,* Chap. IX.

Bibliography

GUIDES TO METHODOLOGY

Alexander, Hubert G. *Language and Thinking: A Philosophical Introduction.* Princeton, N.J.: Van Nostrand, 1967.

Arnold, Carroll C. "Oral Rhetoric, Rhetoric, and Literature." *Philosophy and Rhetoric* 1 (Fall, 1968):191–210.

Baldwin, Charles Sears, *Ancient Rhetoric and Poetic.* New York: Crowell-Collier and Macmillan, 1924.

Barnouw, Victor. *Culture and Personality.* Homewood, Ill.: Dorsey Press, 1963.

Bateson, Gregory. *Naven.* Stanford: Stanford University Press, rev., 1958.

Benedict, Ruth. *The Chrysanthemum and the Sword.* Boston: Houghton Mifflin, 1946.

Bitzer, Lloyd F. "The Rhetorical Situation." *Philosophy and Rhetoric* 1 (January, 1968):1–14.

Boulding, Kenneth E. *The Image: Knowledge in Life and Society.* Ann Arbor: University of Michigan Press, 1956.

Brown, Ina Corinne. *Understanding Other Cultures.* Englewood Cliffs, N.J.: Prentice-Hall, 1963.

Bryant, Donald C. "Rhetoric: Its Function and Its Scope." *Quarterly Journal of Speech* 39 (December, 1953):401–24.

Bryson, Lyman, ed. *The Communication of Ideas.* New York: Harper, 1948.

——, et al., eds. *Symbols and Society.* New York: Harper and Row, 1955.

——, et al., eds. *Symbols and Values.* New York: Harper and Row, 1954.

Burckhardt, Jacob. *Force and Freedom: Reflections on History.* New York: Pantheon, 1943.

Burke, Kenneth. *A Rhetoric of Motives.* Englewood Cliffs, N.J.: Prentice-Hall, 1950.

Campbell, Donald T., and LeVine, Robert A. "A Proposal for Cooperative Cross-Cultural Research on Ethnocentrism." *Journal of Conflict Resolution* 5 (1961):82–108.

Cooper, Lane, trans., *The Rhetoric of Aristotle.* New York: Appleton-Century-Crofts, 1932.

291

Dewey, John, and Bentley, Arthur. *Knowing and the Known*. Boston: Beacon Press, 1949.

Duncan, Hugh Dalziel. *Communication and the Social Order*. New York: Bedminster Press, 1962.

——. "The Search for a Social Theory of Communication in American Sociology." In *Human Communication Theory*, edited by Frank E. X. Dance, pp. 236–63 and 310–32. New York: Holt, Rinehart and Winston, 1967.

Ehninger, Douglas. "On Systems of Rhetoric." *Philosophy and Rhetoric* 1 (Summer, 1968):131–44.

Empson, William. *Seven Types of Ambiguity*. Cleveland: World, rev., 1949.

Eubanks, Ralph T., and Baker, Virgil L. "Toward an Axiology of Rhetoric." *Quarterly Journal of Speech* 48 (April, 1962):157–68.

Fogarty, Daniel. *Roots for a New Rhetoric*. New York: Teachers College of Columbia University, Bureau of Publications, 1959.

Goffman, Erving. *The Presentation of the Self in Everyday Life*. New York: Doubleday Anchor Original, 1959.

Hall, Calvin, and Lindzey, Gardner. *Theories of Personality*. New York: Wiley, 1957.

Hall, Edward T. *The Hidden Dimension*. Garden City, N.Y.: Doubleday, 1966.

Hymes, Dell. "The Anthropology of Communication." In *Human Communication Theory*, edited by Frank E. X. Dance. New York: Holt, Rinehart and Winston, 1967.

Kaplan, Abraham. *The New World of Philosophy*. New York: Random House, Vintage Book, 1963.

Kroeber, Alfred L. *Style and History*. Ithaca, N.Y.: Cornell University Press, 1957.

——, and Kluckhohn, Clyde. *Culture: A Critical Review of Concepts and Definitions*. New York: Random House, Vintage Book, 1966.

Kuntz, Paul G. *The Concept of Order*. Seattle: University of Washington Press, 1963.

Langer, Susanne K. *Philosophy in a New Key*. Cambridge, Mass.: Harvard University Press, 1942.

McBride, Glen. *A General View of Social Organization and Behavior*. St. Lucia, Australia: University of Queensland Press, 1964.

McLuhan, Marshall. *The Gutenberg Galaxy*. Toronto: University of Toronto Press, 1963.

McNally, James R. "Toward a Definition of Rhetoric." *Philosophy and Rhetoric* 3 (Spring, 1970):71–81.

Madden, Edward H. "The Enthymeme: Crossroads of Logic, Rhetoric and Metaphysics." *Philosophical Review* 61 (1952):368–76.

Maslow, A. H. *Motivation and Personality*. New York: Harper, 1954.

Mead, Margaret, and Metraux, Rhoda. *The Study of Culture at a Distance*. Chicago: University of Chicago Press, 1953.

Murphy, Richard. "Preface to an Ethic of Rhetoric." In *The Rhetorical Idiom*, edited by Donald C. Bryant, pp. 125–43. Ithaca, N.Y.: Cornell University Press, 1958.

Murray, Elwood. "The Semantics of Rhetoric." *Quarterly Journal of Speech* 30 (February, 1944):31–41.

Nakamura, Hajime. *Ways of Thinking of Eastern Peoples: India, China, Tibet, Japan.* Edited by Philip P. Wiener. Honolulu, Hawaii: East-West Center Press, rev., 1964.

Natanson, Maurice, and Johnstone, Henry W., Jr. *Philosophy, Rhetoric and Argumentation.* Foreword by Robert T. Oliver. University Park: Pennsylvania State University Press, 1965.

Nichols, Marie Hochmuth. *Rhetoric and Criticism.* Baton Rouge: Louisiana State University Press, 1963.

Northrop, F. S. C. *The Meeting of East and West.* New York: Macmillan, 1946.

Oliver, Robert T. *Culture and Communication.* Springfield, Ill.: Charles C Thomas, 1962.

——. "Culture and Communication." *Vital Speeches of the Day* 29 (September 15, 1963):721–24.

——. *Verdict in Korea.* State College, Pa.: Bald Eagle Press, 1952.

Pareto, Alfredo. *The Mind and Society.* 4 vols. Translated by A. Bongiorno and A. Livingston. New York: Harcourt, Brace, 1935.

Parsons, Talcott, *et al.*, eds. *The Theories of Society.* 2 vols. New York: Free Press of Glencoe, 1961.

Perelman, Chaim, and Olbrechts-Tyteca, L. *The New Rhetoric: A Treatise of Argumentation.* Translated by John Wilkinson and Purcell Weaver. Notre Dame, Ind.: University of Notre Dame Press, 1969.

Plato. *Collected Dialogues of Plato.* Edited by Edith Hamilton and Huntington Cairns. New York: Pantheon Books, Bollingen Series, 1961.

Prosser, Michael, ed. "Communication and Non-Western Cultures." *Today's Speech* 17 (February, 1969):1–65.

Polanyi, Michael. *Personal Knowledge: Towards a Post-Critical Philosophy.* Chicago: University of Chicago Press, 1958.

Reid, Loren. "The Perils of Rhetorical Criticism." *Quarterly Journal of Speech* 30 (December, 1944):416–22.

Richards, I. A. *The Philosophy of Rhetoric.* New York: Oxford University Press, 1936.

Schwartz, Joseph, and Rycenga, John A., eds. *The Province of Rhetoric.* New York: Ronald Press, 1965.

Sinclair, Angus. *The Conditions of Knowing: An Essay Towards a Theory of Knowledge.* New York: Harcourt, Brace, 1951.

Smith, Alfred G., ed. *Communication and Culture.* New York: Holt, Rinehart and Winston, 1966.

Strelka, Joseph, ed. *Problems of Literary Evaluation: Yearbook of Compara-*

tive Criticism. University Park: Pennsylvania State University Press, 1969.

Thonssen, Lester, and Baird, A. Craig. *Speech Criticism: The Development of Standards for Rhetorical Appraisal.* New York: Ronald Press, 1948.

Vaihinger, Hans. *The Philosophy of 'As If.'* Translated by C. K. Ogden. London: Routledge and Kegan Paul, 1924.

Whitehead, A. N. *Modes of Thought.* New York: Macmillan, 1938.

———. *Symbolism: Its Meaning and Effect.* New York: Macmillan, 1927.

Whorf, Benjamin Lee. *Language, Thought and Reality.* Edited by John B. Carroll. New York: Wiley, 1956.

Winterowd, W. Ross. *Rhetoric: A Synthesis.* New York: Holt, Rinehart and Winston, 1968.

Zaner, Richard M. "Philosophy and Rhetoric: A Critical Discussion." *Philosophy and Rhetoric* 1 (Spring, 1968):61–77.

INDIA

Abbott, J. *The Keys of Power: A Study of Indian Ritual and Belief.* London: Methuen, 1932.

Aiyangar, K. V. R. *Considerations of Some Aspects of Ancient Indian Polity.* Madras: Madras University, 1914, 1935.

Aiyar, K. N. *The Purānas in the Light of Modern Science.* Madras: Theosophical Society, 1916.

———. *Thirty Minor Upanishads.* Madras: Madras University, 1914.

Akhilānanda, Swami. *Hindu Psychology: Its Meaning for the West.* New York: Harper, 1946.

———. *Mental Health and Hindu Psychology.* London: George Allen and Unwin, 1952.

Allan, J., Haig, T. W., and Dodwell, H. H. *Cambridge Shorter History of India.* New York: Macmillan, 1934.

Banks, Michael. "Caste in Jaffna." In *Aspects of Caste in South India, Ceylon and North-West Pakistan,* edited by E. R. Leach. Cambridge: University Press, 1962.

Barnett, L. D., trans. and ed. *Bhagavad-Gita or The Lord's Song.* London: Dent, 1928.

Basham, Arthur Llewellyn. *History and Doctrines of the Ajīvikas.* London: Luzac and Co., 1951.

———. *The Wonder that Was India.* London: Sidgwick and Jackson, 1954.

Belvalkar, S. K., and Ranade, R. D. *History of Indian Philosophy.* Poona: Bilvakunja Publishing House, 1927.

Bhandarkar, D. R. *Some Aspects of Ancient Indian Polity.* Benaras: Hindu University, 1929.

Blunt, E. A. H. *The Caste System of Northern India.* London: Oxford University Press, 1931.

Burglingame, E. W. *Buddhist Parables.* New Haven: Yale University Press, 1922.

Burtt, E. A., trans. and ed. *The Teachings of the Compassionate Buddha.* New York: New American Library, Mentor Religious Classic, 1958.

Carstairs, G. Morris. *The Twice-Born.* Bloomington: Indiana University Press, 1958.

Chakladar, H. C. *Social Life in Ancient India.* Calcutta: Greater India Society, 1929.

Chakravarti, Sures Chandra. *The Philosophy of the Upanishads.* Calcutta: University of Calcutta Press, 1935.

Conze, Edward, ed. *Buddhism: Its Essence and Development.* Oxford: Bruno Cassirer, 1951; and New York: Harper Torchbooks, 1959.

——, ed. *Buddhist Scriptures.* Baltimore: Penguin Books, 1959.

——, ed. *Buddhist Thought in India.* London: George Allen and Unwin, 1962.

——, *et al.*, eds. *Buddhist Texts through the Ages.* New York: Harper Torchbooks, 1964, and Oxford: Bruno Cassirer, 1954.

Coomaraswamy, Ananda. *Buddha and the Gospel of Buddhism.* Bombay: Asia Publishing House, 1956.

——. *Hinduism and Buddhism.* New York: Philosophical Library, 1943.

——. "Play and Seriousness." *Journal of Philosophy* 39 (1942):450–52.

Cowell, E. B., ed. *The Jātaka: Stories of the Buddha's Former Births.* 6 vols. Cambridge: University Press, 1880, 1925.

Das, A. C. *Rigvedic Culture.* Calcutta: R. Cambray, 1925.

Das, S. K. *The Educational System of the Ancient Hindus.* Calcutta: Mitra Press, 1930.

Dasgupta, Surendranath. *History of Indian Philosophy.* Cambridge: Cambridge University Press, 1922.

Davids, C. A. F. Rhys. *The Birth of Indian Psychology and Its Development in Buddhism.* London: Luzac, 1936.

Davids, T. W. Rhys. *Buddhist Birth Stories.* Cambridge: University Press, 1880, 1925.

——. *Buddhist India.* London: T. Fisher Unwin, 1911.

——. *Buddhist Suttas.* Oxford: Clarendon Press, 1900.

——, and Carpenter, J. E., eds. *Dīgha Nikāya.* 3 vols. London: Pali Text Society, 1890–1911.

——, with Davids, C. A. F. Rhys, trans. and eds. *Dialogues of the Buddha.* 4 vols. London: Luzac, 1910, 1951.

de Bary, William Theodore, *et al.*, eds. *Sources of Indian Tradition.* New York: Columbia University Press, 1958.

Deussen, Paul. *The Philosophy of the Upanishads.* Edinburgh: Clark, 1906.

Dubois, Abbe J. A. *Hindu Manners, Customs, and Ceremonies.* 3rd ed. Translated by Henry K. Beauchamp. Oxford: Clarendon Press, 1906.

Dunbar, Sir George. *A History of India from Earliest Times to Nineteen Thirty-Nine*. 4th ed. London: Nicholson and Watson, 1949.

Durant, Will. *Our Oriental Heritage*. New York: Simon and Schuster, 1942.

Dutt, Nalinaksha. *Early History of the Spread of Buddhism and the Buddhist Schools*. London: Luzac, 1925.

Dutt, Nripendra Kumar. *Origin and Growth of Caste in India*. 2 vols. London: Kegan Paul, Trench, Trubner and Co., 1931.

Dutt, Sukumar. *Buddhist Monks and Monasteries in India*. London: George Allen, 1962.

Edgerton, Franklin, trans. and ed. *Bhagavad Gita*. Cambridge: Harvard University Press, 1944.

Edwardess, Michael. *A History of India from the Earliest Times to the Present Day*. New York: Farrar, Straus and Cudahy, 1961.

Eliot, Sir Charles. *Hinduism and Buddhism: An Historical Sketch*. 3 vols. London: Routledge and Kegan Paul, 1921.

Fick, R. *The Social Organization of India in Buddha's Time*. Translated by S. K. Maitra. Calcutta: University of Calcutta, 1920.

Foucher, A. *The Life of Buddha*. Translated by S. B. Boas. Middletown, Conn.: Wesleyan University Press, 1963.

Fuchs, Stephen. *The Children of Hari*. Vienna: Verlag Herold, 1950.

Gambhīrananda, Swami. *Eight Upanishads*. 2 vols. Calcutta: Advaita Ashrama, 1957.

Gard, Richard A. *Buddhism*. New York: George Braziller, 1961.

Garratt, G. I., ed. *The Legacy of India*. Oxford: Clarendon Press, 1937.

Gokhale, B. G. *Ancient India: History and Culture*. New York: Asia Publishing House, 1962.

Govinda, Lama Anagarika. *The Psychological Attitude of the Early Buddhist Philosophy*. London: Rider and Co., 1961.

Hare, E. M., trans. and ed. *Woven Cadences of Early Buddhists*. Colombo, Ceylon: Sacred Books of the Buddhists, Vol. 15, 1944; reprinted, London: Oxford University Press, 1945, under the title, *Sutta Nipāta: Dialogues or Discourses of Gautama Buddha*.

Hughes, R. M. [Madame La Meri]. *The Gesture Language of the Hindu Dance*. New York: Columbia University Press, 1941.

Hutton, J. H. *Caste in India: Its Nature, Function, and Origins*. London: Oxford University Press, rev., 1961.

Hume, Robert Ernest. *The Thirteen Principal Upanishads*. 2nd ed. London: Oxford University Press, 1931.

Jaina, Jagmanderlal. *Outlines of Jainism*. Cambridge: University Press, 1916.

Jayatilleke, K. N. *Early Buddhist Theory of Knowledge*. London: George Allen and Unwin, 1963.

Jayawickrama, N. A. *The Inception of Discipline and the Vinaya Nidāna*. London: Luzac, 1962.

Kasambi, D. D. *Ancient India: A History of Its Culture and Civilization*. New York: Pantheon Books, 1965.

Keith, Arthur Berriedale, ed. *Harvard Oriental Series.* 32 vols. Cambridge, Mass.: Harvard University Press, 1925.

Mahajan, V. D. *Early History of India.* Delhi: S. Chand, 1965.

Majumdar, D. M. *Caste and Communication in an Indian Village.* New York: Asia Publishing House, 1958.

Majumdar, R. C., ed. *The History and Culture of the Indian People.* 11 vols. London: George Allen and Unwin, 1951–.

Majumdar, R. C., Raychaudhuri, H. C., and Datta, Kalikinkar. *Ancient India.* 2nd ed. London: Macmillan, 1963.

Majumdar, R. J., and Pusalkar, A. D., eds. *The Vedic Age.* London: George Allen and Unwin, 1951.

Mascaro, Juan, trans. and ed. *The Bhagavad Gita.* Baltimore: Penguin Books, 1962.

——. *The Upsanishads.* Baltimore, Md.: Penguin Books, 1965.

Mayer, Adrian C. *Caste and Kinship in Central India: A Village and Its Region.* Berkeley: University of California Press, 1960.

Müller, Max, trans. and ed. *Dhammapada.* Oxford: Clarendon Press, 1881.

——. *Sacred Books of the Buddhists.* 23 vols. London: Henry Frowde, Oxford University Press, 1895–1964.

——, ed. *Sacred Books of the East.* 50 vols. London: Oxford University Press, 1894; republished, Delhi: Motilal Banarsidass, 1963.

Nanavati, Manilal B., and Vakil, C. N. *Group Prejudices in India.* Bombay: Vora and Co., 1951.

Nehru, Jawaharlal. *The Discovery of India.* London: Meridian Books, 1956.

Nikhilinanda, Swami. *The Upanishads.* 4 vols. New York: Harper, 1949.

Northrop, F. S. C. *Meeting of East and West,* Chaps. 9–10. New York: Macmillan, 1946.

Oldenberg, Hermann. *The Grihya-sûtras: Rules of Vedic Domestic Ceremonies.* 2 vols. Oxford: Clarendon Press, 1886, 1892.

——. *Vinaya Pitika.* 5 vols. London: Oxford University Press, 1929.

Prabhavananda, Swami, and Isherwood, Christopher, trans. *The Song of God: Bhagavad-Gita.* New York: New American Library, Mentor Book, 1954.

Prabhu, Pandharinath H. *Hindu Social Organization.* 4th ed. Bombay: Practical Prakashan, 1963.

Radhakrishnan, S. *Indian Philosophy.* 2 vols. London: George Allen and Unwin, 1939.

——. *Philosophy of the Upaniṣads.* London: George Allen and Unwin, 1924.

——. *The Hindu View of Life.* London: George Allen and Unwin, 1928.

Ragazin, Z. A. *Vedic India.* 3rd ed. London: Unwin, 1895.

Ranade, R. D. *A Constructive Survey of Upanishadic Philosophy.* Poona: Vol. 2 of Encyclopaedic History of Indian Philosophy, 1926.

Rapson, E. J., ed. *Cambridge History of Ancient India.* Cambridge: University Press, 1922.

Rawlinson, Hugh George. *India: A Short Cultural History*. Rev. ed. New York: Praeger, 1952.

Russell, Robert V., and Lal, R. B. H. *The Tribes and Castes of the Central Provinces of India*. 4 vols. London: Macmillan, 1916.

Sharma, Ran Sharan. *Sudras in Ancient India*. Delhi: Motilal Banarsidass, 1958.

Sinha, Jadunath. *Indian Psychology*. 2 vols. Calcutta: Sinha Publishing House, 1958.

Smith, Vincent Arthur. *The Early History of India from 600 B.C. to the Muhamedan Conquest*. Oxford: Clarendon Press, 1924.

———. *The Oxford History of India*. 3rd ed. Edited by Percival Spear. Oxford: Clarendon Press, 1967.

Tatia, Nathmal. *Studies in Jaina Philosophy*. Banaras: Jain Cultural Research Society, 1951.

Thomas, Edward J. *The History of Buddhist Thought*. New York: Knopf, 1933.

———. *The Life of Buddha as Legend and History*. London: Routledge and Kegan Paul, 1927.

Ward, C. H. S. *Buddhism*. Rev. ed. 2 vols. London: Epworth Press, 1947.

Winternitz, M. *A History of Indian Literature*. Calcutta: University of Calcutta, 1959.

Zürcher, E. *Buddhism*. New York: St. Martin's Press, 1962.

CHINA

Bard, Émile. *Chinese Life in Town and Country*. Translated by H. Twitchell. London: G. P. Putnam's Sons, 1905.

Beck, L. M. *The Story of Oriental Philosophy*. New York: Cosmopolitan Book Corp., 1928.

Blakney, R. B., trans. *Lao Tzu*. New York: New American Library, Mentor Book, 1955.

Bloodworth, Dennis. *The Chinese Looking Glass*. New York: Farrar, Straus and Giroux, 1969.

Bodde, Derk. *China's Cultural Tradition: What and Whither?* New York: Rinehart, 1957.

———. *China's First Unifier: A Study of the Ch'in Dynasty as Seen in the Life of Li-Ssu*. Leiden: E. J. Brill, 1938.

———, trans. *Statesman, Patriot and General in Ancient China*. New Haven, Conn.: American Oriental Society, 1940.

Boulger, D. C. *History of China*. 3 vols. London: H. W. Allen, 1881–84.

Burkhardt, V. R. *Chinese Creeds and Customs*. 3 vols. Hong Kong: South China *Morning Post*, 1953–58.

Bynner, Witter. *The Way of Life According to Laotzu*. New York: John Day, 1944.

Carus, Paul, trans. *Tao-Teh-King*. Chicago: Open Court Pub. Co., 1898.

Chai Ch'u, and Chai, Winberg, eds. *The Humanist Way in Ancient China: Essential Works of Confucianism*. New York: Bantam Books, 1965.

——. *The Story of Chinese Philosophy*. New York: Washington Square Press, 1961.

Chan, Wing-tsit. *An Outline and Annotated Bibliography of Chinese Philosophy*. New Haven: Yale University Far Eastern Publications, 1959.

——. *Confucianism*. New York: Barron, Religions of the World Series, 1969.

——. *Source Book in Chinese Philosophy*. Princeton, N.J.: Princeton University Press, 1963.

Chang, Carsun. *The Development of Neo-Confucian Thought*. New York: Bookman Associates, 1957.

Chavannes, Édouard, trans. and ed. *Les Memoires Historiques de Se-Ma Ts'ien*. 5 vols. Leiden: E. J. Brill, 1967.

Ch'ên, Shou-Yi. *Chinese Literature: A Historical Introduction*. New York: Ronald Press, 1961.

Cheng, T'ien-Hsi. *China Moulded by Confucius*. London: Stevens and Sons, 1946.

——, ed. *A Source Book in Chinese Philosophy*. Princeton, N.J.: Princeton University Press, 1963.

Ch'ien, Ssu-Ma. *Records of the Grand Historian of China*. 2 vols. Translated and edited by Burton Watson. New York: Columbia University Press, 1961.

Christy, Arthur S., ed. *The Asian Legacy and American Life*. New York: John Day, 1942.

Chü, T'ung-tsu. *Han Social Structure*. Seattle: University of Washington Press, 1969.

Cottrell, Leonard. *The Tiger of Ch'in*. London: Pan Books, 1964.

Creel, Herrlee Glessner. *Chinese Thought from Confucius to Mao Tze-tung*. Chicago: University of Chicago Press, 1953; reprinted, New York: New American Library, Mentor Book, 1960.

——. *Confucius and the Chinese Way*. New York: Harper Torchbooks, 1960; originally, *Confucius: Man and Myth*, New York: John Day, 1949.

——. *The Birth of China: A Study in the Formative Period of Chinese Civilization*. New York: F. Ungar, 1937, 1964.

——. *The Origins of Statecraft in China*. Chicago: University of Chicago Press, 1970.

——. "What is Taoism?" *Journal of American Oriental Society* 76 (July-September, 1956).

Crump, J. I. *Intrigues: Studies of the Chan-Kuo Tze.* Ann Arbor: University of Michigan Press, 1964.

Crump, J. I., and Dreher, John J. "Peripatetic Rhetors of the Warring Kingdoms," *Central States Speech Journal* 2 (March, 1951):15–17.

de Bary, William Theodore, Chan, Wing-tsit, and Watson, Burton, eds. *Sources of Chinese Tradition.* New York: Columbia University Press, 1960.

Doolittle, Justus. *Social Life of the Chinese.* 2 vols. New York: Harper, 1865; reprinted New York: Paragon Book Gallery, 1966.

Dreher, John, and Crump, J. I. "Pre-Han Persuasion: The Legalist School." *Central States Speech Journal* 3 (March, 1952):10–14.

Dubs, Homer H., trans. *History of the Former Han Dynasty by Pan Ku.* 3 vols. Baltimore: Waverly Press, 1938–55.

——. *Hsüntze: Moulder of Ancient Confucianism.* London: Probsthain, 1927.

——. "The Date and Circumstances of Lao-dz." *Journal of American Oriental Society* 61 (1941):215–21; 62 (1942):8–13 and 300–304; and 64 (1944):24–27.

——, trans. *The Works of Hsüntze.* London: Probsthain, 1928.

Duyvendak, J. J. L., trans. *The Book of Lord Shang.* London: Probsthain, 1928.

——, trans. *Tao Teh Ching.* London: John Murray, 1954.

Du Halde, P. F. B. *Description of the Empire of China.* London: Edward Cave, I, 1738; II, 1741.

Eberhard, Wolfram. *A History of China.* 3rd ed. Translated by E. W. Dickes. Berkeley: University of California Press, 1969.

Faber, E., trans. and ed. *The Mind of Mencius.* Translated into English by A. B. Hutchinson. London: Trübner's Oriental Series, 1878.

Fairbank, John K., ed. *Chinese Thought and Institutions.* Chicago: University of Chicago Press, 1957.

Fitzgerald, C. P. *China: A Short Cultural History.* Rev. ed. London: Cresset Press, 1950.

Fung Yu-lan. *A History of Chinese Philosophy.* 2 vols. Translated by Derk Bodde. Princeton, N.J.: Princeton University Press, 1953.

——. *The Spirit of Chinese Philosophy.* Translated by E. R. Hughes. London: Kegan Paul, 1947.

Giles, Herbert A. *A Chinese Biographical Dictionary.* Cambridge: Cambridge University Press, 1898; reprinted, New York: Paragon Book Gallery, 1966.

——. *A History of Chinese Literature.* New York: Appleton, 1923; reprinted, New York: F. Ungar, 1967.

——. *Chuang-Tzu: Taoist Philosopher and Chinese Mystic.* Shanghai: Kelly and Walsh, 1926.

——. *Confucianism and Its Rivals.* London: George Allen and Unwin, 1915.

Giles, Lionel, trans. *Lao Tzu*. London: Wisdom of the East Series, 1904.

——, trans. *Musings of a Chinese Mystic: Selections from Chuang-Tzu*. London: Wisdom of the East Series, 1906.

——, trans. *Sun Tzu on the Art of War*. London: Luzac, 1910.

——, trans. *The Book of Mencius*. London: John Murray, 1942.

——, trans. *The Sayings of Confucius*. London: Wisdom of the East Series, 1907.

Goodrich, Luther. *A Short History of the Chinese People*. London: George Allen and Unwin, 1948.

Gray, John Henry. *China: A History of the Laws, Manners and Customs of the People*. 2 vols. London: Macmillan, 1878.

Hsu, Leonard Shihlien. *The Political Philosophy of Confucianism*. London: G. Routledge and Sons, 1932.

Hughes, E. R., ed. *Chinese Philosophy in Classical Times*. London: Dent, 1942.

——. *The Great Learning and the Mean-in-Action*. London: Dent, 1942.

——. *Two Chinese Poets: Vignettes of Han Life and Thought*. Princeton, N.J.: Princeton University Press, 1960.

Hu, Shih. "Ch'an (Zen) Buddhism in China: Its History and Method." *Philosophy East and West* 3 (April, 1953).

——. *Development of the Logical Method in Ancient China*. 3rd ed. Shanghai: Oriental Books, 1928.

Kaisuka, Shigeki. *Confucius*. London: George Allen and Unwin, 1956.

Karlgren, Bernard, trans. *Shu Ching: The Book of Documents*. Stockholm: Museum of Far Eastern Antiquities, 1950.

Kramers, Robert Paul. *The School Sayings of Confucius*. Leiden: E. J. Brill, 1945.

Lau, D. C. *Lao Tzu: Tao Te Ching*. Baltimore: Penguin Books, 1963.

Latourette, Kenneth Scott. *The Chinese: Their History and Culture*. 3rd ed. 2 vols. New York: Macmillan, 1946.

Legge, James, trans. and ed. *The Chinese Classics*. 5 vols. London: Oxford University Press, 1893–95; reprinted, Hong Kong: University of Hong Kong Press, 1960.

——, trans. and ed. *Li Chi: Book of Rites*. Edited by Ch'u Chai and Winberg Chai. Hyde Park, N.Y.: University Books, 1967.

——, trans. and ed. *The Four Books*. New York: Paragon Book Gallery, 1966.

——, trans. and ed. *The Texts of Taoism*. 2 vols. Sacred Books of the East Series, edited by Max Müller. Oxford: Clarendon Press, 1891; reprinted, New York: Julian Press, 1959.

Levenson, Joseph R. *Confucian China and Its Modern Fate*. Berkeley: University of California Press, 1958.

Levenson, Joseph R., and Schurmann, Franz. *China: An Interpretive History from the Beginnings to the Fall of Han*. Berkeley: University of California Press, 1969.

Li, Chi. *The Beginnings of Chinese Civilization.* Seattle: University of Washington Press, 1957.

Liang, Chi-Chan. *History of Chinese Political Thought during the Early Tsin Period.* Translated by L. T. Chen. London: Kegan Paul, 1930.

Liao, W. K., trans. *The Complete Works of Han Fei Tzu.* 2 vols. London: Probsthain, 1928.

Lin, Yutang, ed. *The Wisdom of China and India.* New York: Random House, Modern Library, 1938.

——, trans. and ed. *The Wisdom of Confucius.* New York: Random House, Modern Library, 1938.

Liu, Wu-chi. *A Short History of Confucian Philosophy.* Bloomington: Indiana University Press.

——. *Confucius: His Life and Time.* New York: Philosophical Library, 1956.

Loewe, Michael. *Everyday Life in Early Imperial China.* New York: Putnam, 1968.

——, trans. and ed. *Records of the Han Administration.* 2 vols. Cambridge: Cambridge University Press, 1967.

Lyall, Leonard, trans. and ed. *Mencius.* London: Longmans, Green, 1932.

——, trans. and ed. *The Sayings of Confucius.* London: Longmans, Green, 1909.

MacNair, H. F., ed. *China.* Berkeley: University of California Press, 1946.

Maverick, Lewis A. *China: A Model for Europe.* San Antonio, Texas: Paul Anderson Co., 1946.

Mei, Yi-Pao. *The Ethical and Political Works of Motse.* London: Probsthain, 1929.

Moore, Charles E., ed. *Philosophy—East and West.* Princeton, N.J.: Princeton University Press, 1949.

——, ed. *The Status of the Individual in East and West.* Honolulu: The University of Hawaii Press, 1968.

Nivinson, David S., and Wright, Arthur F., eds. *Confucianism in Action.* Stanford: Stanford University Press, 1959.

Old, W. G., trans. and ed. *The Shu King.* New York: John Lane, 1904.

——, trans. and ed. *The Simple Way: The Tao-Teh-King.* London: Philip Welby, 1905; reprinted as *Lao Tze: The Tao-Teh-King,* London: Rider and Co., 8th ed., 1943.

Pierre, Do Dinh. *Confucianism and Chinese Humanism.* Translated by C. L. Markmann. New York: Funk and Wagnalls, 1969.

Pyun, Yung-tai, trans. and ed. *The Analects of Confucius.* Seoul, Korea: Minjungsugwan Press, n.d. (1956).

Richards, I. A. *Mencius on the Mind: Experiments in Multiple Definition.* London: Kegan Paul, Trench, Trubner & Co., 1932.

Shryock, John K. *The Origin and Development of the State Cult of Confucius.* New York: Century, 1932; reprinted, Paragon Book Gallery, 1966.

Siu, R. G. H. *The Man of Many Qualities: A Legacy of the I Ching*. Cambridge: MIT Press, 1968.

Smith, Arthur H. *Chinese Characteristics*. Rev. ed. New York: Fleming H. Revell, 1894.

——. *Proverbs and Common Sayings from the Chinese*. New York: Paragon Book Gallery, reprint, 1965.

Soothill, William E., trans. *The Analects, or The Conversations of Confucius with His Disciples and Certain Others*. Edited by Lady Hosie. London: Oxford University Press, reprint, 1937.

Steele, John, trans. and ed. *The I-Li, or Book of Etiquette and Ceremonial*. 2 vols. London: Probsthain, 1917.

Suzuki, Daisetz T. *A Brief History of Chinese Philosophy*. London: Probsthain, 1914.

——. *The Essentials of Zen Buddhism*. Edited by Bernard Phillips. New York: Dutton, 1962.

T'an, Po-Fu, and Kung-Wen, Wen, trans. *Economic Dialogues in Ancient China—Selections from the Kuan Tzu*. New Haven, Conn.: Yale University Far Eastern Publications, 1954.

Tomkinson, L. "The Early Legalist School of Chinese Political Thought." *Open Court* 45 (1931).

Tseu, Augustinus A. *The Moral Philosophy of Mo-Tze*. Taipei: China Printing, 1965.

Tsui, Chi. *A Short History of Chinese Civilization*. London: Gollancz, 1942.

Waley, Arthur, trans. and ed. *Analects of Confucius*. London: George Allen and Unwin, 1938.

——. *The Way and Its Power*. London: George Allen and Unwin, 1934; reprinted, New York: Grove Press, Evergreen Books, n.d.

——. *Three Ways of Thought in Ancient China*. London: George Allen and Unwin, 1939.

Wang, Gung-Hsing. *The Chinese Mind*. New York: John Day, 1946.

Watson, Burton, trans. and ed. *Basic Writings of Mo Tzu, Hsün Tzu and Han Fei Tzu*. New York: Columbia University Press, 1967.

——. *Early Chinese Literature*. New York: Columbia University Press, 1962.

Ware, James R., trans. and ed. *The Sayings of Chuang Chou*. New York: New American Library, Mentor Classic, 1963.

——, trans. and ed. *The Sayings of Mencius*. New York: New American Library, Mentor Classic, 1960.

Watts, Alan W. *The Way of Zen*. New York: Pantheon Books, 1957; reprinted, New York: New American Library, Mentor Book, 1959.

Wei, Francis Cho Min. *The Spirit of Chinese Culture*. New York: Scribners, 1947.

Welch, Holmes. *The Parting of the Way: Lao Tzu and the Taoist Movement*. London: Methuen, 1958.

Wilhelm, Richard. *Confucius and Confucianism*. Translated by G. E. Danton and A. P. Danton. New York: Kennikat, 1931.

——, trans. *The I Ching or Book of Changes*. Translated into English by Cary F. Baynes. Princeton, N.J.: Princeton University Press, Bollingen Series, 1961.

Wittfogel, Karl A., and Chia-Shêng, Fêng. *History of Chinese Society*. New York: Philosophical Library, 1946.

Wright, Arthur F. *Buddhism in Chinese History*. Stanford: Stanford University Press, 1959; reprinted, New York: Atheneum, 1965.

——, ed. *Confucianism and Chinese Civilization*. New York: Atheneum, 1964.

——, ed. *Studies in Chinese Thought*. Chicago: University of Chicago Press, 1953.

——, et al., eds. *The Confucian Persuasion*. Stanford: Stanford University Press, 1960.

Wu, John Ching Hsiung, trans. *Tao Teh Ching*. New York: St. John's University Press, 1961.

Yorke, Anton, trans. *Yang Chu's Garden of Pleasure*. London: John Murray, 1912.

Index

NAMES AND TITLES

305

TOPICS